Tactical and Strategic Missile Guidance
Second Edition

Tactical and Strategic Missile Guidance
Second Edition

Paul Zarchan
Charles Stark Draper Laboratory, Inc.
Cambridge, Massachusetts

Volume 157
PROGRESS IN
ASTRONAUTICS AND AERONAUTICS
A Volume in the AIAA Tactical Missile Series

A. Richard Seebass, Editor-in-Chief
University of Colorado at Boulder
Boulder, Colorado

Published by the American Institute of Aeronautics and Astronautics, Inc.
370 L'Enfant Promenade, SW, Washington, DC 20024-2518

Second Printing

ISSN 0079-6050

Acknowledgments

Although many of the devices discussed in *Tactical and Strategic Missile Guidance* work in a vacuum, I do not. In this section I would like to take the opportunity to acknowledge those individuals who contributed in some way to the content and publication of this text.

First, I would like to thank Dr. Donald C. Fraser, former Executive Vice President of The Charles Stark Draper Laboratory, Inc. (CSDL) for recommending me as an author for the AIAA Progress in Astronautics and Aeronautics series. He knew of my desire to write a book on missile guidance and through his efforts the dream is now a reality. During the last nine years Mr. John M. Elwell, former Guidance, Navigation & Control Director at CSDL, provided me with numerous technical opportunities that expanded my missile guidance background. The technical thread running throughout the text is based on those technical opportunities. The highly competent staff and superb technical environment of CSDL provided the atmosphere that not only made this project possible but also fun. In particular, I would like to thank CSDL technical staff members Dr. Owen Deutsch, Mr. Steven L. Nelson, and Dr. Richard E. Phillips for our many valuable technical discussions. Much of the material in the strategic interceptor chapters was a consequence of our valuable technical interchanges. Some of the material in several of the chapters pertaining to tactical missile guidance was based on knowledge gained during my employment at Raytheon. Here, I not only learned tactical interceptor guidance and control fundamentals from the people who first made radar homing missiles a reality, but also learned of and developed an appreciation for the hard work involved in converting theory to something that works.

Next, I would like to acknowledge those associated with AIAA responsible for the inception and completion of this project. I would like to thank Dr. Allen E. Fuhs, AIAA Progress in Astronutics and Aeronautics Editorial Board Member, for inviting me to participate in the Progress Series and then helping me formulate an outline from which a manuscript could be written. His kind and constructive review of the initial draft led to numerous changes, all of which improved the overall quality of the text. Mr. John Newbauer, former AIAA Administrator of Scientific Publications, provided me with excellent examples of the standards expected of a Progress Series volume and, in addition, helped outline the preface. Mrs. Jeanne Godette, AIAA Director of Book Publications, and her very competent staff not only taught me a great deal about grammar but, in addition, moved this project forward very rapidly.

Finally, I wish to express my love and gratitude to my wife Maxine for having patience and understanding, while our home fell into a state of disrepair, for not complaining while I put in the many hours required in writing this text.

Table of Contents

Preface to Second Edition xiii

Introduction 1

Chapter 1.   Numerical Techniques 9

Introduction.. 9
Laplace Transforms and Differential Equations................... 9
Numerical Integration of Differential Equations 12
Computer Languages... 15
FORTRAN Comparison 18
Whetstone Benchmarking 19
Reduced Instruction Set Computer 21
References 23

Chapter 2.   Fundamentals of Tactical Missile Guidance 25

Introduction... 25
What Is Proportional Navigation? 26
Simulation of Proportional Navigation in Two Dimensions........ 26
Two-Dimensional Engagement Simulation.......................... 30
Linearization 34
Linearized Engagement Simulation 36
Important Closed-Form Solutions 38
Proportional Navigation and Zero Effort Miss................... 41
Summary 43
References 43

Chapter 3.   Method of Adjoints and the Homing Loop 45

Introduction... 45
Homing Loop 45
Single Time Constant Guidance System 46
How to Construct an Adjoint 49
Adjoint Mathematics 52
Adjoints for Deterministic Systems 53
Deterministic Adjoint Example 55
Adjoint Closed-Form Solutions 58
Normalization 63
Summary 66
References 66

Chapter 4. Noise Analysis **67**

Introduction... 67
Basic Definitions.. 67
Gaussian Noise Example................................... 70
Computational Issues...................................... 74
More Basic Definitions 76
Response of Linear System to White Noise............... 77
Low-Pass-Filter Example.................................. 78
Adjoints for Noise-Driven Systems 81
Shaping Filters and Random Processes................... 82
Example of a Stochastic Adjoint 86
Closed-Form Solution for Random Target Maneuver 91
Summary 92
References 93

Chapter 5. Covariance Analysis and the Homing Loop **95**

Background 95
Theory 95
Low-Pass Filter Example................................... 96
Numerical Considerations................................. 97
Homing Loop Example...................................... 100
Acceleration Adjoint 106
Summary 110
References 110

Chapter 6. Proportional Navigation and Miss Distance **111**

Introduction... 111
System Order.. 111
Design Relationships 113
Optimal Target Evasive Maneuvers........................ 120
Practical Evasive Maneuvers.............................. 122
Saturation 124
Parasitic Effects 127
Thrust Vector Control 131
Summary 135
References 136

**Chapter 7. Digital Fading Memory Noise Filters
in the Homing Loop** **137**

Introduction 137
Fading Memory Filters 137
Fading Memory Filter in Homing Loop 139
Mixed Continuous Discrete Adjoint Theory 145
Using Adjoints to Evaluate Filter Performance 149
Some Properties of Fading Memory Filters 152

Estimating Target Maneuver 155
Summary 159
References 159

Chapter 8.   Advanced Guidance Laws 161

Introduction 161
Review of Proportional Navigation 161
Augmented Proportional Navigation 163
Derivation of Augmented Proportional Navigation 168
Influence of Time Constants 171
Optimal Guidance 174
Summary 179
References 180

Chapter 9.   Kalman Filters and the Homing Loop 181

Introduction 181
Theoretical Equations 181
Application to Homing Loop 183
Kalman Gains 185
Numerical Examples 187
Experiments with Optimal Guidance 196
Summary 202
References 202

Chapter 10.   Other Forms of Tactical Guidance 203

Introduction 203
Proportional Navigation Command Guidance 203
Beam Rider Guidance 210
Command to Line-of-Sight Guidance 219
Summary 223
References 223

Chapter 11.   Tactical Zones 225

Introduction 225
Velocity Computation 225
Drag 228
Acceleration 233
Gravity 234
Summary 238
References 238

Chapter 12.   Strategic Considerations **239**

Introduction 239
Background 239
Gravitational Model 239
Polar Coordinate System 246
Closed-Form Solutions 249
Hit Equation 257
Flight Time 260
Summary 263
References 263

Chapter 13.   Boosters **265**

Introduction 265
Review 265
Staging 267
Booster Numerical Example 270
Gravity Turn 271
Summary 279
Reference 279

Chapter 14.   Lambert Guidance **281**

Introduction 281
Statement of Lambert's Problem 281
Solution to Lambert's Problem 282
Numerical Example 285
Speeding Up Lambert Routine... 288
Booster Steering 291
General Energy Management (GEM) Steering 297
Summary 305
References 305

Chapter 15.   Strategic Intercepts **307**

Introduction 307
Guidance Review 307
Ballistic Engagement Simulation 309
Boosting Target Considerations 320
Summary 329
Reference 329

Chapter 16.   Miscellaneous Topics **331**

Introduction 331
Gravity Compensation 331
Predictive Guidance 335
Booster Estimation with Range and Angle Measurements 343
Pulsed Guidance... 351

Chapter 17. Ballistic Target Properties **361**

Introduction.. 361
Ballistic Target Model 361
Ballistic Target Experiments..................................... 363
Closed-Form Solution for Ballistic Targets 366
Missile Aerodynamics 370
Intercepting a Ballistic Target................................... 373
Summary 380
References 381

**Chapter 18. Extended Kalman Filtering and Ballistic
    Coefficient Estimation**...................................... **383**

Introduction.. 383
Theoretical Equations 383
Differential Equation for One-Dimensional Ballistic Target................. 385
Extended Kalman Filter for One-Dimensional Ballistic Target.............. 387
Numerical Example 389
Summary 397
References 397

Chapter 19. Ballistic Target Challenges **399**

Introduction.. 399
Miss Distance Due to Noise 399
Fifth-Order Binomial Guidance System Miss Distances.................... 404
Minimum Guidance System Time Constant............................ 405
Missile Turning Rate Time Constant................................ 408
Checking Minimum Guidance System Time Constant Constraints 409
Miss Due to Noise for Aircraft and Ballistic Targets..................... 411
Summary 415
References 415

Appendix A. Tactical and Strategic Missile Guidance Software **417**

Introduction.. 417
Software Details 417
Integration Example... 418
Random Number Example 420
Pursuit Guidance 422
Multiple Target Problem... 426
Sensitivity of Optimal Guidance to Time to Go Errors.................... 429
Efficient Lambert Subroutine...................................... 432
Alternative Formulation of Radome Effects 434
Another Way of Generating Random Numbers 437
Sampling Experiments 437
References 439

Appendix B. Units.. **441**

List of Series Volumes.. **443**

Preface to Second Edition

Since *Tactical and Strategic Missile Guidance* was introduced in 1990, a very significant event relating to missile guidance has occurred—the 1991 Persian Gulf War. The deadly Iraqi Scud attacks on civilian population centers made the importance of theater missile defense obvious to all and is best summed up by G. Canavan ("Strategic Defense In Past and Future Conflicts," *The Journal of Practical Applications in Space,* Vol. 2, No. 3, Spring 1991, pp. 1–42):

"In a way, television coverage may have been the most important factor, not because of sensationalism or exaggeration, but because it simply let people see with their own eyes that there were indeed world leaders who would use weapons of mass destruction on civilians without qualms or hesitation. Television helped make strategic defense understandable and real to millions of people....But no one who watched Scuds falling on Riyadh or Tel Aviv could miss the point that there, but for a factor of 10 in range, go I."

This Second Edition includes three new chapters on the fundamentals of endoatmospheric ballistic targets and shows why they are challenging from a missile guidance system point of view. The new chapters are based on material from the AIAA Continuing Education short course "Fundamentals of Tactical and Strategic Missile Guidance" that I have been teaching since 1990. The ballistic target material was omitted from the First Edition because of page limitation and time constraints. As with other material in the text, the new topics are treated from both analytical and simulation points of view so that readers with different backgrounds and learning styles can appreciate the unique challenges of ballistic targets.

In addition, for analytically inclined readers, a new chapter has been added showing how covariance analysis can be used to analyze missile guidance systems and how the adjoint method can be extended to yield acceleration as well as miss distance error budgets. A novel numerical method has been added to the chapter pertaining to Lambert guidance, speeding up the brute force approach of the First Edition by more than two orders of magnitude!

As a special feature of the Second Edition, the many FORTRAN source code listings presented in the text are now included with the book on both Macintosh and IBM compatible formatted disks. For those readers who do not have or cannot afford FORTRAN compilers for running the code, versions of all of the text's source code are also included on the disks in the more popular QuickBASIC language (i.e., a QuickBASIC compiler is one-tenth the cost of a FORTRAN compiler).

Two Appendices have been added to the Second Edition. Appendix A not only serves as a user's guide for the software but also provides examples of how the source code can be modified to explore issues beyond the scope of the text. The examples in Appendix A will also be of interest to those readers who have no interest in the source code. Appendix B offers a conversion table for the various units included in the text.

On a personal note, it has been very gratifying for me to learn that many people working with or having to learn about missile guidance have found *Tactical and Strategic Missile Guidance* useful. In fact, some individuals who previously thought that the subject of missile guidance was a minor engineering detail have learned that "the devil is in the details." It is my hope that this Second Edition, with its included software, additional chapters, and examples, will be of value not only to new readers, but also to those who have already read the First Edition.

Paul Zarchan
April 1994

Introduction

The requirements for tactical missile guidance systems were born at the end of World War II as a result of the highly effective kamikaze attacks on U.S. vessels. After the war it was clear that naval guns using unguided shells were not adequate for shooting down hostile aircraft making suicidal attacks against U.S. ships. To counter kamikaze-like threats, the U.S. Navy initiated the development of the Lark guided missile in 1944. Approximately six years of hard work was required before the first successful intercept, made by the Lark against an unmanned aircraft, occurred on Dec. 2, 1950. A very readable history of this significant event, told by one of the engineering participants, can be found in a work by M. W. Fossier ("The Development of Radar Homing Missiles," *Journal of Guidance, Control, and Dynamics*, Vol. 7, Nov.–Dec. 1984, pp. 641–651).

Operational endoatmospheric tactical missile systems, using the same guidance principles as those used by the Lark, have now been in existence for approximately three decades. These missiles use guidance concepts that work well not only against stationary or predictable targets but also are effective against responsive threats (i.e., aircraft executing evasive maneuvers) whose future position is highly uncertain. In the tactical arena current guidance law technology appears to be adequate if the flight time is long compared to the effective time constant of the guidance system and if the missile enjoys a considerable acceleration advantage over the target. In fact, it is not uncommon for a tactical missile to have an acceleration advantage of more than 5 against an aircraft target. This advantage is more than adequate for a successful intercept with current guidance law technology.

Strategic ballistic missiles are different from tactical guided missiles because they travel much longer distances and are designed to intercept stationary targets whose location is known precisely. A tactical homing missile acquires the target with a seeker and then guides all the way to intercept, whereas a strategic interceptor does not require a seeker since all of its guidance is in the boost phase. Since the boost phase represents only a small fraction of the total flight of a strategic ballistic missile, the interceptor glides most of the way toward the stationary target. In this type of strategic application, precise instrumentation is necessary so that the interceptor can steer to the correct position and velocity states at the end of the boost phase. With the correct states the missile will be able to glide ballistically, without further corrective maneuvers, toward the target.

The concept of long-range strategic ballistic missiles was also born during World War II with the highly effective V-2 rocket developed by German scientists at Peenemünde. The first combat round, launched on Sept. 6, 1944, represented the culmination of nearly 14 years of work (G. P., Kennedy, *Rockets, Missiles and Spacecraft of the National Air and Space Museum*, Smithsonian Institution Press, Washington DC, 1983). The range of the V-2 was only a few hundred miles, and a 2000-lb warhead compensated somewhat for its lack of accuracy. After World War II some of the German scientists from Peenemünde were brought to the United States, along with 80 missiles, in order to advance the V-2 technology. Guidance accuracy was improved by more than an order of magnitude by incorporating precise inertial sensors into the guidance system design. The short-range Redstone missile became the first U.S. ballistic missile with a highly accurate inertial guidance system. More precise and smaller inertial sensor hardware and improved guidance software were achieved with the U.S. medium-range Jupiter missile. An eyewitness account of this advance in strategic missile technology can be found in a work by W. Haeussermann ("Developments in the Field of Automatic Guidance and Control of Rockets," *Journal of Guidance, Control, and Dynamics*, Vol. 4, No. 3, May–June 1981, pp. 225–239). Today's highly accurate strategic ballistic missiles travel at intercontinental ranges at near-orbital speeds.

In newer systems, such as those being considered by the Strategic Defense Initiative (SDI), interceptors will have to make use of and improve on yesterday's tactical and strategic missile technology. Tomorrow's interceptors will have to fly strategic distances against moving and possibly accelerating targets whose future position is highly uncertain. In these applications it is not sufficient to apply only ballistic missile technology. Some type of homing guidance system is required after the interceptor boost phase to take out the inevitable errors. However, it is not clear whether tactical guidance law technology is appropriate for the homing phase of these strategic interceptors. Unlike tactical endoatmospheric interceptors, which maneuver by generating lift, the newer exoatmospheric interceptors require fuel for the missile divert engines in order to maneuver or divert in response to guidance commands. If all of the divert fuel is consumed, the interceptor cannot maneuver. In addition, fuel is at a premium, since, according to the rocket equation, interceptor weight grows exponentially with fuel weight. Therefore, unlike tactical endoatmospheric missiles, the newer exoatmospheric interceptors require guidance laws that minimize fuel consumption. In addition, because of practical limits on achievable divert engine thrust-to-weight ratios, the newer interceptors may no longer enjoy the tactical missile's acceleration advantage over the target. In fact, strategic exoatmospheric interceptors may be working at an *acceleration disadvantage* against a booster target!

With this perspective, this book attempts to lay the foundation for meeting today's new challenges. The principles of both tactical and strategic missile guidance are presented in a common language, notation, and perspective. The mathematics, arguments, and examples presented in the text are intended to be nonintimidating so that the designers working in the tactical world will be able to understand and appreciate the difficulty of the strategic problem and vice versa. Numerous examples are presented to illustrate all of the concepts presented in the text. In later chapters of the book, examples are presented showing elementary ways in which tactical and strategic guidance principles can be combined. In this way the potential for a cross-fertilization of ideas, which is necessary for today's challenges in guidance technology, is increased.

The book is written with both the expert and novice in mind. Proven methods of guidance in both the tactical and strategic world are presented from several points of view. The guidance laws are usually first derived mathematically, then explained from a heuristic point of view, and finally a numerical example, along with a FORTRAN listing, is included to prove that the guidance law performs as expected. The numerical example is usually chosen to highlight the strengths and weaknesses of the guidance law. In this way the novice can understand the principles of a particular guidance approach. The expert or more interested reader, using the FORTRAN listing with a suitable compiler, cannot only get a deeper understanding of the principles involved but can also explore issues beyond the scope of the text. All of the graphs presented in the text were generated with the FORTRAN listings.

It might appear from glancing at the many block diagrams scattered throughout the text that the subject matter requires a control system background. *This is not true!* The block diagrams are offered as a pictorial description of differential equations. The reader can always ignore the block diagrams and just read the differential equations. In fact, relief from block diagrams can be found in Chapters 11–19. The only assumption made in the text is that the reader has either an engineering or physics background. All of the numerical and mathematical techniques used in the text are explained in earlier chapters.

Chapter 1 presents the basis of most of the numerical techniques used throughout the text. The utility of Laplace transforms in solving and representing differential equations is explained. It is then shown how differential equations can be solved using the second-order numerical Runge-Kutta integration technique. FORTRAN code for a representative example is presented so that the reader can better understand how numerical integration is actually applied. The code is written so that it is easy to apply to problems involving other differential equations without changing more than a few lines of code. In fact, most of this sample code is repeated throughout the text when the differential equations representing the system under consideration change. The representative example in this chapter is also used to compare several popular computer languages and various computing platforms. It should be clear at the end of Chapter 1 why FORTRAN was chosen as the language of choice for this text.

Chapter 2 introduces the reader to the most important and widely used tactical missile guidance law: proportional navigation. A simplified engagement simulation is developed in order to show how proportional navigation operates and why it is an effective guidance law. Next, linearization techniques are used to get a deeper understanding of how proportional navigation works and to form an analytical foundation from which guidance theory can be advanced. Closed-form solutions for the required missile acceleration due to heading error and target maneuver disturbances are derived so that the reader can see how these important errors influence total system performance. It is then demonstrated that the derived closed-form solutions are not only analytically convenient but are in fact accurate indicators of the expected system performance.

Chapter 3 introduces one of the most important methods used in analyzing tactical missile guidance systems: the method of adjoints. The rules for constructing an adjoint are presented and the necessary mathematics required to understand why adjoints are useful are included in this chapter. A numerical example involving a missile guidance system is used both as a practical application of the theory and to ensure that the reader fully understands how to apply the adjoint technique. The numerical results of the adjoint example are compared to traditional simulation results so that the reader can appreciate both the power and utility of this very elegant technique. New closed-form solutions are derived using adjoints so that the reader can also begin to appreciate the relationship between miss distance, the guidance system time constant, and the error source.

Chapter 4 reviews all of the necessary theory so that the reader can understand how measurement noise and random phenomenon influence the performance of a missile guidance system. Basic definitions are reviewed and numerical examples are presented showing the reader how theory is used in practice. The method of adjoints, which was introduced in Chapter 3 for deterministic systems, is extended so that a missile guidance system can be analyzed if the error sources are random. A numerical example is presented showing how the method of adjoints can be used to obtain statistical performance projections in only *one computer run*. These results are compared to multiple-run Monte Carlo projections (i.e., repeated simulation trials with ensemble averaging of the resultant output data).

Another popular computerized analytical technique, known as covariance analysis, is introduced in Chapter 5. It is shown that covariance analysis can also be used to yield exact statistical performance projections of a missile guidance system in the presence of random error sources in one computer run. The numerical requirements for the successful implementation of covariance analysis are discussed and compared to the adjoint method. Chapter 5 also shows how the adjoint technique can be extended to yield acceleration as well as miss distance information.

Chapter 6 presents most of the important properties of a proportional navigation guidance system. It is shown that an accurate dynamic model of the guidance system is crucial in obtaining accurate miss distance performance projections. Normalized design curves are developed for a high-order canonical guidance system so that an engineer can quickly estimate system performance given a minimum amount of information. The concept of an optimal target evasive maneuver is developed. It is shown how one can compute the maximum miss distance that a maneuvering target can induce. This type of information is important in determining the vulnerability of a guidance system. Finally, the influence of saturation and parasitic effects on system performance are considered. Design curves are presented showing how to size the missile to target acceleration advantage so that the interceptor will be effective. It is also shown in this chapter that parasitic effects such as radome place fundamental limits on the attainable speed and gain of the guidance system.

The missile seeker provides a noisy measurement of the line-of-sight angle. Chapter 7 demonstrates how simple digital fading memory filters can be used as part of a missile guidance system to provide an estimate of the line-of-sight angle and rate from the noisy measurement. Adjoint theory is again extended to handle systems with continuous and digital parts so that a mixed continuous-discrete missile guidance system can be analyzed efficiently. Some of the more important properties of fading memory filters are illustrated via numerical examples. This chapter also shows that, if range measurements are available, it is possible to estimate target acceleration with a fading memory filter.

Chapter 8 reviews proportional navigation concepts and sets up the mathematical foundation so that more advanced tactical guidance laws can be derived. Augmented proportional navigation is derived from some properties of the Schwartz inequality. It is then shown, via a numerical example, how guidance system time constants can degrade miss distance performance of both proportional and augmented proportional navigation. Recognizing the cause of the miss distance degradation, a new guidance law is derived. It is demonstrated that, as long as the missile guidance system dynamics is known, the new guidance law can effectively eliminate miss distance degradation due to a guidance system time constant.

Chapter 9 introduces a class of optimal digital noise filters known as Kalman filters. Using the theoretical Kalman filtering equations, the chapter develops, in detail, a digital Kalman filter that is very useful for missile guidance system applications. It is shown, in detail, how a Kalman filter can be used in conjunction with an optimal guidance law to improve system performance and to relax missile acceleration requirements. Various experiments are conducted in order to illustrate important filtering and guidance concepts.

Chapter 10 introduces other forms of tactical guidance. A command guidance implementation of proportional navigation is compared to a homing guidance implementation in terms of system noise propagation. Beam riding and command to line-of-sight methods of guidance are introduced and compared to proportional navigation. It is shown that, although the performance of these new methods of guidance are geometry-dependent, they can be made to work rather effectively.

Chapter 11 wraps up the discussion of tactical interceptors with consideration of the missile's operational zone. Reach considerations, based on the rocket equation and drag effects, are presented. Gravitational effects, which were previously neglected, are offered as another phenomenon that further limits the zone. Numerical examples are used to illustrate important effects considered in this chapter.

Chapter 12 introduces strategic interceptor concepts from a tactical point of view. A gravitational model, based on Newton's law of universal gravitation, is developed for strategic flight. Comparisons between a flat-Earth gravitational model and a strategic gravitational model are made. Although strategic engagement simulation models are presented in the text in a Cartesian Earth-centered coordinate system, a polar coordinate system is also introduced so that important closed-form solutions can be derived. Key formulas for velocity and flight time for an impulsive ballistic missile to travel a fixed distance, given an initial flight-path angle, are developed using the polar coordinate system. A Cartesian Earth-centered simulation is used to confirm the analytical results.

Chapter 13 shows how preliminary strategic booster sizing can be done with the rocket equation. Simplified booster sizing examples are presented in order to clarify the concepts. The rocket equation is extended so that the virtues of staging can be illustrated via a numerical example. Finally, the gravity turn maneuver is introduced as the simplest possible steering method a booster can employ in traveling from its launch point to a desired destination.

Starting from the closed-form solutions derived in Chapter 12, the concepts of Lambert steering, which is fundamental to booster and spacecraft steering, are developed in Chapter 14. A simple to understand but numerically inefficient way of solving Lambert's problem is derived. A numerical example is presented showing how the numerical solution to Lambert's problem can be implemented. A novel use of the secant method is demonstrated to speed up the solution to Lambert's problem by more than two orders of magnitude! It is then shown how the implemented solution can be modified with a simple feedback scheme to steer an interceptor, during its boost phase, to its intended target. Another subset of Lambert steering, known as general energy management (GEM) steering, is also derived and demonstrated. A numerical example highlighting the similarities and differences between Lambert and GEM steering is presented.

Chapter 15 shows elementary but fundamental methods of combining the tactical missile guidance concepts of Chapters 2–10 with the strategic notions of Chapters 12–14. Unifying numerical examples are used to illustrate the strengths and weaknesses of the combined approach. Previously derived closed-form solutions for the required missile acceleration to hit a target by a tactical interceptor are converted to strategic lateral divert formulas. Nonlinear strategic engagement simulation results are used to show that the divert formulas for prediction error, apparent target maneuver, and guidance law are not only useful because of their simplicity but are in fact accurate indicators of strategic interceptor requirements.

Chapter 16 presents some additional concepts that are very important to the strategic world. It is shown how compensating for known gravity effects in the guidance law can considerably reduce interceptor lateral divert requirements. Next, predictive guidance is introduced as the ultimate guidance law. It is shown that, if accurate a priori information exists concerning the target, then predictive guidance can be used to substantially alleviate interceptor lateral divert requirements. All of the homing guidance concepts introduced have assumed that strategic interceptor divert engines were effectively throttleable. A pulsed guidance law is developed assuming that guidance commands can only be issued with a few discrete burns. The performance of the pulsed guidance law is compared to that of proportional navigation.

In Chapter 17, the focus of the text switches to endoatmospheric ballistic targets. Closed-form solutions are derived and validated, based on the properties of ballistic targets, showing how the magnitude of endoatmospheric ballistic target deceleration varies with speed, altitude, and re-entry angle. It is demonstrated that unless advanced guidance techniques are used, the high deceleration levels of a ballistic target make it difficult to hit under all engagement conditions.

Advanced guidance techniques and fire control logic for endoatmospheric intercepts require knowledge of the target's ballistic coefficient. Using a simplified extended Kalman filter as an example, the challenges of estimating a target's ballistic coefficient are demonstrated in Chapter 18. Common filter design pitfalls and their engineering fixes are illustrated in easy-to-understand examples. Guidelines for making an extended Kalman filter robust to large initialization errors are presented.

Finally, Chapter 19 integrates many of the text's concepts to further explain why endoatmospheric ballistic targets are challenging. Formulas are derived showing the geometry dependence of noise induced miss distance. The dependence of the minimum achievable guidance system time constant on radome slope, geometry, and missile aerodynamic properties is shown. Numerical examples are presented in order to highlight missile performance differences for both aircraft and ballistic target threats.

This text attempts to present many of the important guidance principles involved in enabling an interceptor to hit its intended target. The utility of these principles are explained and demonstrated with pictures, equations, and computer code. However, missing from the text is the intensity, challenge of the unknown, and plain hard work that it takes in going from a paper design to something that not only flies but also meets the system objectives. In light of the new challenges facing today's guidance engineer, it is very appropriate to quote from the work by M. W. Fossier:

On joining Raytheon as a young engineer, I found an intensity of spirit that I had never experienced before. I felt myself carried along in what seemed almost a crusade, sharing a burning commitment to succeed against an immense challenge.

As a result of this shared feeling, each triumph led to a broad-based feeling of great elation. I still vividly recall the first flight test by Lark against a low-flying drone aircraft in 1951 over the ocean at Point Mugu. The intercept was a relatively short range and was the first to be in full view of the handful of observers permitted on the beach. When the missile homed unerringly to a spectacular direct hit on the drone, the human explosion matched the one in the air. The formal celebration ended in the wee hours of the morning, but the emotional wave lasted for months.

On the other hand, I can still feel the despair that resulted when a technician inadvertently connected B+ (250 V) to the filament string, blowing out every tube in an early Sparrow being prepared for flight test. At that time, the best flight test engineers we had took about a month of 12-hour days to check out a missile. The resulting delay was felt at a personal level in every corner of the organization.

For years I attributed this intensity to the relative youth of most of the participants. However, I found that age has served mainly to mute their exuberance, but not their intensity, and I was forced to seek another source. My current view is that the intensity was (and is) a result of the intellectual challenge of the unknown. It is the characteristic of the engineering profession that there are always new problems waiting in the wings to replace the old ones as they are solved. The constant element is the challenge itself, which demands that we do our utmost and rewards us only when we do.

Chapter 1

Numerical Techniques

Introduction

THE numerical techniques introduced in this chapter involve the use of Laplace transforms for manipulating and displaying differential equations and numerical integration for solving the differential equations. These techniques form the basis of all the numerical methods used throughout the text. A numerical example will be presented that will illustrate a practical application of the use of Laplace transforms and numerical integration.

Computer languages, which are required for the practical implementation of numerical integration, will be discussed, and it will be shown why FORTRAN was chosen for simulation and for the presentation of listings in the text. Finally, a comparison will be performed on various hardware platforms to show the reader that all examples presented in this text can be run on computers ranging from an 8-bit desktop computer to a mainframe supercomputer. A chart will be presented enabling the reader to predict simulation running time as a function of hardware platform.

Laplace Transforms and Differential Equations

Transform methods are often useful because certain operations in one domain are different and often simpler operations in the other domain. For example, ordinary differential equations in the time domain become algebraic expressions in the s domain after being Laplace transformed. In control system engineering Laplace transforms are used both as a shorthand notation and as a method for solving linear differential equations. In this text we will frequently use Laplace transform notation to represent subsystem dynamics in tactical missile guidance systems.

If we define $F(s)$ as the Laplace transform of $f(t)$, then the Laplace transform has the following definition:

$$F(s) = \int_0^\infty f(t)\, e^{-st}\, \mathrm{d}t$$

With this definition it is easy to show that a summation in the time domain is also a summation in the Laplace transform or frequency domain. For example, if $f_1(t)$ and $f_2(t)$ have Laplace transforms $F_1(s)$ and $F_2(s)$, respectively, then

$$\mathcal{L}[f_1(t) \pm f_2(t)] = F_1(s) \pm F_2(s)$$

9

Again, using the definition of the Laplace transform, it is easy to show that differentiation in the time domain is equivalent to frequency multiplication in the Laplace transform domain, or

$$\mathcal{L}\left(\frac{df(t)}{dt}\right) = sF(s) - f(0)$$

where $f(0)$ is the initial condition on $f(t)$. The Laplace transform of the nth derivative of a function is given by

$$\mathcal{L}\left(\frac{d^n f(t)}{dt^n}\right) = s^n F(s) - s^{n-1} f(0) - s^{n-2}\frac{df(0)}{dt} - \cdots$$

From the preceding equation we can see that, for zero initial conditions, the nth derivative in the time domain is equivalent to a multiplication by s^n in the Laplace transform domain.

Laplace transforms can also be used to convert the input-output relationship of a differential equation to a shorthand notation called a transfer function representation. For example, given the second-order equation

$$\frac{d^2 y(t)}{dt^2} + 2\frac{dy(t)}{dt} + 4y(t) = x(t)$$

with zero initial conditions, or

$$\frac{dy(0)}{dt} = 0, \qquad y(0) = 0$$

we can find the same differential equation in the Laplace transform domain to be

$$s^2 Y(s) + 2sY(s) + 4Y(s) = X(s)$$

Combining like terms in the preceding equation to get a fractional relationship between the output and input, known as a transfer function, yields

$$\frac{Y(s)}{X(s)} = \frac{1}{s^2 + 2s + 4}$$

Similarly, given a transfer function, we can go back to the differential equation form. Consider the second-order transfer function

$$\frac{Y(s)}{X(s)} = \frac{1 + 2s}{1 + 2s + s^2}$$

We know that, according to the chain rule, the transfer function can also be expressed as

$$\frac{Y(s)}{X(s)} = \frac{E(s)}{X(s)}\frac{Y(s)}{E(s)}$$

Therefore, we can break the relationship into the following two equivalent transfer functions:

$$\frac{E(s)}{X(s)} = \frac{1}{1 + 2s + s^2}, \qquad \frac{Y(s)}{E(s)} = 1 + 2s$$

Cross multiplication results in

$$s^2 E(s) + 2sE(s) + E(s) = X(s)$$

and

$$2sE(s) + E(s) = Y(s)$$

Converting the first equation to the time domain yields the second-order differential equation

$$\frac{d^2 e(t)}{dt^2} + 2\frac{de(t)}{dt} + e(t) = x(t)$$

and converting the second equation yields the output relationship

$$y(t) = 2\frac{de(t)}{dt} + e(t)$$

The implication from the transfer function notation is that the initial conditions on the second-order differential equation are zero, or

$$\frac{de(0)}{dt} = 0, \qquad e(0) = 0$$

Often we will use Laplace transform notation and, for shorthand, drop the functional dependence on s in the notation [i.e., F is equivalent to $F(s)$]. Similarly, when we are in the time domain, the functional dependence on t will often be dropped [i.e., f is equivalent to $f(t)$]. In addition, block diagrams and program listings will frequently use the overdot notation to represent time derivatives. With this notation, each overdot represents a derivative. For example,

$$\dot{y} = \frac{dy}{dt}, \qquad \ddot{y} = \frac{d^2 y}{dt^2}, \qquad \dddot{y} = \frac{d^3 y}{dt^3}, \qquad \text{etc.}$$

Therefore, converting

$$\frac{d^2 e(t)}{dt^2} + 2\frac{de(t)}{dt} + e(t) = x(t)$$

to the overdot notation yields

$$\ddot{e} + 2\dot{e} + e = x$$

Occasionally, we shall either convert time functions to Laplace transforms or vice versa, by inspection. Some common transfer functions,[1] along with their time domain equivalents, appear in Table 1.1. A more extensive listing of inverse Laplace transforms can be found in Ref. 1.

Numerical Integration of Differential Equations

Throughout this text we will be simulating both linear and nonlinear ordinary differential equations. Since, in general, these equations have no closed-form solutions, it will be necessary to resort to numerical integration techniques to solve or simulate these equations. Many numerical integration techniques[2] exist for solving differential equations. However, we shall use the second-order Runge-Kutta technique throughout the text because it is simple to understand, easy to program, and, most importantly, yields accurate answers for all of the examples presented in this text.

The second-order Runge-Kutta numerical integration procedure is easy to state. Given a first-order differential equation of the form

$$\dot{x} = f(x, t)$$

where t is time, we seek to find a recursive relationship for x as a function of time. With the second-order Runge-Kutta numerical technique, the value

Table 1.1 Common inverse Laplace transforms

$F(s)$	$f(t)$
$\dfrac{K}{s}$	K
$\dfrac{K}{s^n} \quad (n = 1,2,...)$	$\dfrac{Kt^{n-1}}{(n-1)!}$
$\dfrac{K}{(s-a)^n} \quad (n = 1,2,...)$	$\dfrac{Kt^{n-1}e^{at}}{(n-1)!}$
$\dfrac{K}{s^2 + a^2}$	$\dfrac{K\sin(at)}{a}$
$\dfrac{Ks}{s^2 + a^2}$	$K\cos(at)$
$\dfrac{K}{(s-a)^2 + b^2}$	$\dfrac{Ke^{at}\sin(bt)}{b}$
$\dfrac{K(s-a)}{(s-a)^2 + b^2}$	$Ke^{at}\cos(bt)$

of x at the next integration interval, h, is given by

$$x_{K+1} = x_K + \frac{hf(x,t)}{2} + \frac{hf(x,t+h)}{2}$$

where the subscript K represents the last interval and $K + 1$ represents the new interval. From the preceding expression we can see that the new value of x is simply the old value of x plus a term proportional to the derivative evaluated at time t and another term with the derivative evaluated at time $t + h$.

The integration step size h must be small enough to yield answers of sufficient accuracy. A simple test, commonly practiced among engineers, is to find the appropriate integration step size by experiment. As a rule of thumb the initial step size is chosen to be several times smaller than the smallest time constant in the system under consideration. The step size is then halved to see if the answers change significantly. If the new answers are approximately the same, the larger integration step size is used to avoid excessive computer running time. If the answers change substantially, then the integration interval is again halved and the process is repeated.

In order to see how the Runge-Kutta technique can be applied to a practical example let us consider the problem of finding the step response of a sixth-order Butterworth filter.[3] A sixth-order Butterworth filter can be represented by the transfer function

$$\frac{y}{x} = \left(1 + \frac{a_1 s}{\omega_0} + \frac{a_2 s^2}{\omega_0^2} + \frac{a_3 s^3}{\omega_0^3} + \frac{a_4 s^4}{\omega_0^4} + \frac{a_5 s^5}{\omega_0^5} + \frac{a_6 s^6}{\omega_0^6}\right)^{-1}$$

where x is the filter input, y the filter output, ω_0 the natural frequency of the filter, and s Laplace transformation notation for a derivative. The coefficients of a sixth-order Butterworth filter are given by

$$a_1 = 3.86$$
$$a_2 = 7.46$$
$$a_3 = 9.13$$
$$a_4 = 7.46$$
$$a_5 = 3.86$$
$$a_6 = 1$$

Cross multiplying the numerator and denominator of the transfer function and solving for the highest derivative, as was shown in the previous section, yields the following sixth-order differential equation:

$$\overset{......}{y} = \frac{\omega_0^6}{a_6}\left(x - y - \frac{a_1 \dot{y}}{\omega_0} - \frac{a_2 \ddot{y}}{\omega_0^2} - \frac{a_3 \dddot{y}}{\omega_0^3} - \frac{a_4 \ddddot{y}}{\omega_0^4} - \frac{a_5 \overset{.....}{y}}{\omega_0^5}\right)$$

where each overdot represents a differentiation. This differential equation can be represented in block diagram form as shown in Fig. 1.1. In this diagram each $1/s$ represents an integration. The output of each integrator has been labeled $x(1)$–$x(6)$.

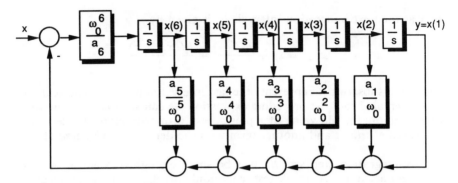

Fig. 1.1   Block diagram representation of sixth-order Butterworth filter.

For numerical integration purposes it is more convenient to express the sixth-order differential equation describing the Butterworth filter by six first-order differential equations. These equations can be obtained from Fig. 1.1 by inspection and are given by

$$\dot{x}(1) = x(2)$$
$$\dot{x}(2) = x(3)$$
$$\dot{x}(3) = x(4)$$
$$\dot{x}(4) = x(5)$$
$$\dot{x}(5) = x(6)$$

$$\dot{x}(6) = \frac{\omega_0^6}{a_6}\left[x - x(1) - \frac{a_1 x(2)}{\omega_0} - \frac{a_2 x(3)}{\omega_0^2} - \frac{a_3 x(4)}{\omega_0^3} - \frac{a_4 x(5)}{\omega_0^4} - \frac{a_5 x(6)}{\omega_0^5}\right]$$

A FORTRAN listing of the simulation of the sixth-order Butterworth filter, using the second-order Runge-Kutta integration technique, appears in Listing 1.1. We can see from the listing that the six first-order differential equations, or derivative information, appear after label 200. We come to this label twice during the integration interval: once to evaluate the derivative at time t and once to evaluate the derivative at time $t + h$. The values of the Butterworth coefficients can be found in the DATA statement.

We can see from the listing that the integration step size H is 0.0001 s. Since the simulation time is 0.5 s, the ratio of the simulation time to the step size is 5000. This means that 10,000 passes are made to the differential equations. The extremely small integration step size was chosen to ensure accurate answers if the natural frequency of the filter was made much larger and to facilitate timing comparisons, which will be discussed later in this chapter. The resultant Butterworth filter transient response, due to a step input ($XIN = 1$), is shown in Fig. 1.2.

Listing 1.1   FORTRAN simulation of sixth-order Butterworth filter

```
        INTEGER ORDER
        DIMENSION X(6),XOLD(6),XD(6)
        INTEGER STEP
        DATA A1,A2,A3,A4,A5,A6,W0/3.86,7.46,9.13,7.46,3.86,1.,50./
        DATA XIN/1./
        ORDER = 6
        W02 = W0*W0
        W03 = W02*W0
        W04 = W03*W0
        W05 = W04*W0
        W06 = W05*W0
        DO 10 I = 1,ORDER
        X(I) = 0.
10      CONTINUE
        T = 0.
        H = .0001
        S = 0.
5       IF(T.GE..5)GOTO 999
        S = S + H
        DO 20 I = 1,ORDER
        XOLD(I) = X(I)
20      CONTINUE
        STEP = 1
        GOTO 200
66      STEP = 2
        DO 30 I = 1,ORDER
        X(I) = X(I) + H*XD(I)
30      CONTINUE
        T = T + H
        GOTO 200
55      CONTINUE
        DO 40 I = 1,ORDER
        X(I) = (XOLD(I) + X(I))/2. + .5*H*XD(I)
40      CONTINUE
        IF(S.GE..004999)THEN
          S = 0.
          WRITE(9,*)T,X(1)
        END IF
        GOTO 5
200     CONTINUE
        XD(1) = X(2)
        XD(2) = X(3)
        XD(3) = X(4)
        XD(4) = X(5)
        XD(5) = X(6)
        XD(6) = W06*(XIN-A5*X(6)/W05-A4*X(5)/W04-A3*X(4)/W03
     1  -A2*X(3)/W02-A1*X(2)/W0-X(1))/A6
        IF(STEP-1)66,66,55
999     CONTINUE
        PAUSE
        END
```

Computer Languages

FORTRAN is known as the cockroach of computer languages because of its age and durability. Although frowned upon by software professionals, FORTRAN is still popular among senior engineers and scientists because it was the first (and probably only) computer language they learned. FORTRAN was the first high-level language introduced on a large scale.[4] It was first proposed in the 1953–1954 time frame by Jim Backus of IBM. The goal of FORTRAN was to demonstrate that a high-order language could be developed that would produce programs as efficient as hand-coded programs in machine language for a wide class of problems. The objective of FORTRAN at that time was to make programming on the IBM/704 computer much faster, cheaper, and more reliable. Originally the FORTRAN

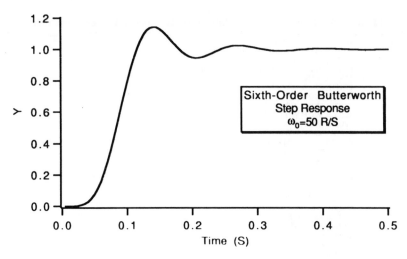

Fig. 1.2   Butterworth filter step response.

language reflected the hardware constraints of the IBM/704. However, because of the popularity of the language, other computer manufacturers developed versions of FORTRAN, tailored to their own hardware. By 1963 virtually all mainframe manufacturers committed themselves to some version of FORTRAN. Since that time FORTRAN has evolved; undesirable features have been eliminated and some elements of structured programming have been added. Today there even exist many excellent FORTRAN compilers in the microcomputer world. These compilers have many of the language extensions found in their minicomputer and mainframe counterparts and, in addition, have graphic extensions for scientific plotting. All of the listings in this text will be in the FORTRAN language so that programs can be run in either the microcomputer, minicomputer, or mainframe worlds.

Pascal was developed in the late 1960s by Niklaus Wirth of Eidgenossische Technische Hochschule in Zurich. The principal aim of Pascal was to make a language available that was suitable for teaching programming as a systematic discipline based on certain fundamental concepts clearly and naturally reflected by the language (structured programming). In addition, it was desired to develop implementations of Pascal that were both reliable and efficient. The first Pascal compiler was available in 1970, and since that time, Pascal has gained widespread acceptance as a teaching language for structured programming. Turbo Pascal, developed by Borland International for the MS DOS microcomputer world, popularized this language by introducing a low-cost advanced compiler technology.

To many engineers BASIC is known as "FORTRAN without grief." BASIC was originally developed in 1963 at Dartmouth College by John Kemeny and Thomas Kurtz. The language was originally designed for beginners with interactive computing in mind. However, by 1970 the language had grown so that it could handle the most sophisticated and complex applications. During the 1970s, as graphics devices became available, easy-to-use graphics commands were added to the language. When microcomputers first appeared, BASIC was the most popular language for implementation on them, because it was clean, simple, and generally included without cost with each microcomputer purchased. Although, commonly implemented as an interpretive language, excellent compilers exist today for BASIC in the microcomputer world. Although generally scorned by computer language gourmets, BASIC continues to be the world's most popular programming language because of its low cost and ease of use.

C is a general purpose programming language. It has been called a "systems programming language" because it is useful for writing operating systems. It has been used in the microcomputer world to write major text processing, desktop publishing, and data base programs. C is a relatively low-level language compared to either FORTRAN or Pascal. This language stems from the language BCPL, developed by Martin Richards. The influence of BCPL on C proceeded indirectly through the language B, which was written by Ken Thompson in 1970 for the first UNIX system on the PDP-7.

For a given hardware platform the choice of language makes a significant difference in the computer running time. Interpretive languages, such as BASIC, are slower than compiled languages, such as FORTRAN. However, interpretive languages, due to the friendly debugging environment, often reduce the program development time. If one has to develop a program quickly and only run it a few times, an interpretive language like BASIC might be the best choice. If the program has many differential equations and will be run many times, a compiled language like FORTRAN might be a better choice.

Several popular microcomputer languages were used on the sample problem of the previous section and the computer running times, circa 1987,[5] on a Macintosh Plus without a math coprocessor are summarized in Table 1.2.

Surprisingly, although during 1987 C was the de facto standard for commercial program development on microcomputers, it is nearly as slow as interpretive BASIC for problems involving floating-point computation. Similarly, although Pascal during the same time frame was the standard in many educational institutions, it is very slow for problems involving the integration of differential equations. The slowness of C and Pascal on the

Table 1.2   FORTRAN is the fastest language for simulation on the Macintosh Plus

Language	Type	Running time, s
MBASIC 2.1	Interpretive	784
Mac Pascal	Interpretive	1804
True BASIC	Intermediate	242
MBASIC 1.0	Compiled	159
Z BASIC	Compiled	412
TML Pascal	Compiled	425
Lightspeed Pascal	Compiled	505
Light Speed C	Compiled	410
Aztec C	Compiled	620
MacFORTRAN	Compiled	61

Macintosh Plus for simulation-type problems is due to floating-point operations. Both C and Pascal use the standard package provided by Apple for floating-point operations which gives high precision (too high for this simple example) but exacts a heavy penalty in speed. However, the implementations of both BASIC and FORTRAN for the Macintosh Plus developed their own software floating-point libraries. In these software libraries there was a choice of either single- or double-precision arithmetic. The user was allowed to trade off reduction in accuracy vs greatly improved speed. The accuracy of both BASIC and FORTRAN in single-precision for the sample Butterworth filter transient response problem was sufficient to get the correct answers. The table also shows that when BASIC is compiled it is faster than either C or Pascal. In the case of the Macintosh Plus without a math coprocessor, FORTRAN is clearly the language of choice when speed is an issue. If a coprocessor is available and the language can take advantage of it, then the speed differences between the compiled languages begin to blur. Although software purists do not like to admit it, the fastest compiler is more a function of who wrote the compiler than a language issue!

FORTRAN Comparison

The simulation of the sixth-order Butterworth filter using the FORTRAN source code of Listing 1.1 is now solved on microcomputers representative of the 8-, 16-, and 32-bit world, and their running times are compared. The machines used in this comparison are the original IBM PC, an improved PC, an IBM AT, a Macintosh Plus, and Macintosh II microcomputers. The performance of the machines are compared with and without math coprocessors. Table 1.3 (Ref. 5) presents the running time comparisons.

Table 1.3 indicates that the original IBM PC is very slow compared to the other machines on the Butterworth simulation example. However, newer versions of the 4.77-Mhz, 8-bit IBM PC and clones are significantly faster (and less expensive too). For example, the IBM AT is about twice as fast as the improved IBM PC, and the Macintosh II is four times faster than the Macintosh Plus. Addressing the math coprocessor significantly improves the speed of both the Macintosh II and the improved IBM PC. However, addressing the math coprocessor on an IBM AT results in negligible speed improvement. The performance improvement for the IBM AT is not as significant because the math coprocessor operates at 4 Mhz whereas the machine is running at 6 Mhz. From Table 1.3 we can see that the 32-bit Macintosh II is nearly 35 times faster than the original 8-bit IBM PC. When the math coprocessor is addressed, it is nearly 70 times faster. Clearly there have been many improvements since the introduction of the first IBM PC.

Table 1.3   FORTRAN running time comparison for Butterworth filter example

Coprocessor	IBM PC	Improved PC	IBM AT	Macintosh Plus	Macintosh II
Out	520 s	75 s	39 s	61 s	15.4 s
In	——	40 s	35 s	——	7.4 s

**Table 1.4   Microcomputer, minicomputer, and mainframe
running time comparison**

IBM PC	IBM AT	Macintosh II	VAX/785	VAX/8600	IBM/3084Q
520 s	35 s	7.4 s	3.1 s	0.74 s	0.61 s

The sample problem was also run in FORTRAN on two super minicomputers and one mainframe computer. The running times are summarized in Table 1.4 (Ref. 5).

In this table the running time for the larger machines corresponds to CPU time with a single-user load on a time-sharing system. Usually large machines are shared among many users, and the CPU time is indicative only of what the user is charged for a session. In addition, on large machines the turnaround time (the elapsed time it takes the user to get the output) may be hours, even though the CPU time may be in seconds. On a microcomputer the CPU time is the turnaround time. Nonetheless, Table 1.4 indicates that the Macintosh II is only 2.4 times slower than the VAX/785 and 12 times slower than the mainframe. Considering that the Macintosh II costs about $6,000, whereas the VAX/785 is about $250,000 and the IBM/3084Q is several million dollars, the comparison is more impressive. More importantly, the sample Butterworth filter problem could be solved on any of the machines in a very reasonable amount of time. In the case of the microcomputers the user gets the answers immediately, whereas on the larger machines the turnaround time may be significantly longer.

The answers for the sample FORTRAN problem were for six differential equations, a simulation time of 0.5 s, and an integration interval of 0.0001 s. Doubling the simulation time, doubling the number of differential equations, or halving the integration interval will work in the direction of doubling the computer running time, regardless of the computer. Figure 1.3 presents computational information so that an engineer can approximate the computer running time for a given problem. All that has to be done is to multiply the number of differential equations by the simulation time and divide by the integration step size in order to compute the abscissa of the figure. The computer running time in seconds is the ordinate.

For example, the simulation of 100 differential equations in FORTRAN for a 10-s simulation with an integration step size of 0.01 s would require a run time of 1730 s on the original IBM PC, 116 s on an IBM AT, 24.7 s on a Macintosh II, 10.3 s on a VAX/785, and 2.03 s on an IBM/3084Q.

Whetstone Benchmarking

The whetstone benchmark, devised in England by H. J. Curnow and B. A. Wichmann in the Feb. 1976 issue of *Computer Journal*,[6] is an attempt to cover a typical mix of all floating-point operations. This benchmark contains linear arrays, and addition, subtraction, multiplication, division, and transcendental operations. Whetstones were originally written in ALGOL, but were later translated to FORTRAN in 1979 by D. Frank. Since that

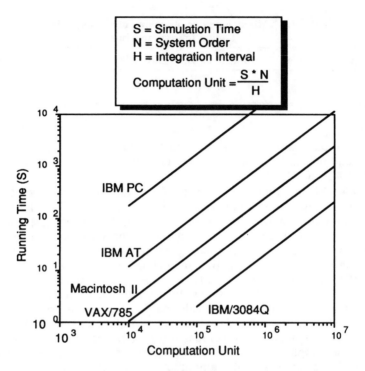

Fig. 1.3   Computer running time for a given problem.

time, many computer manufacturers have rated their machines in terms of thousands of whetstones per second or kilowhetstones per second. Higher whetstone ratings mean more powerful machines. Table 1.5 (Refs. 7,8) presents single-precision and double-precision whetstone ratings for a variety of microcomputers, minicomputers, and mainframes. In addition, ratios referenced to Macintosh II speed are indicated in the table. A ratio of 1.7 means that the computer is 1.7 times faster than the Macintosh II. All computers, with the exception of the Macintosh Plus, have math coprocessors or floating-point accelerators. The poor double-precision whetstone rating of the Macintosh Plus, relative to the IBM PC, may be one of the reasons there was a scarcity of scientific software for the Macintosh in the 1987 time frame and a plethora of scientific software for the IBM PC.

The whetstone results of Table 1.5 [with no input/output (I/O)] can be compared to the Butterworth simulation results (with considerable I/O and more representative of a realistic engineering application) of Ref. 5. Figure 1.4 shows that all of the benchmarks, whether they are whetstones or Butterworth simulation results, yield about the same relative machine performance. Only the Macintosh Plus seems to yield results that are significantly benchmark dependent. It yields worse performance on the whetstones because of its lack of a math coprocessor.

The performance comparison of Fig. 1.4 can be placed into proper perspective when the cost of the host computer is considered. For simplicity,

Table 1.5   Whetstone ratings for a variety of machines

Microcomputer	Single-precision, kwhet/s	Ratio	Double-precision, kwhet/s	Ratio
Macintosh Plus[a]	42.8	0.083	18.7	0.04
IBM PC	57.8	0.11	52.5	0.11
IBM AT	98	0.19	89	0.18
IBM RT	200	0.39	188	0.39
Compaq 386	241	0.47	219	0.45
Macintosh II	515	1	485	1
Micro VAX 2	880	1.7	655	1.35
VAX 11/780	1191	2.3	734	1.5
VAX 11/785	1800	3.5	1157	2.4
VAX 8650	6100	11.8	3895	8
IBM/3084Q	5850	11.4	5680	11.7
IBM/3090	18,000	35	15,000	30.9

[a]No math coprocessor.

computer cost can be considered to be the machine's purchase price only. This neglects the cost of the small army of technicians required to operate the larger machines and the cost of software leasing agreements. We can see from Fig. 1.5 (Ref. 7) that generally higher cost computers yield faster performance. However, the cost is not always commensurate with the performance. For example, a VAX 11/780 is only 1.5 times as fast as a Macintosh II and yet is 40 times more expensive. An IBM/3084Q is 11.7 times faster than a Macintosh II and is 500 times more expensive. On the microcomputer side an IBM RT is 2.5 times slower than a Macintosh II and yet costs twice as much.

If we normalize the computer performance as measured by double-precision whetstones per second to the computer purchase price, we can generate "bang for the buck" information. More bang for the buck means that the computer yields a higher double-precision whetstone rating for less cost. Figure 1.6 presents this cost effectiveness information and shows that the Compaq 386, Macintosh II and Micro VAX 2 are very cost effective, with the Macintosh II yielding the most "bang for the buck" during the 1987 time frame. The curve also indicates that, if a microcomputer can do the job, it is more cost effective from a performance point of view than a mainframe.

Reduced Instruction Set Computer

Based on the results of the previous section, it seems that increasing computer chip clock rates is the most effective way of increasing personal computer speeds. However, since physics places an upper limit of 100–150 MHz on achievable clock rates with silicon, it would appear that personal computer speeds could only increase by less than a factor of 10 over their 1987 levels. Fortunately reduced instruction set computer (RISC) based platforms offer much greater performance increases. RISC is a style of computer architecture that advocates shifting complexity from hard-

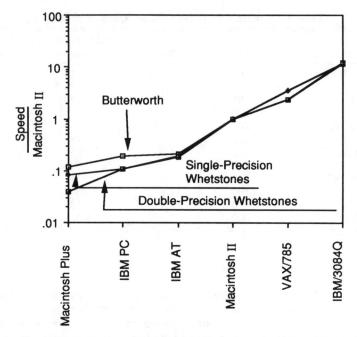

Fig. 1.4   Relative machine performance is approximately independent of benchmark.

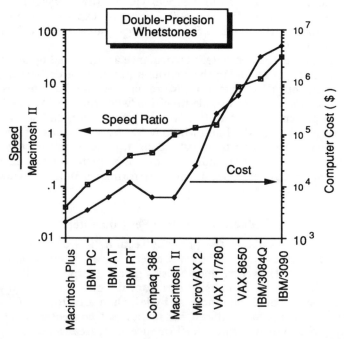

Fig. 1.5   Microcomputers are more cost effective than larger machines.

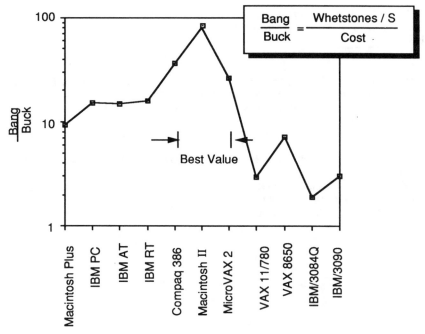

Fig. 1.6   Microcomputers are very cost effective.

ware and program run time to software and program compile time. With RISC most instructions are effectively executed in a single machine cycle and only those features that measurably affect performance are implemented in hardware.

The first RISC machine was the IBM/801 minicomputer built in 1979. This computer, which was not a commercial product, had a very fast memory and fixed format instructions that could execute in a single clock cycle. The IBM RT PC work station was a commercial product introduced in 1986 based on the 801 technology. However, the original RT was a failure commercially, possibly because of the absence of high-level language support.

Reference 9 describes how one particular RISC board and FORTRAN compiler sped up a Macintosh II by a factor of 30 on programs such as the ones in this text. Based on the results of Table 1.5 we can see that this type of speed increase places RISC personal computers in mainframe territory without the need for nitrogen bottles or elements of superconductivity. In fact, the 1993 68040-based Macintosh and 80486-based IBM compatible computers have elements of RISC in them, making them an order of magnitude faster than their counterparts in Table 1.5. During the 1993 time frame, 80486-based IBM compatible computers yielded the most "bang for the buck" since complete systems could be purchased for under $2000.

References

[1]Selby, S. M., *Standard Mathematical Tables—Twentieth Edition,* Chemical Rubber Co., Cleveland, OH, 1972.

[2]Press, N. H., Flannery, B. P., Teukolsky, S. A., and Vetterling, W. T., *Numerical Recipes: The Art of Scientific Computation,* Cambridge Univ. Press, London, 1986.

[3]Karni, S., *Network Theory: Analysis and Synthesis,* Allyn & Bacon, London, 1966.

[4]MacLennan, B. J., *Principles of Programming Languages: Design, Evaluation, and Implementation,* Holt, Rinehart, & Winston, New York, 1983.

[5]Zarchan, P., "New Mac Workstation Potential," *MacTutor,* Vol. 3, No. 3, March 1987, pp. 15-21.

[6]Curnow, H. J., and Wichmann, B. A., "Synthetic Benchmark," *Computer Journal,* Vol. 19, Feb. 1976, pp. 43-49.

[7]Zarchan, P., "Benchmarks Re-Visited," *MacTutor,* Vol. 3, Sept. 1987, pp. 78-80.

[8]Marshall, T., Jones, C., and Kluger, S., "Definicon 68020 Coprocessor," *BYTE,* Vol. 11, July 1986, pp. 120-144.

[9]Zarchan, P., "The Mac II on Steroids," *MacTutor,* Vol. 6, Sept. 1990, pp. 78–82.

Chapter 2

Fundamentals of Tactical Missile Guidance

Introduction

TACTICAL guided missiles apparently had their origin in Germany. For example, the Hs. 298 was one of a series of German air-to-air guided missiles developed by the Henschel Company during World War II.[1] A high-thrust first stage accelerated the missile from the carrier aircraft, whereas a low-thrust, long-burning sustainer, maintained the vehicle's velocity. The Hs. 298, which was radio-controlled from the parent aircraft, was to be released either slightly above or below the target. Apparently the height differential made it easier to aim and guide the missile. This first air-to-air missile weighed 265 lb and had a range of nearly 3 miles. On December 22, 1944, three missiles were test flown from a JU 88G aircraft. All three tests resulted in failure. Although 100 of these air-to-air missiles were manufactured, none was used in combat.

The Rheintochter (R-1) was a surface-to-air missile also developed in Germany during World War II.[1] This unusual looking two-stage radio-controlled missile weighed nearly 4000 lb and had three sets of plywood fins: one for the booster and two for the sustainer. Eighty-two of these missiles flew before production was halted in December 1944. The missile was ineffective because Allied bombers, which were the R-1's intended target, flew above the range (about 20,000 ft) of this surface-to-air missile.

Although proportional navigation was apparently known by the Germans during World War II at Peenemünde, no applications on the Hs. 298 or R-1 missiles using proportional navigation were reported.[2] The Lark missile, which had its first successful test in December 1950, was the first missile to use proportional navigation. Since that time proportional navigation guidance has been used in virtually all of the world's tactical radar, infrared (IR), and television (TV) guided missiles.[3] The popularity of this interceptor guidance law is based upon its simplicity, effectiveness, and ease of implementation. Apparently, proportional navigation was first studied by C. Yuan and others at the RCA Laboratories during World War II under the auspices of the U.S. Navy.[4] The guidance law was conceived from physical reasoning and equipment available at that time. Proportional navigation was extensively studied at Hughes Aircraft Company[5] and implemented in a tactical missile using a pulsed radar system. Finally, proportional navigation was more fully developed at Raytheon and implemented in a tactical continuous wave radar homing missile.[6] After World War II, the U.S. work on proportional navigation was declassified and first appeared in the *Journal of Applied Physics*.[7] Mathematical derivations of the "optimality" of proportional navigation came more than 20 years later.[8]

Keeping with the spirit of the origins of proportional navigation, we shall avoid mathematical proofs in this chapter on deriving the guidance law, but shall, instead, concentrate first on proving to the reader that the guidance technique works. Next we shall investigate some properties of the guidance law that we shall both observe and derive. Finally, we shall show how this classical guidance law provides the foundation for more advanced techniques of interceptor guidance.

What Is Proportional Navigation?

Theoretically, the proportional navigation guidance law issues acceleration commands, perpendicular to the instantaneous missile-target line-of-sight, which are proportional to the line-of-sight rate and closing velocity. Mathematically, the guidance law can be stated as

$$n_c = N' V_c \dot{\lambda}$$

where n_c is the acceleration command (in ft/s^2), N' a unitless designer chosen gain (usually in the range of 3–5) known as the effective navigation ratio, V_c the missile-target closing velocity (in ft/s), and λ the line-of-sight angle (in rad). The overdot indicates the time derivative of the line-of-sight angle or the line-of-sight rate.

In tactical radar homing missiles using proportional navigation guidance, the seeker provides an effective measurement of the line-of-sight rate, and a Doppler radar provides closing velocity information. In tactical IR missile applications of proportional navigation guidance, the line-of-sight rate is measured, whereas the closing velocity, required by the guidance law, is "guesstimated."

In tactical endoatmospheric missiles, proportional navigation guidance commands are usually implemented by moving fins or other control surfaces to obtain the required lift. Exoatmospheric strategic interceptors use thrust vector control, lateral divert engines, or squibs to achieve the desired acceleration levels.

Simulation of Proportional Navigation in Two Dimensions

In order to better understand how proportional navigation works, let us consider the two-dimensional, point mass missile-target engagement geometry of Fig. 2.1. Here we have an inertial coordinate system fixed to the surface of a flat-Earth model (i.e., the 1 axis is downrange and the 2 axis can either be altitude or crossrange). Using the inertial coordinate system of Fig. 2.1 means that we can integrate components of the accelerations and velocities along the 1 and 2 directions without having to worry about additional terms due to the Coriolis effect. In this model it is assumed that both the missile and target travel at constant velocity. In addition, gravitational and drag effects have been neglected for simplicity.

We can see from the figure that the missile, with velocity magnitude V_M, is heading at an angle of $L + HE$ with respect to the line of sight. The angle

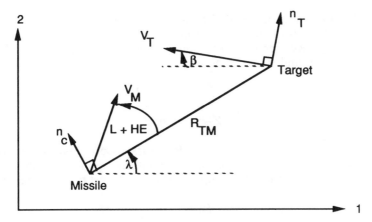

Fig. 2.1   Two-dimensional missile-target engagement geometry.

L is known as the missile lead angle. The lead angle is the theoretically correct angle for the missile to be on a collision triangle with the target. In other words, if the missile is on a collision triangle, no further acceleration commands are required for the missile to hit the target. The angle HE is known as the heading error. This angle represents the initial deviation of the missile from the collision triangle.

In Fig. 2.1 the imaginary line connecting the missile and target is known as the line of sight. The line of sight makes an angle of λ with respect to the fixed reference, and the length of the line of sight (instantaneous separation between missile and target) is a range denoted R_{TM}. From a guidance point of view, we desire to make the range between missile and target at the expected intercept time as small as possible (hopefully zero). The point of closest approach of the missile and target is known as the miss distance.

The closing velocity V_c is defined as the negative rate of change of the distance from the missile to the target, or

$$V_c = -\dot{R}_{TM}$$

Therefore, at the end of the engagement, when the missile and target are in closest proximity, the sign of V_c will change. In other words, from calculus we know that the closing velocity will be zero when R_{TM} is a minimum (i.e., the function is either minimum or maximum when its derivative is zero). The desired acceleration command n_c, which is derived from the proportional navigation guidance law, is perpendicular to the instantaneous line of sight.

In our engagement model of Fig. 2.1 the target can maneuver evasively with acceleration magnitude n_T. Since target acceleration n_T in the preceding model is perpendicular to the target velocity vector, the angular velocity of the target can be expressed as

$$\dot{\beta} = \frac{n_T}{V_T}$$

where V_T is the magnitude of the target velocity. The components of the target velocity vector in the Earth or inertial coordinate system can be found by integrating the differential equation given earlier for the flight-path angle of the target, β, and substituting in

$$V_{T1} = -V_T \cos\beta$$

$$V_{T2} = V_T \sin\beta$$

Target position components in the Earth fixed coordinate system can be found by directly integrating the target velocity components. Therefore, the differential equations for the components of the target position are given by

$$\dot{R}_{T1} = V_{T1}$$

$$\dot{R}_{T2} = V_{T2}$$

Similarly, the missile velocity and position differential equations are given by

$$\dot{V}_{M1} = a_{M1}$$

$$\dot{V}_{M2} = a_{M2}$$

$$\dot{R}_{M1} = V_{M1}$$

$$\dot{R}_{M2} = V_{M2}$$

where a_{M1} and a_{M2} are the missile acceleration components in the Earth coordinate system. In order to find the missile acceleration components, we must first find the components of the relative missile-target separation. This is accomplished by first defining the components of the relative missile-target separations by

$$R_{TM1} = R_{T1} - R_{M1}$$

$$R_{TM2} = R_{T2} - R_{M2}$$

We can see from Fig. 2.1 that the line-of-sight angle can be found, using trigonometry, in terms of the relative separation components as

$$\lambda = \tan^{-1} \frac{R_{TM2}}{R_{TM1}}$$

If we define the relative velocity components in Earth coordinates to be

$$V_{TM1} = V_{T1} - V_{M1}$$

$$V_{TM2} = V_{T2} - V_{M2}$$

we can calculate the line-of-sight rate by direct differentiation of the expression for line-of-sight angle. After some algebra we obtain the expression for the line-of-sight rate to be

$$\dot{\lambda} = \frac{R_{TM1}V_{TM2} - R_{TM2}V_{TM1}}{R_{TM}^2}$$

The relative separation between missile and target, R_{TM}, can be expressed in terms of its inertial components by application of the distance formula, as

$$R_{TM} = (R_{TM1}^2 + R_{TM2}^2)^{\frac{1}{2}}$$

Since the closing velocity is defined as the negative rate of change of the missile target separation, it can be obtained by differentiating the preceding equation, yielding

$$V_c = -\dot{R}_{TM} = \frac{-(R_{TM1}V_{TM1} + R_{TM2}V_{TM2})}{R_{TM}}$$

The magnitude of the missile guidance command n_c can then be found from the definition of proportional navigation, or

$$n_c = N'V_c\dot{\lambda}$$

Since the acceleration command is perpendicular to the instantaneous line of sight, the missile acceleration components in Earth coordinates can be found by trigonometry using the angular definitions from Fig. 2.1. The missile acceleration components are

$$a_{M1} = -n_c \sin\lambda$$

$$a_{M2} = n_c \cos\lambda$$

We have now listed all the differential equations required to model a complete missile-target engagement in two dimensions. However, some additional equations are required for the initial conditions on the differential equations in order to complete the engagement model.

A missile employing proportional navigation guidance is not fired at the target but is fired in a direction to lead the target. The initial angle of the missile velocity vector with respect to the line of sight is known as the missile lead angle L. In essence we are firing the missile at the expected intercept point. We can see from Fig. 2.1 that, for the missile to be on a collision triangle (missile will hit target if both continue to fly along a straight-line path at constant velocities), the theoretical missile lead angle can be found by application of the law of sines, yielding

$$L = \sin^{-1}\frac{V_T \sin(\beta + \lambda)}{V_M}$$

In practice, the missile is usually not launched exactly on a collision triangle, since the expected intercept point is not known precisely. The location of the intercept point can only be approximated because we do not know in advance what the target will do in the future. In fact, that is why a guidance system is required! Any initial angular deviation of the missile from the collision triangle is known as a heading error HE. The initial missile velocity components can therefore be expressed in terms of the theoretical lead angle L and actual heading error HE as

$$V_{M1}(0) = V_M \cos(L + HE + \lambda)$$

$$V_{M2}(0) = V_M \sin(L + HE + \lambda)$$

Two-Dimensional Engagement Simulation

In order to witness and understand the effectiveness of proportional navigation, it is best to simulate the guidance law and test its properties under a variety of circumstances. A two-dimensional missile-target engagement simulation was set up using the differential equations derived in the previous section. The simulation inputs are the initial location of the missile and target, speeds, flight time, and effective navigation ratio. The user can vary the level of the two error sources considered: target maneuver and heading error.

A FORTRAN tactical missile-target engagement simulation appears in Listing 2.1. We can see from the listing that the missile and target differential equations are solved using the second-order Runge-Kutta numerical integration technique. As was the case in the Butterworth filter simulation of Chapter 1, the differential equations appear after label 200. All computation in the simulation is performed in single-precision arithmetic. The integration step size is fixed for most of the flight ($H = 0.01$ s) but is made smaller near the end of the flight ($H = 0.0002$ s when $R_{TM} < 1000$ ft) to accurately capture the magnitude of the miss distance. The program is terminated when the closing velocity changes sign, since this means that the separation between the missile and target is a minimum. At this time the missile-target separation is the miss distance. Nominally the program is set up without errors. We can see from the listing that errors can be introduced by changing values in the data statements. Status of the missile and target location, along with acceleration and separation information, is displayed every 0.1 s.

A sample case was run in which the only disturbance was a 20-deg heading error ($HEDEG = -20.$). Sample trajectories for effective navigation ratios of 4 and 5 are depicted in Fig. 2.2. We can see from the figure that initially the missile is flying in the wrong direction because of the heading error. Gradually the guidance law forces the missile to home on the target. The larger effective navigation ratio enables the missile to remove the initial heading error more rapidly, thus causing a much tighter trajectory. In both cases, proportional navigation appears to be an effective guidance law because the missile hits the target (near zero miss distance with the simulation).

Listing 2.1   Two-dimensional tactical missile-target engagement simulation

```
            DATA VM,VT,XNT,HEDEG,XNP/3000.,1000.,0.,-20.,3./
            DATA RM1,RM2,RT1,RT2/0.,10000.,40000.,10000./
            BETA = 0.
            VT1 = - VT*COS(BETA)
            VT2 = VT*SIN(BETA)
            HE = HEDEG/57.3
            T = 0.
            S = 0.
            RTM1 = RT1 - RM1
            RTM2 = RT2 - RM2
            RTM = SQRT(RTM1**2 + RTM2**2)
            XLAM = ATAN2(RTM2,RTM1)
            XLEAD = ASIN(VT*SIN(BETA + XLAM)/VM)
            THET = XLAM + XLEAD
            VM1 = VM*COS(THET + HE)
            VM2 = VM*SIN(THET + HE)
            VTM1 = VT1 - VM1
            VTM2 = VT2 - VM2
            VC = - (RTM1*VTM1 + RTM2*VTM2)/RTM
   10       IF(VC<0.)GOTO 999
            IF(RTM<1000.)THEN
                H = .0002
            ELSE
                H = .01
            ENDIF
            BETAOLD = BETA
            RT1OLD = RT1
            RT2OLD = RT2
            RM1OLD = RM1
            RM2OLD = RM2
            VM1OLD = VM1
            VM2OLD = VM2
            STEP = 1
            GOTO 200
   66       STEP = 2
            BETA = BETA + H*BETAD
            RT1 = RT1 + H*VT1
            RT2 = RT2 + H*VT2
            RM1 = RM1 + H*VM1
            RM2 = RM2 + H*VM2
            VM1 = VM1 + H*AM1
            VM2 = VM2 + H*AM2
            T = T + H
            GOTO 200
   55       CONTINUE
            BETA = .5*(BETAOLD + BETA + H*BETAD)
            RT1 = .5*(RT1OLD + RT1 + H*VT1)
            RT2 = .5*(RT2OLD + RT2 + H*VT2)
            RM1 = .5*(RM1OLD + RM1 + H*VM1)
            RM2 = .5*(RM2OLD + RM2 + H*VM2)
            VM1 = .5*(VM1OLD + VM1 + H*AM1)
            VM2 = .5*(VM2OLD + VM2 + H*AM2)
            S = S + H
            IF(S<.09999)GOTO 10
            S = 0.
            WRITE(9,*)T,RT1,RT2,RM1,RM2,XNC,RTM
            GOTO 10
  200       CONTINUE
            RTM1 = RT1 - RM1
            RTM2 = RT2 - RM2
            RTM = SQRT(RTM1**2 + RTM2**2)
            VTM1 = VT1 - VM1
            VTM2 = VT2 - VM2
            VC = - (RTM1*VTM1 + RTM2*VTM2)/RTM
            XLAM = ATAN2(RTM2,RTM1)
            XLAMD = (RTM1*VTM2 - RTM2*VTM1)/(RTM*RTM)
            XNC = XNP*VC*XLAMD
            AM1 = - XNC*SIN(XLAM)
            AM2 = XNC*COS(XLAM)
            VT1 = - VT*COS(BETA)
            VT2 = VT*SIN(BETA)
            BETAD = XNT/VT
            IF(STEP - 1)66,66,55
  999       CONTINUE
            WRITE(9,*)T,RT1,RT2,RM1,RM2,XNC,RTM
            PAUSE
            END
```

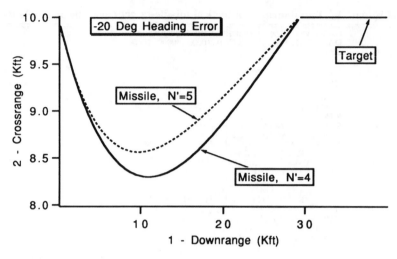

Fig. 2.2   Increasing effective navigation ratio causes heading error to be removed more rapidly.

The resultant missile acceleration histories, displayed in Fig. 2.3, for both cases are somewhat different. The quicker removal of heading error in the higher effective navigation ratio case ($N' = 5$) results in larger missile accelerations at the beginning of the flight and lower accelerations near the end of the flight. In both cases the acceleration profiles for the required missile acceleration to take out the heading error and to hit the target is monotonically decreasing and zero at the end of the flight. Thus, a property of a proportional navigation guidance system is to start taking out heading error as soon as possible but also gradually throughout the *entire* flight. In Chapter 16 we shall study a guidance system that tries to remove the entire

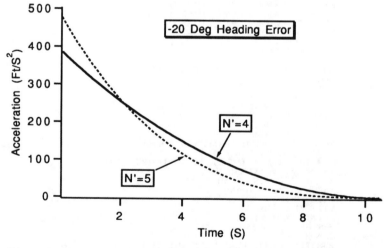

Fig. 2.3   Increasing effective navigation ratio causes more acceleration initially.

heading error immediately. By increasing the effective navigation ratio, we are allowing the missile to take out heading error more rapidly.

Another sample case was run in which the only disturbance was a 3-g target maneuver ($XNT = 96.6$, $HEDEG = 0$). In this scenario the missile and target are initially on a collision triangle and flying along the down-range component of the Earth fixed coordinate system (cross-range velocity components of both interceptor and target are zero). Therefore, the target velocity vector is initially along the line of sight, and at first all 3 g of the target acceleration are perpendicular to the line of sight. As the target maneuvers, the magnitude of the target acceleration perpendicular to the line of sight diminishes due to the turning of the target. Sample missile-target trajectories for this case with effective navigation ratios of 4 and 5 are depicted in Fig. 2.4. We can see that the higher effective navigation ratio causes the missile to lead the target slightly more than the lower navigation ratio case. Otherwise the trajectories are virtually identical. In both cases, the proportional navigation guidance law enabled the missile to hit the maneuvering target.

However, Fig. 2.5 shows that there are significant differences between the acceleration profiles for the maneuvering target case. Although both acceleration profiles are virtually monotonically increasing for the entire flight, the higher effective navigation ratio requires less acceleration capability of the missile. In addition, we can see that the peak acceleration required by the missile to hit the target is significantly higher than the maneuver level of the target (96.6 ft/s^2).

In both simulation examples we have seen the effectiveness of proportional navigation guidance. First we saw that proportional navigation is able to hit a target, even if it is initially launched in the wrong direction by 20 deg. Then we observed that the guidance law was also effective in hitting a maneuvering target. In both cases certain acceleration levels were required

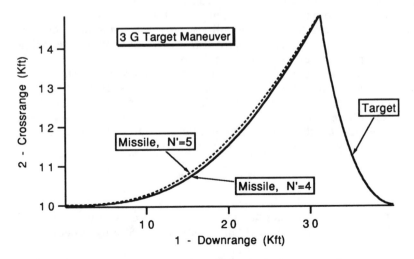

Fig. 2.4   **Proportional navigation works against maneuvering target.**

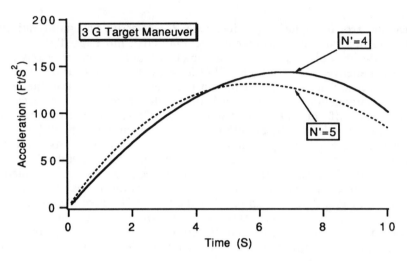

Fig. 2.5   Higher navigation ratio yields less acceleration to hit maneuvering target.

of the missile in order for it to hit the target. The levels were dependent on the type of error source and the effective navigation ratio. If the missile does not have the acceleration required by the guidance law, a miss will result.

Linearization

Thus far our understanding of the effectiveness of proportional naviga-tion has come from the numerical simulation results of the two-dimensional engagement simulation. It is critical for the analysis, understanding, and development of design relationships to temporarily depart from the nonlin-ear missile-target simulation and develop a simpler model. Therefore, we will linearize the two-dimensional engagement model in the hope of gaining more understanding. This does not mean that we will abandon the nonlinear engagement model. In fact, we will always use the nonlinear engagement model to verify the insights generated by powerful analytical techniques to be used on the linearized engagement model.

The linearization of the missile-target geometry can easily be accom-plished if we define some new relative quantities as shown in Fig. 2.6. Here y is the relative separation between the missile and target perpendicular to the fixed reference.

The relative acceleration (difference between missile and target accelera-tion) can be written by inspection of Fig. 2.6 as

$$\ddot{y} = n_T \cos\beta - n_c \cos\lambda$$

If the flight-path angles are small (near head-on or tail chase case), the cosine terms are approximately unity, and the preceding equation becomes

$$\ddot{y} = n_T - n_c$$

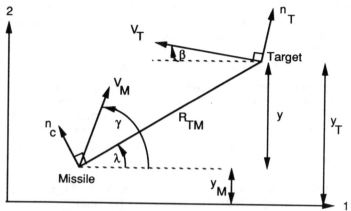

Fig. 2.6 Engagement model for linearization.

Similarly, the expression for the line-of-sight angle can also be linearized using the small-angle approximation, yielding

$$\lambda = y/R_{TM}$$

For a head-on case we can approximate the closing velocity as

$$V_c = V_M + V_T$$

whereas in a tail chase case the closing velocity can be approximated as

$$V_c = V_M - V_T$$

Therefore, in a linearized analysis we will treat the closing velocity as a positive constant. Since closing velocity has also been previously defined as the negative derivative of the range from the missile to target, and since the range must go to zero at the end of the flight, we can also linearize the range equation with the time-varying relationship

$$R_{TM} = V_c(t_F - t)$$

where t is current time and t_F the total flight time of the engagement. Note that t_F is also now a constant. The quantity $t_F - t$ is the time to go until the end of the flight. Therefore, the range from the missile to the target is also the closing velocity multiplied by the time to go until intercept. Since range goes to zero at the end of the flight by definition, we must reexamine the definition of miss distance. The linearized miss distance is taken to be the relative separation between missile and target, y, at the end of the flight, or

$$\text{Miss} = y(t_F)$$

Since the linearized miss is not obtained from the distance formula, it is only an approximation to the actual miss. However, we shall soon see that the miss distance approximation is very accurate.

Linearized Engagement Simulation

In the previous section we developed linearized equations for the missile-target engagement. In this section we will see if the resultant linearized equations give performance projections that have trends similar to those of the nonlinear engagement equations. If they do not, then there is no point in developing design relationships based on a meaningless model. If they do, then there may be a point for the interested reader to continue reading this text!

The linearized proportional navigation engagement FORTRAN simulation appears in Listing 2.2. In this simulation the flight time t_F is an input rather than output. We can see from the listing that the simulation only consists of two differential equations: one for relative velocity and the other for relative acceleration. These differential equations are also solved using the second-order Runge-Kutta numerical integration technique. The linearized differential equations appear in the listing after label 200. Unlike the nonlinear engagement simulation, the integration step size in the linear simulation can be kept fixed for the entire flight ($H = 0.01$ s). The program is stopped when the current time equals the flight time. Nominally the

Listing 2.2   Linearized engagement simulation

```
         DATA VC,XNT,Y,VM,HEDEG,TF,XNP/4000.,0.,0.,3000., − 20.,10.,3./
         YD = − VM*HEDEG/57.3
         T = 0.
         H = .01
         S = 0.
10       IF(T > (TF − .0001))GOTO 999
         YOLD = Y
         YDOLD = YD
         STEP = 1
         GOTO 200
66       STEP = 2
         Y = Y + H*YD
         YD = YD + H*YDD
         T = T + H
         GOTO 200
55       CONTINUE
         Y = .5*(YOLD + Y + H*YD)
         YD = .5*(YDOLD + YD + H*YDD)
         S = S + H
         IF(S < .09999)GOTO 10
         S = 0.
         WRITE(9,*)T,Y,YD,XNC
         GOTO 10
200      CONTINUE
         TGO = TF − T + .00001
         XLAMD = (Y + YD*TGO)/(VC*TGO*TGO)
         XNC = XNP*VC*XLAMD
         YDD = XNT − XNC
         IF(STEP − 1)66,66,55
999      CONTINUE
         WRITE(9,*)T,Y,YD,XNC
         CLOSE (2)
         PAUSE
         END
```

program is set up without errors. Errors can be introduced by changing values in the data statements. The status of the relative position and velocity, along with missile acceleration information, is displayed every 0.1 s.

In order to verify that the linearized engagement model is a reasonable approximation to the nonlinear engagement model, cases that were run for the nonlinear engagement model were repeated using the simulation of Listing 2.2. A sample run was made with the linearized engagement model in which the only disturbance was a − 20-deg heading error (*HEDEG* = − 20.). In this case the effective navigation ratio was 4. Acceleration profile comparisons for both the linear and nonlinear engagement models are presented in Fig. 2.7. The figure clearly shows that, even for a relatively large heading error disturbance, the resultant acceleration profiles are virtually indistinguishable. Thus, the linearized model is an excellent approximation to the nonlinear engagement model in the case of a heading error disturbance.

Another sample run was made with the linear engagement model; this time with a 3-*g* target maneuver disturbance. Figure 2.8 shows that this time the linearized model overestimates the missile acceleration requirements. The reason for the discrepancy is that the linear model assumes that the target acceleration magnitude, perpendicular to the line of sight, is always the same and equal to the magnitude of the maneuver. In reality, as the target maneuvers, the component of acceleration perpendicular to the line of sight decreases because the target is turning. Therefore, the nonlinear acceleration requirements due to a maneuvering target are somewhat less than those predicted by the linearized engagement model. However, it is important to note that the linear engagement model accurately predicts the monotonically increasing trend (for most of the flight) for the missile acceleration profile due to a target maneuver.

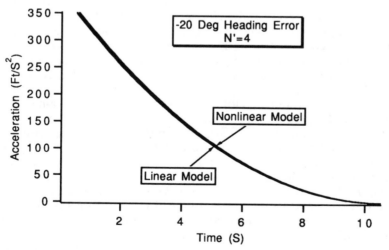

Fig. 2.7 Linearized engagement model yields accurate performance projections for heading error disturbance.

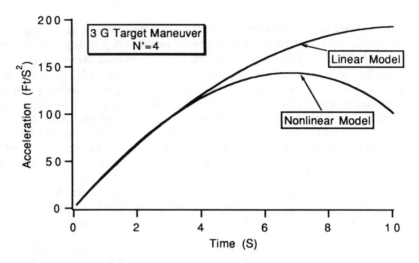

Fig. 2.8   Linear model overestimates missile acceleration due to target maneuver.

At this point we can conclude that the linearized engagement model yields performance projections of sufficient accuracy to make it worthwhile to proceed with the development of design relationships. We will test the validity of those relationships throughout the text in a variety of environments.

Important Closed-Form Solutions

The linearization of the engagement model is important for two reasons. First, with a linear model, powerful computerized techniques such as the method of adjoints (described in Chapters 3 and 4) can be used to analyze the missile guidance system both statistically and deterministically in one computer run. With this technique, error budgets are automatically generated so that key system drivers can be identified and a balanced guidance system design can be achieved. The linear model is also important because, under special circumstances, closed-form solutions can be obtained. These solutions can be used as system sizing aids. In addition, the form of the solutions will suggest how key parameters influence system performance.

Let us consider obtaining closed-form solutions for the two important cases we have already considered in both the linear and nonlinear engagement simulations. The first case is the missile acceleration required to remove a heading error, and the second case is the missile acceleration required to hit a maneuvering target. In the absence of target maneuver the relative acceleration (target acceleration minus missile acceleration) can be expressed as

$$\ddot{y} = -N'V_c\dot{\lambda}$$

Integrating the preceding differential equation once yields

$$\dot{y} = -N' V_c \lambda + C_1$$

where C_1 is the constant of integration. Substitution of the linear approximation to the line-of-sight angle in the preceding expression yields the following time-varying first-order differential equation:

$$\frac{dy}{dt} + \frac{N'y}{t_F - t} = C_1$$

Since a first-order differential equation of the form

$$\frac{dy}{dt} + a(t)y = h(t)$$

has the solution[9-12]

$$y = \exp\left[-\int_0^t a(T)\,dT\right]\left\{\int_0^t h(n)\exp\left[\int_0^n a(T)\,dT\right]dn + C_2\right\}$$

we can solve the linearized trajectory differential equation exactly. Note that the first constant of integration C_1 is contained in $h(t)$ while the second constant of integration C_2 appears in the preceding equation. Both constants of integration can be found by evaluating initial conditions on y and its derivative. Let us assume that the initial condition on the first state is zero, or

$$y(0) = 0$$

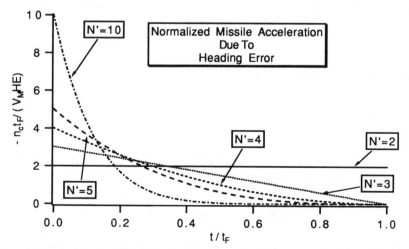

Fig. 2.9 Normalized missile acceleration due to heading error for proportional navigation guidance.

and that the initial condition on the second state is related to the heading error by

$$\dot{y}(0) = -V_M HE$$

where V_M is the missile velocity and HE the heading error in radians. Under these circumstances, after much algebra, we find that the closed-form solution for the missile acceleration due to heading error is given by

$$n_c = \frac{-V_M HE \, N'}{t_F} \left(1 - \frac{t}{t_F}\right)^{N'-2}$$

where t_F is the flight time and N' the effective navigation ratio. We can see that the magnitude of the initial acceleration is proportional to the heading error and missile velocity and inversely proportional to the flight time. Doubling the velocity or heading error will double the initial missile acceleration, whereas doubling the flight time or time available for guidance will halve the initial missile acceleration. In addition, the closed-form solution for the miss distance $y(t_F)$ is zero. In other words, as long as the missile has sufficient acceleration capability, there is no miss due to heading error!

The closed-form solution for the missile acceleration response due to heading error is displayed in normalized form in Fig. 2.9. We can see that higher effective navigation ratios require more acceleration at the beginning of flight than at the end of the flight and less acceleration as the flight progresses. From a system sizing point of view, the designer usually wants to ensure that the acceleration capability of the missile is adequate at the beginning of flight so that saturation can be avoided. For a fixed missile acceleration capability, Fig. 2.9 shows how requirements are placed on minimum guidance or flight time and maximum allowable heading error and missile velocity.

Similarly, if the only disturbance is a target maneuver the appropriate second-order differential equation becomes

$$\ddot{y} = -N'V_c\dot{\lambda} + n_T$$

with initial conditions

$$y(0) = 0$$

$$\dot{y}(0) = 0$$

After conversion to a first-order differential equation and much algebra, the solution can be found to be

$$n_c = \frac{N'}{N'-2}\left[1 - \left(1 - \frac{t}{t_F}\right)^{N'-2}\right]n_T$$

It appears that something "magical" happens to the acceleration when the effective navigation ratio is two. Application of L'Hopital's rule elimi-

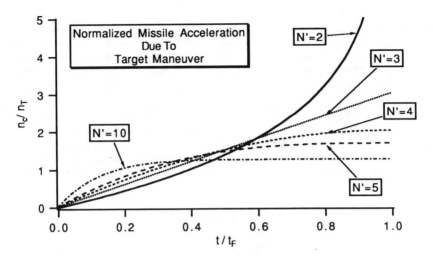

Fig. 2.10   Normalized missile acceleration due to target maneuver for proportional navigation guidance.

nates the division by zero in the preceding formula and indicates that

$$\lim_{N' \to 2} n_c = -2 \log \left(\frac{t_F - t}{t_F} \right)$$

This is approximately the same solution as if we simply let $N' = 2.01$ or $N' = 1.99$ in the original closed-form solution for the acceleration as a function of the effective navigation ratio. As with the heading error case, the closed-form solution indicates that the miss distance due to target maneuver is exactly zero!

Unlike the heading error case, missile acceleration due to maneuver is independent of flight time and missile velocity and only depends on the magnitude of the maneuver and the effective navigation ratio. Doubling the maneuver level of the target doubles the missile acceleration requirements.

The closed-form solution for the missile acceleration response due to target maneuver is displayed in normalized form in Fig. 2.10. We can see that higher effective navigation ratios relax the acceleration requirements at the end of the flight. Unlike the heading error response, the missile acceleration required to hit a maneuvering target increases as the flight progresses. From a system sizing point of view, the designer must ensure that the acceleration capability of the missile is adequate at the end of flight so that saturation can be avoided so that the missile can hit the target.

Proportional Navigation and Zero Effort Miss

Thus far we have seen from simulation results and closed-form solutions that proportional navigation appears to be effective, but we do not know why. Although it is possible to construct geometric arguments showing that it is very logical to issue acceleration commands proportional to the line-of-sight rate (i.e., zero line-of-sight rate means we are on a collision triangle and therefore no further commands are necessary), it is not obvious what is happening. The concept of zero effort miss is not only useful in explaining proportional navigation but is also useful in deriving and understanding more advanced guidance laws.

We can define the zero effort miss to be the distance the missile would miss the target if the target continued along its present course and the missile made no further corrective maneuvers. Therefore, if the target does not maneuver, the two components, in the Earth fixed coordinate system, of the zero effort miss can be expressed in terms of the previously defined relative quantities as

$$ZEM_1 = R_{TM1} + V_{TM1}t_{go}$$

$$ZEM_2 = R_{TM2} + V_{TM2}t_{go}$$

where t_{go} is the time to go until intercept. Thus, we can see that in this case the zero effort miss is just a simple prediction (assuming constant velocities and zero acceleration) of the future relative separation between missile and target. From Fig. 2.1 we can see that the component of the zero effort miss that is perpendicular to the line of sight, ZEM_{PLOS}, can be found by trigonometry and is given by

$$ZEM_{PLOS} = -ZEM_1 \sin\lambda + ZEM_2 \cos\lambda$$

Expansion and simplification of the preceding equation yields

$$ZEM_{PLOS} = \frac{t_{go}(R_{TM1}V_{TM2} - R_{TM2}V_{TM1})}{R_{TM}}$$

Comparing the preceding expression to the expression for line-of-sight rate, we can see that the line-of-sight rate can be expressed in terms of the component of the zero effort miss perpendicular to the line of sight or

$$\dot{\lambda} = \frac{ZEM_{PLOS}}{R_{TM}t_{go}}$$

If we assume that the relative separation between missile and target and closing velocity are approximately related to the time to go by

$$R_{TM} = V_c t_{go}$$

then the proportional navigation guidance command can be expressed in terms of the zero effort miss perpendicular to the line of sight as

$$n_c = \frac{N' \, ZEM_{PLOS}}{t_{go}^2}$$

Thus, we can see that the proportional navigation acceleration command that is perpendicular to the line of sight is not only proportional to the line-of-sight rate and closing velocity but is also proportional to the zero effort miss and inversely proportional to the square of time to go. We shall later see that this is a very powerful concept, since the zero effort miss can be computed by a variety of methods, including the on-line numerical integration of the assumed nonlinear differential equations of the missile and target.

Summary

In this chapter we have developed and shown the results of a simple two-dimensional proportional navigation missile-target engagement simulation. Results have shown that the proportional navigation law is effective in a variety of cases. Linearization of the nonlinear missile-target geometry was shown to be an accurate approximation to the actual geometry. Closed-form solutions were derived, based on the linearized geometry, for the missile acceleration requirements due to heading error and target maneuver. From these solutions it was shown how the effective navigation ratio influences system performance. Finally, the concept of zero effort miss was introduced, and it was shown how the proportional navigation guidance law could be expressed in terms of this concept. In later chapters we shall develop more advanced guidance laws based upon the zero effort miss concept.

References

[1]Kennedy, G. P., *Rockets, Missiles and Spacecraft of the National Air and Space Museum,* Smithsonian Institution Press, Washington, DC, 1983.

[2]Benecke, T., and Quick, A. W. (eds.), "History of German Guided Missile Development," Proceedings of AGARD First Guided Missile Seminar, 1956.

[3]Nesline, F. W., and Zarchan, P., "A New Look at Classical Versus Modern Homing Guidance," *Journal of Guidance and Control,* Vol. 4, Jan.–Feb. 1981, pp. 78–85.

[4]Yuan, C. L., "Homing and Navigation Courses of Automatic Target-Seeking Devices," RCA Labs., Princeton, NJ, Rept. PTR-12C, Dec. 1942.

[5]Bennett, R. R., and Mathews, W. E., "Analytical Determination of Miss Distance For Linear Homing Navigation Systems," Hughes Aircraft Co., Culver City, CA, TN-260, March 1952.

[6]Fossier, M. W., "The Development of Radar Homing Missiles," *Journal of Guidance, Control, and Dynamics,* Vol. 7, Nov.–Dec. 1984, pp. 641–651.

[7]Yuan, C. L., "Homing and Navigation Courses of Automatic Target-Seeking Devices," *Journal of Applied Physics,* Vol. 19, Dec. 1948, pp. 1122–1128.

[8]Bryson, A. E., and Ho, Y. C., *Applied Optimal Control,* Blaisdell, Waltham, MA, 1969.

[9]Regan, F. J., *Re-Entry Vehicle Dynamics,* AIAA Education Series, AIAA, New York, 1984.

[10]Locke, A. S., *Guidance,* D. Van Nostrand, Toronto, 1955.

[11]Jerger, J. J., *System Preliminary Design,* Van Nostrand, Princeton, NJ, 1960.

[12]Garnell, P., and East, D. J., *Guided Weapon Control System,* Pergamon, Oxford, 1977.

Chapter 3

Method of Adjoints and the Homing Loop

Introduction

ALTHOUGH direct simulation is always used in evaluating missile system designs, the adjoint technique has historically been the main computerized analysis and design tool used in tactical missile guidance system design. The adjoint technique goes back at least to Vito Volterra,[1] circa 1870, and was used particularly by the ballisticians in connection with their theoretical studies of artillery hit dispersions.[2] The adjoint was popularized by Laning and Battin in the 1950s.[3]

The adjoint technique is based on the system impulse response and can be used to analyze linear time-varying systems such as the missile homing loop. With the adjoint method, exact performance projections of any quantity at a particular time and information showing how all disturbance terms contribute to the performance are available.[4,5] In other words, error budgets are automatically generated with the adjoint technique. Although this technique has mainly been used in missile guidance system design and analysis, its application potential is much broader.

In this chapter we shall show how to construct an adjoint model from a missile guidance system homing loop. Numerical examples will be presented that demonstrate the power and utility of the adjoint approach. Performance projection comparisons will be made from nonlinear engagement simulation results and adjoint solutions.

Homing Loop

It is convenient to take the linearized engagement equations of Chapter 2 and draw them in block diagram form as is shown in Fig. 3.1. This type of block diagram is known as a homing loop because it is drawn as a feedback control system. In this diagram missile acceleration is subtracted from target acceleration to form a relative acceleration. After two integrations we have relative position, which at the end of the flight is the miss distance. A division by range (or the closing velocity multiplied by the time to go until intercept) yields the geometric line-of-sight angle where the time to go is defined as

$$t_{\text{go}} = t_F - t$$

The missile seeker, which is represented in Fig. 3.1 as a perfect differentiator, attempts to track the target. Effectively the seeker takes the deriva-

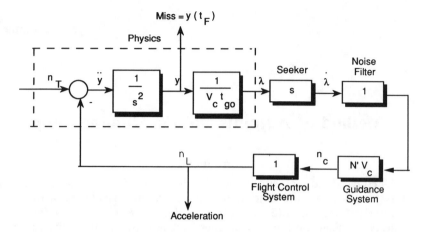

Fig. 3.1 Simplest possible proportional navigation guidance homing loop.

tive of the geometric line-of-sight angle, thus providing a measurement of the line-of-sight rate. The noise filter must process the noisy line-of-sight rate measurement of the seeker and provide an estimate of the line-of-sight rate. A guidance command is generated, based on the proportional navigation guidance law, from the noise filter output. In tactical aerodynamic missiles the flight control system (which is represented by unity gain in Fig. 3.1) must, by moving control surfaces, cause the missile to maneuver in such a way that the achieved acceleration matches the desired acceleration.

Figure 3.1 presents the simplest possible proportional navigation homing loop. In this perfect homing loop, models of the seeker, noise filter, guidance, and flight control systems have been considered to be perfect and without dynamics. Such a block diagram is known as a zero-lag guidance system. The miss distance will always be zero in a zero-lag proportional navigation homing loop.

Guidance system lags or subsystem dynamics will cause miss distance. As long as the lags can be represented by either linear differential or difference equations, the homing loop will still remain linear and more powerful methods of analysis, such as the method of adjoints, can be used to determine system performance and behavior.

Single Time Constant Guidance System

Thus far, in our homing loop analysis, the missile has always hit the target. The strength of proportional navigation is that, in the absence of acceleration saturation effects, zero miss distance can be achieved if there are no lags within the homing loop. If the flight control system dynamics were modeled as a single lag, or

$$\frac{n_L}{n_c} = \frac{1}{1 + sT}$$

where n_L is the achieved missile acceleration, n_c the commanded missile acceleration, and T the flight control system time constant. Note that the relative acceleration equation in Fig. 3.1 would also have to be modified to

$$\ddot{y} = n_T - n_L$$

In order to determine how flight control system time constant influences miss distance, a massive simulation experiment was conducted. Both the linear and nonlinear engagement simulations, developed in Chapter 2, were run for many different flight times. Each simulation trial had a 1-s flight control system time constant ($T = 1$ s), an effective navigation ratio of 4, a -20-deg heading error, and a different flight time. The flight times ranged from 0.1 s to 10 s in steps of 0.1 s.

In the linearized model the miss distance $y(t_F)$ can be either positive or negative, whereas in the nonlinear model the miss can only be positive. A positive linear miss means that the target is above the missile, whereas a negative linear miss means the opposite. For comparison with the nonlinear engagement simulation results, where the miss is always positive, the sign of the miss in the linear engagement model was always taken as positive.

The miss distance results for each run representing a different flight time, for both the linear and nonlinear engagement models, were recorded. Figure 3.2 displays miss distance as a function of flight time for both the linear and nonlinear engagement simulation results. First, the figure shows that a 1-s flight control system time constant can have a profound influence on the miss distance. In order for the miss distance to be negligible, the flight time must be large when compared to the flight control system time constant. In addition, we can see from Fig. 3.2 that the linearized engagement model and nonlinear engagement model results are in close proximity, which demon-

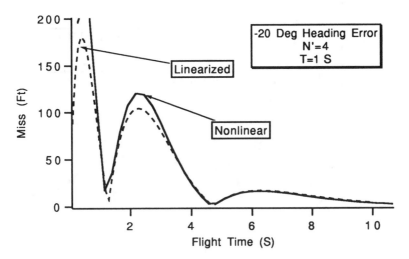

Fig. 3.2   Both models show that heading error miss approaches zero as flight time increases.

strates that the linearized model accurately captures the interaction between guidance system dynamics (flight control system time constant) and miss distance for the heading error disturbance.

Another important disturbance is target maneuver. We saw in Chapter 2 that the linearization of the engagement model in the case of target maneuver was not as accurate as it was for heading error. It is important to determine if the inaccuracy in linearization leads to false conclusions concerning system performance. Both the linear and nonlinear engagement simulations were run for many different flight times, each run having a 1-s flight control system time constant, an effective navigation ratio of 4, and a 3-g target maneuver. Figure 3.3 displays miss distance as a function of the flight time. Again we can see that the miss due to a constant target maneuver is only negligible if the flight time is much larger than the flight control system time constant. In addition, Fig. 3.3 shows that the linearized guidance system model accurately captures the effect of flight control system time constant on miss distance. The jaggedness in the nonlinear results is due to the approximate way in which the miss distance is computed. At the end of the flight, the integration step size is reduced to 0.0002 s. This means that, for the case considered, where the closing velocity is 4000 ft/s, the nonlinear miss distance computation is only good to 0.8 ft (4000*0.0002).

In this section we have shown the very important result that, when the homing loop has guidance system dynamics, the linearized guidance system model yields very accurate miss distance performance projections for both heading error and target maneuver disturbances. Therefore, techniques that depend on the linearized engagement model for miss distance projections should also be accurate.

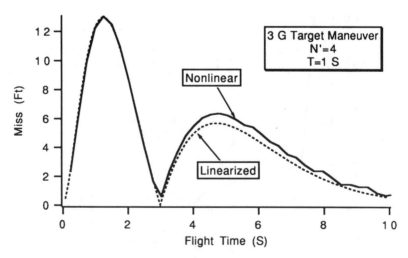

Fig. 3.3   Linear model accurately captures relationship between miss and flight time.

How to Construct an Adjoint

In this section we will see how the miss distance results of Figs. 3.2 and 3.3, which were generated from many simulation trials, can be obtained in one computer run using the method of adjoints. However, we must first learn how to construct an adjoint model from the original system.

For every linear deterministic system there exists an adjoint system that can be constructed from the original system, given in block diagram form, by application of the following rules[3-6]:

Rule 1: Convert All System Inputs to Impulses

In order to construct an adjoint we must have impulsive inputs in the original system. Since impulsive inputs may not exist in the original system, block diagram manipulation of the actual inputs of the original system may be necessary. For example, deterministic inputs can be converted to impulsive inputs by judicious use of integrators. Figure 3.4 shows that a step input and an integrator-driven impulse are equivalent at the integrator output. The figure also shows that an initial condition is equivalent at the integrator output to an integrator with an impulsive input.

Rule 2: Replace t by $t_F - t$ in the Arguments of All Time-Varying Coefficients

Often a linear system has a gain that can be expressed as a function of time, either in analytical or tabular form. Care must be taken with time-varying gains when applying the method of adjoints. Figure 3.5 shows, by example, how both a time-varying gain and a gain expressed as a tabular function of time can be converted to the adjoint domain. Notice that the adjoint of a table which is a function of time is the same table with the gains reversed. Otherwise, gains that are a function of time simply have t replaced by $t_F - t$ when the adjoint is taken, where t_F is the final time or time of flight.

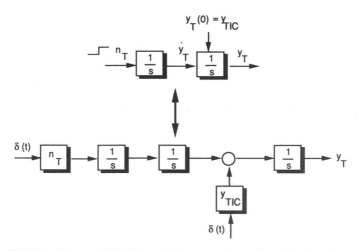

Fig. 3.4 Steps and initial conditions can be replaced by impulses.

System \ Function	Original System	Adjoint System
Time Varying Gain	$K(t) = at + b$ $K(t) = \dfrac{1}{a(t_F - t) + b}$	$K(t_F - t) = a(t_F - t) + b$ $K(t_F - t) = \dfrac{1}{at + b}$
Table	$\begin{array}{c|c} t & K \\ \hline 0 & 8 \\ 1 & 4 \\ 2 & 3 \\ 3 & 9 \end{array}$	$\begin{array}{c|c} t & K \\ \hline 0 & 9 \\ 1 & 3 \\ 2 & 4 \\ 3 & 8 \end{array}$

Fig. 3.5   Taking the adjoint of a time-varying gain.

Rule 3: Reverse All Signal Flow, Redefining Nodes as Summing Junctions and Vice Versa

Figure 3.6 shows how summing junctions and nodes are converted in going from the original to the adjoint system. Note that all original system inputs become adjoint outputs and vice versa. This simple relationship between the two systems enables one to take an adjoint by first drawing the original block diagram and then using tracing paper to construct the adjoint model.

Figure 3.7 presents an example of a single-lag, proportional navigation homing loop in which a step target maneuver disturbance has been converted to an impulsive input by the use of an extra integrator. In addition,

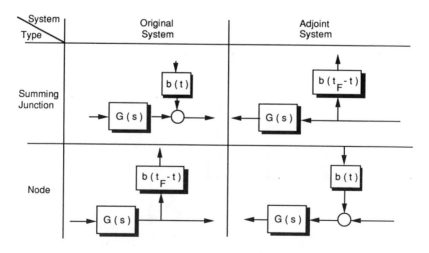

Fig. 3.6   Adjoints redefine branch points and nodes.

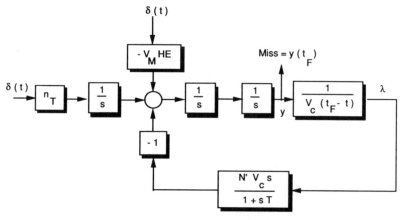

Fig. 3.7   Single lag proportional navigation homing loop.

a heading error initial condition has also been converted to an impulsive input. The output of interest is the miss distance or $y(t_F)$. A simulation of this block diagram will yield y as a function of time, $y(t)$, and the last value of y will be the miss distance, $y(t_F)$. In order to find the miss due to a target maneuver disturbance, we would have to set the heading error disturbance to zero, and in order to find the miss due to an initial heading error, the target maneuver disturbance would have to be set to zero.

The adjoint of this homing loop, obtained by following the rules for constructing an adjoint, is shown in Fig. 3.8. Here the original output of interest [miss distance or $y(t_F)$] becomes an impulsive input to the adjoint system, and the two original system inputs (target maneuver and heading error) become two adjoint outputs. A simulation of the adjoint block diagram will yield y as a function of flight time, $y(t_F)$. This means that in an

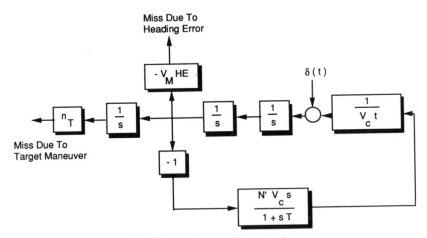

Fig. 3.8   Adjoint of homing loop.

adjoint simulation we obtain the miss distances due to both a step target maneuver and initial heading error for various flight times—all obtained in *one* computer run!

Adjoint Mathematics

The impulse response of the adjoint system, h^*, and the impulse response of the original system, h, are related by

$$h^*(t_F - t_I, t_F - t_O) = h(t_O, t_I)$$

where t_I and t_O are the impulse application and observation times, respectively, of the original system. This equation means that applying an impulse at time t_I and observing the output at time t_O of the original system is equivalent to applying an impulse to the adjoint system at time $t_F - t_O$ and observing the adjoint output at time $t_F - t_I$. The importance of this fundamental relationship becomes more apparent when it is desired to observe the impulse response of the original system at time t_F due to various impulse application times. This means that in order to generate $h(t_F, t_I)$ it becomes necessary to simulate the system response for each impulse application time as shown in Fig. 3.9.

However, since the observation time is the final time ($t_O = t_F$), only one adjoint response need be generated, since the fundamental adjoint relationship simplifies to

$$h^*(t_F - t_I, 0) = h(t_F, t_I)$$

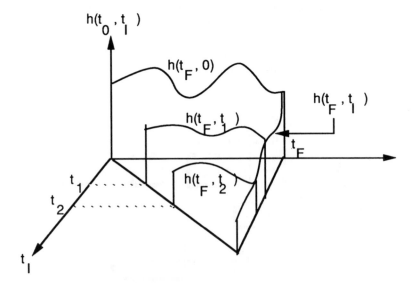

Fig. 3.9 Impulse response of original system for different application times.

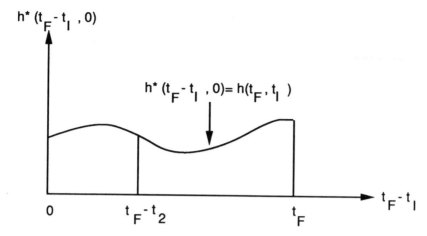

Fig. 3.10   Impulse response of adjoint system is related to impulse response of original system.

Therefore, an impulse applied at any time t_I and observed only at the final time t_F in the original system is equivalent to applying an impulse at time zero in the adjoint system and monitoring the output at time $t_F - t_I$. Figure 3.10 shows that the adjoint impulse response is identical to the impulse response of the original system, except that it is generated backwards!

Adjoints for Deterministic Systems

In order to fully understand the utility of adjoints, let us consider the convolution integral, or

$$y(t) = \int_{-\infty}^{t} x(\tau)h(t, \tau)\, d\tau$$

where x is the system input and h the system impulse response. For physically realizable (noncausal) systems, this integral becomes

$$y(t) = \int_{0}^{t} x(\tau)h(t, \tau)\, d\tau$$

A step input of magnitude a changes the preceding equation to

$$y(t) = a \int_{0}^{t} h(t, \tau)\, d\tau$$

Therefore, this equation states that the step response of a system can be found by integrating the impulse response. A closer examination reveals that this revelation is of no practical utility because the variable of integration is with respect to τ. This means that many impulse responses, each with a different application time, would have to be generated. Then the results would have to be saved and then integrated—just to get a system step response! Of course, it would be much easier to avoid the convolution integral and to just simulate the system with the step input and observe the output in order to get the system step response.

Let us now see if the method of adjoints can be useful in the case where the system has a step input. We can substitute the fundamental relationship between the original and adjoint system impulse responses into the convolution integral, yielding

$$y(t) = a \int_0^t h^*(t_F - \tau, t_F - t) \, d\tau$$

Variables can be changed according to

$$x = t_F - \tau$$

$$dx = -d\tau$$

Hence, we obtain

$$y(t) = a \int_{t_F - t}^{t_F} h^*(x, t_F - t) \, dx$$

If the observation time of interest is the final time ($t = t_F$), the preceding relationship simplifies to

$$y(t_F) = a \int_0^{t_F} h^*(x, 0) \, dx$$

Note that the integration in the adjoint system is with respect to the observation time rather than the impulse application time. This means that the original system step response output at time t_F can be obtained by using an impulsive input in the adjoint system at time zero and then integrating the output. The resultant one computer run adjoint solution obtains the step response value at the final time for *all* final time values! For time-invariant systems the original system step response, for all final times, could also have been obtained in one computer run. However, for time-varying systems, many original system computer runs would have been required to obtain the same information as that provided by the adjoint response.

In order to see further benefits from the method of adjoints, let us consider many step input disturbances to the original system as shown in Fig. 3.11. Here, not only would many computer runs be required to find the system step response for different flight times, but also information showing how each disturbance contributed to the total output would require many more computer runs. In order to generate this type of error budget in the original system for N disturbances, N computer runs would be required (each run only having that disturbance), and then superposition could be invoked (add up all responses) to get the total step response. However, original system inputs become adjoint outputs; thus, only one adjoint run would be required to get the total step response value at the final time and to also automatically generate an error budget. Only the adjoint outputs (original system inputs) have to be monitored, as shown in Fig. 3.11, and

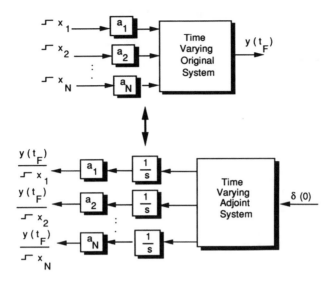

Fig. 3.11   Equivalence between adjoint and original systems for deterministic step disturbances.

superposition allows the total output to be expressed as

$$y(t_F) = \frac{y(t_F)}{\int x_1} + \frac{y(t_F)}{\int x_2} + \cdots + \frac{y(t_F)}{\int x_N}$$

Thus, when there are many deterministic disturbances to the original system, one adjoint computer run yields the system response for all final times, along with a detailed error budget showing how each disturbance influenced total system performance.

Deterministic Adjoint Example

In order to demonstrate the practical utility of adjoint theory for a system with deterministic inputs, let us reconsider the proportional navigation homing loop example of Fig. 3.7. After following the rules for constructing an adjoint, we obtain the detailed adjoint model shown in Fig. 3.12.

All of the integrator inputs and outputs are marked in Fig. 3.12 for the purpose of understanding the adjoint simulation. With the exception of the two adjoint outputs, none of the quantities shown in the adjoint model has any physical meaning. The impulse required for adjoint initiation can also be represented as an initial condition on the $x3$ integrator. The output $x1$ is the miss distance sensitivity (multiply by n_T to get miss) due to a step target maneuver, whereas the output $x2$ is related to the miss sensitivity (multiply by $-V_M HE$) due to an initial heading error.

Listing 3.1 presents the FORTRAN adjoint simulation of Fig. 3.12. Here the four differential equations of Fig. 3.12 (which appear after label 200 in

Listing 3.1   Single-lag adjoint with second-order Runge-Kutta integration

```
          INTEGER STEP
          DATA XNT,XNP,TAU,TF,VM,HEDEG/ 96.6,4.,1.,10.,3000., − 20./
          T = 0.
          S = 0.
          TP = T + .00001
          X1 = 0
          X2 = 0
          X3 = 1
          X4 = 0
          H = .02
          HE = HEDEG/57.3
10        IF(TP > (TF − .00001))GOTO 999
          S = S + H
          X1OLD = X1
          X2OLD = X2
          X3OLD = X3
          X4OLD = X4
          STEP = 1
          GOTO 200
66        STEP = 2
          X1 = X1 + H*X1D
          X2 = X2 + H*X2D
          X3 = X3 + H*X3D
          X4 = X4 + H*X4D
          TP = TP + H
          GOTO 200
55        CONTINUE
          X1 = (X1OLD + X1)/2 + .5*H*X1D
          X2 = (X2OLD + X2)/2 + .5*H*X2D
          X3 = (X3OLD + X3)/2 + .5*H*X3D
          X4 = (X4OLD + X4)/2 + .5*H*X4D
          IF(S < .09999)GOTO 10
          S = 0.
          XMNT = ABS(XNT*X1)
          XMHE = ABS( − VM*HE*X2)
          WRITE(9,*)TP,XMNT,XMHE
          GOTO 10
200       CONTINUE
          X1D = X2
          X2D = X3
          Y1 = (X4 − X2)/TAU
          TGO = TP + .00001
          X3D = XNP*Y1/TGO
          X4D = − Y1
          IF(STEP − 1)66,66,55
999       CONTINUE
          PAUSE
          END
```

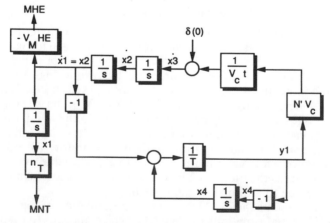

Fig. 3.12   Adjoint simulation model of single-lag guidance system.

listing) are integrated using the second-order Runge-Kutta method with an integration step size of 0.02 s. The integration step size is small enough in this sample program to get fairly accurate answers. Note that in this example the effective navigation ratio is four, the guidance time constant is 1 s, there is -20 deg of heading error, and the maneuver level is 96.6 ft/s^2 or 3 g. Absolute values of adjoint outputs are taken to conform to our convention in which all miss distances are treated as positive quantities.

The adjoint output due to a 3-g step target maneuver appears in Fig. 3.13 along with results from the linearized engagement simulation (run for many different flight times). The figure shows that the adjoint simulation yields accurate miss distance projections for many different flight times in one computer run. Since the adjoint is linear, we can apply superposition to the results. Doubling the target maneuver acceleration level doubles the miss. The abscissa of Fig. 3.13 can either be interpreted as flight time or the time to go until intercept at which the target initiates its maneuver. Therefore, in this example, a 3-g maneuver causes nearly 12 ft of miss if the flight time is only 1 s or if the maneuver occurs at 1 s to go before intercept. The figure also shows that long flights (flight time large compared to guidance system time constant), or flights with maneuver initiation occurring at the beginning of flight (large time to go), result in virtually zero miss.

Another adjoint output, from the same simulation trial, also yields miss distance information for a heading error disturbance. These results, along with linearized engagement simulation results (run for many different flight times) appear in Fig. 3.14. We can see that the adjoint also yields accurate performance projections in the case of the heading error disturbance.

Therefore, we can see that a great deal of information is available from one adjoint run representing a system with many deterministic disturbances.

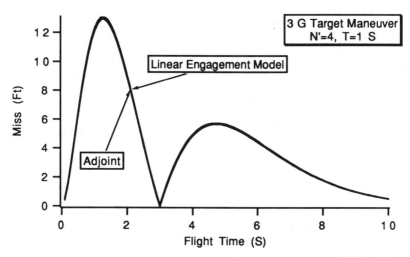

Fig. 3.13 Adjoint yields accurate miss distance information for all flight times in one run.

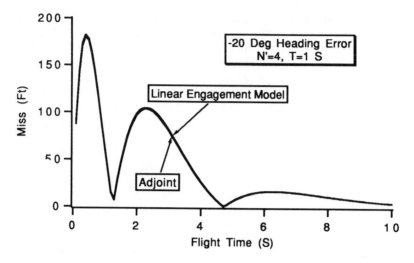

Fig. 3.14   Adjoint also yields accurate heading-error-induced miss information for all flight times in one run.

Miss distance sensitivity data for a variety of disturbances and for all flight times can be obtained in a single adjoint run. We can also tell from the adjoint output when the guidance system is most sensitive to an error source. In addition, the shape of the adjoint output also provides information concerning system behavior. For example, if the adjoint output for a deterministic input does not approach zero as the flight time increases, then we know that the missile cannot guide effectively.

Adjoint Closed-Form Solutions[7,8]

If there are no dynamics in a proportional navigation homing loop, then the resultant miss distance should always be zero. Guidance system dynamics cause miss distance. Under special circumstances it is possible to obtain closed-form solutions for the miss distance when there are dynamics in the homing loop. These closed-form solutions can be used to gain insight into the effectiveness of homing and also be used to check the accuracy of computerized adjoints. In addition, we shall see later that the normalization factors developed from simpler systems are also valid for more complex systems.

Consider the generalized homing loop diagram of Fig. 3.15. In this figure there are three disturbances that have been represented in impulse form, so that the method of adjoints can be applied. The disturbances are 1) an impulse in target jerk (or step target maneuver), 2) an impulse in target velocity (or step target position displacement), and 3) an impulse in missile acceleration (or heading error). In Fig. 3.15, n_T represents the magnitude of the target maneuver (in ft/s²), HE represents heading error (in rad), and V_M represents interceptor velocity (in ft/s).

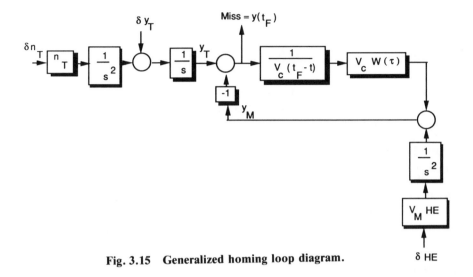

Fig. 3.15   Generalized homing loop diagram.

The guidance system is represented in the time domain by $W(\tau)$. For convenience we will often express the guidance system in terms of Laplace transform notation. For example, in a zero-lag proportional navigation guidance system, W can be represented in the frequency domain by

$$W(s)_{\text{zero lag}} = N'/s$$

The effective integration of the perfect guidance system is due to a differentiation to get line-of-sight rate and two integrations to get from missile acceleration to missile position. A single-lag guidance system can be repre-

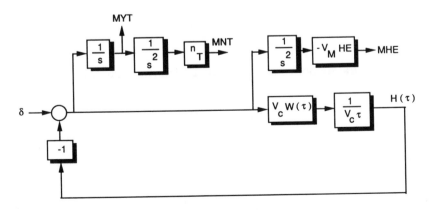

Fig. 3.16   Generalized homing loop adjoint.

sented by

$$W(s)_{\text{single lag}} = \frac{N'}{s(1 + sT)}$$

where T is the effective time constant of the guidance system.

Following the rules for constructing adjoints discussed at the beginning of the chapter, we can construct the generalized homing loop adjoint shown in Fig. 3.16. The impulsive inputs of the original system become adjoint outputs. In other words, MYT represents the miss due to a unit step in target position displacement, MNT represents the miss due to a step target maneuver of magnitude n_T, and MHE represents the miss due to a heading error of magnitude HE. The miss distance output of the original system is now replaced by an impulsive input as shown in Fig. 3.16.

For convenience, $H(\tau)$ is also indicated as an adjoint signal of interest. From the convolution integral we can relate the adjoint output to the input by

$$H(\tau) = \frac{1}{\tau} \int W(x)[\delta(\tau - x) - H(\tau - x)] \, dx$$

Converting from the time to the frequency domain (Laplace transform notation), we can express the preceding relationship as

$$\frac{-dH(s)}{ds} = W(s)[1 - H(s)]$$

since

$$\frac{d}{ds} [1 - H(s)] = \frac{-dH(s)}{ds}$$

For convenience let us allow $H(s)$ to be replaced by H and $W(s)$ to be replaced by W. Therefore, substitution yields

$$\int \frac{d(1 - H)}{1 - H} = \int W \, ds$$

Finally, integrating both sides of the preceding equations yields the important conclusion

$$1 - H = c \exp\left(\int W \, ds\right)$$

where c is a constant of integration. We can evaluate c by first recognizing from Fig. 3.16 that a miss due to a unit step in target displacement, MYT, can be expressed in Laplace transform notation as

$$MYT(s) = \frac{1 - H(s)}{s}$$

We know that in the time domain the miss due to a unit step target displacement at flight time zero is unity. Therefore, using the initial value theorem, which relates the time domain with the Laplace transform domain, we can say that

$$MYT(0) = 1 = \lim_{s \to \infty} s\left(\frac{1 - H}{s}\right)$$

Therefore c is chosen to make

$$\lim_{s \to \infty} \left[c \, \exp\left(\int W \, ds\right)\right] = 1$$

Since the simplest possible guidance system has at least one integration, the constant of integration becomes unity ($c = 1$).

In order to demonstrate that we have enough analytical tools to find closed-form solutions under special circumstances, let us find the miss due to a step target maneuver for a single-lag guidance system. As mentioned before, the guidance system transfer function in this case is

$$W(s) = \frac{N'}{s(1 + sT)}$$

where N' is the effective navigation ratio and T the guidance system time constant. Since

$$1 - H = \exp\left(\int W \, ds\right)$$

we get after integration

$$1 - H(s) = \left[s \middle/ \left(s + \frac{1}{T}\right)\right]^{N'}$$

Therefore, the miss due to a step maneuver of magnitude n_T is given by

$$\frac{MNT}{n_T}(s) = \frac{1 - H(s)}{s^3} = \frac{1}{s^3}\left[s \middle/ \left(s + \frac{1}{T}\right)\right]^{N'}$$

For an effective navigation ratio of 4, the miss, in Laplace transform notation, is given by

$$\left.\frac{MNT}{n_T}\right|_{N' = 4}(s) = \frac{s}{\left(s + \dfrac{1}{T}\right)^4}$$

Taking the inverse Laplace transform of the preceding expression yields the miss due to a step target maneuver in the adjoint time domain as

$$\left.\frac{MNT}{n_T}\right|_{N' = 4}(\tau) = \tau^2 \, e^{-\tau/T}\left(0.5 - \frac{\tau}{6T}\right)$$

where τ is adjoint time and can be interpreted as either time of flight (t_F) or time to go at which the maneuver occurs.

The single-lag adjoint simulation of Listing 3.1 was run for a case in which the target maneuver level was 3 g, the guidance system time constant was 1 s, and the effective navigation ratio was 4. Figure 3.17 displays the adjoint simulation results along with the closed-form solution. We can see from the figure that both the adjoint results and closed-form solution results are virtually identical, which proves that it is possible for theory and simulation to agree.

The nonlinear engagement simulation of Chapter 2 was rerun for the same case (3-g target maneuver, $N' = 4$ and $T = 1$ s) for many different flight times. The nonlinear results and the closed-form solution results are compared in Fig. 3.18. We can see that the miss distance projections from the closed-form solution are in excellent agreement with the nonlinear results.

Similarly, a closed-form expression can be found for the miss due to an initial heading error. The generalized formula for the heading error miss is given by

$$\frac{MHE}{HE}(s) = \frac{-V_M[1 - H(s)]}{s^2}$$

Following a similar procedure to that of the target maneuver case and assuming an effective navigation ratio of 4 for a single-lag guidance system, we obtain a closed-form solution for the heading error miss:

$$\left.\frac{MHE}{HE}\right|_{N'=4}(\tau) = -V_M\tau\,e^{-\tau/T}\left(1 - \frac{\tau}{T} + \frac{\tau^2}{6T^2}\right)$$

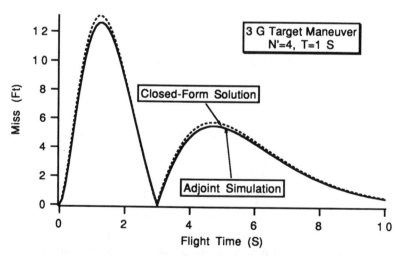

Fig. 3.17 **Closed-form solution agrees with computerized adjoint for step target maneuver.**

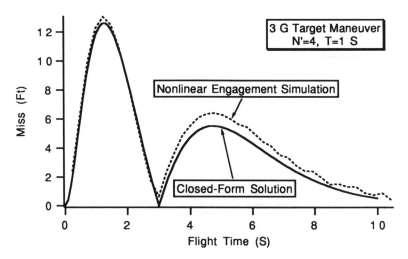

Fig. 3.18 Miss distance formula and nonlinear simulation results are in close agreement.

The adjoint simulation results for a −20-deg heading error and the closed-form solution results are displayed in Fig. 3.19. Again we can see that the adjoint simulation results are in complete agreement with the closed-form solution.

Normalization

In the previous section we showed how closed-form solutions for the heading error and target maneuver could be derived for a single time constant guidance system. Specific solutions were derived for the case in which the effective navigation ratio was 4. Following the same procedure outlined in the previous section, closed-form solutions were derived for the miss due to a target maneuver when the effective navigation ratio varied between 3 and 5. The solutions are

$$\left.\frac{\text{Miss}}{n_T}\right|_{N'=3} = 0.5\ t_F^2\ e^{-t_F/T}$$

$$\left.\frac{\text{Miss}}{n_T}\right|_{N'=4} = t_F^2\ e^{-t_F/T}\left(0.5 - \frac{t_F}{6T}\right)$$

$$\left.\frac{\text{Miss}}{n_T}\right|_{N'=5} = t_F^2\ e^{-t_F/T}\left(0.5 - \frac{t_F}{3T} + \frac{t_F^2}{24T^2}\right)$$

where n_T is the maneuver level of the target (in ft/s^2), t_F is the flight time (in s), T is the guidance system time constant (in s), and Miss is the miss distance (in ft).

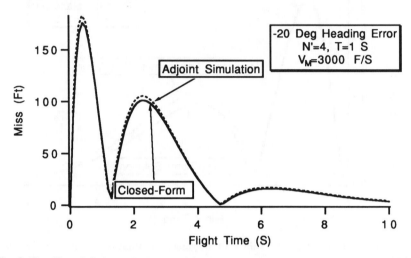

Fig. 3.19   Closed-form solution agrees with computerized adjoint for heading error.

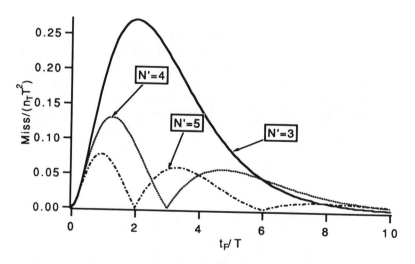

Fig. 3.20   Normalized miss due to target maneuver for single time constant guidance system.

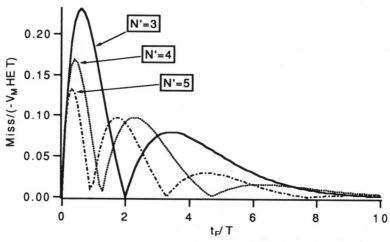

Fig. 3.21   Normalized miss due to heading error for single time constant guidance system.

In a similar way, miss distance formulas can be derived for heading error in a single time constant guidance system. The formulas are

$$\left.\frac{\text{Miss}}{-V_M HE}\right|_{N'=3} = t_F \, e^{-t_F/T}\left(1 - \frac{t_F}{2T}\right)$$

$$\left.\frac{\text{Miss}}{-V_M HE}\right|_{N'=4} = t_F \, e^{-t_F/T}\left(1 - \frac{t_F}{T} + \frac{t_F^2}{6T^2}\right)$$

$$\left.\frac{\text{Miss}}{-V_M HE}\right|_{N'=5} = t_F \, e^{-t_F/T}\left(1 - 1.5\frac{t_F}{T} + \frac{t_F^2}{2T^2} - \frac{t_F^3}{24T^3}\right)$$

where V_M is the missile velocity (in ft/s) and HE the heading error (in rad).

The closed-form solutions for both the target maneuver and heading error miss can be normalized for conciseness. For example, Fig. 3.20 displays the target maneuver miss sensitivity, in normalized form, for various effective navigation ratios. From the normalization factor it becomes obvious that, as the ratio of the flight time to the guidance system time constant (t_F/T) becomes large, the miss eventually goes to zero. From the normalization on the ordinate it becomes obvious that, for a given ratio of flight time to guidance time constant, doubling the guidance system time constant quadruples the miss!

Figure 3.21 displays the heading error miss sensitivity, in normalized form, for various effective navigation ratios. In this case too, it is obvious from the figure that, as the ratio of the flight time to the guidance system time constant (t_F/T) becomes large, the miss eventually goes to zero. From the normalization on the ordinate, we can see that, for a given ratio of flight time to guidance time constant, doubling the guidance system time constant only doubles the heading error miss.

Summary

In this chapter we have seen the power and accuracy of linearization. First we showed that the method of adjoints could be applied to the linearized homing loop. The adjoint technique permitted us to obtain miss distance performance projections as a function of flight time, in error budget form, for many inputs in a single adjoint computer run. The method was shown to be accurate when compared to linear performance projections obtained by massive simulation. It was also shown how the adjoint method could be used to derive miss distance formulas. These closed-form solutions agreed closely with results obtained by massive simulation trials of the nonlinear engagement simulation.

References

[1]Goldsmith, J. L., "A Discussion of the Adjoint Technique of System Analysis," Raytheon, Bedford, MA, Memo SDD-74-525, Oct. 1974.

[2]Bliss, G. A., *Exterior Ballistics,* Univ. of Chicago Press, Chicago, 1925.

[3]Laning, J. H., and Battin, R. H., *Random Processes in Automatic Control,* McGraw-Hill, New York, 1956.

[4]Zarchan, P., "Complete Statistical Analysis of Nonlinear Missile Guidance Systems—SLAM," *Journal of Guidance and Control,* Vol. 2, Jan.–Feb. 1979, pp. 71–78.

[5]Peterson, E. L., *Statistical Analysis and Optimization of Systems,* Wiley, New York, 1961.

[6]Zarchan, P., "Comparison of Statistical Digital Simulation Methods," *Advisory Group for Aerospace Research and Development,* AGARDograph No. 273, July 1988, pp. 2-1-2-16.

[7]Travers, P., "Interceptor Dynamics," unpublished lecture notes, Raytheon, circa 1971.

[8]Bennett, R. R., and Mathews, W. E., "Analytical Determination of Miss Distance for Linear Homing Navigation Systems," Hughes Aircraft Co., Culver City, CA, TM-260, March 1952.

Chapter 4

Noise Analysis

Introduction

THE concept of noise is important to the guidance system engineer. For example, in a radar homing tactical missile the seeker measurement of the line-of-sight rate signal, required for the implementation of proportional navigation guidance, is not perfect but is corrupted by noise. In order to extract the signal from the measurement, an understanding of the concept of noise and its various properties are mandatory. In addition, in order to evaluate system performance in the presence of noise, we must first know how to simulate noise and then how to conduct and interpret experiments with repeated simulation trials. The concepts developed and illustrated in this chapter will be used throughout the text for filtering and evaluating system performance in the presence of noise or other random phenomenon.

Basic Definitions[1]

In this section we will depart from our usual guidance discussions and start by defining some important quantities related to random variables. Since random variables have unknown specific values, they are usually quantified according to their statistical properties. One of the most important statistical properties of any random function x is its probability density function $p(x)$. This function is a measure of the likelihood of occurrence of each value of x and is defined such that

$$p(x) \geq 0$$

and

$$\int_{-\infty}^{\infty} p(x) \, \mathrm{d}x = 1$$

This means that there is a probability that x will occur, and it is certain that the value of x is somewhere between plus and minus infinity. The probability that x is between a and b can be expressed in terms of the probability density function as

$$\text{Prob}(a \leq x \leq b) = \int_{a}^{b} p(x) \, \mathrm{d}x$$

Another important quantity related to random variables is the distribution function. A distribution function, $P(x)$, is the probability that a random variable is less than or equal to x. Therefore, if the probability density function is known, the distribution function can be found by integration as

$$P(x) = \int_{-\infty}^{x} p(u) \, du$$

The mean or expected value of x is defined by

$$m = E(x) = \int_{-\infty}^{\infty} xp(x) \, dx$$

Therefore, the mean can also be thought of as the first moment of x. We can also think of the mean value of x as the sum (integral) of all values of x, each being weighted by its probability of occurrence. It can be shown that, if random variables $x_1, \ldots, x_n$ are independent, then the expectation of the sum is the sum of the expectations, or

$$E(x_1 + x_2 + \cdots + x_n) = E(x_1) + E(x_2) + \cdots + E(x_n)$$

The second moment or mean squared value of x is defined as

$$E(x^2) = \int_{-\infty}^{\infty} x^2 p(x) \, dx$$

Therefore, the rms of x can be obtained by taking the square root of the preceding equation, or

$$\text{rms} = [E(x^2)]^{1/2}$$

The variance of x, σ^2, is defined as the expected squared deviation of x from its mean value. Mathematically, the variance can be expressed as

$$\sigma^2 = E\{[x - E(x)]^2\} = E(x^2) - E^2(x)$$

We can see that the variance is the difference between the mean squared value of x and the square of the mean of x. If we have independent random variables $x_1, \ldots, x_n$ then the variance of the sum can be shown to be the sum of the variances, or

$$\sigma^2 = \sigma_1^2 + \sigma_2^2 + \cdots + \sigma_n^2$$

The square root of the variance σ is also known as the standard deviation. In general, the rms value and standard deviation are not the same unless the random process under consideration has a zero mean.

An example of a probability density function is the uniform distribution, which is depicted in Fig. 4.1. With this probability density function all values of x between a and b are equally likely to occur. An important practical example of the uniform distribution, which should be familiar to any engineer who has programmed on a personal computer, is the BASIC language random number generator (RND). The BASIC RND statement supplies a uniformly distributed random number, on each call, between 0 and 1. Soon we will see how random numbers with different probability

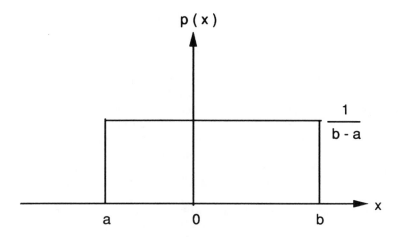

$p(x)$

$\dfrac{1}{b\text{-}a}$

a   0   b

x

Fig. 4.1   Uniform probability distribution.

density functions can be constructed from random numbers following the uniform distribution. From our previous definitions we can see that the mean value of a uniform distribution is

$$m = \int_{-\infty}^{\infty} xp(x)\,\mathrm{d}x = \frac{1}{b-a}\int_{a}^{b} x\,\mathrm{d}x = \frac{b+a}{2}$$

This makes sense, since the expected or mean value is halfway between a and b. The variance of a uniform distribution can also be found from our previous definitions and can be shown to be

$$\sigma^2 = E(x^2) - m^2 = \frac{b^3 - a^3}{3(b-a)} - \left(\frac{b+a}{2}\right)^2 = \frac{(b-a)^2}{12}$$

This means that, if the random numbers from a uniform distribution vary from 0 to 1, the mean of the resultant set of numbers should be 1/2 and the variance should be 1/12. We will use this property of a uniform distribution later in this chapter for constructing random numbers with different probability density functions.

Another important probability density function is the Gaussian or normal distribution. In the missile homing loop we shall often treat the sensor noise disturbances as having a Gaussian distribution. The probability density function for this distribution is shown in Fig. 4.2 and is given by the formula

$$p(x) = \exp\left[-\frac{(x-m)^2}{2\sigma^2}\right]\bigg/[\sigma(2\pi)^{0.5}]$$

where m and σ are parameters. By using our basic definitions it is easy to show that the expected or mean value of a Gaussian distribution is given by

$$E(x) = m$$

and its variance is

$$E(x^2) - m^2 = \sigma^2$$

Therefore, m and σ in the expression for the Gaussian probability density function correspond to the mean and standard deviation, respectively.

We can see from Fig. 4.2 that this "bell-shaped" distribution is virtually zero after three standard deviations ($\pm 3\sigma$). Integration of the probability density function, to find the distribution function, shows that there is a 68% probability that the Gaussian random variable is within one standard deviation ($\pm \sigma$) of the mean, 95% probability it is within two standard deviations of the mean, and 99% probability that it is within three standard deviations of the mean.

It can be shown that the resultant probability density function of a sum of Gaussian distributed random variables is also Gaussian. In addition, under certain circumstances, it can also be shown that the sum of independent random variables, regardless of individual density function, tends toward Gaussian as the number of random variables gets larger (an illustration of this phenomenon will be illustrated in the next section). That is in fact why so many random variables are Gaussian distributed.

Gaussian Noise Example

In order to simulate noise or random events we have to know how to generate, via the computer, pseudorandom numbers with the appropriate probability density function. The FORTRAN language does not come with a random number generator. However, many microcomputer implementations of FORTRAN provide extensions from which noise, with the desired probability density function, can be constructed. For example, in Macintosh Absoft FORTRAN, the statement TOOLBX(RANDOM) produces a uni-

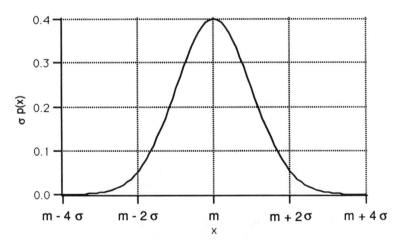

Fig. 4.2 Gaussian or normal probability density function.

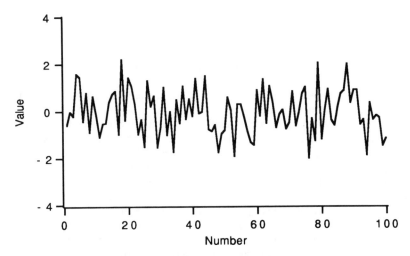

Fig. 4.3   One hundred random numbers with Gaussian distribution.

formly distributed integer between ± 32768. It can be shown from the central limit theorem that the addition of many uniformly distributed variables produces a Gaussian distributed variable.

The first step in constructing random numbers with the desired probability density function is to normalize the uniform noise generator so that random numbers between − 0.5 and 0.5 are produced. The second step is to add 12 uniformly distributed random variables in order to obtain a zero-mean Gaussian variable with unity standard deviation (since the variance of one uniformly distributed random variable is 1/12, the variance of 12 must be 1). The FORTRAN listing for the generation of 100 Gaussian-distributed random numbers with zero mean and unity variance is shown in Listing 4.1.

Figure 4.3 displays the values of each of the 100 random numbers, generated via the program of Listing 4.1, in graphic form. A quick glance at the plot indicates that the data appear to have approximately zero mean. The standard deviation of the data can be "eyeballed" by looking at the maxi-

Listing 4.1   Gaussian random number generator

```
      INTEGER BIN,RANDOM,SUM
      INTEGER*4 TOOLBX
      N = 100
      DO 10 I = 1,N
      SUM = 0
      DO 14 J = 1,12
      IRAN = TOOLBX(RANDOM)
      SUM = SUM + IRAN
14    CONTINUE
      X = SUM/65536.
      WRITE(9,*)I,X
10    CONTINUE
40    CONTINUE
      PAUSE
      END
```

mum excursions (99% chance that data is within the 3σ values) and using the simplified relationship

$$\sigma_{approx} = (\text{peak to peak})/6 = 4/6 = 0.67$$

Thus, the eyeballed value of σ does not quite meet the theoretical expectations of unity standard deviation.

In order to get an idea of the resultant probability density function of the computer-generated 100 random numbers, another FORTRAN program was written and appears in Listing 4.2. Essentially each random number is placed in a bin in order to calculate the frequency of occurrence and hence the probability density function.[2] Also included in the listing, for comparative purposes, is the theoretical formula for the probability density function of a zero-mean, unity variance, Gaussian distribution.

Figure 4.4 presents the calculated probability density function in graphic form. Superimposed on the figure is a plot of the theoretical Gaussian distribution. The figure indicates that, with a sample size of only 100 random numbers, it is not immediately obvious that the computer-generated probability density function follows a Gaussian distribution.

Increasing the sample size from 100 random numbers to 1000 random numbers will clarify the "goodness" of the computer-generated random numbers. Figure 4.5 displays each of the 1000 random numbers generated.

Listing 4.2   FORTRAN program used to generate probability density function

```
         INTEGER BIN,RANDOM,SUM
         INTEGER*4 TOOLBX
         DIMENSION H(10000),X(10000)
         PARAMETER (RANDOM = Z'86140000')
         XMAX = 6.
         XMIN = -6.
         RANGE = XMAX-XMIN
         TMP = 1./SQRT(6.28)
         N = 100
         BIN = 50
         DO 10 I = 1,N
         SUM = 0
         DO 14 J = 1,12
         IRAN = TOOLBX(RANDOM)
         SUM = SUM + IRAN
14       CONTINUE
         X(I) = SUM/65536.
10       CONTINUE
         DO 20 I = 1,BIN
         H(I) = 0
20       CONTINUE
         DO 30 I = 1,N
         K = INT(((X(I) - XMIN)/RANGE)*BIN) + .99
         IF(K<1)K = 1
         IF(K>BIN)K = BIN
         H(K) = H(K) + 1
30       CONTINUE
         DO 40 K = 1,BIN
         PDF = (H(K)/N)*BIN/RANGE
         AB = XMIN + K*RANGE/BIN
         TH = TMP*EXP(-AB*AB/2.)
         WRITE(9,*)AB,PDF,TH
40       CONTINUE
         PAUSE
         END
```

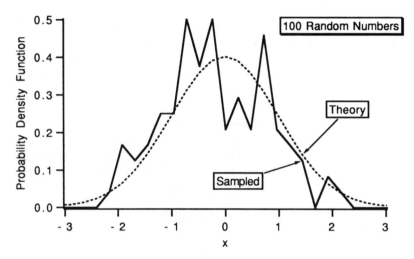

Fig. 4.4 Sampled Gaussian distribution does not closely follow theory for 100 random numbers.

The figure demonstrates that, although the mean of the random numbers is still about zero, we now have larger excursions (numbers vary between $\pm 3\sigma$) and the approximate value of the standard deviation is

$$\sigma_{approx} = (\text{peak to peak})/6 = 6/6 = 1$$

which is the theoretically correct value.

Finally, Fig. 4.6 now shows that when the sample size is increased to 1000 numbers the resultant probability density function closely follows the theoretical ''bell-shaped'' curve. Thus, we have seen how a Gaussian distribution can be constructed from the summation of 12 uniformly distributed

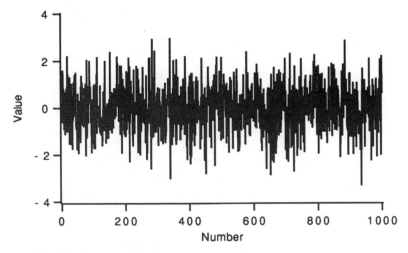

Fig. 4.5 One thousand random numbers with Gaussian distribution.

random variables. This is a practical application of the central limit theorem. In practice, to save on computer running time, we can add fewer than 12 uniformly distributed numbers to get a Gaussian-distributed random number. In the rest of the text we will only add six uniformly distributed numbers to get the desired Gaussian distribution.

Computational Issues

Often, from simulation outputs, we wish to compute some of the basic random variable properties (i.e., mean, variance, etc.). Stated more mathematically, we wish to compute these basic random variable properties from a finite set of data, x_i, when only n samples are available. The discrete equivalent of the previously presented formulas for basic random variable properties are presented in the following equations:

$$\text{mean} = \sum_{i=1}^{n} x_i / n$$

$$\text{mean square} = \sum_{i=1}^{n} x_i^2 / (n-1)$$

$$\text{standard deviation} = \left\{ \left[\sum_{i=1}^{n} (x_i - \text{mean})^2 \right] \middle/ (n-1) \right\}^{\frac{1}{2}}$$

We can see from these equations that integrals from the theoretical or continuous formulas have been replaced with summations in their discrete equivalents. In order for the theoretical and calculated random variable properties to be equal, the number of samples in the discrete computations must be infinite. Since the sample size is finite, the discrete or calculated

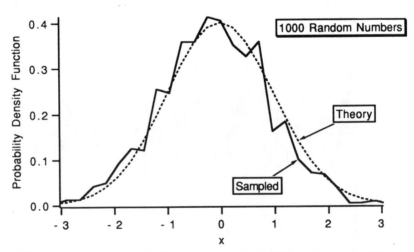

Fig. 4.6 Sampled Gaussian distribution more closely follows theory for 1000 random numbers.

formulas are approximations. In fact, the answers generated from these formulas have statistics of their own.

Recognizing that simulation outputs based upon random inputs can vary, the Monte Carlo approach[3] will often be used in this text to obtain system performance. The Monte Carlo method is approximate and is simply repeated simulation trials plus postprocessing of the resultant data in order to do ensemble averaging (using the preceding formulas) to get the mean and standard deviation. Usually a large number of simulation trials are required in order to provide confidence in the accuracy of the results. However, because of its simplicity and generality, the Monte Carlo approach is probably the most popular computerized method of statistical analysis.

In order to demonstrate that our computed statistics are not precise and in fact are random variables with statistics, a FORTRAN simulation of the Gaussian noise was generated, and Listing 4.3 shows the computation of the sampled standard deviation. The number of i samples used in the program computation was made a parameter in the study and varied from 1 to 100.

Figure 4.7 shows that the computed standard deviation (actual standard deviation is unity) obtained from the FORTRAN program is a function of the sample size used. Large errors in the standard deviation estimate occur when there are less than 20 samples. The accuracy of the computation improves significantly when many samples are used in computing the standard deviation. In this example, we need more than 100 samples for the computed standard deviation to be within 5% of the theoretical value of unity. When we begin to evaluate system performance, when the inputs are random, we will take this information into account in determining how many simulation trials (Monte Carlo runs) will be required to get reasonably

Listing 4.3   Program for computing sampled standard deviation

```
        INTEGER BIN,RANDOM,SUM
        INTEGER*4 TOOLBX
        DIMENSION Z(100)
        PARAMETER (RANDOM = Z'86140000')
        Z1 = 0.
        DO 10 I = 1,100
        SUM = 0
        DO 14 J = 1,12
        IRAN = TOOLBX(RANDOM)
        SUM = SUM + IRAN
14      CONTINUE
        X = SUM/65536.
        Z(I) = X
        Z1 = Z(I) + Z1
        XMEAN = Z1/I
10      CONTINUE
        SIGMA = 0.
        Z1 = 0.
        DO 20 I = 1,100
        Z1 = (Z(I) - XMEAN)**2 + Z1
        IF(I = 1)THEN
            SIGMA = 0.
        ELSE
        SIGMA = SQRT(Z1/(I - 1))
        ENDIF
        WRITE(9,*)I,SIGMA
20      CONTINUE
        PAUSE
        END
```

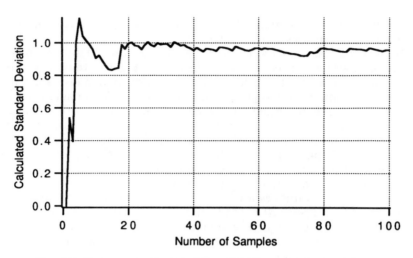

Fig. 4.7 **Large errors occur when only a few samples are taken.**

accurate results. Usually we will consider 50 runs to be sufficient in the tradeoff between computer running time and numerical accuracy.

More Basic Definitions[1]

A few more definitions are required before we can build up the tools required for the analysis of noise-driven systems. Thus far we have discussed the second-order statistics of random processes. However, in practice, we are limited to even less information than that given by the probability density function. Often, only the first moment of these random processes are measured. One such moment is the autocorrelation function, which is defined by

$$\phi_{xx}(t_1, t_2) = E[x(t_1) x(t_2)]$$

The Fourier transform of the autocorrelation function is called the power spectral density and is defined as

$$\Phi_{xx} = \int_{-\infty}^{\infty} \phi_{xx}(\tau) e^{-j\omega\tau} \, d\tau$$

where the power spectral density, using these definitions, has dimensions of unit squared per Hertz. In all of the statistical work presented throughout this text, the power spectral density will have those units.

One simple and useful form for the power spectral density is that of white noise, in which the power spectral density is constant, or

$$\Phi_{xx} = \Phi_0 \qquad \text{(white noise)}$$

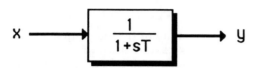

Fig. 4.8 Low-pass filter with white noise input.

The autocorrelation function for white noise is a delta function given by

$$\phi_{xx} = \Phi_0\, \delta(\tau) \qquad \text{(white noise)}$$

Although white noise is not physically realizable, it can be used to serve as an invaluable approximation to situations in which a disturbing noise is wideband compared to the system bandwidth. In addition, white noise is useful for analytical operations because of the impulsive nature of the autocorrelation function (it makes integrals disappear).

Response of Linear System to White Noise

Often we are interested in finding the response of a linear system to noise. If the system is linear, with impulse response $h(t,\tau)$, the output $y(t)$ can be expressed in terms of the input $x(t)$ via the convolution integral, or

$$y(t) = \int_{-\infty}^{t} x(\tau)h(t,\tau)\, \mathrm{d}\tau$$

Squaring both sides of the preceding equation yields

$$y^2(t) = \int_{-\infty}^{t} x(\tau_1)h(t,\tau_1)\, \mathrm{d}\tau_1 \int_{-\infty}^{t} x(\tau_2)h(t,\tau_2)\, \mathrm{d}\tau_2$$

If $x(t)$ is random, we can take expectations of both sides, or

$$E[y^2(t)] = \int_{-\infty}^{t}\int_{-\infty}^{t} h(t,\tau_1)\, h(t,\tau_2) E[x(\tau_1)x(\tau_2)]\, \mathrm{d}\tau_1\, \mathrm{d}\tau_2$$

In addition, if the input $x(t)$ is white noise with power spectral density Φ, the double integral of the preceding equation can be simplified because of the impulsive nature of the autocorrelation function, or

$$E[x(\tau_1)x(\tau_2)] = \Phi\delta(\tau_1 - \tau_2)$$

Substitution yields

$$E[y^2(t)] = \Phi\int_{-\infty}^{t} h^2(t,\tau)\, \mathrm{d}\tau$$

Therefore, the mean square response of a linear system driven by white noise with power spectral density Φ (where Φ has the dimensions of unit^2/Hz) is proportional to the integral of the square of the impulse response. The preceding equation is a general relationship and is valid for both time-varying and time-invariant linear systems driven by white noise.

Low-Pass-Filter Example

In order to illustrate the utility of the mean square response equation, let us find the response of a low-pass filter to white noise as shown in Fig. 4.8. Here the input x is white noise with power spectral density Φ. Since this system is time-invariant and physically realizable (noncausal), the fundamental noise relationship simplifies to

$$E[y^2(t)] = \Phi \int_0^t h^2(\tau)\, d\tau$$

We can find the system impulse response in the preceding integral by first recognizing that the transfer function of the low-pass filter, shown in Fig. 4.8, is given by

$$H(s) = \frac{1}{1 + sT}$$

Therefore, its inverse Laplace transform is

$$h(t) = \mathcal{L}^{-1}[H(s)] = \frac{e^{-t/T}}{T}$$

Substitution yields

$$E[y^2(t)] = \frac{\Phi}{T^2} \int_0^t e^{-2\tau/T}\, d\tau$$

Evaluation of the upper and lower limits results in the final answer:

$$E[y^2(t)] = \frac{\Phi(1 - e^{-2t/T})}{2T}$$

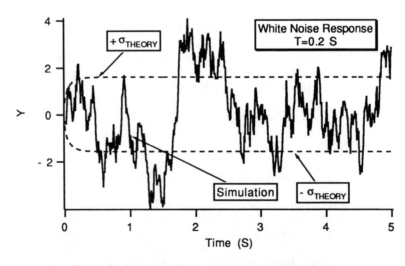

Fig. 4.9   Low-pass filter output agrees with theory.

Listing 4.4   Simulation of low-pass filter driven by white noise

```
        INTEGER BIN,RANDOM,SUM
        INTEGER STEP
        DATA TAU,PHI/.2,1./
        T = 0.
        H = .01
        SIG = SQRT(PHI/H)
        Y = 0.
10      IF(T > 4.999)GO TO 999
        CALL GAUSS(X,SIG)
        YOLD = Y
        STEP = 1
        GOTO 200
66      STEP = 2
        Y = Y + H*YD
        T = T + H
        GOTO 200
55      CONTINUE
        Y = (YOLD + Y)/2. + .5*H*YD
        SIGPLUS = SQRT(PHI*(1. − EXP(− 2.*T/TAU))/(2.*TAU))
        SIGMINUS = − SIGPLUS
        WRITE(9,*)T,Y,SIGPLUS,SIGMINUS
        GOTO 10
200     CONTINUE
        YD = (X − Y)/TAU
        IF(STEP − 1)66,66,55
999     CONTINUE
        PAUSE
        END

        SUBROUTINE GAUSS(X,SIG)
        INTEGER RANDOM,SUM
        INTEGER*4 TOOLBX
        PARAMETER (RANDOM = Z'86140000')
        SUM = 0
        DO 14 J = 1,12
        IRAN = TOOLBX(RANDOM)
        SUM = SUM + IRAN
14      CONTINUE
        X = SUM/65536.
        X = X*SIG
        RETURN
        END
```

In the steady state, the exponential term drops out, yielding

$$E[y^2(\infty)] = \frac{\Phi}{2T}$$

We can write a FORTRAN program to simulate the problem and to see how the theoretical results and simulation results agree. In order to do this we must be able to simulate Gaussian white noise. We already know how to simulate Gaussian random numbers. Since the Gaussian distributed random numbers are independent, the resultant Gaussian random numbers will look white to the low-pass filter if its bandwidth is much greater than the filter bandwidth. In a simulation of the continuous system of Fig. 4.8, the equivalent Gaussian noise generator is called every integration interval, h. Since the integration interval is always chosen to be at least several times smaller than the smallest system time constant T ($h \ll T$ in order to get correct answers with numerical integration techniques), the noise will look white to the system.

The standard deviation of the pseudowhite noise (actual white noise has infinite standard deviation) is related to the desired white noise spectral density Φ and integration interval h according to[3]

$$\sigma = \sqrt{\frac{\Phi}{h}}$$

where Φ has dimensions of units squared per Hertz. The FORTRAN simulation listing of this white-noise-driven low-pass filter is shown in Listing 4.4. It is important to note that this listing will run as is on any Macintosh microcomputer using the Absoft FORTRAN compiler. Other computers and FORTRAN compilers will use slightly different methods for generating uniformly distributed random variables. We can see from the listing that the Gaussian noise with unity standard deviation is modified to get the desired pseudowhite noise spectral density ($\Phi = 1$). The approximate white noise enters the system every integration interval. A sample output for a correlation time of 0.2 s is shown in Fig. 4.9. Also shown in the listing and figure are the theoretical results obtained from the previously derived formula for the output standard deviation of a white-noise-driven low-pass filter, which is

$$\sigma_{\text{theory}} = \pm \sqrt{\frac{\Phi[1 - e^{-2t/T}]}{2T}}$$

We can see from this figure that the simulation results, based upon the FORTRAN listing, agree with theory in the sense that the simulation results lie within the $\pm \sigma$ bounds approximately 68% of the time. Therefore, we can say that the experimental and theoretical results are in agreement.

Increasing the correlation time constant increases the smoothing action of the low-pass filter. Figure 4.10 shows the filter output when the correlation time constant is increased from 0.2 s to 1 s. Here we can see that the larger filter time constant not only provides more filtering action but also tends to

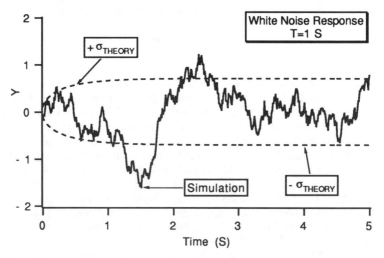

Fig. 4.10   Increasing filter time constant reduces the noise transmission.

correlate the noise. In other words, the randomness of the noise is starting to disappear as the filter time constant increases. Again, this figure shows that the simulated results appear to be within the $\pm \sigma$ bounds about 68% of the time.

It is important to note that both the simulated time domain results and the theoretical second-order statistical results provided invaluable visual information. The use of both theory and simulation can be used to not only verify results but also to provide a deeper understanding of the processes involved.

Adjoints for Noise-Driven Systems[4,5]

In the previous chapter we saw that the method of adjoints could be very useful in analyzing linear time-varying deterministic systems. We shall now demonstrate that adjoints can also be of great utility in analyzing linear time-varying systems driven by white noise. It was shown before that the mean square response of a linear time-varying system driven by white noise is given by

$$E[y^2(t)] = \Phi \int_0^t h^2(t,\tau) \, d\tau$$

where Φ is the white noise power spectral density and $h(t,\tau)$ the impulse response of the linear time-varying system. In this case τ is the impulse application time and t the observation time. The previous section presented a simple example demonstrating the practical utility of this equation. However, for time-varying systems this equation is not as useful because the integration is with respect to the impulse application time τ. As with the deterministic case, this means that many computer runs would have to be made, each having a different impulse application time, in order to evaluate the preceding equation.

If we go back to the fundamental relationship between the original and adjoint systems, we can say that

$$E[y^2(t)] = \Phi \int_0^t [h^*(t_F - \tau, \, t_F - t)]^2 \, d\tau$$

After making the substitution

$$x = t_F - \tau$$

$$dx = -d\tau$$

we obtain

$$E[y^2(t)] = \Phi \int_{t_F-t}^{t_F} [h^*(x, \, t_F - t)]^2 \, dx$$

If the final time is of interest ($t = t_F$), the preceding equation can be rewritten as

$$E[y^2(t)] = \Phi \int_0^t [h^*(x, 0)]^2 \, dx$$

Since the integration is now with respect to the observation time, this new equation is quite useful. Therefore, we can find the mean square response

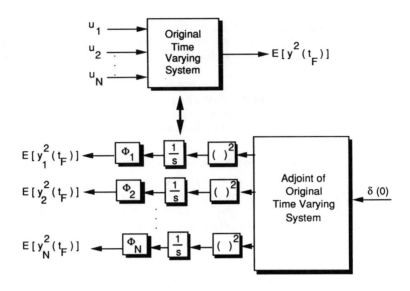

where Φ_1, Φ_2 and Φ_N are power spectral densities of

white noise sources $u_1, u_2,$ and u_N

Fig. 4.11   Equivalence between adjoint and original systems for stochastic inputs.

of a linear, time-varying system driven by white noise by squaring and integrating the output of the impulsively driven adjoint system *in one computer run!*

The benefits of the adjoint approach become even more dramatic when we consider many white noise inputs to the original system as shown in Fig. 4.11.

As with the deterministic inputs, white noise inputs to the original system become outputs in the adjoint system. Therefore, by superposition, one adjoint run yields an exact statistical analysis of the noise-driven system plus a statistical error budget showing how each white noise error source contributed to the total performance projection. In Fig. 4.11 the total mean square response is computed from

$$E[y^2(t)] = E[y_1^2(t)] + E[y_2^2(t)] + \cdots + E[y_N^2(t)]$$

Shaping Filters and Random Processes[6,7]

Thus far we have seen the importance of target maneuver on system performance. In this section we will show how shaping filters can be used to accurately represent aircraft evasive maneuvers. The purpose of the shaping filter approach is to allow us to use efficient and effective means of performance analysis such as the method of adjoints.

The concept of "shaping filter" has been used for many years in the analysis of physical systems because it allows a system with a random input to be replaced by an augmented system (the original system plus the shaping filter) excited only by white noise. An example of this is the replacement of the random telegraph signal by white noise through a simple lag network. This approach is generally applied to problems where mean square values of outputs are of prime importance. In such cases only second-order statistics are important, and rather complex input processes can sometimes be represented by very simple shaping filters. This is due to the fact that random processes that have the same mean and autocorrelation are mathematically equivalent. This is true even though the associated probability density functions of the random processes may be quite different. In other words, a random phenomenon and its shaping filter equivalent are indistinguishable as far as their second-order statistics are concerned. The concept of shaping filter can also be applied to the statistical representation of signals with known form but random starting time. Consider a signal of known form $h(t)$ with random starting time so that the resultant signal $x(t)$ is given by

$$x(t) = h(t - T)u(t - T)$$

where the probability density function of T is given by $p_T(t)$, and $u(t)$ is the unit step function. Note that, although $h(t)$ is deterministic, $x(t)$ is random because of the random starting time. It can be shown that the white-noise-driven shaping network of Fig. 4.12 has the same mean and autocorrelation functions as those of the preceding equation. Here we can see that the white noise has a power spectral density equal to the probability density function of the random starting time and that the inverse Laplace transform of the shaping filter is equal to the deterministic signal.

The output of the shaping network and the actual random process are equivalent in terms of second-order statistics. If either process is passed through a linear physical system, the outputs would be indistinguishable if second-order statistics are being observed (i.e., mean square values).

Consider a step target maneuver which has a starting time that is uniformly distributed over the flight time. Mathematically speaking, the maneuver can be modeled as a constant signal of magnitude n_T, which starts at

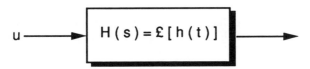

$$u \longrightarrow \boxed{H(s) = \mathcal{L}[h(t)]} \longrightarrow$$

where u is white noise with power spectral density Φ_u

and

$$\Phi_u = p_T(t)$$

Fig. 4.12 Shaping network representation of deterministic signal with random starting time.

time T, or

$$x(t) = n_T u(t - T)$$

where $u(t - T)$ is a unit step function defined by

$$u(t - T) = 0 \qquad \text{for} \qquad t < T$$

$$= 1 \qquad \text{otherwise}$$

Let us assume that the initiation of the maneuver is equally likely to occur anywhere during the flight. More precisely, we can say that the starting time T is uniformly distributed over the flight time t_F, with probability density function

$$p_T(t) = 1/t_F \qquad \text{for} \qquad 0 \le t \le t_F$$

$$= 0 \qquad \text{otherwise}$$

Therefore, the autocorrelation function of this signal with random starting time is given by

$$\phi_{xx}(t_1, t_2) = \int_{-\infty}^{\infty} x(t_1) x(t_2) p_T(T) \, dT$$

or

$$\phi_{xx}(t_1, t_2) = \int_0^{t_F} n_T u(t_1 - T) n_T u(t_2 - T) \frac{dT}{t_F}$$

Assuming that

$$0 < t_1 < t_2 < t_F$$

the autocorrelation function simplifies to

$$\phi_{xx}(t_1, t_2) = \frac{n_T^2}{t_F} \int_0^{t_1} dT$$

It is important to note that the output autocorrelation function of a linear time-invariant system with impulse response $h(t)$ driven by white noise can be expressed as

$$\phi_{yy}(t_1, t_2) = \int_{-\infty}^{t_1} h(t_1 - \tau_1) \int_{-\infty}^{t_2} h(t_2 - \tau_2) \phi_{uu}(\tau_1, \tau_2) \, d\tau_1 \, d\tau_2$$

The autocorrelation function of the white noise input is

$$\phi_{uu}(\tau_1, \tau_2) = \Phi_u(\tau_1) \delta(\tau_1 - \tau_2)$$

where the spectral density of the white noise, Φ_u, is a function of time. Substitution of the white noise autocorrelation function into the preceding integral equation eliminates one of the integrals. After some manipulations and assuming $t_1 < t_2$, we obtain

$$\phi_{yy}(t_1, t_2) = \int_{-\infty}^{t_1} \Phi_u(\tau_1) h(t_1 - \tau_1) h(t_2 - \tau_1) \, d\tau_1$$

If the spectral density takes on values of

$$\Phi_u(t) = \Phi_u, \qquad 0 \le t \le t_F$$

$$= 0 \qquad \text{otherwise}$$

and we assume that

$$0 < t_1 < t_2 < t_F$$

then we can say that

$$\phi_{yy}(t_1, t_2) = \Phi_u \int_0^{t_1} h(t_1 - \tau_1) h(t_2 - \tau_2) \, d\tau_1$$

Therefore, we can say that the two different expressions for the autocorrelation function are equivalent if

$$\Phi_u = n_T^2 / t_F$$

and

$$h(t) = 1$$

In summary, a step maneuver of amplitude n_T, whose starting time is uniformly distributed over the flight time t_F has the same autocorrelation function as a linear network with transfer function

$$H(s) = \frac{1}{s}$$

driven by white noise with power spectral density

$$\Phi_u = n_T^2 / t_F \qquad 0 < t < t_F$$

$$= 0 \qquad \text{otherwise}$$

The uniformly distributed step maneuver is shown in Fig. 4.13 and its shaping filter equivalent is shown in Fig. 4.14.

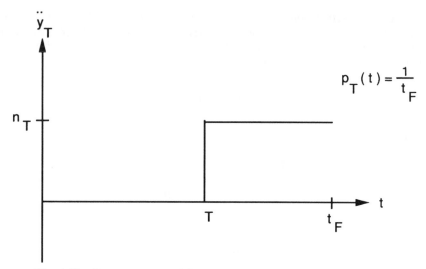

Fig. 4.13   Step maneuver with uniformly distributed starting time.

Example of a Stochastic Adjoint

In order to show how the adjoint can also be used to analyze linear systems driven by stochastic or random disturbances, let us revisit the single-lag proportional navigation homing loop. However, this time we will consider a target maneuver with a random starting time (starting time that is uniformly distributed over the flight time) as the error source. A single-lag proportional navigation homing loop with the stochastic input is shown in Fig. 4.15.

In Fig. 4.15 the target maneuver is a constant from flight to flight (either plus or minus n_T). However, on a given flight its initiation time is equally likely to occur anywhere during the flight (uniformly distributed over the flight time). A FORTRAN Monte Carlo simulation of Fig. 4.15 with the random target maneuver appears in Listing 4.5. We can see from the listing that there are two main loops. The outer loop varies the flight time from 1

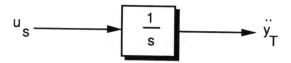

u_s is White Noise With Power Spectral Density

$$\Phi_s = \frac{n_T^2}{t_F}$$

Fig. 4.14   Shaping filter equivalent of random starting time step maneuver.

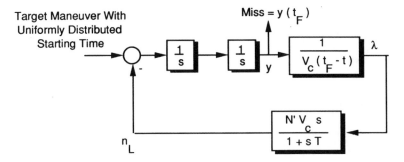

Fig. 4.15 Single-lag homing loop with stochastic inputs.

to 10 s in increments of 1 s. The inner loop performs 50 sets of runs on a particular case. In each of these cases the starting time of the maneuver is chosen from a uniform distribution. After each Monte Carlo set, the standard deviation and mean of the 50 miss distances are computed according to the formulas developed in this chapter.

A case was run for the single-time-constant guidance system in which the time constant was set to 1 s and the effective navigation ratio was set to 3. Fifty-run Monte Carlo sets for 10 different flight times were run for this single case, which actually encompassed a total of 500 runs (50 × 10). The standard deviation of the miss for each flight time was calculated and is displayed as a function of flight time in Fig. 4.16. We can see that the miss distance is small for both small and large flight times. The miss is small for short flight times because the miss distance does not have enough time to develop. At the larger flight times there is a good chance that the target

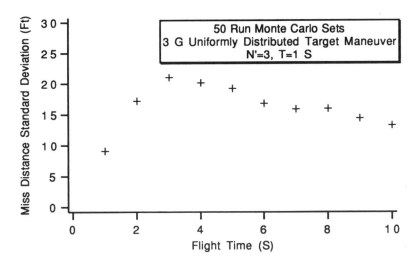

Fig. 4.16 Monte Carlo results for uniformly distributed target maneuver.

Listing 4.5   Simulation of homing loop with random target maneuver

```
        DIMENSION Z(1000)
        INTEGER RUN
        VC = 4000.
        XNT = 96.6
        VM = 3000.
        XNP = 3.
        TAU = 1.
        RUN = 50
106     CONTINUE
        DO 60 TF = 1,10
        Z1 = 0.
        DO 20 I = 1,RUN
        CALL UNIFORM(SUM)
        TSTART = TF*SUM
        CALL UNIFORM(PZ)
        PZ = PZ - .5
        IF(PZ>0.)THEN
            COEF = 1.
        ELSE
            COEF = - 1.
        ENDIF
        Y = 0.
        YD = 0.
        T = 0.
        H = .01
        S = 0.
        XNC = 0.
        XNL = 0.
10      IF(T>(TF - .0001))GOTO 999
        IF(T<TSTART)THEN
            XNT = 0.
        ELSE
            XNT = COEF*96.6
        ENDIF
        YOLD = Y
        YDOLD = YD
        XNLOLD = XNL
        STEP = 1
        GOTO 200
66      STEP = 2
        Y = Y + H*YD
        YD = YD + H*YDD
        XNL = XNL + H*XNLD
        T = T + H
        GOTO 200
55      CONTINUE
        Y = .5*(YOLD + Y + H*YD)
        YD = .5*(YDOLD + YD + H*YDD)
        XNL = .5*(XNLOLD + XNL + H*XNLD)
        S = S + H
        GOTO 10
200     CONTINUE
        TGO = TF - T + .00001
        RTM = VC*TGO
        XLAMD = (RTM*YD + Y*VC)/(RTM**2)
        XNC = XNP*VC*XLAMD
        XNLD = (XNC - XNL)/TAU
        YDD = XNT - XNL
        IF(STEP - 1)66,66,55
999     CONTINUE
        Z(I) = Y
        Z1 = Z(I) + Z1
        XMEAN = Z1/I
20      CONTINUE
        SIGMA = 0.
        Z1 = 0.
        DO 50 I = 1,RUN
        Z1 = (Z(I) - XMEAN)**2 + Z1
        IF(I = 1)THEN
            SIGMA = 0.
        ELSE
            SIGMA = SQRT(Z1/(I - 1))
        ENDIF
```

(Listing 4.5 continued on next page.)

Listing 4.5   (cont.) Simulation of homing loop with random target maneuver

```
50     CONTINUE
       WRITE(9,*)TF,SIGMA,XMEAN
60     CONTINUE
       PAUSE
       END

       SUBROUTINE UNIFORM(SUM)
       INTEGER*4 TOOLBX
       INTEGER RANDOM
       PARAMETER (RANDOM = Z'86140000')
       IRAN = TOOLBX(RANDOM)
       SUM = IRAN/65536. + .5
       RETURN
       END
```

maneuver initiation time will be at a long time to go, relative to the guidance system time constant, and will therefore induce a smaller miss distance.

We have seen in the previous section that the shaping filter equivalent for a uniformly distributed target maneuver is white noise, with spectral density Φ_s through an integrator. The spectral density of the white noise is related to the maneuver level and the flight time according to

$$\Phi_s = \frac{n_T^2}{t_F}$$

An adjoint model can be constructed from the original system by following the rules for constructing stochastic adjoints.[4,5] The only additional rule for stochastic systems is that all stochastic inputs to the original system must be modeled as white noise inputs, which then become outputs in the adjoint system. Since the input to the original system can be modeled as white noise through an integrator, the adjoint model will reverse the signal flow and

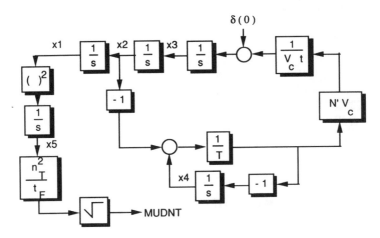

Fig. 4.17   Adjoint model for stochastic example.

square and integrate the output. The resultant adjoint model is shown in Fig. 4.17. The impulsive input can be replaced by an initial condition of unity on integrator $x3$.

An adjoint FORTRAN simulation of the model in Fig. 4.17 appears in Listing 4.6. We can see that we have a loop around the entire program in which the flight time is varied. Normally, adjoint time can be interpreted as either flight time or time to go at which the disturbance occurs. Since the maneuver is uniformly distributed over the flight time, the adjoint output must be interpreted as the time to go, for a given flight time, at which the maneuver occurs. Therefore, multiple adjoint runs have to be made in this case to get flight time information.

Listing 4.6 Adjoint model using shaping filter approach

```
        INTEGER STEP
        DATA XNT,XNP,TAU,TF/ 96.6,3,1,10/
        T = 0.
        S = 0.
        TP = T + .00001
        X1 = 0
        X2 = 0
        X3 = 1
        X4 = 0
        X5 = 0.
        H = .02
        DO 20 TF = 1.,10.,.1
10      IF(TP > (TF - .00001))GOTO 999
        S = S + H
        X1OLD = X1
        X2OLD = X2
        X3OLD = X3
        X4OLD = X4
        X5OLD = X5
        STEP = 1
        GOTO 200
66      STEP = 2
        X1 = X1 + H*X1D
        X2 = X2 + H*X2D
        X3 = X3 + H*X3D
        X4 = X4 + H*X4D
        X5 = X5 + H*X5D
        TP = TP + H
        GOTO 200
55      CONTINUE
        X1 = (X1OLD + X1)/2 + .5*H*X1D
        X2 = (X2OLD + X2)/2 + .5*H*X2D
        X3 = (X3OLD + X3)/2 + .5*H*X3D
        X4 = (X4OLD + X4)/2 + .5*H*X4D
        X5 = (X5OLD + X5)/2 + .5*H*X5D
        GOTO 10
200     CONTINUE
        X1D = X2
        X2D = X3
        Y1 = (X4 - X2)/TAU
        TGO = TP + .00001
        X3D = XNP*Y1/TGO
        X4D = - Y1
        X5D = X1*X1
        IF(STEP - 1)66,66,55
999     CONTINUE
        XMUDNT = XNT*SQRT(X5/TF)
        WRITE(9,*)TP,XMUDNT
20      CONTINUE
        PAUSE
        END
```

The adjoint simulation was run using the input parameters shown in Listing 4.6. The adjoint results for this example are shown in Fig. 4.18. Superimposed on the plot are the Monte Carlo results previously generated. We can see that the adjoint and Monte Carlo results are in close proximity, thus experimentally confirming the shaping filter approach and demonstrating the utility of stochastic adjoints. Although the adjoint had to have a flight time loop, it gave the equivalent of 50-run Monte Carlo sets in one adjoint run!

Closed-Form Solution for Random Target Maneuver

If we closely investigate Fig. 4.17, we can see that the miss due to a target maneuver with uniformly distributed starting time can be found by squaring the sensitivity due to a step target maneuver and then integrating and taking the square root of the resultant adjoint signal. If we define the miss due to a step target maneuver as *MNT,* the miss due to a uniformly distributed target maneuver can be expressed mathematically as

$$MUDNT = n_T \sqrt{\frac{1}{t_F} \int_0^{t_F} MNT^2 \, d\tau}$$

where n_T is the target maneuver level and t_F the flight time. For a single-lag guidance system with an effective navigation ratio of 3, we have already shown in Chapter 3 that the miss due to a step target maneuver is given by

$$MNT\Big|_{N'=3} = 0.5 \, t_F^2 \, e^{-t_F/T}$$

where T is the guidance system time constant. Substitution of the step target maneuver solution into the expression for the uniformly distributed target

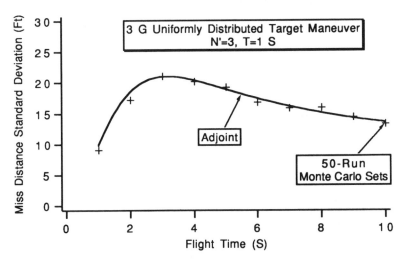

Fig. 4.18   Shaping filter adjoint and Monte Carlo results are in close agreement.

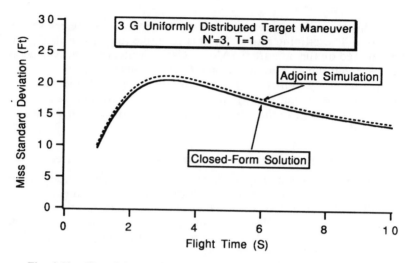

Fig. 4.19   Closed-form solution and adjoint simulation results agree.

maneuver yields

$$MUDNT\Big|_{N'=3} = n_T \sqrt{\frac{1}{t_F} \int_0^{t_F} 0.25\tau^4 \, e^{-2\tau/T} \, d\tau}$$

After integration by parts and much algebra we obtain the closed-form expression, valid for an effective navigation ratio of 3, for the uniformly distributed target maneuver:

$$MUDNT\Big|_{N'=3} = \frac{n_T}{4} \sqrt{\frac{T^5}{t_F} [3 - e^{-2x}(2x^4 + 4x^3 + 6x^2 + 6x + 3)]}$$

where x is defined as normalized time, or

$$x = \frac{t_F}{T}$$

Figure 4.19 displays the closed-form solution for the case in which the guidance system time constant is 1 s. Superimposed on the plot are the previously presented adjoint results for a uniformly distributed target maneuver. We can see from the close proximity of the two curves that both solutions are in close agreement.

Summary

Starting from basic definitions of random variables, we have shown how to simulate random phenomena and properly interpret the simulation results. Throughout this chapter we have shown two ways of doing problems: the theoretical way, which only works under certain circumstances, and simulation, which is always valid. Numerical examples have been presented that not only demonstrate that theory and simulation agree but also show how each method offers new insights. Finally, it was shown how the method of adjoints can be extended to evaluate system performance in the presence of random disturbances.

References

[1]Gelb, A., *Applied Optimal Estimation,* MIT Press, Cambridge, MA, 1974.

[2]Zarchan, P., "Engineering Tips For Plotting," *MacTutor,* Vol. 4, Feb. 1988, pp. 78–82.

[3]Zarchan, P., "Comparison of Statistical Digital Simulation Methods," *Advisory Group for Aerospace Research and Development,* AGARDograph No. 273, July 1988, pp. 2-1-2-16.

[4]Laning, J. H., and Battin, R. H., *Random Processes in Automatic Control,* McGraw-Hill, New York, 1956.

[5]Zarchan, P., "Complete Statistical Analysis of Nonlinear Missile Guidance Systems—SLAM," *Journal of Guidance and Control,* Vol. 2, Jan.-Feb. 1979, pp. 71–78.

[6]Zarchan, P., "Representation of Realistic Evasive Maneuvers By the Use of Shaping Filters," *Journal of Guidance and Control,* Vol. 2, July–Aug. 1979, pp. 290–295.

[7]Fitzgerald, R. J., "Shaping Filters for Disturbances With Random Starting Times," *Journal of Guidance and Control,* Vol. 2, March–April 1979, pp. 152–154.

Chapter 5

Covariance Analysis and the Homing Loop

Background

COVARIANCE analysis is another useful computerized tool that can be used to analyze time-varying linear systems driven by random inputs. Covariance analysis, like the adjoint technique, is an exact method of analysis that is restricted to linear systems. With this method, the covariance matrix of the system state vector is propagated as a function of time by the direct integration of a nonlinear matrix differential equation. Exact statistical performance projections of any state or combination of states as a function of time can be obtained with this technique. Covariance analysis is quite popular in problems associated with inertial navigation and optimal estimation. We shall show that the covariance analysis technique can also be used to get exact statistical performance projections in a missile guidance system.

Theory

So far we are accumstomed to writing computer programs directly from inspection of the system block diagram. To apply covariance analysis, we must first change our method of operation and convert the system block diagram to state space notation or an equivalent set of first-order differential equations expressed in matrix form.

The dynamics of any linear system driven by white noise inputs can be converted to the following first-order vector differential equation:

$$\dot{x}(t) = F(t)x(t) + u(t)$$

where $x(t)$ is the system state vector, $F(t)$ is the system dynamics matrix, and $u(t)$ is a white noise vector with spectral density matrix, $Q(t)$, or

$$Q(t) = E\left[u(t)u^T(t)\right]$$

The matrix differential equation for the propagation of the covariance of this general system is[1,2]

$$\dot{X}(t) = F(t)X(t) + \left[F(t)X(t)\right]^T + Q(t)$$

where the covariance matrix $X(t)$ is related to the state $x(t)$ according to

$$X(t) = E\left[x(t)x^T(t)\right]$$

The diagonal elements of the covariance matrix represent the variances of the state variables if the disturbance processes are zero mean. The off-diagonal elements of the covariance matrix represent the degree of correlation between the various state variables.

Low-Pass Filter Example

In order to demonstrate the application of covariance analysis, let us revisit the example of Chapter 4 in which a low-pass filter with a white noise input has been redrawn in block diagram form as shown in Fig. 5.1. In this example the input u_S is white noise with power spectral density Φ_S, T is the time constant of the low-pass filter, and x is the filter output. We want to find the variance of x as a function of time.

By inspection of Fig. 5.1 we can write the first-order differential equation of the low-pass filter in state space form as

$$\dot{x} = -\frac{x}{T} + \frac{u_S}{T}$$

Therefore, for this example, the system dynamic matrix and spectral density matrix are time-invariant scalars and can be written by inspection of the preceding differential equation as

$$F = \frac{-1}{T}$$

$$Q = \frac{\Phi_S}{T^2}$$

The differential equation for the propagation of the covariance simplifies to the linear equation

$$\dot{X} = \frac{-2}{T} X + \frac{\Phi_S}{T^2}$$

The solution to the preceding linear covariance analysis differential equation can be found, using standard differential equation solution techniques,

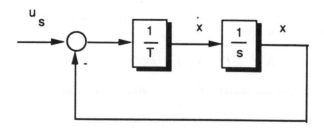

Fig. 5.1   Low-pass filter with white noise input.

to be

$$X = \frac{\Phi_S}{2T}\left[1 - e^{-2t/T}\right]$$

Since X represents the mean square value of x, we recognize that the preceding answer is identical to the answer obtained in Chapter 4 using the impulse response technique.

Numerical Considerations

In all of the systems simulated in the text, the second-order Runge-Kutta numerical integration method is used to solve the necessary differential equations. Although more accurate numerical integration techniques exist, the second-order Runge-Kutta technique is adequate for getting the correct answers. When the equations associated with covariance analysis are solved numerically, higher order integration methods are required to get the desired accuracy.

Let us again consider the Butterworth filter simulation of Chapter 1 (i.e., Fig. 1.1 and Listing 1.1) in which the second-order Runge-Kutta numerical integration technique was used. In that simulation the integration step size was made very small ($h = 0.0001$ s) for platform timing experiments. If we arbitrarily increase the integration step size we can see from Fig. 5.2 that the accuracy of the answers begins to degrade.

It is apparent from Fig. 5.2 that $h = 0.01$ s is about the largest the integration step size can be made without severely degrading accuracy. This is not surprising since the natural frequency of the Butterworth filter in this example is 50 r/s. This means that the approximate time constant of the system under consideration is 0.02 s ($1/50 = 0.02$). Making the integration step size

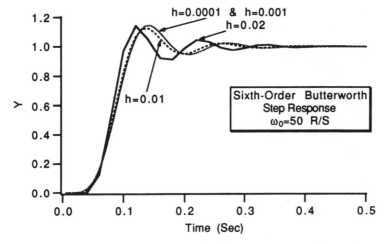

Fig. 5.2   Increasing integration step size eventually degrades accuracy.

Listing 5.1   Simulation of sixth-order Butterworth filter with fourth-order Runge-Kutta integration technique

```
        INTEGER ORDER,STEP
        DIMENSION X(6),XOLD(6),XD(6)
        REAL K0(6),K1(6),K2(6),K3(6)
        DATA A1,A2,A3,A4,A5,A6,W0/3.86,7.46,9.13,7.46,3.86,1.,50./
        DATA XIN/1./
        ORDER = 6
        W02 = W0*W0
        W03 = W02*W0
        W04 = W03*W0
        W05 = W04*W0
        W06 = W05*W0
        DO 10 I = 1,ORDER
        X(I) = 0.
10      CONTINUE
        T = 0.
        H = .02
        S = 0.
5       IF(T.GE..5)GOTO 999
        S = S + H
        DO 20 I = 1,ORDER
        XOLD(I) = X(I)
20      CONTINUE
        STEP = 1
        GOTO 200
40      STEP = 2
        DO 50 I = 1,ORDER
        K0(I) = XD(I)
50      CONTINUE
        TNEW = T + .5*H
        DO 60 I = 1,ORDER
        X(I) = XOLD(I) + .5*H*K0(I)
60      CONTINUE
        GOTO 200
41      STEP = 3
        DO 70 I = 1,ORDER
        K1(I) = XD(I)
70      CONTINUE
        TNEW = T + .5*H
        DO 75 I = 1,ORDER
        X(I) = XOLD(I) + .5*H*K1(I)
75      CONTINUE
        GOTO 200
42      STEP = 4
        DO 80 I = 1,ORDER
        K2(I) = XD(I)
80      CONTINUE
        TNEW = T + H
        DO 85 I = 1,ORDER
        X(I) = XOLD(I) + H*K2(I)
85      CONTINUE
        GOTO 200
43      DO 90 I = 1,ORDER
        K3(I) = XD(I)
90      CONTINUE
        T = TNEW
        DO 95 I = 1,ORDER
        X(I) = XOLD(I) + H*(K0(I) + 2.*(K1(I) + K2(I)) + K3(I))/6.
95      CONTINUE
        IF(S.GE..01999)THEN
          S = 0.
          WRITE(9,*)T,X(1)
        END IF
        GOTO 5
200     CONTINUE
        XD(1) = X(2)
        XD(2) = X(3)
        XD(3) = X(4)
        XD(4) = X(5)
        XD(5) = X(6) XD(6) = W06* (XIN-A5*X(6)/W05-A4*X(5)/W04-A3*X(4)/W03
1       -A2*X(3)/W02-A1*X(2)/W0-X(1))/A6
```

(Listing 5.1 continued on next page.)

Listing 5.1   (cont.) Simulation of sixth-order Butterworth filter with fourth-order Runge-Kutta integration technique

```
        IF (STEP.EQ.1) THEN
              GOTO 40
        ELSEIF (STEP.EQ.2) THEN
              GOTO 41
        ELSEIF (STEP.EQ.3) THEN
              GOTO 42
        ELSE
              GOTO 43
        ENDIF
999     CONTINUE
        PAUSE
        END
```

equal to or larger than 0.02 s means that we will be missing the effect of the small time constant. We can see from Fig. 5.2 that even when the integration step size is 0.01 s the answers also deviate from the exact solution.

Better accuracy can be achieved with the fourth-order Runge-Kutta numerical integration technique.[3,4] Given a first-order differential equation of the form

$$\dot{x} = f(x, t)$$

where t is time, we want to find a numerical integration recursive relationship for x as a function of time. With the fourth-order Runge-Kutta numerical integration technique, the value of x at the next integration inverval h is given by

$$x_{k+1} = x_k + \frac{h}{6} \left[K_0 + 2K_1 + 2K_2 + K_3 \right]$$

where

$$K_0 = f(x_k, t_k)$$

$$K_1 = f(x_k + 0.5K_0, t + 0.5h)$$

$$K_2 = f(x_k + 0.5K_1, t + 0.5h)$$

$$K_3 = f(x_k + K_2, t + h)$$

From the preceding expressions we can see that the new value of x is simply the old value of x plus terms proportional to the derivative evaluated at various times between t and $t + h$. Using the relationships for the fourth-order Runge-Kutta integration technique, we can write a program to simulate the sixth-order Butterworth filter as shown in Listing 5.1. We can see that the structure of this program is identical to the one of Listing 1.1 (i.e., differential equations appear after statement label 200) except extra steps have been added to the integration procedure.

Figure 5.3 shows that when we simulate the Butterworth filter with Listing 5.1 using fourth-order rather than second-order Runge-Kutta numerical

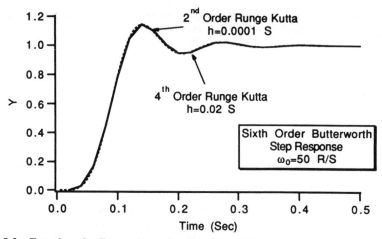

Fig. 5.3   Fourth-order Runge-Kutta integration yields adequate accuracy with large integration step sizes.

integration we can use a much larger integration step size to get the same accuracy. In this example, a step size as large as 0.02 s was adequate for getting the correct solution.

Homing Loop Example

To demonstrate the utility of covariance analysis for a more relevant example let us revisit the single-lag homing loop example of Chapter 4 in which the random error source is a uniformly distributed target maneuver. The homing loop model of Fig. 4.15 is redrawn in Fig. 5.4 for convenience. In Fig. 5.4 the uniformly distributed target maneuver has been replaced by its shaping filter equivalent which is white noise through an integrator. The spectral density of the white noise input u_S is given by Φ_S, which was shown in Chapter 4 to be

$$\Phi_S = \frac{n_T^2}{t_F}$$

where n_T is the magnitude of the target maneuver and t_F is the flight time over which the maneuver is equally likely to occur.

In order to apply covariance analysis to the homing loop of Fig. 5.4, we must convert this block diagram to state space form. To perform the conversion the homing loop equations must first be expressed as a set of first-order linear differential equations or

$$\ddot{y} = \ddot{y}_T - N'V_c\dot{D} = \ddot{y}_T - \frac{N'V_c}{T}\left[\frac{y}{V_c(t_F-t)} - D\right]$$

$$\ddot{y}_T = u_S$$

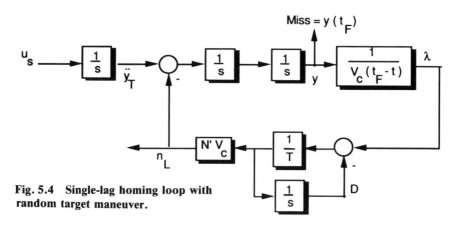

Fig. 5.4 Single-lag homing loop with random target maneuver.

$$\dot{D} = \frac{1}{T}\left[\frac{y}{V_c(t_F - t)} - D\right]$$

Since the preceding set of first-order differential equations are functions of the states they can be written in state space form by inspection as

$$
\begin{bmatrix} \dot{y} \\ \ddot{y} \\ \dddot{y}_T \\ \dot{D} \end{bmatrix} =
\begin{bmatrix} 0 & 1 & 0 & 0 \\ \dfrac{-N'}{T(t_F - t)} & 0 & 1 & \dfrac{N'V_c}{T} \\ 0 & 0 & 0 & 0 \\ \dfrac{1}{TV_c(t_F - t)} & 0 & 0 & \dfrac{-1}{T} \end{bmatrix}
\begin{bmatrix} y \\ \dot{y} \\ \ddot{y}_T \\ D \end{bmatrix} +
\begin{bmatrix} 0 \\ 0 \\ u_S \\ 0 \end{bmatrix}
$$

By comparing the preceding matrix differential equation with the generalized state space equation we can see that the state vector for this example is

$$
x = \begin{bmatrix} y \\ \dot{y} \\ \ddot{y}_T \\ D \end{bmatrix}
$$

and the system dynamic matrix is given by

$$
F = \begin{bmatrix} 0 & 1 & 0 & 0 \\ \dfrac{-N'}{T(t_F - t)} & 0 & 1 & \dfrac{N'V_c}{T} \\ 0 & 0 & 0 & 0 \\ \dfrac{1}{TV_c(t_F - t)} & 0 & 0 & \dfrac{-1}{T} \end{bmatrix}
$$

From the homing loop state space equation we can also see that $u(t)$ is

$$u = \begin{bmatrix} 0 \\ 0 \\ u_S \\ 0 \end{bmatrix}$$

and therefore and the spectral density matrix $Q(t)$ becomes

$$Q = \begin{bmatrix} 0 & 0 & 0 & 0 \\ 0 & 0 & 0 & 0 \\ 0 & 0 & \Phi_S & 0 \\ 0 & 0 & 0 & 0 \end{bmatrix}$$

where Φ_S has been previously defined.

Integration of the covariance analysis nonlinear matrix differential equation yields statistical information for all of the states. For this homing loop example, the standard deviation of the relative trajectory y can be found by taking the square root of the first diagonal element of the covariance matrix X or

$$\sigma_y(t) = \sqrt{X(1,1)}$$

The source code listing of the homing loop covariance analysis program appears in Listing 5.2. We can see from the listing that both double-precision arithmetic and fourth-order Runge-Kutta integration are used to get the necessary accuracy. Standard transposition, multiplication, and addition matrix subroutines[4] have been added to conveniently form the covariance matrix differential equations after statement label 200. From Listing 5.2 we can see that the only error source in the guidance system is a 3-g uniformly distributed target maneuver.

The homing loop covariance analysis program of Listing 5.2 was run and Fig. 5.5 presents the resultant standard deviation of the relative separation between the missile and target [i.e., square root of first diagonal element of covariance matrix represents $\sigma_y(t)$] for the entire 10-s flight. At the end of the flight the relative separation between the missile and target is the miss distance [i.e., $\sigma_{\text{Miss}} = \sigma_y(t_F)$]. In this example the covariance analysis program indicates that the standard deviation of the miss distance is 13.3 ft, which is identical to the adjoint results of Chapter 4 (i.e., see Fig. 4.18). Unlike the adjoint technique, covariance analysis does not provide miss distance error budget information for all different flight times in a single computer run. However, as can be seen from Fig. 5.5, covariance analysis does provide relative trajectory information at all times for a given flight time. If many random error sources are present, one covariance analysis computer run yields a total statistical performance projection. If learning how each error source contributed to the total performance is desired,

Listing 5.2   Homing loop covariance analysis program

```
         IMPLICIT REAL*8(A-H)
         IMPLICIT REAL*8(O-Z)
         REAL*8 F(4,4),X(4,4),FX(4,4),FXT(4,4),FXFXT(4,4)
         REAL*8 XOLD(4,4),K0(4,4),Q(4,4)
         REAL*8 K1(4,4),K2(4,4),K3(4,4),XD(4,4)
         REAL*8 A(1,4),AT(4,1),AX(1,4),AXAT(1,1)
         INTEGER ORDER,STEP
         ORDER = 4
         T = 0.
         TNEW = T
         S = 0.
         H = .01
         XNP = 3.
         TAU = 1.
         XNT = 96.6
         VC = 4000.
         TF = 10.
         TGO = TF-T + .00001
         PHIS = XNT*XNT/TF
         DO 10 I = 1,ORDER
         DO 10 J = 1,ORDER
         F(I,J) = 0.
         X(I,J) = 0.
         Q(I,J) = 0.
10       CONTINUE
         F(1,2) = 1.
         F(2,1) = -XNP/(TAU*TGO)
         F(2,3) = 1.
         F(2,4) = XNP*VC/TAU
         F(4,1) = 1./(TAU*VC*TGO)
         F(4,4) = -1./TAU
         Q(3,3) = PHIS
5        IF (T.GE.TF) GOTO 999
         DO 20 I = 1,ORDER
         DO 20 J = 1,ORDER
         XOLD(I,J) = X(I,J)
20       CONTINUE
         STEP = 1
         GOTO 200
40       STEP = 2
         DO 50 I = 1,ORDER
         DO 50 J = 1,ORDER
         K0(I,J) = XD(I,J)
50       CONTINUE
         TNEW = T + .5*H
         DO 60 I = 1,ORDER
         DO 60 J = 1,ORDER
         X(I,J) = XOLD(I,J) + .5*H*K0(I,J)
60       CONTINUE
         GOTO 200
41       STEP = 3
         DO 70 I = 1,ORDER
         DO 70 J = 1,ORDER
         K1(I,J) = XD(I,J)
70       CONTINUE
         TNEW = T + .5*H
         DO 75 I = 1,ORDER
         DO 75 J = 1,ORDER
         X(I,J) = XOLD(I,J) + .5*H*K1(I,J)
75       CONTINUE
         GOTO 200
42       STEP = 4
         DO 80 I = 1,ORDER
         DO 80 J = 1,ORDER
         K2(I,J) = XD(I,J)
80       CONTINUE
         TNEW = T + H
         DO 85 I = 1,ORDER
         DO 85 J = 1,ORDER
         X(I,J) = XOLD(I,J) + H*K2(I,J)
85       CONTINUE
         GOTO 200
43       DO 90 I = 1,ORDER
         DO 90 J = 1,ORDER
         K3(I,J) = XD(I,J)
```

(Listing 5.2 continued on next page.)

Listing 5.2   (cont.) Homing loop covariance analysis program

```
 90    CONTINUE
       T = TNEW
       DO 95 I = 1,ORDER
       DO 95 J = 1,ORDER
       X(I,J) = XOLD(I,J) + H*(K0(I,J) + 2.*(K1(I,J) + K2(I,J)) + K3(I,J))/6.
 95    CONTINUE
       S = S + H
       IF(S.LE..09999)GOTO 5
       S = 0.
       A(1,1) = XNP/(TAU*TGO)
       A(1,2) = 0.
       A(1,3) = 0.
       A(1,4) = -XNP*VC/TAU
       CALL MATMUL(A,1,ORDER,X,ORDER,ORDER,AX)
       CALL MATTRN(A,1,ORDER,AT)
       CALL MATMUL(AX,1,ORDER,AT,ORDER,1,AXAT)
       SIGY = SQRT(X(1,1))
       SIGNL = SQRT(AXAT(1,1))
       WRITE(9,*)T,SIGY,SIGNL
       GOTO 5
200    TGO = TF-TNEW + .00001
       F(2,1) = -XNP/(TAU*TGO)
       F(4,1) = 1./(TAU*VC*TGO)
       CALL MATMUL(F,ORDER,ORDER,X,ORDER,ORDER,FX)
       CALL MATTRN(FX,ORDER,ORDER,FXT)
       CALL MATADD(FX,ORDER,ORDER,FXT,FXFXT)
       CALL MATADD(FXFXT,ORDER,ORDER,Q,XD)
       IF(STEP.EQ.1)THEN
           GOTO 40
       ELSEIF(STEP.EQ.2)THEN
           GOTO 41
       ELSEIF(STEP.EQ.3)THEN
           GOTO 42
       ELSE
           GOTO 43
       ENDIF
999    CONTINUE
       PAUSE
       END

       SUBROUTINE MATTRN(A,IROW,ICOL,AT)
       IMPLICIT REAL*8 (A-H)
       IMPLICIT REAL*8 (O-Z)
       REAL*8 A(IROW,ICOL),AT(ICOL,IROW)
       DO 105 I = 1,IROW
       DO 105 J = 1,ICOL
       AT(J,I) = A(I,J)
105    CONTINUE
       RETURN
       END
       SUBROUTINE MATMUL(A,IROW,ICOL,B,JROW,JCOL,C)
       IMPLICIT REAL*8 (A-H)
       IMPLICIT REAL*8 (O-Z)
       REAL*8 A(IROW,ICOL),B(JROW,JCOL),C(IROW,JCOL)
       DO 110 I = 1,IROW
       DO 110 J = 1,JCOL
           C(I,J) = 0.
           DO 110 K = 1,ICOL
               C(I,J) = C(I,J) + A(I,K)*B(K,J)
110    CONTINUE
       RETURN
       END

       SUBROUTINE MATADD(A,IROW,ICOL,B,C)
       IMPLICIT REAL*8 (A-H)
       IMPLICIT REAL*8 (O-Z)
       REAL*8 A(IROW,ICOL),B(IROW,ICOL),C(IROW,ICOL)
       DO 120 I = 1,IROW
       DO 120 J = 1,ICOL
           C(I,J) = A(I,J) + B(I,J)
120    CONTINUE
       RETURN
       END
```

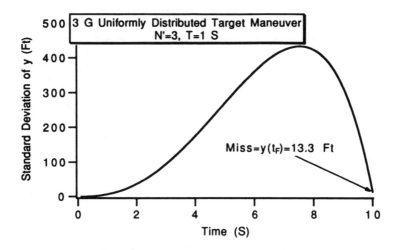

Fig. 5.5   Covariance analysis miss distance results agree with adjoint.

additional computer runs must be made—each one run with one error source at a time!

Covariance analysis also has the capability of providing information concerning other quantities in the same computer run. For example, covariance analysis could also show us how the standard deviation of the missile acceleration varies with time in the same computer run. However, we must first express the missile acceleration as a function of the states. From Fig. 5.4 we can see that the missile acceleration is related to the states according to

$$n_L = \frac{N' V_c}{T} \left[\frac{y}{V_c(t_F - t)} - D \right]$$

or more concisely, in matrix form we can say that

$$n_L = Ax$$

where x is the system state vector, and for this example A is given by

$$A = \left[\frac{N'}{T(t_F - t)} \quad 0 \quad 0 \quad \frac{-N' V_c}{T} \right]$$

Therefore the variance of the missile acceleration is given by

$$E\left[n_L n_L^T \right] = \sigma_{n_L}^2 = AXA^T$$

where X is the covariance matrix and the standard deviation of the acceleration is simply the square root of the preceding expression. From Listing 5.2 we can see that A and the variance of the acceleration are defined before the *WRITE* statement preceding statement label 200. Figure 5.6 displays the resultant missile acceleration profile, using the preceding expression in the

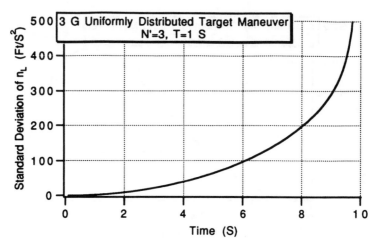

Fig. 5.6   Covariance analysis also provides acceleration profile information.

covariance analysis program, for the entire flight. We can see that the standard deviation of the missile acceleration is monotonically increasing for the 10-s flight. If we make the Gaussian assumption, we can infer that 68% of the time 15 g (i.e., 483 ft/s^2) or 5 times the acceleration of the target is required to avoid acceleration saturation. In more pessimistic terms we can also say that if the missile only has a 15-g capability there is a 32% probability that the missile will acceleration saturate for this example. This example demonstrates that although covariance analysis does not provide all of the information of the adjoint, it does provide extra useful information which can be used to access system performance. In addition, the covariance analysis technique can be used to provide an independent check of the accuracy of an adjoint simulation.

Acceleration Adjoint

We stated in Chapter 3 that the impulse response of the original system and adjoint system are related according to

$$h^*(t_F - t_I, t_F - t_o) = h(t_o, t_I)$$

where h denotes the impulse responses of the original system and h^* is the impulse response of the adjoint system. This important relationship means that putting an impulse into the original system at time t_I and observing the output at time t_o is identical to putting an impulse into the adjoint system at time $t_F - t_o$ and observing the output at time $t_F - t_I$, where t_F is the final time or flight time. In all of the adjoint applications discussed so far, the observation time was always the final time t_F since we were only interested in the miss distance. If all disturbances occur at time zero in the original system but the observation time is not the final time, the fundamental adjoint relationship simplifies to

$$h^*(t_F, t_F - t_o) = h(t_o, 0)$$

The preceding relationship means that applying an impulse to the original system at time zero and observing the output at time t_0 is equivalent to initiating the impulse at time $t_F - t_o$ in the adjoint system and observing the output at time t_F. *In other words, if we would like to develop other types of adjoints it is only necessary to change the impulse application time and the location of the impulse application. The adjoint block diagram remains unchanged!*

Figure 5.7 is the adjoint block diagram of the single-lag homing loop of Fig. 5.4. This adjoint diagram is identical to Fig. 4.17 (adjoint model in Chapter 4) except that it is noted that certain initial conditions are used if a miss distance adjoint is desired and other initial conditions are used for an acceleration adjoint. If a miss distance adjoint is being run, an initial condition of unity is applied at time zero on the $x3$ integrator. If an acceleration

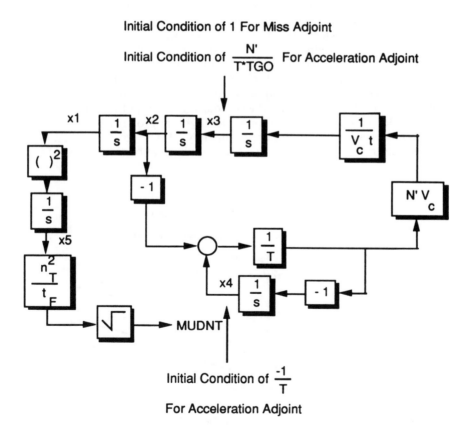

Fig. 5.7   Adjoint model for miss distance and acceleration.

adjoint is required, initial conditions are applied at time $t_F - t_o$ to the $x3$ and $x4$ integrators. In this case time $t_F - t_o$ corresponds to the time to go until intercept in which we desire to observe the acceleration in the original system. In other words, if we desire to observe acceleration in the original system at time 8 s for a 10-s flight, that is the same as observing the acceleration at 2 s to go (i.e., $10 - 8 = 2$). Therefore the impulse (or initial conditions on appropriate integrators) is applied at time 2 s in the adjoint system and the output is observed at 10 s in the adjoint system. Changing the observation time in the adjoint system corresponds to observing acceleration at 2 s to go for different flight times in the original system.

The source code listing for the adjoint program, which can be used for both miss distance and acceleration computaion, appears in Listing 5.3. In this program *TINT* represents the time to go in the original system in which we wish to observe the quantity of interest. If we want to compute miss distance, *MISS* should be set to *.TRUE.* and *TINT* set to zero. For an acceleration adjoint, *MISS* should be set to *.FALSE.* and *TINT* set to a number representing the time to go at which we want to observe the acceleration. The adjoint program of Listing 5.3 is set to run as an acceleration adjoint in which acceleration levels correspond to 0.5 s to go in the original system (*TINT* = 0.5).

The preceding acceleration adjoint program was run for values of observation time in the original system corresponding to 0.5, 1, and 2 s to go (*TINT* = 0.5, 1, 2) and the results for the three adjoint runs are displayed in Fig. 5.8. We can interpret the abscissa of the plot as either adjoint time or flight time. The curve representing acceleration at 0.5 s to go, *TINT* = 0.5 (labeled $t_{go} = 0.5$), indicates that the standard deviation of the missile acceleration is 388 ft/s² at 0.5 s to go for a 10-s flight, approximately 300 ft/s² at 0.5 s to go for a 6-s flight, and approximately 50 ft/s² for a 2-s flight. The missile acceleration values for a 10-s flight at observation times to go of 0.5,

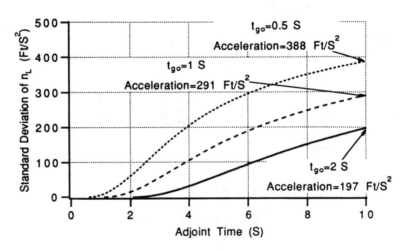

Fig. 5.8   Adjoint and covariance analysis acceleration results agree.

Listing 5.3   Acceleration and miss distance adjoint program

```
      INTEGER STEP
      LOGICAL MISS
      DATA XNT,XNP,TAU,TF/ 96.6,3,1,10/
      T = 0.
      S = 0.
      TINT = .5
      MISS = .FALSE.
      TP = T + .00001 + TINT
      X1 = 0
      X2 = 0
      X5 = 0.
      IF(MISS)THEN
          X3 = 1.
          X4 = 0.
      ELSE
          X3 = XNP/(TAU*TINT)
          X4 = -1./TAU
      ENDIF
      H = .01
      TF = 10.
10    IF(TP > (TF-.00001))GOTO 999
      S = S + H
      X1OLD = X1
      X2OLD = X2
      X3OLD = X3
      X4OLD = X4
      X5OLD = X5
      STEP = 1
      GOTO 200
66    STEP = 2
      X1 = X1 + H*X1D
      X2 = X2 + H*X2D
      X3 = X3 + H*X3D
      X4 = X4 + H*X4D
      X5 = X5 + H*X5D
      TP = TP + H
      GOTO 200
55    CONTINUE
      X1 = (X1OLD + X1)/2 + .5*H*X1D
      X2 = (X2OLD + X2)/2 + .5*H*X2D
      X3 = (X3OLD + X3)/2 + .5*H*X3D
      X4 = (X4OLD + X4)/2 + .5*H*X4D
      X5 = (X5OLD + X5)/2 + .5*H*X5D
      IF(S.LE..09999)GOTO 10
      S = 0.
      XMUDNT = XNT*SQRT(X5/TF)
      WRITE(9,*)TP,XMUDNT
      GOTO 10
200   CONTINUE
      X1D = X2
      X2D = X3
      Y1 = (X4-X2)/TAU
      TGO = TP + .00001
      X3D = XNP*Y1/TGO
      X4D = -Y1
      X5D = X1*X1
      IF(STEP-1)66,66,55
999   CONTINUE
      PAUSE
      END
```

1, and 2 s (388, 291, and 197 ft/s^2) respectively agree exactly with the single run covariance analysis results of Fig. 5.6.

Summary

In this chapter we have shown how the covariance analysis technique can be applied to a missile guidance system. Double-precision arithmetic and the fourth-order Runge-Kutta numerical integration technique were required in order to obtain performance projections of the desired accuracy. Although covariance analysis techniques do not yield error budget information as does the adjoint technique, exact performance projects can be obtained for all quantities of interest in a single run. It was also shown how the adjoint technique could be extended to yield acceleration as well as miss distance information.

References

[1] Gelb, A., *Applied Optimal Estimation,* MIT Press, Cambridge, MA, 1974.

[2] Bryson, A. E., and Ho, Y. C., *Applied Optimal Control,* Blaisdell, Waltham, MA, 1969.

[3] Press, W. H., Flannery, B. P., Teukolsky, S. A., and Vetterling, W. T., *Numerical Recipes: The Art of Scientific Computation,* Cambridge, University Press, London, 1986.

[4] Wolf, P. M., and Koelling, C. P., *Basic Engineering, Science and Business Programs for the Apple II and IIe,* Bradly Communications Co. Inc., Bowie, MD, 1984.

Chapter 6

Proportional Navigation and Miss Distance

Introduction

THE relationship between proportional navigation and miss distance will be investigated more extensively in this chapter. First we will demonstrate, via numerical examples, that it is important to have an accurate guidance system model in order to get performance projections that are meaningful and not overly optimistic. Normalized design curves will be presented that allow an analyst to rapidly predict system behavior given a minimum of information. Curves of this type are invaluable in preliminary system design. The influence of optimal target maneuvers on system performance will be evaluated to highlight potential guidance system weaknesses. Finally, the influence of saturation and parasitic effects will be demonstrated to help the designer place realistic bounds on achievable system performance.

System Order[1]

Thus far, the work presented has concerned itself with either a zero- or single-lag guidance system. We have seen that, if the flight time is *not* significantly larger than the guidance system time constant, then the difference between the performance of a zero- and single-lag guidance system can be significant. Both the single- and zero-lag guidance systems are convenient analytical models but do not quite match reality. It is important to determine if a higher-order guidance system representation would influence system performance. In order to separate time constant and system order effects, it is convenient to use a binomial representation of the guidance system:

$$\frac{n_L}{\lambda} = (N' V_c) \Big/ \left[\left(1 + \frac{sT}{n} \right)^n \right]$$

In the preceding representation, T is the effective guidance system time constant and n the system order. If $n = 1$, the binomial expansion reduces to the single-lag guidance system which we have already previously studied. This particular form of the binomial representation is useful, although not especially realistic, because an expansion of the guidance system denominator always yields

$$\left(1 + \frac{sT}{n} \right)^n = 1 + sT + \cdots$$

111

which means that T is always the approximate time constant of the guidance system, regardless of system order.

Figure 6.1 shows how the miss distance due to a 3-g target maneuver varies with flight time and system order for a binomial guidance system in which the effective navigation ratio is 4 and the effective guidance system time constant is 1 s. We can see that the performance projections resulting from a single-lag guidance system model are a serious underestimate of the influence of target maneuver on miss when the flight time is not an order of magnitude greater than the guidance system time constant. The importance of system order and its influence on system performance becomes less important as system order increases. The experiment conveys the importance of accurately modeling the guidance system (which is generally not a binomial) under consideration if accurate performance projections are required.

An experiment was also conducted to determine if, in the presence of guidance system dynamics, the linearized model of the homing loop still gives accurate performance projections. Fifth-order binomial guidance system models were included in both the linearized and nonlinear engagement simulations. Cases were run for both simulations in the case of a 3-g target maneuver disturbance for various flight times, and the resultant miss distances were monitored. Figure 6.2 shows that the linearized model of the homing loop gives very accurate performance projections. Thus, we can feel confident in using our linearized guidance system model for studies involving a binomial representation of the guidance system.

Normally a missile guidance system is represented by n different time constants for an n-state system. If the time constants are widely separated, then the slowest time constant will usually dictate system performance. If the time constants are closely spaced, one must evaluate the guidance system to get accurate performance projections.

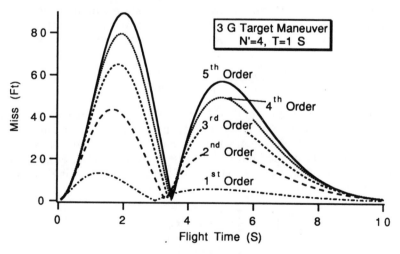

Fig. 6.1   System order has a profound influence on system performance.

Design Relationships

We have just seen that target maneuver can play a major role in determining missile system performance. Target maneuver can induce very large miss distances if the effective guidance time constant is too large or if the flight time is very short. In addition, we have seen in Chapter 2 that target maneuver induces large missile acceleration levels. This may lead to acceleration saturation, which will significantly further increase the induced miss distance. The purpose of this section is to quantify the influence of target maneuver on system performance in a form that will be of value to an analyst in preliminary system design.

In the previous section we established that the linearized model of the guidance system gave accurate performance projections in terms of miss distance induced by target maneuver. Performance projections were obtained by running both the linear and nonlinear engagement simulation for many times of flight and the resultant data were plotted. The same results could have been obtained by making one adjoint run as shown in Fig. 6.3.

In Chapter 3 a closed-form solution was developed for the miss distance induced by target maneuver in a single time constant representation of the guidance system. Although the miss distance formula will change for varying effective navigation ratios and canonic system form and order, the normalization for miss due to target maneuver will be the same. In this section we will use the method of adjoints to develop design curves that may be of use in preliminary system sizing. We will chose a guidance system form that has only one parameter: the guidance system time constant.

The model to be used for the development of normalized design curves is the fifth-order binomial proportional navigation system. This guidance sys-

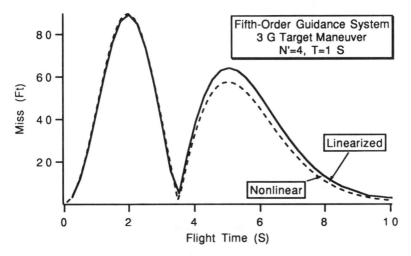

Fig. 6.2   Linearized guidance system model gives very accurate performance projections.

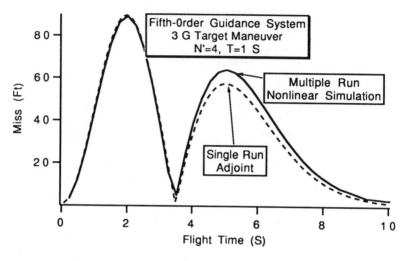

Fig. 6.3   One adjoint run gives the same result as many runs with nonlinear engagement simulation.

tem, which is depicted in Fig. 6.4, has guidance system transfer function

$$\frac{n_L}{\lambda} = (N' V_c s) \bigg/ \left[\left(1 + \frac{sT}{5}\right)^5 \right]$$

where T is the guidance system time constant. In this canonic model, one time constant represents the seeker, another represents the noise filter, and the three time constants represent the flight control system. Hopefully, the simplicity of this model will shed some light on fundamental issues and be of value for other guidance system forms.

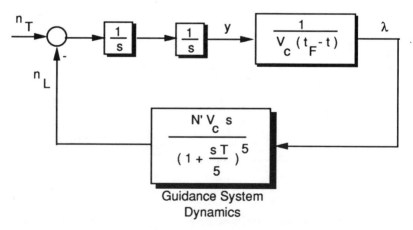

Fig. 6.4   Fifth-order binomial guidance system.

Figure 6.5 presents the adjoint model of the fifth-order binomial guidance system. The adjoint model consists of three outputs that are related to three input disturbances in the original system. The miss due to a step target maneuver is represented by MNT, the miss due to a ramp target maneuver is represented by $MNTD$, and the miss due to a parabolic maneuver is denoted $MNTDD$. In the figure each integrator output is denoted by variables $x1$ to $x10$. The impulse needed to start a miss distance adjoint is represented by a unity initial condition on integrator $x3$.

An adjoint simulation can be derived from the model of Fig. 6.5. Listing 6.1 presents a FORTRAN adjoint program of this fifth-order binomial guidance system. We can see from the listing that the nominal value of the target maneuver is 1 g, the value of target jerk, $XNTD$, is 1 g/s, and the value of target yank, $XNTDD$, is 1 g/s^2. As in our other simulations, the differential equations describing the adjoint system can be found after statement label 200. All integrator initial conditions are zero, except for integrator $x3$. We can see from the listing that this integrator has a unity initial condition in order to make a miss distance adjoint. We can also see from the listing that a small number is added to adjoint time so that we can avoid a division by zero. This is a practical way of applying L'Hopital's rule.

The adjoint program is set up to generate normalized results by choosing the guidance system time constant TAU to be unity and the step target maneuver disturbance XNT to be 1 g or 32.2 ft/s^2. The value of closing velocity is not important, since there is a cancellation of this term in the guidance loop. Normalized adjoint results can be generated by running the program once for a value of unity guidance system time constant. The normalization factors, derived in Chapter 3 for a single-lag guidance system, are also valid for the fifth-order binomial guidance system. Therefore, the adjoint program only has to be rerun for each effective navigation ratio,

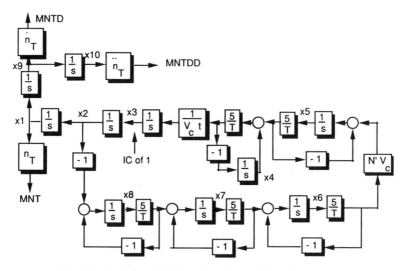

Fig. 6.5   Adjoint of fifth-order binomial guidance system.

Listing 6.1 Adjoint of fifth-order binomial guidance system

```
        INTEGER STEP
        DATA XNT,XNP,TAU,TF,VC/ 32.2,3,1,10.,4000./
        DATA XNTD,XNTDD/32.2,32.2/
        T = 0.
        S = 0.
        TP = T + .00001
        X1 = 0
        X2 = 0
        X3 = 1
        X4 = 0
        X5 = 0.
        X6 = 0.
        X7 = 0.
        X8 = 0.
        X9 = 0.
        X10 = 0.
        H = .02
10      IF(TP > (TF − .00001))GOTO 999
        S = S + H
        X1OLD = X1
        X2OLD = X2
        X3OLD = X3
        X4OLD = X4
        X5OLD = X5
        X6OLD = X6
        X7OLD = X7
        X8OLD = X8
        X9OLD = X9
        X10OLD = X10
        STEP = 1
        GOTO 200
66      STEP = 2
        X1 = X1 + H*X1D
        X2 = X2 + H*X2D
        X3 = X3 + H*X3D
        X4 = X4 + H*X4D
        X5 = X5 + H*X5D
        X6 = X6 + H*X6D
        X7 = X7 + H*X7D
        X8 = X8 + H*X8D
        X9 = X9 + H*X9D
        X10 = X10 + H*X10D
        TP = TP + H
        GOTO 200
55      CONTINUE
        X1 = (X1OLD + X1)/2 + .5*H*X1D
        X2 = (X2OLD + X2)/2 + .5*H*X2D
        X3 = (X3OLD + X3)/2 + .5*H*X3D
        X4 = (X4OLD + X4)/2 + .5*H*X4D
        X5 = (X5OLD + X5)/2 + .5*H*X5D
        X6 = (X6OLD + X6)/2 + .5*H*X6D
        X7 = (X7OLD + X7)/2 + .5*H*X7D
        X8 = (X8OLD + X8)/2 + .5*H*X8D
        X9 = (X9OLD + X9)/2 + .5*H*X9D
        X10 = (X10OLD + X10)/2 + .5*H*X10D
        IF(S < .09999)GOTO 10
        S = 0.
        XMNT = ABS(XNT*X1)
        XMNTD = ABS(XNTD*X9)
        XMNTDD = ABS(XNTDD*X10)
        WRITE(9,*)TP,XMNT,XMNTD,XMNTDD
        GOTO 10
200     CONTINUE
        X1D = X2
        X2D = X3
        Y1 = 5.*(5.*X5/TAU + X4)/TAU
        TGO = TP + .00001
        X3D = Y1/(VC*TGO)
        X4D = − Y1
        X5D = − 5.*X5/TAU + 5.*X6*XNP*VC/TAU
        X6D = − 5.*X6/TAU + 5.*X7/TAU
        X7D = − 5.*X7/TAU + 5.*X8/TAU
        X8D = − 5.*X8/TAU − X2
        X9D = X1
        X10D = X9
        IF(STEP − 1)66,66,55
999     CONTINUE
        PAUSE
        END
```

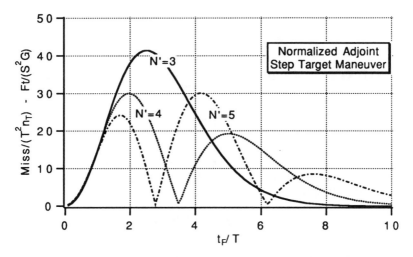

Fig. 6.6   Normalized miss due to step target maneuver.

XNP. For example, Fig. 6.6 presents the normalized system response to a step in target acceleration. The abscissa can be interpreted as either normalized time of flight for a step maneuver occurring at the beginning of flight or the normalized time to go at which the disturbance occurs. We can see from Fig. 6.6 that for long normalized flight times the miss approaches zero and for small normalized flight times the miss can be quite large. Increasing the effective navigation ratio tends to reduce the miss for small normalized flight times and increases the miss at the larger normalized flight times.

In order to illustrate the use of the normalized miss distance results of Fig. 6.6, let us consider a numerical example. If the guidance time constant is 0.5 s, and the time of flight is 2.5 s, then the normalized flight time

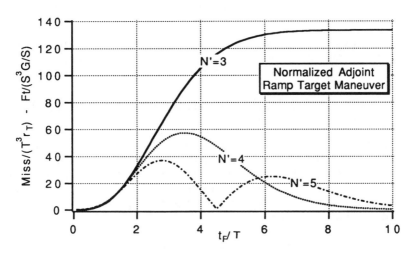

Fig. 6.7   Normalized miss due to ramp target maneuver.

is 5, or

$$t_F/T = 2.5/0.5 = 5$$

For an effective navigation ratio of 3 the normalized miss can be read from Fig. 6.6 as 12, or

$$\frac{\text{Miss}}{T^2 n_T} = 12$$

In order to compute the actual miss distance in this example, we must assume a target maneuver level, n_T. With a 4-g maneuver level the actual miss distance becomes

$$\text{Miss} = 12T^2 n_T = 12*0.5^2*4 = 12 \text{ ft}$$

Increasing the guidance system time constant can substantially influence the miss distance. For example, if we increase the guidance system time constant from 0.5 s to 1 s, the normalized flight time becomes

$$t_F/T = 2.5/1 = 2.5$$

Keeping the effective navigation ratio to 3 yields a new normalized miss of approximately 42, or

$$\frac{\text{Miss}}{T^2 n_T} = 42$$

which means that for a 4-g maneuver the actual miss is

$$\text{Miss} = 42T^2 n_T = 42*1^2*4 = 168 \text{ ft}$$

In other words, for this case doubling the guidance system time constant increased the miss distance by more than an order of magnitude!

By integrating the miss due to a step target maneuver in the adjoint program, we can also find the normalized miss due to a ramp maneuver. Figure 6.7 presents normalized miss distance results for a ramp maneuver disturbance. Again, the abscissa has the same interpretation as before. Here we can see that the effective navigation ratio must be greater than 3 for the miss to approach zero for long flight times. This means that, if the actual maneuver is a ramp, we need an effective navigation ratio of more than 3 to hit the target. In addition, we can see from Fig. 6.7 that the normalization on the ordinate is different from that in the case of a step target maneuver.

If we had a ramp maneuver that reached the 4-g level in 2.5 s, then its acceleration rate would be

$$r_T = n_T/t_F = 4/2.5 = 1.6 \text{ } g/s$$

With the same inputs as before (i.e., $T = 0.5$ s) we can read the normalized miss from Fig. 6.7 as

$$\frac{\text{Miss}}{T^3 r_T} = 120$$

Therefore, the actual miss distance is

$$\text{Miss} = 120 T^3 r_T = 120*0.5^3*1.6 = 24 \text{ ft}$$

We can see that, although the ramp maneuver only reaches the 4-g level by the end of the flight, its influence on miss distance, for this example, is much greater than that of the step maneuver. Increasing the effective navigation ratio to 4 reduces the normalized miss to

$$\frac{\text{Miss}}{T^3 r_T} = 40$$

which reduces the actual miss to

$$\text{Miss} = 40*0.5^3*1.6 = 8 \text{ ft}$$

This numerical example illustrates the need for larger effective navigation ratios in a proportional navigation guidance system for nonconstant target maneuvers.

Integrating the adjoint ramp maneuver output yields the miss due to a parabolic maneuver. Figure 6.8 presents the normalized miss distance induced by a parabolic target maneuver. Here we can see that an effective navigation ratio of 5 is required for the miss to go to zero for long flight times.

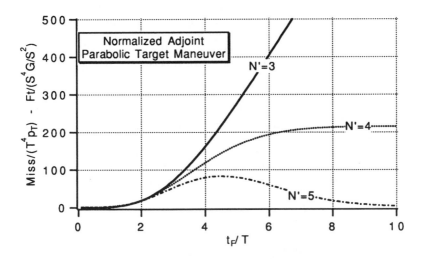

Fig. 6.8   Normalized miss due to parabolic target maneuver.

For consistency, let us consider a case in which all numerical values are related to the previous cases considered. If the parabolic maneuver reaches the 4-g level in 2.5 s, the acceleration jerk will be

$$p_T = n_T/t^2 = 4/2.5^2 = 0.64 \ g/s^2$$

For the same inputs as before, the miss for a navigation ratio of 3 becomes

$$\text{Miss}\,|_{N'\,=\,3} = 300T^4p_T = 300*0.5^4*0.64 = 12 \ \text{ft}$$

Increasing the navigation ratio reduces the miss, as we can see from

$$\text{Miss}\,|_{N'\,=\,4} = 150*0.5^4*0.64 = 6 \ \text{ft}$$

$$\text{Miss}\,|_{N'\,=\,5} = 75*0.5^4*0.64 = 3 \ \text{ft}$$

In summary, we can say that increasing the effective navigation ratio and decreasing the guidance system time constant work in the direction of reducing the miss due to target maneuver. We shall see later that increasing the navigation ratio also increases the miss due to noise and parasitic effects. Variable maneuver levels such as ramps and parabolas may cause more miss than constant maneuvers because the navigation ratio may not be set at a high enough level.

Optimal Target Evasive Maneuvers[2-6]

We have seen that the effective navigation ratio has a strong influence on missile guidance system performance against all types of target maneuvers. Let us consider the influence of step target maneuver on a fifth-order binomial guidance system in more detail. From a target's point of view an optimal maneuver is one that induces the most miss distance. Figure 6.9 shows that, when the effective navigation ratio is 3, the normalized miss distance curve has a maxima at a normalized flight time of 2.5. Since flight time and time to go are interchangeable for this system, we can interpret the abscissa of Fig. 6.9 as normalized time to go. Therefore, as shown in Fig. 6.9, the target can induce the most miss distance by first executing $+ n_T g$ (normalized time to go is large) and then rolling 180 deg at a normalized time to go of 2.5 so that the target will be executing $- n_T g$. As far as the missile is concerned, the target appears to be executing a maneuver of magnitude $2n_T$! The optimality of this maneuver is proven mathematically in Ref. 2 using a combination of optimal control theory and adjoint theory.

We can see from Fig. 6.9 that the induced miss distance caused by this optimal maneuver will be

$$\text{Miss}\,|_{opt,N'\,=\,3} = 41.4*(2n_T)T^2 = 82.8T^2n_T$$

For a maneuver level of 4 g and a guidance system time constant of 0.5 s, the largest miss distance the target maneuver can induce for an effective

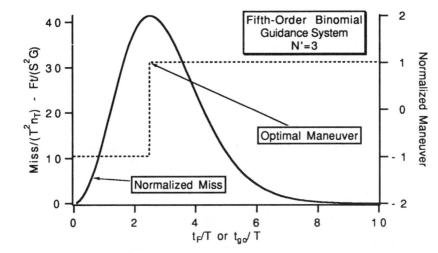

Fig. 6.9   Optimal maneuver policy for effective navigation ratio of 3.

navigation ratio of 3 is

$$\text{Miss}|_{\text{opt},N'\,=\,3} = 82.8*0.5^2*4 = 82.8 \text{ ft}$$

This miss distance is considerably larger than 12 ft, which was previously obtained with a step target maneuver occurring at a normalized time to go of 5 s.

If the effective navigation ratio is 4, the miss response has maxima indicated in Fig. 6.10. Therefore, in this case, the optimal maneuver policy is for the target to begin with a maneuver level of $-n_T g$ until $t_{\text{go}}/T = 5$, then rolling 180 deg in order to execute $+n_T g$ and then finally at $t_{\text{go}}/T = 2$, rolling another 180 deg in order to execute $-n_T g$. We can see from Fig. 6.10 that the induced miss in this case will be

$$\text{Miss}|_{\text{opt},N'\,=\,4} = (19.1 + 29.8)*(2n_T)T^2 = 97.8T^2 n_T$$

If the navigation ratio is 5, the miss response has three maxima, as shown in Fig. 6.11. The optimal maneuver strategy is superimposed on this figure, and the optimal induced miss turns out to be

$$\text{Miss}|_{\text{opt},N'\,=\,5} = (8.4 + 29.9 + 24)*(2n_T)T^2 = 124.6T^2 n_T$$

It is interesting to note that, as we increase the effective navigation ratio, the optimal miss due to a step target maneuver also increases because of the increased number of maxima in the miss distance sensitivity curve.

The concept of an optimal maneuver is useful in that it identifies the largest possible miss distance that the target can induce and possibly aid in the selection of the missile guidance system time constant. Of course, this optimal maneuver assumes unrealistically that the target has precise knowledge of the time to go until intercept and of the missile guidance system dynamics. It is readily apparent from the preceding miss distance curves that the missile guidance time constant must be minimized if the miss distance due to target maneuver is to be kept small. However, we shall see later that noise and parasitic effect place a practical lower limit on the minimum achievable guidance system time constant.

Practical Evasive Maneuvers

In the previous section we showed that optimal target evasive maneuvers could induce very large miss distances if a priori information concerning the missile guidance system was available. In this section we shall demonstrate that when a priori information is lacking, practical periodic target evasive maneuvers can also generate very large miss distances. Two such practical evasive periodic maneuver policies are the barrel roll and the Vertical-S.

The barrell roll can be described in one dimension as a sinusoid with radian frequency ω or period T and amplitude n_T as given by

$$\ddot{y}_T = n_T \sin \omega t = n_T \sin \frac{2\pi}{T} t$$

From the preceding relationship we can see that the barrel roll only yields maximum acceleration levels some of the time. With the Vertical-S maneuver, however, the aircraft is always at maximum acceleration and the sign of the acceleration is periodically reversed by rolling the aircraft through 180 deg. With a theoretically infinite roll rate, this maneuver policy can be approximated by a periodic square wave in one dimension. The barrel roll and Vertical-S maneuver policies do not require information about the missile guidance system. The amplitudes of both target maneuvers are cho-

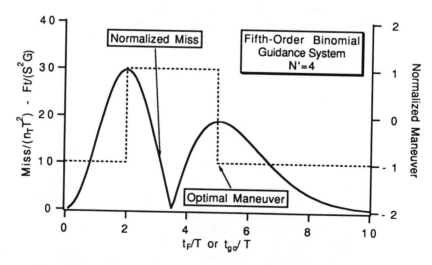

Fig. 6.10 Optimal maneuver policy for effective navigation ratio of 4.

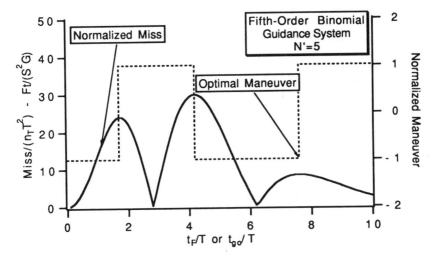

Fig. 6.11   Optimal maneuver policy for effective navigation ratio of 5.

sen to reflect the maximum acceleration capability of the aircraft, whereas the frequencies of both maneuvers are chosen to be physiologically possible for a human pilot and robust enough to cause any missile guidance system problems.

Both the barrel roll and Vertical-S maneuver policies are illustrated in Fig. 6.12 where, for illustrative purposes, it is assumed that the maneuver amplitude n_T is $4\,g$ and the maneuver frequency ω is 1 rad/s. Figure 6.12 confirms that the effective maneuver period T is 6.28 s.

For comparative purposes, the preceding maneuver policies were evaluated on the fifth-order proportional navigaiton binomial guidance system.

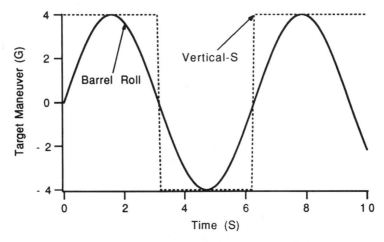

Fig. 6.12   More realistic evasive maneuver policies.

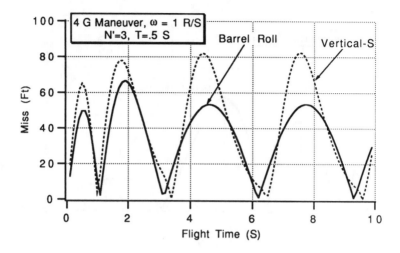

Fig. 6.13   Realistic maneuvers can induce very large miss distances.

The guidance system time constant was 0.5 s, the target maneuver amplitude was 4 g, and the effective navigation ratio considered was three so that comparisons could be made with the optimal evasive maneuver induced miss distances. With these numbers it was shown in the previous section that the optimal miss distance was 82.8 ft. Figure 6.13 shows how the miss distances vary with flight time for both the barrel roll and Vertical-S maneuver policies. It is apparent that the Vertical-S maneuver generates the largest miss distances because the target is always at maximum acceleration. We can also see from Fig. 6.13 that, on the average, the miss distances for both maneuver policies are quite high. For this example the Vertical-S maneuver yields miss distances which approach that of the optimal maneuver when the flight times are 0.5, 1.8, 4.4, or 7.5 s. Of course, if the pilot is not lucky and the flight time is 1.0, 3.4, 6.5, or 9.5 s, the miss distance will be quite small. In these cases the aircraft is hitting the missile rather than the missile hitting the target!

More details on the influence of practical evasive maneuver strategies on miss distance can be found in Ref. 5. In addition, Ref. 5 derives the shaping filter equivalent for many practical maneuvers, so that the method of adjoints can be used to assess system performance in a single computer run.

Saturation[2]

Thus far we have seen normalized miss distance curves for a fifth-order proportional navigation binomial guidance system. The results presented have implicitly assumed that the missile had adequate acceleration capability in order to guide and hit the target. If adequate acceleration capability is not available, the missile acceleration saturates, which results in additional miss distance. In endoatmospheric interceptors, angle-of attack constraints limit maximum achievable accelerations at high altitudes, whereas the missile structure limits achievable acceleration levels at the lower altitudes. The lateral engine thrust-to-weight ratio limits the acceleration level in exoatmospheric interceptors.

The basic homing loop can be modified and made nonlinear to account for acceleration saturation as shown in Fig. 6.14. In this figure the guidance system is also represented as a fifth-order binomial guidance system with guidance time constant T. Two of the time constants are devoted to the seeker and noise filter, and the other three time constants are devoted to the flight control system. The acceleration limit is on the acceleration command n_c, and the resultant acceleration command is denoted n_{CLIM}.

The first question that must be answered again is whether or not linearizing the geometry in the presence of the nonlinear acceleration saturation model is adequate for capturing important miss distance effects. For convenience, let us define the acceleration ratio as the ratio between the missile acceleration limit to the maneuver level of the target. Figure 6.14 will only be linear if the acceleration ratio is infinity.

Figure 6.15 represents the results of running both the nonlinear engagement simulation with saturation effects modeled and an engagement simulation of the model shown in Fig. 6.14. In the case considered, the guidance time constant was 1 s, the effective navigation ratio was 4, and the level of the target maneuver was 3 g. The acceleration ratio considered was 3. This means that since the target maneuver level is 3 g, the effective acceleration limit of the missile is 9 g. We can see from Fig. 6.15 that the miss distance results for both the linearized geometry model and nonlinear geometry models are virtually identical. Therefore, we can conclude that the linearized geometry model is adequate for investigating saturation effects. By comparing Fig. 6.15 with the nonsaturation case of Fig. 6.6, we can also conclude that even with a missile-to-target acceleration advantage of 3, considerable miss distance is contributed by saturation, especially for the shorter flight times.

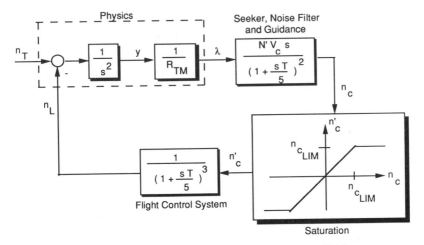

Fig. 6.14   Homing loop with acceleration saturation.

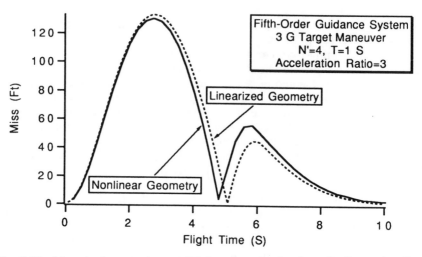

Fig. 6.15 Linearized geometry model is adequate for investigating saturation effects.

Using the missile to target acceleration capability (n_{CLIM}/n_T) and the normalization factors for miss due to a constant target maneuver, we can derive normalized miss distance curves by the method of brute force (running engagement model with nonlinear saturation effect for many different flight times and noting the miss distance). In other words, we can generate normalized design curves by simulating all of the possibilities. We can then infer performance by making extrapolations from the normalized design curves. Figure 6.16 presents the normalized miss distance due to a step target maneuver when the effective navigation ratio is 3. This figure shows that miss distance always increases with increasing flight time if the acceleration ratio is only 2. For acceleration ratios of 4 or more, the miss is virtually 0 for flight times approximately 10 times greater than the guidance time constant. An acceleration ratio of about 5 closely follows the infinite ratio or linear case.

Let us do a numerical example in order to clarify the use of these curves. If the guidance time constant is 0.5 s and the flight time is 2.5 s, we get a normalized flight time of

$$t_F/T = 2.5/0.5 = 5$$

Assuming a target maneuver level of 4 g, we can then calculate the miss distances for various acceleration limits as

$$\text{Miss}\,|_{\infty g} = 12.0T^2 n_T = 12.0*0.5^2*4 = 12.0 \text{ ft}$$

$$\text{Miss}\,|_{20g} = 18.9T^2 n_T = 18.9*0.5^2*4 = 18.9 \text{ ft}$$

$$\text{Miss}\,|_{16g} = 31.1T^2 n_T = 31.1*0.5^2*4 = 31.1 \text{ ft}$$

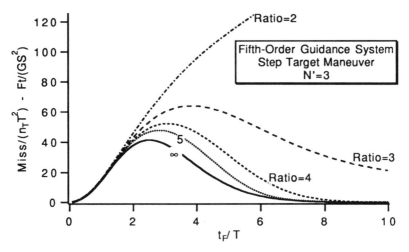

Fig. 6.16   Normalized miss due to target maneuver with saturation effects ($N' = 3$).

$$\text{Miss}|_{12g} = 58.1T^2n_T = 58.1*0.5^2*4 = 58.1 \text{ ft}$$

$$\text{Miss}|_{8g} = 112T^2n_T = 112*0.5^2*4 = 112 \text{ ft}$$

Therefore, we can see that the miss goes up by nearly a factor of 5 from the linear case if the missile-to-target acceleration advantage is only 3 and by a factor of 10 if the acceleration advantage is only 2.

Increasing the effective navigation ratio tends to reduce the acceleration requirements as shown in the normalized curves of Figs. 6.17 and 6.18.

Parasitic Effects[7-10]

Thus far, from all of the results presented it would appear that the guidance system designer has an easy job, since all the graphs indicate that smaller time constants and larger effective navigation ratios appear to improve system performance. Actually, parasitic or unwanted feedback paths within the homing loop will work in the direction of larger time constants and smaller effective navigation ratios to get acceptable performance. One of the most serious unwanted feedback paths is created in tactical radar homing missile applications by the missile radome. The radome causes a refraction or bending of the incoming radar wave, which in turn gives a false indication of the target location. A parameter associated with missile maneuverability, which has a significant interaction with radome effects, is the turning rate time constant T_α. If we consider the basic geometry of Fig. 6.19, the turning rate time constant can be defined as the amount of time it takes to turn the missile flight-path angle γ through an equivalent angle of attack α, or

$$T_\alpha = \frac{\alpha}{\dot{\gamma}}$$

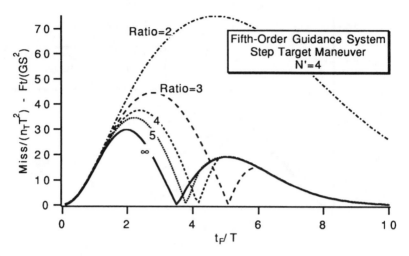

Fig. 6.17   Normalized miss due to target maneuver with saturation effects ($N' = 4$).

where the angle of attack and the flight-path angle are defined in Fig. 6.19. Generally the turning rate time constant increases with increasing missile altitude and decreasing missile velocity.

In order to see how the turning rate time constant enters into the homing loop, we must see how it is related to other important quantities. From Fig. 6.19 we can see that the missile pitch angle θ can be expressed as

$$\theta = \gamma + \alpha$$

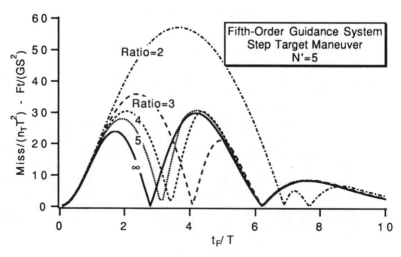

Fig. 6.18   Normalized miss due to target maneuver with saturation effects ($N' = 5$).

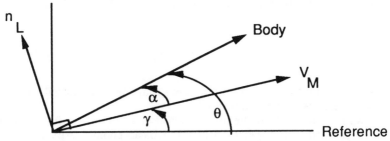

Fig. 6.19   Geometry for turning rate time constant.

Taking derivatives of both sides of the equation yields

$$\dot{\theta} = \dot{\gamma} + \dot{\alpha} = \dot{\gamma} + \frac{s\alpha\dot{\gamma}}{\dot{\gamma}}$$

Since the missile acceleration is perpendicular to the missile velocity, we can say that

$$n_L = V_M\dot{\gamma}$$

Therefore, we can express the missile pitch rate in terms of the missile acceleration as

$$\dot{\theta} = \frac{n_L}{V_M} + sT_\alpha \frac{n_L}{V_M}$$

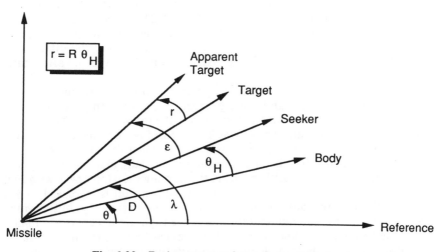

Fig. 6.20   Basic geometry for radome analysis.

Dividing both sides by the missile acceleration yields the missile pitch rate transfer function,

$$\frac{\dot{\theta}}{n_L} = \frac{1}{V_M}(1 + T_\alpha s)$$

This aerodynamic transfer function shows that there is a missile body rate whenever the missile is accelerating.

Now we need to see how the missile aerodynamic transfer function interacts with the radome slope. Consider the basic geometry of Fig. 6.20 in which the seeker is not pointed at the actual target because of seeker dynamics and radome effects.

The radome refraction angle r varies with the missile gimbal angle θ_H. For preliminary analysis it is usually assumed that the refraction angle is linearly proportional to the gimbal angle, or

$$r = R\theta_H$$

where R is constant known as the radome slope (see Appendix A for alternative definition). The radome slope is a function of the radome material, radome diameter, and fineness ratio, and the wavelength of the incoming signal. From Fig. 6.20 we can see that it is possible to express the missile boresight error ϵ as

$$\epsilon = \lambda - \theta - \theta_H + r = \lambda - \theta - \theta_H + R\theta_H$$

A block diagram of the homing loop with the radome unwanted feedback path is indicated in Fig. 6.21. We can see that without radome effects ($R = 0$) we would have a fifth-order binomial guidance system transfer function. The missile aerodynamic transfer function[11] provides the unwanted feedback path in the guidance system.

Listing 6.2 presents an engagement simulation with the fifth-order binomial model, including radome effects, of Fig. 6.21. The simulation is set to run multiple cases with the flight time as a parameter so that miss distance sensitivity curves can be generated by brute force. Again, the differential equations representing the guidance system of Fig. 6.21 appears after statement label 200.

In order to see how the turning rate time constant influences system performance, a case was run for a 1-g target maneuver disturbance in which the guidance system time constant was 0.5 s, the radome slope was -0.01, and the effective navigation ratio was 3. The turning rate time constant was varied from 0 to 10 s. Figure 6.22 shows that when the turning rate time constant is zero the miss distance response is virtually identical to the case in which there are no parasitic paths in the homing loop (compare with Fig. 6.6, for example). When the turning rate time constant is increased to 5 s, the miss distance response begins to become more oscillatory, but the miss distances are still small and tend to zero as the flight time increases. Finally, when the turning rate time constant is increased to 10 s, the miss distance response becomes unstable. Thus, we can see that we have to be concerned about radome effects from both a miss distance and stability point of view.

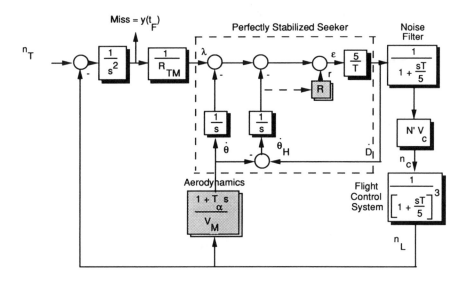

Fig. 6.21   Fifth-order binomial model of guidance system with radome effects.

As was mentioned previously, the magnitude of the effective radome slope is determined by the physical characteristics of the radome and the wavelength of the incoming signal. For a given radome, the guidance designer has only two parameters (i.e., guidance system time constant and effective navigation ratio) under control to get acceptable performance and meet stability requirements. Figure 6.23 shows how miss distance due to a 1-*g* target maneuver varies with flight time for two different values of effective navigation ratio in the presence of a negative radome slope ($R = -0.01$). We can see that the higher effective navigation ratio has a destabilizing effect. This is not unreasonable since we are essentially increasing the guidance system gain. Thus, the guidance system designer desires to keep the effective navigation ratio as small as possible to meet the stability requirements and yet large enough so that homing will be effective.

Figure 6.24 shows that, in the presence of a large effective navigation ratio and negative radome slope, increasing the guidance system time constant from 0.5 s to 0.75 s has a stabilizing effect.

In tactical missile design the guidance system time constant is generally made larger at the higher altitudes because the turning rate time constant is largest at the higher altitudes. Of course, the penalty for such a decision is that miss distances tend to increase with increasing guidance system time constant. Therefore, the guidance system designer attempts to make the guidance system time constant as small as possible subject to meeting guidance system stability requirements.

Thrust Vector Control

We saw in the previous section that, if the turning rate time constant of a tactical aerodynamic missile was large, radome effects caused stability

Listing 6.2 Engagement simulation with radome effects

```
          VC = 4000.
          XNT = 32.2
          YIC = 0.
          VM = 3000.
          HEDEG = 0.
          TAU = 1.
          XNP = 3.
          TA = 0.
          R = -.01
          TF = 10.
          DO 20 TF = .1,10.,.1
          Y = YIC
          YD = -VM*HEDEG/57.3
          YDIC = YD
          ELAMDH = 0.
          X4 = 0.
          X5 = 0.
          TH = 0.
          THH = 0.
          T = 0.
          H = .01
          S = 0.
10        IF(T>(TF - .0001))GOTO 999
          YOLD = Y
          YDOLD = YD
          XNLOLD = XNL
          ELAMDHOLD = ELAMDH
          X4OLD = X4
          X5OLD = X5
          THOLD = TH
          THHOLD = THH
          STEP = 1
          GOTO 200
66        STEP = 2
          Y = Y + H*YD
          YD = YD + H*YDD
          XNL = XNL + H*XNLD
          ELAMDH = ELAMDH + H*ELAMDHD
          X4 = X4 + H*X4D
          X5 = X5 + H*X5D
          TH = TH + H*THD
          THH = THH + H*THHD
          T = T + H
          GOTO 200
55        CONTINUE
          Y = .5*(YOLD + Y + H*YD)
          YD = .5*(YDOLD + YD + H*YDD)
          XNL = .5*(XNLOLD + XNL + H*XNLD)
          ELAMDH = .5*(ELAMDHOLD + ELAMDH + H*ELAMDHD)
          X4 = .5*(X4OLD + X4 + H*X4D)
          X5 = .5*(X5OLD + X5 + H*X5D)
          TH = .5*(THOLD + TH + H*THD)
          THH = .5*(THHOLD + THH + H*THHD)
          S = S + H
          GOTO 10
200       CONTINUE
          TGO = TF - T + .00001
          XLAM = Y/(VC*TGO)
          EPS = XLAM - TH - THH + R*THH
          DD = 5.*EPS/TAU
          ELAMDHD = 5.*(DD - ELAMDH)/TAU
          XNC = XNP*VC*ELAMDH
          X4D = 5.*(XNC - X4)/TAU
          X5D = 5.*(X4 - X5)/TAU
          XNLD = 5.*(X5 - XNL)/TAU
          THD = XNL/VM + TA*XNLD/VM
          THHD = DD - THD
          YDD = XNT - XNL
          IF(STEP - 1)66,66,55
999       CONTINUE
          Y = ABS(Y)
          WRITE(9,*)TF,Y
20        CONTINUE
          PAUSE
          END
```

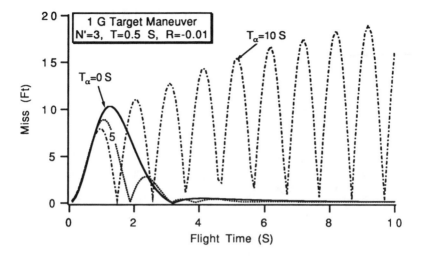

Fig. 6.22   Miss degrades with increasing turning rate time constant.

problems and miss distance deterioration. This problem is not confined to only tactical aerodynamic missiles. Consider a missile that operates outside the atmosphere and uses thrust vector control to maneuver. Figure 6.25 presents a diagram of a thrust vector controlled missile with all important angles indicated. The missile acceleration n_L needed to maneuver in accordance with guidance commands is obtained from the component of the thrust T perpendicular to the missile body.

For simplicity we are neglecting the fact that, if the thrust does not go through the center of gravity, the missile will tumble. The rate of change of the missile flight-path angle γ is related to the missile acceleration and velocity according to

$$\dot{\gamma} = \frac{n_L}{V_M}$$

where n_L is the missile acceleration and V_M the missile velocity. From Fig. 6.25 we can see that the flight-path rate can also be expressed as

$$\dot{\gamma} = \frac{n_L}{V_M} = \frac{Tg \sin\alpha}{WV_M}$$

where T is thrust (in lb), g is the gravitational acceleration (in ft/s^2), α is the angle of attack, and W is the missile weight. For small angles of attack we can approximate the flight-path rate to be

$$\dot{\gamma} = \frac{Tg\,\alpha}{WV_M}$$

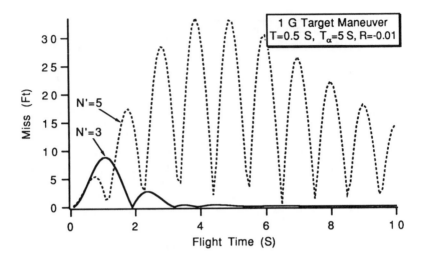

Fig. 6.23 **Increasing effective navigation ratio has destabilizing effect in presence of negative radome slope.**

Recalling that the turning rate time constant is the ratio of the angle of attack to the flight-path rate, we obtain

$$T_\alpha = \frac{\alpha}{\dot{\gamma}} = \frac{WV_M}{Tg}$$

This means that the effective turning rate time constant for a thrust vector controlled missile is proportional to the missile weight and velocity and inversely proportional to the thrust.

In order to illustrate the importance of turning rate time constant to a thrust vector controlled missile, let us work a numerical example. Consider a missile traveling at 20,000 ft/s and requiring a 5-deg angle of attack in order to generate 5 g of acceleration. In order to generate 5 g of acceleration at 5-deg angle of attack, the missile must have a thrust-to-weight ratio given by

$$\frac{T}{W} = \frac{n_L/g}{\alpha} = \frac{5}{5/57.3} = 57.3$$

This means that the effective turning rate time constant is

$$T_\alpha = \frac{V_M}{(T/W)g} = \frac{20,000}{57.3*32.2} = 10.8 \text{ s}$$

The turning rate time constant in this example is quite large compared to values indicated in the previous section. However, since the thrust vector controlled missile operates outside the atmosphere, the shape of the missile

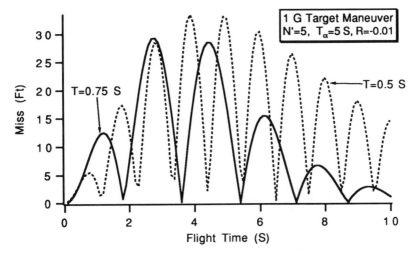

Fig. 6.24 **Increasing guidance system time constant has stabilizing effect in presence of negative radome slope.**

nose can be made near-hemispherical. This means that the effective randome slope will be close to zero. For a thrust vector controlled missile the guidance system designer must pay close attention to the product of the radome slope and turning rate time constant to ensure adequate stability margins in the resultant design. If the design yields unacceptable stability margins, the guidance system time constant must be increased to yield a workable design.

Summary

In this chapter we have shown how system order, optimal target maneuvers, saturation, and parasitic effects all influence miss distance. Miss dis-

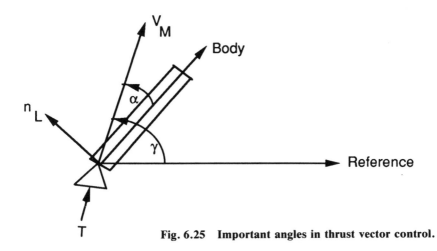

Fig. 6.25 **Important angles in thrust vector control.**

tance design curves were presented to aid the guidance system designer in predicting preliminary system performance. These curves could also be used to ensure that the interceptor had adequate acceleration capability. Examples were presented showing the conflicting tradeoffs the guidance system designer must confront in choosing acceptable guidance system parameters.

References

[1]Nesline, F. W., and Zarchan, P., "Miss Distance Dynamics in Homing Missiles," *Proceedings of AIAA Guidance and Control Conference,* AIAA, New York, Aug. 1984.

[2]Shinar, J., and Steinberg, D., "Analysis of Optimal Evasive Maneuvers Based on a Linearized Two-Dimensional Model," *Journal of Aircraft,* Vol. 14, Aug. 1977, pp. 795–802.

[3]Bennett, R. R., and Mathews, W. E., "Analytical Determination of Miss Distance for Linear Homing Navigation Systems," Hughes Aircraft Co., Culver City, CA, TM-260, March 1952.

[4]Travers, P., *Interceptor Dynamics,* unpublished lecture notes, Raytheon Co., circa 1971.

[5]Zarchan, P., "Representation of Realistic Evasive Maneuvers by the Use of Shaping Filters," *Journal of Guidance and Control,* Vol. 2, July–Aug. 1979, pp. 290–295.

[6]Howe, R. M., "Guidance," *System Engineering Handbook*, edited by R. E. Machol, W. P. Tanner Jr., and S. N. Alexander, McGraw-Hill, New York, 1965, Chap. 19.

[7]Nesline, F. W., and Zarchan, P., "Radome Induced Miss Distance in Aerodynamically Controlled Homing Missiles," *Proceedings of AIAA Guidance and Control Conference,* AIAA, New York, Aug. 1984.

[8]Youngren, F. R., "Minimizing Boresight Errors in Aerodynamic Radomes," *Electronic Design,* Dec. 20, 1961, pp. 152–157.

[9]Peterson, E. L., *Statistical Analysis and Optimization of Systems,* Wiley, New York, 1961.

[10]Eichblatt, E. (ed), *Test and Evaluation of the Tactical Missile,* Vol. 119, Progress in Astronautics and Aeronautics, AIAA, Washington, DC, 1989, p. 415.

[11]Hemsch, M. J., and Nielsen, J. N. (eds), *Tactical Missile Aerodynamics,* Vol. 104, Progress in Astronautics and Aeronautics, AIAA, New York, 1986, p. 858.

Chapter 7

Digital Fading Memory Noise Filters in the Homing Loop

Introduction

THUS far, we have assumed in our analysis that the geometric line-of-sight rate was available for guidance purposes. Actually, the seeker measurement of the line-of-sight angle is corrupted by noise. Therefore, in order to derive the line-of-sight rate estimate required by proportional navigation guidance, it is necessary to use a digital noise filter in an onboard guidance system. Although we shall later study optimal digital noise filters, we shall first consider simple constant gain filters, known as fading memory filters, to derive the line-of-sight rate estimate. We will investigate, by example, some of the properties of digital fading memory filters and their influence on system performance. Fading memory filters will serve as the foundation for more advanced digital filters, known as Kalman filters.

Fading Memory Filters[1]

A simple digital noise filter is known as a fading memory filter. This filter is recursive and weights new measurements more heavily than older measurements. First-, second-, and third-order fading memory filters and their gains are tabulated in recursive form in Table 7.1. We can see from the table that the filter estimate is essentially the old estimate plus a gain times a residual (difference between current measurement and previous estimate). Table 7.1 also shows that the fading memory filter gains are constant and are a function of only one parameter, β. This parameter is associated with the memory length of the filter and is a constant between zero and unity. Increasing β tends to decrease the bandwidth of the filter and enables the filter to "remember" more about previous measurements.

We can see from Table 7.1 that the fading memory filter assumes a polynomial model for the actual process. If the polynomial process of the filter is an underestimate of the polynomial degree of the actual process, then there will be a filter truncation error. The lowest order filter does the best job of removing the noise from the signal. However, it also has the potential for having the most truncation error. The filter designer must select the appropriate filter order to trade off filter variance reduction vs truncation error buildup. Fading memory filters are quite popular in radar tracking applications but, as we shall see, can also be made to work in tactical missile homing applications.

137

Table 7.1　Different order digital fading memory filters

Filter	Gains
$\hat{x}_n = \hat{x}_{n-1} + G[x_n^* - \hat{x}_{n-1}]$	$G = 1 - \beta$
$\hat{x}_n = \hat{x}_{n-1} + \hat{\dot{x}}_{n-1}T_s + G[x_n^* - (\hat{x}_{n-1} + \hat{\dot{x}}_{n-1}T_s)]$	$G = 1 - \beta^2$
$\hat{\dot{x}}_n = \hat{\dot{x}}_{n-1} + \dfrac{H}{T_s}[x_n^* - (\hat{x}_{n-1} + \hat{\dot{x}}_{n-1}T_s)]$	$H = (1 - \beta)^2$
$\hat{x}_n = \hat{x}_{n-1} + \hat{\dot{x}}_{n-1}T_s + 0.5\hat{\ddot{x}}_{n-1}T_s^2$ $+ G[x_n^* - (\hat{x}_{n-1} + \hat{\dot{x}}_{n-1}T_s + 0.5\hat{\ddot{x}}_{n-1}T_s^2)]$	$G = 1 - \beta^3$
$\hat{\dot{x}}_n = \hat{\dot{x}}_{n-1} + \hat{\ddot{x}}_{n-1}T_s + \dfrac{H}{T_s}[x_n^* - (\hat{x}_{n-1} + \hat{\dot{x}}_{n-1}T_s$ $+ 0.5\hat{\ddot{x}}_{n-1}T_s^2)]$	$H = 1.5(1 - \beta)^2(1 + \beta)$
$\hat{\ddot{x}}_n = \hat{\ddot{x}}_{n-1} + \dfrac{2K}{T_s^2}[x_n^* - (\hat{x}_{n-1} + \hat{\dot{x}}_{n-1}T_s + 0.5\hat{\ddot{x}}_{n-1}T_s^2)]$	$K = 0.5(1 - \beta)^3$

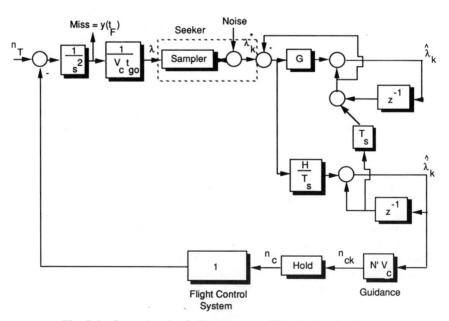

Fig. 7.1　Second-order fading memory filter in homing loop.

Fading Memory Filter in Homing Loop

Figure 7.1 shows an example of how a second-order fading memory filter can be included in the homing loop. In this loop the actual line-of-sight angle λ is sampled with noise added every T_s seconds, thus providing an idealized seeker model. Estimates of the line-of-sight angle and rate are made with a digital two-state fading memory filter's measurement of the noisy line-of-sight angle λ_k^*. The notation z^{-1} is Z transform notation for a pure delay of T_s seconds. A guidance command is generated, using the proportional navigation guidance law from the estimated line-of-sight rate. The resultant command is passed through a "hold" network that converts the digital signal to a continuous signal for the flight control system. The diagram shows a unity gain for an idealized representation of the flight control system.

Listing 7.1 is a FORTRAN engagement simulation of the homing loop shown in Fig. 7.1. Zero-mean Gaussian noise, independent from sample to sample, with standard deviation, SIGNOISE, is added to the measured line-of-sight angle every T_s seconds. We can see from the listing that the program consists of two separate parts. The first part, which represents the real world, consists of differential equations and the second-order Runge-Kutta numerical integration technique, and the second part, which represents an onboard guidance system, has the difference equations for the second-order digital fading memory filter. We solve the differential equations every H seconds, and the difference equations are solved every T_s seconds. It is important to note that the ratio T_s/H must be a large integer so that effects in between sampling instants be treated properly and accurately. Note that the Gaussian noise generator consists of the sum of six uniform noise generators as was discussed in Chapter 4.

The engagement simulation was exercised and a nominal case was run in which β of the fading memory filter was set to 0.8. Figure 7.2 compares the

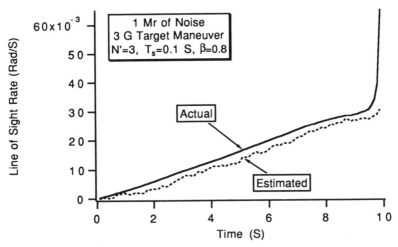

Fig. 7.2   Filter is sluggish and lags signal when $\beta = 0.8$.

Listing 7.1   Engagement simulation with second-order fading memory filter

```
        VC = 4000.
        XNT = 96.6
        YIC = 0.
        VM = 3000.
        HEDEG = 0.
        BETA = .3
        XNP = 3.
        SIGNOISE = .001
        TF = 10.
        TS = .1
        NOISE = 1
        Y = YIC
        YD = − VM*HEDEG/57.3
        YDIC = YD
        T = 0.
        H = .01
        S = 0.
        GFILTER = 1. − BETA**2
        HFILTER = (1. − BETA)**2
        XLAMH = 0.
        XLAMDH = 0.
        XNC = 0.
10      IF(T > (TF − .0001))GOTO 999
        YOLD = Y
        YDOLD = YD
        STEP = 1
        GOTO 200
66      STEP = 2
        Y = Y + H*YD
        YD = YD + H*YDD
        T = T + H
        GOTO 200
55      CONTINUE
        Y = .5*(YOLD + Y + H*YD)
        YD = .5*(YDOLD + YD + H*YDD)
        S = S + H
C       COLLECT DATA PERIODICALLY
        IF(S < (TS − .0001))GOTO 10
        S = 0.
        IF(NOISE = 1)THEN
            CALL GAUSS(XLAMNOISE,SIGNOISE)
        ELSE
            XLAMNOISE = 0.
        ENDIF
        RES = XLAM − (XLAMH + TS*XLAMDH) + XLAMNOISE
        XLAMH = GFILTER*RES + XLAMH + TS*XLAMDH
        XLAMDH = HFILTER*RES/TS + XLAMDH
        XNC = XNP*VC*XLAMDH
        Y = ABS(Y)
        WRITE(9,*)T,Y,XNC,XLAMD,XLAMDH
        GOTO 10
200     CONTINUE
        TGO = TF − T + .00001
        RTM = VC*TGO
        XLAM = Y/(VC*TGO)
        XLAMD = (RTM*YD + Y*VC)/(RTM**2)
        YDD = XNT − XNC
        IF(STEP − 1)66,66,55
999     CONTINUE
        Y = ABS(Y)
        WRITE(9,*)T,Y,XNC,XLAMD,XLAMDH
        PAUSE
        END
        SUBROUTINE GAUSS(X,SIG)
        INTEGER RANDOM,SUM
        INTEGER*4 TOOLBX
        PARAMETER (RANDOM = Z'86140000')
        SUM = 0
        DO 14
        J = 1,6
        IRAN = TOOLBX(RANDOM)
        SUM = SUM + IRAN
14      CONTINUE
        X = SUM/65536.
        X = 1.414*X*SIG
        RETURN
        END
```

actual line-of-sight rate to the filter estimate of the derivative of the measurement. We can see that the filter estimate of the line-of-sight rate is smooth but lags the actual line-of-sight rate, indicating that the filter is sluggish.

Figure 7.3 indicates that we can effectively increase the bandwidth of the fading memory filter by decreasing β. Here we can see that the line-of-sight rate estimate no longer lags the actual signal when β is reduced from 0.8 to 0.3. However, we can see from the figure that the noisiness of the line-of-sight rate estimate is the price paid for reducing β. In other words, decreasing β increases the fading memory filter's noise transmission.

The results presented thus far are for a single flight with a particular noise stream. Answers will change for another flight with a different noise stream. In order to get accurate performance projection in terms of miss distance, we must run the program in the Monte Carlo mode. That is, repeated simulation trials must be conducted for each flight time of interest. The resultant miss distance data must be postprocessed, as was done in Chapter 4 when dealing with the random target maneuver, to calculate the mean and standard deviation of the resultant miss distances. Listing 7.2 presents a modification to the engagement simulation of Listing 7.1. Here two loops are added to the program. One loop executes 50 simulation trials (RUN = 50) for each flight time of interest, and the other loop selects different flight times (*TF* ranges from 0.5 to 10 s in increments of 0.5 s). In other words, the simulation of Listing 7.2 runs Monte Carlo sets for engagements in which the flight time is a parameter. Postprocessing of the resultant data is conducted after statement label 999 in accordance with the formulas and routines developed in Chapter 4.

A nominal case was considered in which there was a constant 3-*g* target maneuver and 1 milliradian (mr) of measurement noise. A filter fading memory factor of 0.8 and a sampling time of 0.1 s were selected for the

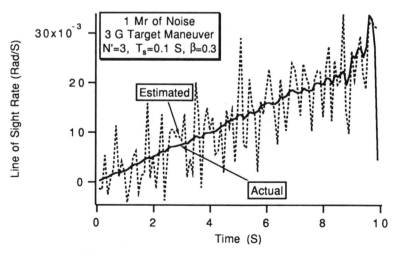

Fig. 7.3   Decreasing β increases noise transmission of fading memory filter.

Listing 7.2   Monte Carlo version of fading memory filter in homing loop

```
          DIMENSION Z(1000)
          INTEGER RUN
          VC = 4000.
          XNT = 96.6
          YIC = 0.
          VM = 3000.
          HEDEG = 0.
          BETA = .8
          XNP = 3.
          SIGNOISE = .001
          TS = .1
          NOISE = 1
          RUN = 50
          IF(NOISE = 0)THEN
              RUN = 1
          ELSE
              WRITE(9,*)
              WRITE(9,*)'NUMBER OF RUNS IN EACH MONTE CARLO SET'
              WRITE(9,*)'RUNS = ',RUN
              WRITE(9,*)
              READ(9,*)RUN
          ENDIF
          DO 60 TF = .5,10.,.5
          Z1 = 0.
          DO 20 I = 1,RUN
          Y = YIC
          YD = - VM*HEDEG/57.3
          YDIC = YD
          T = 0.
          H = .01
          S = 0.
          GFILTER = 1. - BETA**2
          HFILTER = (1. - BETA)**2
          XLAMH = 0.
          XLAMDH = 0.
          XNC = 0.
10        IF(T > (TF - .0001))GOTO 999
          YOLD = Y
          YDOLD = YD
          STEP = 1
          GOTO 200
66        STEP = 2
          Y = Y + H*YD
          YD = YD + H*YDD
          T = T + H
          GOTO 200
55        CONTINUE
          Y = .5*(YOLD + Y + H*YD)
          YD = .5*(YDOLD + YD + H*YDD)
          S = S + H
C         COLLECT DATA PERIODICALLY
          IF(S < (TS - .0001))GOTO 10
          S = 0.
          IF(NOISE = 1)THEN
              CALL GAUSS(XLAMNOISE,SIGNOISE)
          ELSE
              XLAMNOISE = 0.
          ENDIF
          RES = XLAM - (XLAMH + TS*XLAMDH) + XLAMNOISE
          XLAMH = GFILTER*RES + XLAMH + TS*XLAMDH
          XLAMDH = HFILTER*RES/TS + XLAMDH
          XNC = XNP*VC*XLAMDH
          GOTO 10
200       CONTINUE
          TGO = TF - T + .00001
          RTM = VC*TGO
          XLAM = Y/(VC*TGO)
          XLAMD = (RTM*YD + Y*VC)/(RTM**2)
          YDD = XNT - XNC
          IF(STEP - 1)66,66,55
```

(Listing 7.2 continued on next page.)

Listing 7.2 (cont.) Monte Carlo version of fading memory filter in homing loop

```
999     CONTINUE
        Z(I) = Y
        Z1 = Z(I) + Z1
        XMEAN = Z1/I
20      CONTINUE
        SIGMA = 0.
        Z1 = 0.
        DO 50 I = 1,RUN
        Z1 = (Z(I) − XMEAN)**2 + Z1
        IF(I = 1)THEN
            SIGMA = 0.
        ELSE
            SIGMA = SQRT(Z1/(I − 1))
        ENDIF
50      CONTINUE
        WRITE(9,*)TF,SIGMA,XMEAN
60      CONTINUE
        PAUSE
        END
        SUBROUTINE GAUSS(X,SIG)
        INTEGER RANDOM,SUM
        INTEGER*4 TOOLBX
        PARAMETER (RANDOM = Z'86140000')
        SUM = 0
        DO 14
        J = 1,6
        IRAN = TOOLBX(RANDOM)
        SUM = SUM + IRAN
14      CONTINUE
        X = SUM/65536.
        X = 1.414*X*SIG
        RETURN
        END
```

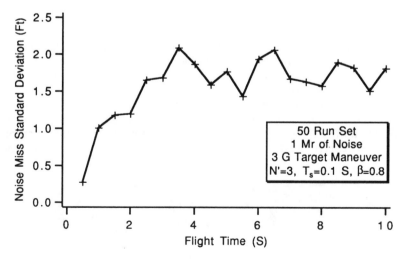

Fig. 7.4 Standard deviation of miss for various flight times.

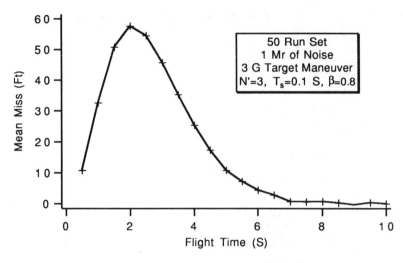

Fig. 7.5   Mean of miss for various flight times.

nominal case. A 50-run Monte Carlo set was run for 20 different values of flight time with the program of Listing 7.2 for a total of 1000 runs! The standard deviation and mean miss were computed for each of the 50-run Monte Carlo sets, and the results are displayed in Figs. 7.4 and 7.5. In this experiment there are only two disturbances. The target maneuver is deterministic (always 3 g), and the noise is a zero-mean random process. Therefore, we can assume that the standard deviation of the miss must be due to the noise, and the mean of the miss must be due to the target maneuver. Figures 7.4 and 7.5 show that for the value of β selected the noise-induced miss is small compared to the target-maneuver-induced miss for most flight times. This is not surprising because we know that the fading memory filter with $\beta = 0.8$ is sluggish.

In order to generate the data of Figs. 7.4 and 7.5, 1000 runs had to be made! One thousand run sets will have to be made each time a parameter of interest is changed. In addition, we were able to separate the contributions to the miss from the measurement noise and the target maneuver in the 1000 run set *only because* the noise was random and the target maneuver was deterministic. In a system with many deterministic and stochastic inputs, one would have to run 1000-run sets for one disturbance at a time in order to generate a miss distance error budget. Fortunately the adjoint technique allows us to get error budget information of this type in only *one* run! Since

Fig. 7.6   Connecting continuous and discrete systems.

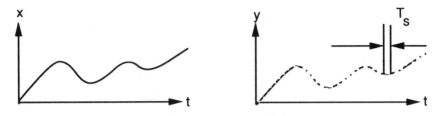

Fig. 7.7   Effect of sampling on continuous signal.

the system under consideration is a mixed continuous discrete system, we have to extend the rules for adjoints which we have already covered in Chapters 3 and 4.

Mixed Continuous Discrete Adjoint Theory[2,3]

The rules for constructing an adjoint of a mixed continuous discrete system are simple and are similar to the adjoint rules for continuous systems. Given a linear time-varying discrete system with impulse response H_D in which the ratio of the time of flight to the sampling time is an integer given by

$$N = t_F/T_s$$

there exists an adjoint system with impulse response $H_D{}^*$. One can construct a mixed continuous discrete adjoint from the original system using the rules of Chapters 3 and 4 and the additional rule given in the next subsection.

Replace n by $N - n$ in the Arguments of all Variable Coefficients

Therefore, the rules for continuous and mixed continuous discrete adjoints are identical in that the signal flow of the original system is reversed and the time-varying gains in the original system are generated backwards for the adjoint system. In mixed continuous discrete systems the adjoint rules get slightly more complicated because additional elements are required for interfacing the continuous and discrete parts of the system. For example, a sampler or analog-to-digital converter is required as shown in Fig. 7.6, to make the connection from a continuous system to a discrete system.

The input/output characteristics of a sampler can easily be illustrated. For example, Fig. 7.7 shows that, if the input signal to the sampler is continuous, the output signal has the same shape but is defined only at each sampling instant by a number. These numbers, or sample points, are spaced T_s seconds apart.

Applying adjoint theory to mixed continuous discrete systems requires taking the adjoint of a sampler. The adjoint of a sampler is depicted in Fig. 7.8. Here the s block represents a pure derivative and the "hold" block will soon be defined. The z^{-1} block is Z transform notation and represents a pure delay of T_s seconds.

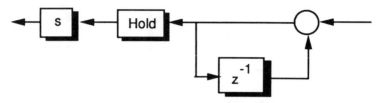

Fig. 7.8   Adjoint of a sampler.

A hold network or digital-to-analog converter is required to connect signal flow from a discrete network to a continuous network as shown in Fig. 7.9.

If the input to the hold is a set of numbers, Fig. 7.10 illustrates the proper input/output characteristics of the hold network. Here we can see that, after a discrete signal has been "held," it becomes continuous.

The adjoint of a hold is shown in Fig. 7.11. Here the $1/s$ term is the Laplace transform representation of an integrator. Again, the z^{-1} term represents a pure delay of T_s seconds.

We now have enough rules to enable us to take the adjoint of a mixed continuous discrete system. Consider the model of Fig. 7.12. In this model there are three continuous linear time-varying networks with impulse responses H_{C1}, H_{C2}, and H_{C3}, respectively. White noise u_C with spectral density Φ_C enters the continuous portion of the system through the shaping network H_{C3}. In addition, a step disturbance of magnitude a also enters the system through the shaping network H_{C1}. The step input has been represented as an impulse through an integrator so that adjoint theory can be applied to this error source.

In this example we are interested in observing the continuous quantity y at the final time t_F. The output of the network H_{C2} is sampled and sent through a discrete network with impulse response H_{D1}. Zero-mean Gaussian noise with variance σ_D^2 enters the discrete portion of the system through shaping network H_{D2}. After the resultant signal goes through the discrete network H_{D1}, the output is held and fed back to the continuous network H_{C1}, thus completing the loop. In this example we seek to find $y(t_F)$ due to each of the disturbances. Adjoint theory can readily be applied to this example.

Following the rules of adjoints we can obtain the adjoint system of Fig. 7.13. Although this adjoint model is driven by an impulse, we have seen in previous chapters that it is not necessary to simulate an impulse. The impulse becomes initial conditions on integrators in its forward path. The impulse is applied at time zero in the adjoint system because the output of

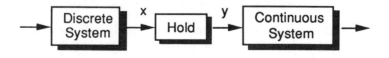

Fig. 7.9   Connecting discrete and continuous systems.

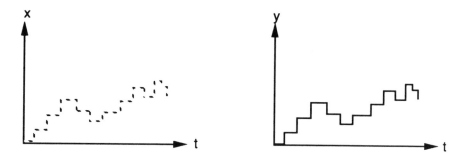

Fig. 7.10   Effects of holding a discrete signal.

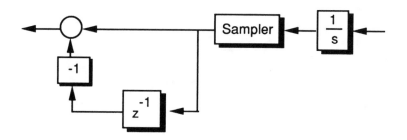

Fig. 7.11   Adjoint of hold.

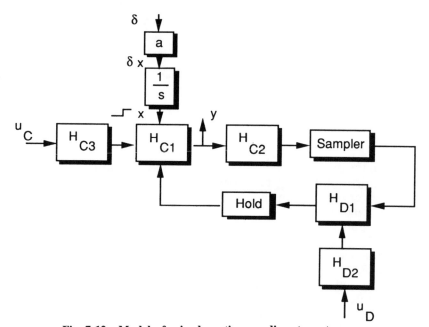

Fig. 7.12   Model of mixed continuous discrete system.

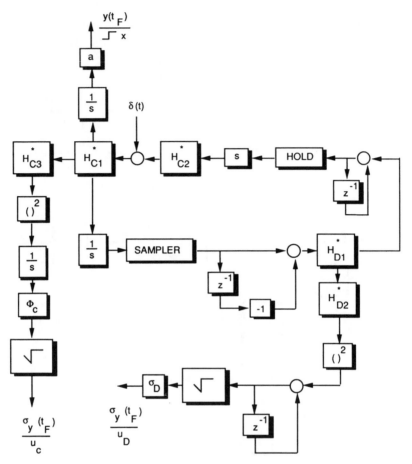

Fig. 7.13   Adjoint of mixed continuous discrete system.

interest in the original system is at the final time. The adjoint model shows a differentiator appearing before $H_{C2}{}^*$. Again, one need not simulate the differentiator but just use block diagram manipulation to eliminate it (i.e., feed it through $H_{C2}{}^*$).

The outputs of the adjoint model represent output sensitivities of the system. They are referred to as sensitivities because a change in their levels does not necessitate a rerunning of the adjoint simulation. As can be seen from Fig. 7.13, the new outputs can be calculated by inspection. Note that, in order to find $y(t_F)$ due to a continuous random disturbance, we square and integrate a continuous signal (i.e., output of $H_{C3}{}^*$). In order to find $y(t_F)$ due to a discrete random disturbance, we square and sum a discrete signal (i.e., output of $H_{D2}{}^*$).

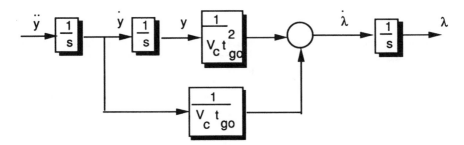

Fig. 7.14   Block diagram for line-of-sight rate.

Using Adjoints to Evaluate Filter Performance

Mixed continuous discrete adjoint theory can be applied to the engagement model of Fig. 7.1, a sample data homing loop containing a two-state fading memory filter. Recall that in this example there are two disturbances: a deterministic target maneuver and measurement noise on the line-of-sight angle. However, before we take the complete adjoint, let us realize that when the adjoint of a "sampler" is taken we will have a pure differentiator in the homing loop. It is desirable, for simulation reasons, to eliminate the differentiator by block diagram manipulation. This can easily be done by modifying the original system to have an extra integrator before the sam-

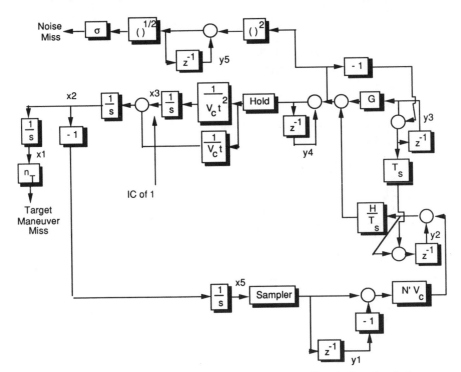

Fig. 7.15   Adjoint of second-order fading memory filter in homing loop.

Listing 7.3   Adjoint engagement simulation with two-state fading memory filter

```
        INTEGER STEP
        DATA XNT,XNP,TF,TS/ 96.6,3.,10.,.1/
        BETA = .8
        SIGNOISE = .001
        VC = 4000.
        T = 0.
        S = 0.
        TP = T + .00001
        X1 = 0
        X2 = 0
        X3 = 1
        X5 = 0.
        Y1OLD = 0.
        Y2OLD = 0.
        Y3OLD = 0.
        Y4OLD = 0.
        Y5OLD = 0.
        H = .01
        GFILTER = 1. − BETA**2
        HFILTER = (1. − BETA)**2
10      IF(TP > (TF − .00001))GOTO 999
        S = S + H
        X1OLD = X1
        X2OLD = X2
        X3OLD = X3
        X5OLD = X5
        STEP = 1
        GOTO 200
66      STEP = 2
        X1 = X1 + H*X1D
        X2 = X2 + H*X2D
        X3 = X3 + H*X3D
        X5 = X5 + H*X5D
        TP = TP + H
        GOTO 200
55      CONTINUE
        X1 = (X1OLD + X1)/2 + .5*H*X1D
        X2 = (X2OLD + X2)/2 + .5*H*X2D
        X3 = (X3OLD + X3)/2 + .5*H*X3D
        X5 = (X5OLD + X5)/2 + .5*H*X5D
        IF(S < (TS − .0001))GOTO 10
        S = 0.
        TEMP1 = (X5 − Y1OLD)*XNP*VC
        TEMP2 = HFILTER*(Y2OLD + TEMP1)/TS + GFILTER*Y3OLD
        Y1NEW = X5
        Y2NEW = TEMP1 + Y2OLD + TS*(Y3OLD − TEMP2)
        Y3NEW = Y3OLD − TEMP2
        Y4NEW = Y4OLD + TEMP2
        Y5NEW = Y5OLD + TEMP2*TEMP2
        Y1OLD = Y1NEW
        Y2OLD = Y2NEW
        Y3OLD = Y3NEW
        Y4OLD = Y4NEW
        Y5OLD = Y5NEW
        XMNOISE = SIGNOISE*SQRT(Y5NEW)
        XMNT = ABS(XNT*X1)
        WRITE(9,*)TP,XMNT,XMNOISE
        GOTO 10
200     CONTINUE
        TGO = TP + .00001
        X1D = X2
        X2D = X3 + Y4OLD/(VC*TGO)
        X3D = (Y4OLD)/(VC*TGO*TGO)
        X5D = − X2
        IF(STEP − 1)66,66,55
999     CONTINUE
        PAUSE
        END
```

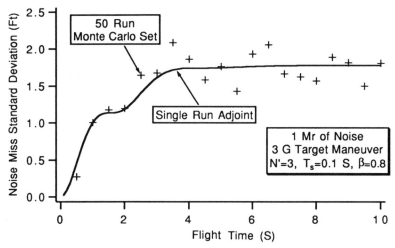

Fig. 7.16 Adjoint noise miss projections are in agreement with Monte Carlo results.

pler. This can be accomplished by first generating the line-of-sight rate and then integrating it to get line-of-sight angle. First we must realize that the line-of-sight angle can be expressed as

$$\lambda = \frac{y}{R_{TM}} = \frac{y}{V_c t_{go}}$$

Taking the derivative of the preceding expression, using the quotient rule, and expressing the result in block diagram form we obtain Fig. 7.14.

The resultant adjoint block diagram for the entire homing loop, following the mixed continuous discrete adjoint rules of the previous section, appears in Fig. 7.15. The two disturbances of the original system become adjoint outputs, whereas the miss distance output of the original system becomes an impulsive input (or initial condition on integrator $x3$) in the adjoint system. Note that, since the noise is digital, the adjoint noise miss distance sensitivity is obtained by squaring and summing the appropriate signal.

Listing 7.3 presents the FORTRAN adjoint program for the engagement model of Fig. 7.15 in which the homing loop contains a second-order fading memory filter. As with the original engagement simulation presented in this chapter, the adjoint program also consists of two sections: one for the differential equations and the other part for the difference equations. Care must also be taken in the adjoint program to ensure that the ratio of the sampling interval to the integration interval be a large integer.

A single adjoint run was made for the nominal case considered at the beginning of the chapter ($\beta = 0.8$). The target maneuver miss and noise miss outputs are plotted separately vs adjoint or flight time in Figs. 7.16 and 7.17. Superimposed on these *single run* adjoint results are the standard deviation and mean of the Monte Carlo miss distance results, obtained with *1000 runs* (50 run sets for 20 flight times). We can see that both methods yield approx-

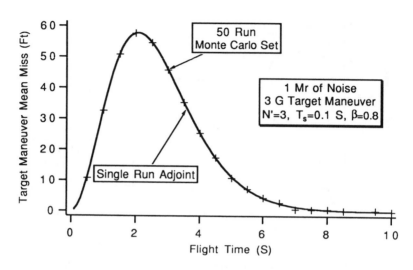

Fig. 7.17   Adjoint target maneuver miss projections are in agreement with Monte Carlo results.

imately the same answers. If there were more error sources, the miss distance performance projections could still have been obtained from the same adjoint run by monitoring additional outputs. Thus, we can see that the adjoint technique is a very powerful method for efficiently generating miss distance error budgets.

Some Properties of Fading Memory Filters

The filter parameter β determines how much the filter will remember about past measurements, which in turn will determine the filter bandwidth or speed of response. Higher values of β yield a filter that remembers a great deal about the past. This type of filter will have low bandwidth and slow speed of response. Low values of β result in a high bandwidth fast filter. Figures 7.18 and 7.19 show, based on adjoint simulation results, how miss distance varies with the fading memory filter parameter β. It is not surprising that Fig. 7.18 shows dramatically improved miss distance results for the wider bandwidth filter (faster guidance systems yield smaller miss distances due to target maneuver). However, it is surprising that Fig. 7.19 shows that there is slightly less miss distance due to line-of-sight angle noise for the faster filter, even though we know that the filter has more noise transmission. In general, reducing the guidance system time constant will reduce the miss for most disturbances in a proportional navigation guidance system in the absence of parasitic and saturation effects. Ultimately excessive noise transmission will lead to saturation and increased miss distance.

Changing the sampling time also effects filter and system performance. Increasing the sampling rate (lower values for T_s) means that the filter has more information per unit time. Therefore, increasing the sampling rate should be beneficial. Figure 7.20 shows, from single flight results, that

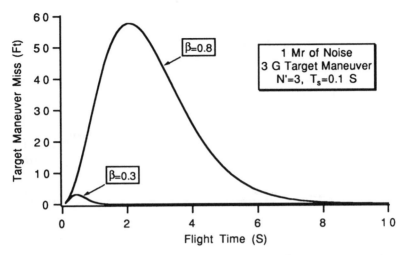

Fig. 7.18   Faster fading memory filter yields less miss due to target maneuver.

increasing the sampling rate (reduce T_s from 0.1 s to 0.05 s) removes the previously noted lag in the line-of-sight rate estimate when β is 0.8 (see Fig. 7.2 for comparison). The noise transmission appears to be about the same, or slightly reduced, from the case when the sampling time was 0.1 s.

From a system performance point of view, increasing the sampling rate should also be beneficial. In essence, we are speeding up the guidance system, which means for the inputs previously considered, miss should decrease. Adjoint results, which are displayed in Fig. 7.21, confirm that doubling the sampling rate (reducing T_s from 0.1 s to 0.05 s) dramatically reduces the miss sensitivity due to target maneuver.

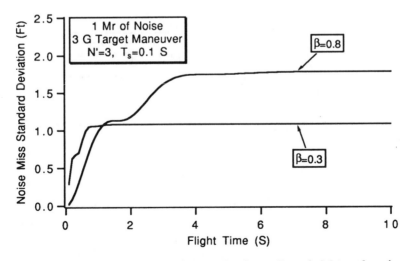

Fig. 7.19   Faster noise filter yields less miss due to line-of-sight angle noise.

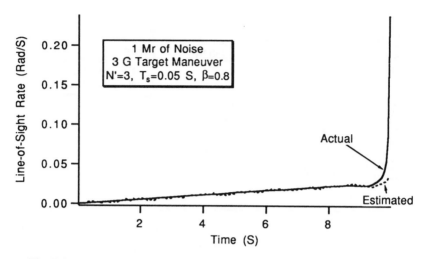

Fig. 7.20   Increasing sampling rate makes fading memory filter faster.

Figure 7.22 also confirms that the miss due to noise decreases with increasing sampling rate. Usually, increased system costs are associated with higher sampling rates. Therefore, financial considerations usually place an upper limit on practical achievable sampling rates.

It is important to note that in the preceding experiment the noise standard deviation remained constant as the data rate changed. In many systems the noise spectral density remains constant and so the noise standard deviation changes with changing data rate. The interested reader is referred to Appendix A for a more complete discussion of this topic.

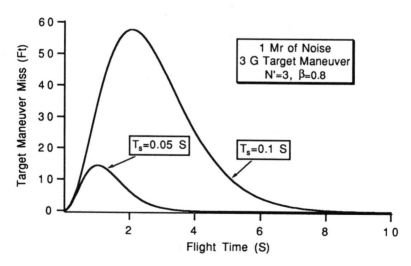

Fig. 7.21   Increasing sampling rate reduces miss due to target maneuver.

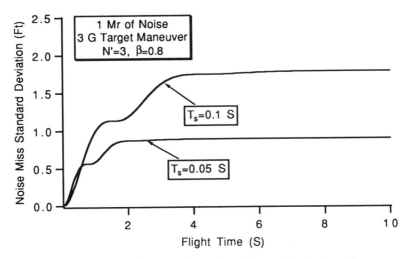

Fig. 7.22   **Increasing sampling rate reduces miss due to noise.**

Estimating Target Maneuver

In Chapter 8 we will investigate more advanced guidance laws. In order to implement more advanced guidance laws, we must have knowledge of all the target states. In other words, we must know what the target is doing. Mathematically stated, we would like to be able to estimate the current maneuver level of the target based on a noisy measurement of the line-of-sight angle. Theoretically it is impossible, without additional measured or a priori information, to estimate the maneuver level of the target based on angle-only measurements from a single sensor. However, many tactical radar homing missiles also measure range and range rate in addition to the line-of-sight angle, which makes target acceleration estimation possible.

Figure 7.23 presents a guidance system that uses a three-state fading memory filter to estimate target acceleration from a measurement of the line-of-sight angle, range, and closing velocity. The noisy measurement of the line-of-sight angle is multiplied by a range measurement to get a pseudomeasurement of relative position $y_k{}^*$. The filter then estimates the derivatives of the measurement. Using knowledge of the missile acceleration, which is assumed to be known precisely, it is then possible to estimate target acceleration from a relative acceleration as shown in Fig. 7.23. With this type of guidance system we also need time to go information, which can be obtained from the range and range rate measurements, to implement either the proportional or augmented proportional navigation guidance law.

Listing 7.4 presents a FORTRAN engagement simulation with the three-state fading memory filter as shown in Fig. 7.23. Note that the three-state filter gains are different from the two-state filter gains.

A nominal case was run with the simulation of Listing 7.4 in which the fading memory factor of the filter was 0.8 and the sampling time was 0.1 s. Figure 7.24 compares the line-of-sight rate estimate of the filter with the

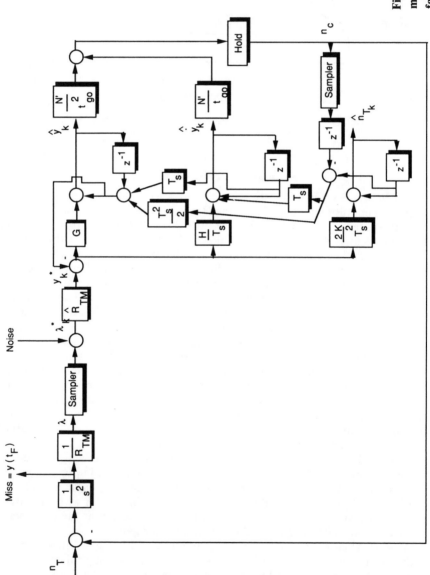

Fig. 7.23 Estimating target maneuver with three-state fading memory filter.

Listing 7.4   Engagement simulation with three-state fading memory filter

```
        REAL KFILTER
        VC = 4000.
        XNT = 96.6
        YIC = 0.
        VM = 3000.
        HEDEG = 0.
        BETA = .8
        XNP = 3.
        SIGNOISE = .001
        TF = 10.
        TS = .1
        NOISE = 1
        Y = YIC
        YD = - VM*HEDEG/57.3
        YDIC = YD
        T = 0.
        H = .01
        S = 0.
        GFILTER = 1. - BETA**3
        HFILTER = 1.5*((1. - BETA)**2)*(1. + BETA)
        KFILTER = .5*((1. - BETA)**3)
        YH = 0.
        YDH = 0.
        XNTH = 0.
        XNC = 0.
10      IF(T > (TF - .0001))GOTO 999
        YOLD = Y
        YDOLD = YD
        STEP = 1
        GOTO 200
66      STEP = 2
        Y = Y + H*YD
        YD = YD + H*YDD
        T = T + H
        GOTO 200
55      CONTINUE
        Y = .5*(YOLD + Y + H*YD)
        YD = .5*(YDOLD + YD + H*YDD)
        S = S + H
C       COLLECT DATA PERIODICALLY
        IF(S < (TS - .0001))GOTO 10
        S = 0.
        IF(NOISE = 1)THEN
            CALL GAUSS(XLAMNOISE,SIGNOISE)
        ELSE
            XLAMNOISE = 0.
        ENDIF
        YSTAR = RTM*(XLAM + XLAMNOISE)
        RES = YSTAR - YH - TS*YDH - .5*TS*TS*(XNTH - XNC)
        YH = GFILTER*RES + YH + TS*YDH + .5*TS*TS*(XNTH - XNC)
        YDH = HFILTER*RES/TS + YDH + TS*(XNTH - XNC)
        XNTH = 2.*KFILTER*RES/(TS*TS) + XNTH
        XLAMDH = (YH + YDH*TGO)/(VC*TGO*TGO)
        XNC = XNP*VC*XLAMDH
        WRITE(9,*)T,Y,XNC,XLAM,XLAMDH,XNT,XNTH
        GOTO 10
200     CONTINUE
        TGO = TF - T + .00001
        RTM = VC*TGO
        XLAM = Y/(VC*TGO)
        XLAMD = (RTM*YD + Y*VC)/(RTM**2)
        YDD = XNT - XNC
        IF(STEP - 1)66,66,55
999     CONTINUE
        Y = ABS(Y)
        WRITE(9,*)T,Y,XNC,XLAMD,XLAMDH,XNT,XNTH
        PAUSE
        END
        SUBROUTINE GAUSS(X,SIG)
        INTEGER RANDOM,SUM
        INTEGER*4 TOOLBX
        PARAMETER (RANDOM = Z'86140000')
        SUM = 0
        DO 14
        J = 1,6
        IRAN = TOOLBX(RANDOM)
        SUM = SUM + IRAN
14      CONTINUE
        X = SUM/65536.
        X = 1.414*X*SIG
        RETURN
        END
```

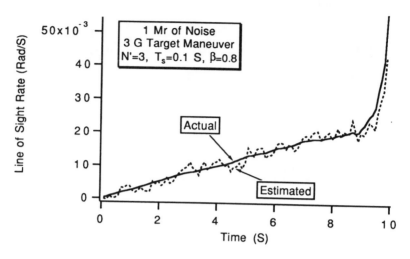

Fig. 7.24   Three-state filter yields excellent estimate of line-of-sight rate.

actual line-of-sight rate for the nominal case. We can see that the filter estimate follows the geometric line-of-sight rate without excessive noise transmission.

Figure 7.25 shows, for the same case, the filter estimate of the target maneuver. Superimposed on the figure is the actual maneuver. We can see that for this case it takes the filter about 5 s to get a reasonable estimate of the maneuver level. A faster filter would have a smaller transient period but much more noise transmission. Estimates of the quality shown in Fig. 7.25 are sufficient for improving guidance system performance.

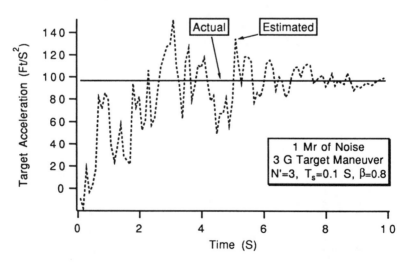

Fig. 7.25   Three-state fading memory filter is able to estimate target maneuver.

Summary

In this chapter it was shown how a simple constant-gain, digital noise filter, known as a fading memory filter, could be implemented in a missile guidance system. It was shown that both filter bandwidth and sampling rate are important parameters in determining overall system performance. The method of adjoints was extended so that it could be used to yield performance projections of a missile guidance system with a digital noise filter. Experiments confirmed that Monte Carlo simulation results were in complete agreement with single-run adjoint performance projections. Finally, it was shown how a fading memory filter could be utilized to provide target acceleration estimates.

References

[1]Morrison, N., *Introduction to Sequential Smoothing and Prediction*, McGraw-Hill, New York, 1969.

[2]Moroney, R., "The Adjoint of Mixed Continuous/Discrete Systems," Raytheon Memo RM-69-1, Jan. 1969.

[3]Zarchan, P., and Warren, R. S., "Discrete Adjoint Simulation," Raytheon Rept., BR-5440-1, Oct. 1969.

Chapter 8

Advanced Guidance Laws

Introduction

THUS far we have used proportional navigation as an interceptor guidance law because it is easy to implement and is very effective. In fact, proportional navigation is used extensively in the tactical missile world. However, there are other more advanced guidance laws. These advanced guidance laws relax the interceptor acceleration requirements and also yield smaller miss distances. The price paid for these more advanced guidance laws is that more information, such as time to go and missile-target range, is required for their successful implementation. The concept of zero effort miss, originally introduced in Chapter 2, will be used to develop and understand new guidance laws. The zero effort miss concept will also be important when we move to the strategic world and encounter predictive guidance. The Schwartz inequality will be used to analytically derive optimal guidance laws.

Review of Proportional Navigation

The basic homing loop for a zero-lag proportional navigation guidance system, which first appeared in Chapter 2, is repeated for convenience in Fig. 8.1. In this zero-lag loop, the seeker, noise filter, and flight control system dynamics have been neglected. As can be seen from the figure, the proportional navigation guidance law can be expressed as

$$n_c = N' V_c \dot{\lambda}$$

where N' is a gain known as the effective navigation ratio, V_c the closing velocity, and λ the line-of-sight angle.

We have already shown in Chapter 2 that closed-form solutions for the required missile acceleration exist for this zero-lag guidance system. The resultant formula for the missile acceleration n_c due to a step target maneuver was derived from the first-order time-varying proportional navigation homing loop differential equation originally presented in Chapter 2. The solution, which is repeated here for convenience, is given by

$$n_c = \frac{N'}{N' - 2} \left[1 - \left(1 - \frac{t}{t_F} \right)^{N' - 2} \right] n_T$$

where t_F is the time of flight, t the time, and n_T the target maneuver level. We can see from the closed-form solution that the required missile acceler-

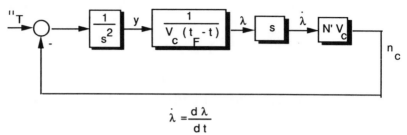

$$\dot{\lambda} = \frac{d\lambda}{dt}$$

Fig. 8.1   Zero-lag proportional navigation homing loop.

ation is directly proportional to the target maneuver acceleration level. Doubling the target acceleration level also doubles the missile acceleration requirements.

In order to convey the maximum amount of information concisely, the closed-form solution for the missile acceleration induced by target maneuver is normalized and displayed in Fig. 8.2 for different values of the effective navigation ratio. We can see that, regardless of the effective navigation ratio, the required missile acceleration induced by a target maneuver is largest at the end of the flight. Increasing the effective navigation ratio tends to reduce the maximum missile acceleration requirement. Of course we have already seen that, due to parasitic effects and possibly noise considerations, there is a practical upper limit on maximum allowable values for the effective navigation ratio.

The missile's maximum required acceleration, which occurs at the end of the flight ($t = t_F$), can be obtained from the closed-form solution as

$$n_{cmax}\Big|_{PN} = \frac{N' n_T}{N' - 2}$$

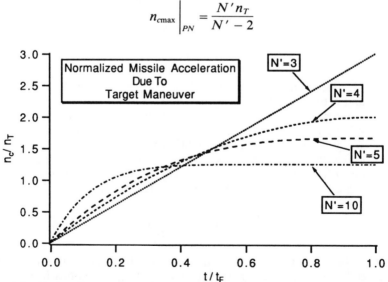

Fig. 8.2   Normalized missile acceleration due to target maneuver for proportional navigation guidance.

Therefore, for an effective navigation ratio of 3, the missile requires three times the acceleration capability of the target for a successful intercept. However, increasing the effective navigation ratio from 3 to 5 reduces the required missile acceleration advantage from 3 to 1.67. Of course, other disturbances plus system dynamics will work in the direction of increasing the required missile acceleration advantage.

Augmented Proportional Navigation

More advanced guidance laws can be developed from the zero-lag homing loop model of Fig. 8.1. First we note that the line-of-sight angle can also be expressed as

$$\lambda = \frac{y}{R_{TM}} = \frac{y}{V_c(t_F - t)}$$

where y is the relative missile-target separation and R_{TM} the range from the missile to the target. We can find the line-of-sight rate by taking the derivative of the preceding expression, using the quotient rule, obtaining

$$\dot{\lambda} = \frac{y + \dot{y}t_{go}}{V_c t_{go}^2}$$

where t_{go} is the time to go until intercept and can be defined as

$$t_{go} = t_F - t$$

Thus, we can also express the proportional navigation guidance law as the mathematically equivalent expression

$$n_c = N'V_c\dot{\lambda} = \frac{N'(y + \dot{y}t_{go})}{t_{go}^2}$$

The expression in the parentheses of the preceding equation represents the future separation between missile and target. More simply, the expression in parentheses is the miss distance that would result if the missile made no further corrective acceleration and the target did not maneuver. This expression is referred to as the zero effort miss ZEM. Therefore, we can also think of proportional navigation as a guidance law in which acceleration commands are issued inversely proportional to the square of time to go and directly proportional to the zero effort miss.

If the target maneuvers the zero effort miss must be augmented by an additional term. The new equation for the zero effort miss, in the presence of a constant target maneuver, is simply

$$ZEM_{TGT\,MVR} = y + \dot{y}t_{go} + 0.5n_T t_{go}^2$$

where n_T is the target maneuver acceleration level. Therefore, a perfectly plausible guidance law, in the presence of target maneuver, would be

$$n_c\bigg|_{APN} = \frac{N'ZEM_{TGT\,MVR}}{t_{go}^2} = N'V_c\dot{\lambda} + \frac{N'n_T}{2}$$

This new guidance law, known as augmented proportional navigation, is proportional navigation with an extra term to account for the maneuvering target.[1]

A zero-lag augmented proportional navigation homing loop is shown in block diagram form in Fig. 8.3. The additional target maneuver term, required by the guidance law, appears as a feedforward term in the homing loop block diagram. As with the proportional navigation guidance law, we can also obtain closed-form solutions for the required missile acceleration due to a constant target maneuver for the zero-lag homing loop depicted in Fig. 8.3. The resultant solution for the required missile acceleration is

$$n_c\bigg|_{APN} = 0.5n_T N'\left(1 - \frac{t}{t_F}\right)^{N'-2}$$

The closed-form solution for the missile acceleration required to hit a maneuvering target with augmented proportional navigation is displayed in normalized form in Fig. 8.4. Here we can see that the required missile acceleration decreases monotonically with time, regardless of the effective navigation ratio, rather than increasing monotonically with time as was the case with proportional navigation. Increasing the effective navigation ratio increases the maximum acceleration at the beginning of the flight but also reduces the time at which the acceleration decays to negligible levels.

The maximum required acceleration required by augmented proportional navigation to hit a maneuvering target is

$$n_{cmax}\bigg|_{APN} = 0.5N'n_T$$

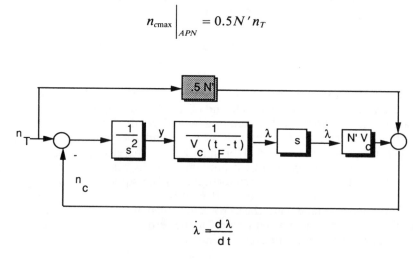

$$\dot{\lambda} = \frac{d\lambda}{dt}$$

Fig. 8.3 Augmented proportional navigation homing loop.

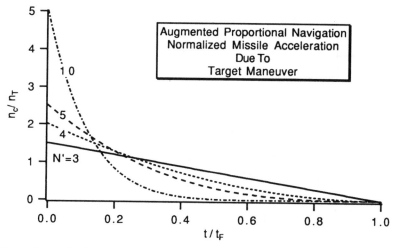

Fig. 8.4 Normalized acceleration for augmented proportional navigation to hit a maneuvering target.

This means that, for a navigation ratio of 3, augmented proportional navigation requires half the acceleration of the missile than with proportional navigation guidance. However, for an effective navigation ratio of 5, augmented proportional navigation requires a larger maximum acceleration compared with proportional navigation guidance.

Comparative plots of proportional and augmented proportional navigation missile acceleration profiles for different values of effective navigation ratio due to a target maneuver appear in Figs. 8.5–8.7. Figure 8.5 shows that, with an effective navigation ratio of 3, augmented proportional navigation requires less acceleration capability of the missile than proportional

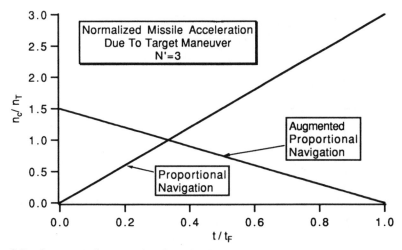

Fig. 8.5 Augmented proportional navigation requires less acceleration capability of missile for $N' = 3$.

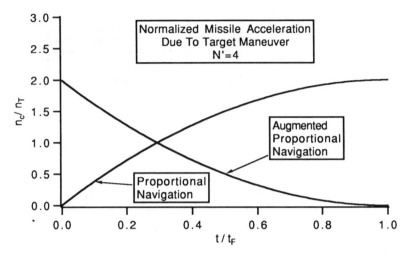

Fig. 8.6   Augmented proportional navigation requires the same acceleration capability of missile for $N' = 4$.

navigation. This figure also indicates that augmented proportional navigation requires much less total acceleration than proportional navigation. This is not surprising because augmented proportional navigation is making use of extra information, namely, knowledge of the target maneuver. It is reasonable that this knowledge should enable the missile to maneuver in a more efficient manner.

Figure 8.6 shows that for an effective navigation ratio of 4 the maximum acceleration required by both guidance laws is the same. The total acceleration begins to be less with augmented proportional navigation at a normalized time of 0.3. This means that 70% of the time-augmented proportional

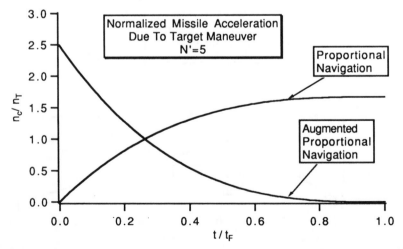

Fig. 8.7   Augmented proportional navigation requires more acceleration capability of missile for $N' = 5$.

navigation requires less acceleration than proportional navigation to hit a maneuvering target.

Figure 8.7 shows that, when the effective navigation ratio is 5, augmented proportional navigation requires a larger maximum acceleration capability of the missile than does proportional navigation. However, about 75% of the time-augmented proportional navigation requires less missile acceleration than proportional navigation.

It appears from Figs. 8.6 and 8.7 that augmented proportional navigation does not appear to relax the maximum missile acceleration requirements imposed by proportional navigation guidance when the effective navigation ratio is greater than or equal to 4. However, in these cases, augmented proportional navigation appears to require less total acceleration than proportional navigation for most of the flight.

In order to quantify this observation more precisely, we need a performance index other than maximum acceleration. One possibility is to consider the total acceleration required or to find the area under the acceleration curve. We shall see in later chapters that strategic missiles require fuel to maneuver since they operate outside the atmosphere (i.e., they cannot generate lift by moving control surfaces). In these cases the missile maneuverability is referred to as a lateral divert capability. Lateral divert is directly related to the amount of fuel required by the interceptor to implement the guidance law and effect an intercept outside the atmosphere. The lateral divert is in fact the total area under the absolute value of the acceleration curve. Since missile acceleration is always positive we can find the lateral divert requirements for proportional navigation by integrating the closed-form solution for the required missile acceleration, or

$$\Delta V_{PN} = \int_0^{t_F} n_c \bigg|_{PN} dt = \int_0^{t_F} \frac{N'}{N'-2} \left[1 - \left(1 - \frac{t}{t_F} \right)^{N'-2} \right] n_T \, dt$$

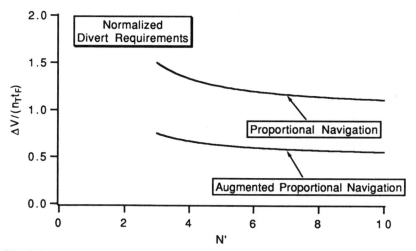

Fig. 8.8 Augmented proportional navigation has reduced divert requirement.

After some algebra we obtain

$$\Delta V_{PN} = \frac{N' n_T t_F}{N' - 1}$$

Thus, we can see that increasing the effective navigation ratio makes the lateral divert requirements smaller. Following the same procedure we can express the lateral divert required for augmented proportional navigation. First we must set up the integral as

$$\Delta V_{APN} = \int_0^{t_F} n_c \bigg|_{APN} dt = \int_0^{t_F} 0.5 n_T N' \left(1 - \frac{t}{t_F}\right)^{N'-2} dt$$

Integration and simplification yields

$$\Delta V_{APN} = \frac{0.5 N' n_T t_F}{N' - 1}$$

Figure 8.8 presents a comparative plot of the total energy or lateral divert required by the interceptor as a function of the effective navigation ratio for both guidance laws. The figure shows that the lateral divert requirements decrease with increasing effective navigation ratio for both guidance laws. We can also see from the formulas and figure that augmented proportional navigation always has one-half the lateral divert requirements of proportional navigation, regardless of the effective navigation ratio. Therefore, for strategic applications, augmented proportional navigation is a more fuel-efficient guidance law than proportional navigation.

Derivation of Augmented Proportional Navigation[4]

Thus far we have given a heuristic argument for the augmented proportional navigation guidance law. This is a good approach if the desire is to understand a guidance law concept, but it is not quite adequate for developing more advanced and complex laws.

Our model of the guidance system, for guidance law development, is shown in Fig. 8.9. In this zero-lag model we are saying that relative acceleration is the difference between target acceleration n_T and missile acceleration n_c.

We seek to find a guidance law that is a function of the system states. There are an infinite number of possible guidance laws; thus, it is necessary to state in mathematical terms what the guidance law should do. Certainly we would like to hit the target! Therefore, one feature of the guidance law

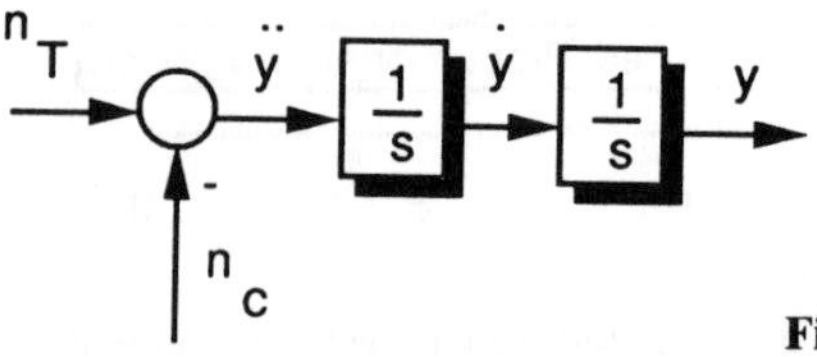

Fig. 8.9   Model for guidance law derivation.

should be a zero miss distance requirement. In addition, we would like to hit the target in an efficient manner. In other words, we desire to use minimal total acceleration. A popular and mathematically convenient way of stating the guidance problem to be solved is that we desire to achieve zero miss subject to minimizing the integral of the square of the acceleration command, or

$$y(t_F) = 0 \text{ subject to minimizing } \int_0^{t_F} n_c^2(t) \, dt$$

Unfortunately, if we minimized a more meaningful performance index such as the integral of the absolute value of n_c, the solution would be mathematically intractable. Typically this type of problem with a quadratic performance index is solved using techniques from optimal control theory.[2,3] However, this class of problem can be solved more easily using the Schwartz inequality.[4] Before we begin let us review a few fundamentals. A system of linear differential equations can always be represented in the following state space form:

$$\dot{x} = Fx + Gu$$

The system of Fig. 8.9 can be expressed in state space form as

$$\begin{bmatrix} \dot{y} \\ \ddot{y} \\ \dot{n}_T \end{bmatrix} = \underbrace{\begin{bmatrix} 0 & 1 & 0 \\ 0 & 0 & 1 \\ 0 & 0 & 0 \end{bmatrix}}_{F} \begin{bmatrix} y \\ \dot{y} \\ n_T \end{bmatrix} + \underbrace{\begin{bmatrix} 0 \\ -1 \\ 0 \end{bmatrix}}_{G} n_c$$

where F is the 3×3 system dynamics matrix and G the 3×1 vector. The solution to the state space vector differential equation is given at the final time t_F by the vector relationship[5]

$$x(t_F) = \Phi(t_F - t)x(t) + \int_t^{t_F} \Phi(t_F - \lambda)G(\lambda)u(\lambda) \, d\lambda$$

where Φ is the fundamental matrix and is related to F according to

$$\Phi(t) = \mathcal{L}^{-1}[(sI - F)^{-1}]$$

where $\mathcal{L}^{-1}$ is the inverse Laplace transform. This means that in order to find the fundamental matrix we must first invert the matrix $sI - F$ and then find the inverse Laplace transform of the resultant matrix expression.

For the model of Fig. 8.9 the fundamental matrix is found to be

$$\Phi(t) = \begin{bmatrix} 1 & t & 0.5t^2 \\ 0 & 1 & t \\ 0 & 0 & 1 \end{bmatrix}$$

Using the preceding fundamental matrix in the solution for the state space vector differential equation and only looking at the first state, we get

$$y(t_F) = y(t) + \dot{y}(t)(t_F - t) + 0.5n_T(t_F - t)^2 - \int_t^{t_F}(t_F - \lambda)n_c(\lambda)\,d\lambda$$

For convenience let us define the terms

$$f_1(t_F - t) = y(t) + \dot{y}(t)(t_F - t) + 0.5n_T(t_F - t)^2$$

and

$$h_1(t_F - \lambda) = t_F - \lambda$$

Then we can say that

$$y(t_F) = f_1(t_F - t) - \int_t^{t_F}h_1(t_F - \lambda)n_c(\lambda)\,d\lambda$$

For the condition in which we have zero miss distance $[y(t_F) = 0]$ we can rewrite the preceding equation as

$$f_1(t_F - t) = \int_t^{t_F}h_1(t_F - \lambda)n_c(\lambda)\,d\lambda$$

If we apply the Schwartz inequality to the preceding expression, we get the relationship

$$f_1^2(t_F - t) \le \int_t^{t_F}h_1^2(t_F - \lambda)\,d\lambda\int_t^{t_F}n_c^2(\lambda)\,d\lambda$$

Expressing the preceding inequality in terms of the desired acceleration command, we get

$$\int_t^{t_F}n_c^2(\lambda)\,d\lambda \ge \frac{f_1^2(t_F - t)}{\int_t^{t_F}h_1^2(t_F - \lambda)\,d\lambda}$$

The integral of the square of the commanded acceleration will be minimized when the equality sign holds in the preceding inequality. According to the Schwartz inequality, the equality sign holds when

$$n_c(\lambda) = kh_1(t_F - \lambda)$$

This means that the integral of the squared acceleration is minimized when

$$k = \frac{f_1(t_F - t)}{\int_t^{t_F}h_1^2(t_F - \lambda)\,d\lambda}$$

Therefore, the commanded acceleration is given by

$$n_c = \left[\frac{f_1(t_F - t)}{\int_t^{t_F}h_1^2(t_F - \lambda)\,d\lambda}\right]h_1(t_F - t)$$

Substitution yields the feedback control guidance law

$$n_c = \frac{3(y + \dot{y}t_{go} + 0.5 n_T t_{go}^2)}{t_{go}^2}$$

where

$$t_{go} = t_F - t$$

We can see that the "optimal" guidance law is simply augmented proportional navigation with an effective navigation ratio of 3. The effective navigation ratio turns out to be 3 because we are minimizing the integral of the square of the acceleration. If we were to minimize another function of acceleration, we would get a different answer for the optimal effective navigation ratio. It is still important to note that the optimal guidance law is proportional to the zero effort miss and inversely proportional to the square of time to go.

Influence of Time Constants

Thus far we have seen that augmented proportional navigation may offer considerable advantages, in terms of required missile acceleration needed to effect an intercept, over the proportional navigation guidance law. It has been demonstrated that, under certain circumstances, augmented proportional navigation may be considered to be an optimal guidance law for a zero-lag guidance system. Let us see how augmented proportional navigation performs when there is a guidance system lag.

Consider a case where the flight time is 10 s, the missile has an effective navigation ratio of 4, and there is a 3-g target maneuver. Figure 8.10 displays the resultant commanded acceleration profile for both proportional

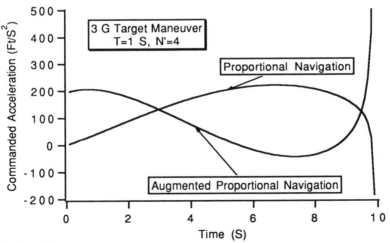

Fig. 8.10 Guidance law acceleration requirements in presence of single-lag guidance system.

and augmented proportional navigation. Since the effective navigation ratio is 4, we can compare these results directly with the normalized zero-lag guidance system results of Fig. 8.6. Figure 8.10 indicates that the lag does not change the value of the maximum value of acceleration for both guidance laws. In addition, the lag does not change the fact that augmented proportional navigation requires less acceleration than proportional navigation about 70% of the time. The lag does slightly alter the shape of both acceleration profiles in the sense that the curves are not completely monotonically decreasing (APN) or monotonically increasing (PN).

Having seen that the lag does not change trends in acceleration, let us use the method of adjoints to perform a miss distance sensitivity analysis for both guidance laws in the presence of the lag. The adjoint block diagram of a single time constant system appears in Fig. 8.11. In this diagram we have proportional navigation if $APN = 0$ and augmented proportional navigation if $APN = 1$.

The FORTRAN listing for the adjoint simulation appears in Listing 8.1. The guidance system time constant is represented in FORTRAN by TAU. The listing shows that an initial condition of unity is applied to the $x3$ integrator to make a miss distance adjoint. The four adjoint differential equations can be found after statement label 200.

Two adjoint runs were made in which proportional navigation ($APN = 0$) and augmented proportional navigation ($APN = 1$) were used. The error source was a 3-g target maneuver in the presence of a 1-s flight control system time constant. The value of the effective navigation ratio was 4. We can see from Fig. 8.12 that neither guidance law is superior from a miss distance point of view (assuming the system is linear and we do not have acceleration saturation). Augmented proportional navigation yields smaller miss distances for shorter flight times, whereas proportional navigation yields smaller miss distances for longer flight times.

Of course in a zero-lag system both guidance laws would always yield zero miss distance. So we can see that, although the lag does not significantly alter the acceleration signature, it does cause miss distance!

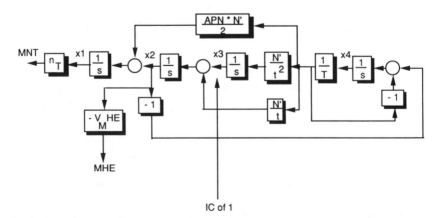

Fig. 8.11   Adjoint for investigating guidance laws in single-lag guidance system.

Listing 8.1   Adjoint simulation for investigating guidance laws

```
        INTEGER STEP
        DATA XNT,XNP,TAU,TF,VM,HEDEG/ 96.6,4,1,10,3000., − 20./
        DATA APN/1./
        T = 0.
        S = 0.
        TP = T + .00001
        X1 = 0
        X2 = 0
        X3 = 1
        X4 = 0
        H = .02
        HE = HEDEG/57.3
10      IF(TP > (TF − .00001))GOTO 999
        S = S + H
        X1OLD = X1
        X2OLD = X2
        X3OLD = X3
        X4OLD = X4
        STEP = 1
        GOTO 200
66      STEP = 2
        X1 = X1 + H*X1D
        X2 = X2 + H*X2D
        X3 = X3 + H*X3D
        X4 = X4 + H*X4D
        TP = TP + H
        GOTO 200
55      CONTINUE
        X1 = (X1OLD + X1)/2 + .5*H*X1D
        X2 = (X2OLD + X2)/2 + .5*H*X2D
        X3 = (X3OLD + X3)/2 + .5*H*X3D
        X4 = (X4OLD + X4)/2 + .5*H*X4D
        IF(S < .09999)GOTO 10
        S = 0.
        XMNT = ABS(XNT*X1)
        XMHE = ABS( − VM*HE*X2)
        WRITE(9,*)TP,XMNT,XMHE
        GOTO 10
200     CONTINUE
        X1D = X2 + X4*XNP*APN/(2.*TAU)
        X2D = X3 + XNP*X4/(TAU*TP)
        X3D = XNP*X4/(TAU*TP*TP)
        X4D = − X4/TAU − X2
        IF(STEP − 1)66,66,55
999     CONTINUE
        PAUSE
        END
```

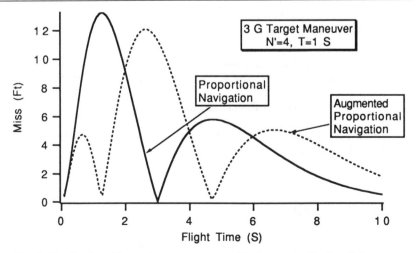

Fig. 8.12   Both guidance laws are comparable in terms of miss distance.

Optimal Guidance[1,3,4]

We have observed that by making use of target acceleration information we could derive a guidance law to reduce the missile acceleration requirements. It has been demonstrated in the previous example that guidance system lags cause miss distance. Generally, larger guidance system time constants yield larger miss distances (except for parasitic effects and some types of noise disturbances). If we had knowledge of the guidance system dynamics, could we derive a guidance law to eliminate miss distance? Mathematically speaking, the answer is yes!

A single-lag guidance system model for guidance law development is presented in Fig. 8.13. This model is identical to the one of Fig. 8.9, except that the guidance system dynamics has been represented by a single lag, or

$$\frac{n_L}{n_c} = \frac{1}{1 + sT}$$

where n_c is the commanded acceleration, n_L the achieved acceleration, and T the guidance system or flight control system time constant.

Figure 8.13 can be expressed in state space form as

$$\begin{bmatrix} \dot{y} \\ \ddot{y} \\ \dot{n}_T \\ \dot{n}_L \end{bmatrix} = \begin{bmatrix} 0 & 1 & 0 & 0 \\ 0 & 0 & 1 & -1 \\ 0 & 0 & 0 & 0 \\ 0 & 0 & 0 & \frac{-1}{T} \end{bmatrix} \begin{bmatrix} y \\ \dot{y} \\ n_T \\ n_L \end{bmatrix} + \begin{bmatrix} 0 \\ 0 \\ 0 \\ \frac{1}{T} \end{bmatrix} n_c$$

Therefore, the fundamental matrix can be found to be

$$\Phi(t) = \begin{bmatrix} 1 & t & 0.5t^2 & -tT + T^2(1 - e^{-t/T}) \\ 0 & 1 & t & -T(1 - e^{-t/T}) \\ 0 & 0 & 1 & 0 \\ 0 & 1 & 0 & e^{-t/T} \end{bmatrix}$$

Recall that we still seek a guidance law that yields zero miss subject to minimizing the integral of the square of the commanded acceleration, or

$$y(t_F) = 0 \text{ subject to minimizing } \int_0^{t_F} n_c^2(t) \, dt$$

Using a procedure similar to that used in the previous section, we can derive the important quantities

$$f_1(t_F - t) = y + \dot{y}(t_F - t) + 0.5 n_T(t_F - t)^2 - T^2 n_L \left[e^{-(t_F - t)/T} + \frac{(t_F - t)}{T} - 1 \right]$$

$$h_1(t_F - \lambda) = t_F - \lambda - T[1 - e^{-(t_F - \lambda)/T}]$$

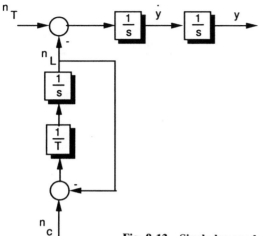

Fig. 8.13 Single-lag model for guidance law development.

Calculating

$$\int_{t}^{t_F} h_1^2(t_F - \lambda) \, d\lambda = T^3\left(0.5 - 0.5 \, e^{-2t_{go}/T} - \frac{2t_{go} \, e^{-t_{go}/T}}{T} - \frac{t_{go}^2}{T^2} + \frac{t_{go}}{T} + \frac{t_{go}^3}{3T^3}\right)$$

and defining

$$x = \frac{t_{go}}{T}$$

we obtain the optimal guidance law

$$n_c = \frac{N'}{t_{go}^2} \, [y + \dot{y}t_{go} + 0.5n_T t_{go}^2 - n_L T^2(e^{-x} + x - 1)]$$

where the bracketed quantity is the zero effort miss, and the effective navigation ratio is no longer a constant but is related to the guidance system time constant and time to go by the relationship

$$N' = \frac{6x^2(e^{-x} - 1 + x)}{2x^3 + 3 + 6x - 6x^2 - 12x \, e^{-x} - 3 \, e^{-2x}}$$

The effective navigation ratio for the optimal guidance law is displayed in normalized form in Fig. 8.14. We can see that at the beginning of the flight (long time to go) the effective navigation ratio is approximately constant and is approaching 3. As we get closer to intercept (small time to go), the effective navigation ratio grows considerably.

In Fig. 8.15 a theoretically optimal guidance law is implemented in a single-lag guidance system. It is assumed that precise knowledge of the target and missile acceleration is available. The only error disturbance shown in this guidance system is target maneuver n_T.

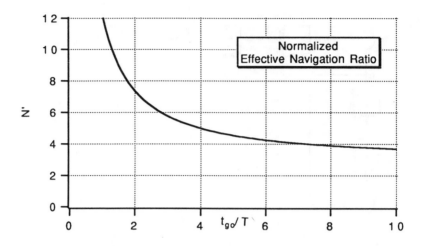

Fig. 8.14   Normalized effective navigation ratio for optimal guidance law.

The guidance law has been represented with control gains C_1–C_4. These gains are functions of the time to go to intercept and the guidance system time constant. They are defined as

$$C_1 = \frac{N'}{t_{go}^2}$$

$$C_2 = \frac{N'}{t_{go}}$$

$$C_3 = 0.5\,N'$$

$$C_4 = \frac{-N'(e^{-x} + x - 1)}{x^2}$$

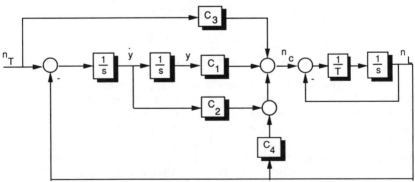

Fig. 8.15   Theoretical optimal single time constant guidance system.

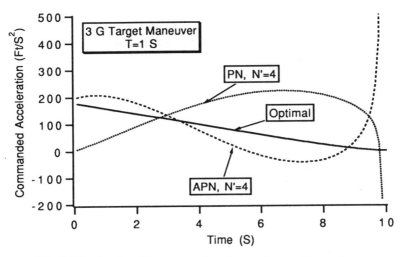

Fig. 8.16 Acceleration comparison for various guidance laws.

where N' is the optimal effective navigation ratio, which has been defined previously.

A case was run for a 1-s guidance system time constant in which the flight time was 10 s and the error disturbance was a 3-g target maneuver. Figure 8.16 shows the acceleration profile for proportional navigation ($N' = 4$), augmented proportional navigation ($N' = 4$), and optimal guidance. If we compare this figure with Fig. 8.5 we can see that the optimal guidance acceleration profile appears to be identical to the augmented proportional navigation acceleration profile *for a zero-lag guidance system and an effective navigation ratio of 3!* This means that the guidance law is dynamically canceling out the guidance system dynamics.

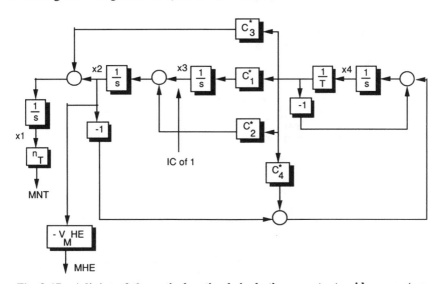

Fig. 8.17 Adjoint of theoretical optimal single time constant guidance system.

Listing 8.2   Adjoint simulation of optimal guidance system

```
      INTEGER STEP,APN
      DATA XNT,XNP,TAU,TF,VM,HEDEG/ 96.6,4,1,10,3000., - 20./
      DATA APN/0/
      T = 0.
      S = 0.
      TP = T + .00001
      X1 = 0
      X2 = 0
      X3 = 1
      X4 = 0
      XNPP = 0.
      H = .02
      HE = HEDEG/57.3
10    IF(TP > (TF - .00001))GOTO 999
      S = S + H
      X1OLD = X1
      X2OLD = X2
      X3OLD = X3
      X4OLD = X4
      STEP = 1
      GOTO 200
66    STEP = 2
      X1 = X1 + H*X1D
      X2 = X2 + H*X2D
      X3 = X3 + H*X3D
      X4 = X4 + H*X4D
      TP = TP + H
      GOTO 200
55    CONTINUE
      X1 = (X1OLD + X1)/2 + .5*H*X1D
      X2 = (X2OLD + X2)/2 + .5*H*X2D
      X3 = (X3OLD + X3)/2 + .5*H*X3D
      X4 = (X4OLD + X4)/2 + .5*H*X4D
      IF(S < .09999)GOTO 10
      S = 0.
      XMNT = ABS(XNT*X1)
      XMHE = ABS( - VM*HE*X2)
      WRITE(9,*)TP,XMNT,XMHE
      GOTO 10
200   CONTINUE
      TGO = TP + .00001
      IF(APN = 0)THEN
          C1 = XNP/(TGO*TGO)
          C2 = XNP/TGO
          C3 = 0.
          C4 = 0.
      ELSEIF(APN = 1)THEN
          C1 = XNP/(TGO*TGO)
          C2 = XNP/TGO
          C3 = .5*XNP
          C4 = 0.
      ELSE
          X = TGO/TAU
          TOP = 6.*X*X*(EXP( - X) - 1. + X)
          BOT1 = 2*X*X*X + 3. + 6.*X - 6.*X*X
          BOT2 = - 12.*X*EXP( - X) - 3.*EXP( - 2.*X)
          XNPP = TOP/(.0001 + BOT1 + BOT2)
          C1 = XNPP/(TGO*TGO)
          C2 = XNPP/TGO
          C3 = .5*XNPP
          C4 = - XNPP*(EXP( - X) + X - 1.)/(X*X)
      ENDIF
      X1D = X2 + C3*X4/TAU
      X2D = X3 + C2*X4/TAU
      X3D = C1*X4/TAU
      X4D = - X4/TAU - X2 + C4*X4/TAU
      IF(STEP - 1)66,66,55
999   CONTINUE
      PAUSE
      END
```

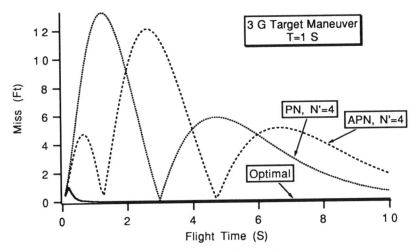

Fig. 8.18   Optimal guidance system does not have miss distance.

If the optimal guidance law were attempting to make the single-lag guidance system appear to be a zero-lag augmented proportional navigation guidance system, then the miss distance should be zero—just as it is in a zero-lag system. To test this theory an adjoint block diagram of a single-lag optimal guidance system was constructed from Fig. 8.15 and appears in Fig. 8.17. The control gains become C^* because they must be reversed in time according to adjoint theory. The miss sensitivities due to target maneuver MNT and heading error MHE are indicated in the figure.

The FORTRAN listing of the adjoint simulation of the optimal single time constant guidance system with various guidance law options appears in Listing 8.2. We can see from the listing that the parameter APN determines the guidance law used. $APN = 0$ denotes proportional navigation, $APN = 1$ represents augmented proportional navigation, and $APN = 2$ defines optimal guidance.

Figure 8.18 shows the miss sensitivity of all the guidance laws to a 3-g step target maneuver in the presence of a single-lag guidance system with a time constant of 1 s. We can see that the optimal guidance law always yields zero miss distance. Therefore, as predicted, the optimal guidance system is attempting to make the single time constant guidance system appear to be a zero-lag augmented proportional navigation guidance system with an effective navigation ratio of 3. The interested reader is referred to Appendix A to see how the optimal guidance system performs when time to go information is degraded.

Summary

In this chapter we have shown how some advanced guidance laws can be derived both heuristically and mathematically. The method of adjoints was used to show the performance advantages of the more advanced guidance laws. In practice, one must also test the advanced guidance concepts in the presence of parasitic effects to ensure that performance is still better than proportional navigation.[1]

References

[1]Nesline, F. W., and Zarchan, P., "A New Look at Classical Versus Modern Homing Guidance," *Journal of Guidance and Control*, Vol. 4, No. 1, Jan.-Feb. 1981, pp. 78–85.

[2]Bryson, A. E., and Ho, Y. C., *Applied Optimal Control*, Blaisdell, Waltham, MA., 1969.

[3]Cottrell, R. G., "Optimal Intercept Guidance for Short-Range Tactical Missiles," *AIAA Journal,* Vol. 9, July 1971, pp. 1414–1415.

[4]Kliger, I., "A Simple Derivation of Certain Optimal Control Laws," Raytheon, Bedford, MA, Memo SAD-1230, Nov. 1970.

[5]Gelb, A., *Applied Optimal Estimation*, MIT Press, Cambridge, MA, 1974.

Chapter 9

Kalman Filters and the Homing Loop

Introduction

KALMAN filtering concepts can be used in the homing loop to produce an optimal digital noise filter. The filter is considered optimal because the errors in the estimates of the system states are minimized in the least-squares sense. We shall see that, for the filter to be truly optimal, the statistics of the measurement and process noise must be known. If this information is lacking or inaccurate, the filter performance will degrade. However, we shall also see that in homing loop applications the Kalman filter cannot only perform very well with significant errors in the knowledge of the statistics, but it may even be desirable to lie to the filter to achieve a desired filter bandwidth. Finally, we shall demonstrate that when Kalman filtering concepts are used it is possible to apply advanced guidance techniques and substantially improve system performance.

Theoretical Equations[1]

For linear systems Kalman filters can provide optimal estimators in the least-squares sense. To apply Kalman filtering theory, our model of the real world must be described by a matrix differential equation of the form

$$\dot{x} = Fx + Gu + w$$

where x is a column vector describing the states of the system, F the system dynamics matrix, u a known control vector, and w a white noise process. There is a process noise matrix Q that is related to the process noise vector according to

$$Q = E[w\ w^T]$$

In other words, Q is the expectation of the white process noise times its transpose. The filter will be optimal if the measurements available are linearly related to the states according to

$$z = Hx + v$$

where z is the measurement vector, H the measurement matrix, and v the white noise measurement. The measurement noise matrix R is related to the measurement noise vector v according to

$$R = E[v\,v^T]$$

The preceding relationships are valid for continuous systems. Since we are not taking measurements continuously but plan to receive information every T_s seconds, we need to discretize our system model. The fundamental matrix Φ is related to the system dynamics matrix according to

$$\Phi(t) = \mathcal{L}^{-1}\{[sI - F]^{-1}\}$$

where I is the identity matrix and $\mathcal{L}^{-1}$ the inverse Laplace transform. For discrete systems we can say that the discrete transition matrix is given by

$$\Phi_k = \Phi(T_s)$$

where T_s is the sampling time. In other words, the discrete fundamental matrix is simply the continuous fundamental matrix evaluated at the sampling time. The discrete form of the measurement equation is now

$$z_k = Hx_k + v_k$$

and

$$R_k = \sigma_n^2$$

where σ_n^2 is the variance of the measurement noise. The resultant form of the discrete Kalman filter is given by the recursive relationship in matrix form

$$\hat{x}_k = \Phi_k\hat{x}_{k-1} + G_k u_{k-1} + K_k(z_k - H\Phi_k\hat{x}_{k-1} - HG_k u_{k-1})$$

where G_k is obtained from

$$G_k = \int_0^{T_s}\Phi(\tau)G\,\mathrm{d}\tau$$

and K_k represents the Kalman gain matrix. The Kalman gains are computed, while the filter is operating, from the matrix Ricatti equations. The Ricatti equations are a set of recursive matrix equations given by

$$M_k = \Phi_k P_{k-1}\Phi_k^T + Q_k$$

$$K_k = M_k H^T[HM_k H^T + R_k]^{-1}$$

$$P_k = (I - K_k H)M_k$$

where P_k is a covariance matrix representing errors in the state estimates before an update, and M_k the covariance matrix representing errors in the state estimates after an update. The discrete process noise matrix Q_k can be found from the continuous process noise matrix Q and the fundamental matrix according to

$$Q_k = \int_0^{T_s} \Phi(\tau)Q\Phi^T(\tau)\,d\tau$$

In order to start the Ricatti equations we need an initial covariance matrix, P_0. This matrix represents the initial uncertainty in the error in the estimate. Choosing appropriate values for this initial matrix is in itself an art.[1]

Application to Homing Loop

In order to demonstrate the utility of Kalman filtering, let us consider the zero-lag homing loop model of Fig. 9.1. In this guidance system we measure noisy relative position y^* and are attempting to estimate relative position, relative velocity, and target acceleration. In our model the missile acceleration n_c is assumed to be known, and the target acceleration is considered to be modeled as a white noise through an integrator. We have shown in Chapter 4 mathematically that the shaping filter equivalent of a target maneuver with constant amplitude but random starting time (where the starting time is uniformly distributed over the flight time) is white noise through an integrator. According to the results of Chapter 4, the spectral density of this white noise process is given by

$$\Phi_s = n_T^2/t_F$$

where n_T is the maneuver level and t_F the flight time. In Chapter 4 we also showed via a numerical experiment that this model is statistically equivalent to a maneuver of constant amplitude whose starting time is equally likely to occur anywhere during the flight.

We can express the model of Fig. 9.1 in state space form as

$$\begin{bmatrix} \dot{y} \\ \ddot{y} \\ \dot{n}_T \end{bmatrix} = \underbrace{\begin{bmatrix} 0 & 1 & 0 \\ 0 & 0 & 1 \\ 0 & 0 & 0 \end{bmatrix}}_{F} \begin{bmatrix} y \\ \dot{y} \\ n_T \end{bmatrix} + \underbrace{\begin{bmatrix} 0 \\ -1 \\ 0 \end{bmatrix}}_{G} n_c + \underbrace{\begin{bmatrix} 0 \\ 0 \\ u_s \end{bmatrix}}_{w}$$

In the previous section we showed that the fundamental matrix could be found from the system dynamics matrix. After some computation the fun-

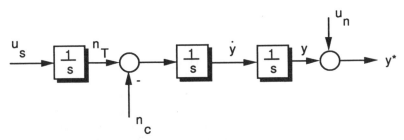

Fig. 9.1 Homing loop model for Kalman filter development.

damental matrix for the model of Fig. 9.1 turns out to be

$$\Phi(t) = \begin{bmatrix} 1 & t & 0.5t^2 \\ 0 & 1 & t \\ 0 & 0 & 1 \end{bmatrix}$$

or in discrete form

$$\Phi_k = \begin{bmatrix} 1 & T_s & 0.5T_s^2 \\ 0 & 1 & T_s \\ 0 & 0 & 1 \end{bmatrix}$$

The measurement equation can also be expressed in discrete form as

$$y_k^* = \underbrace{[100]}_{H} \begin{bmatrix} y_k \\ \dot{y}_k \\ n_{Tk} \end{bmatrix} + u_k$$

where the variance of u_k, known as R_k, is given by σ_n^2. The discrete form of G can be found from

$$G_k = \int_0^{T_s} \Phi(\tau)G(\tau)\, d\tau = \begin{bmatrix} -0.5T_s^2 \\ -T_s \\ 0 \end{bmatrix}$$

The Kalman filter for the model of Fig. 9.1 can now be expressed in matrix form as

$$\begin{bmatrix} \hat{y}_k \\ \hat{\dot{y}}_k \\ \hat{n}_{Tk} \end{bmatrix} = \begin{bmatrix} 1 & T_s & 0.5T_s^2 \\ 0 & 1 & T_s \\ 0 & 0 & 1 \end{bmatrix} \begin{bmatrix} \hat{y}_{k-1} \\ \hat{\dot{y}}_{k-1} \\ \hat{n}_{Tk-1} \end{bmatrix} + \begin{bmatrix} -0.5T_s^2 \\ -T_s \\ 0 \end{bmatrix} n_{c_{k-1}}$$

$$+ \begin{bmatrix} K_1 \\ K_2 \\ K_3 \end{bmatrix} \left[y_k^* - [100] \begin{bmatrix} 1 & T_s & 0.5T_s^2 \\ 0 & 1 & T_s \\ 0 & 0 & 1 \end{bmatrix} \begin{bmatrix} \hat{y}_{k-1} \\ \hat{\dot{y}}_{k-1} \\ \hat{n}_{Tk-1} \end{bmatrix} - [100] \begin{bmatrix} -0.5T_s^2 \\ -T_s \\ 0 \end{bmatrix} n_{c_{k-1}} \right]$$

This Kalman filter is shown in block diagram form as part of the homing loop in Fig. 9.2. In this diagram z^{-1} represents a pure delay so that $z^{-1} y_k$ means y_{k-1}. In our model the measurement of the line-of-sight angle λ_k^* is corrupted by noise. We create a pseudomeasurement of relative position y_k^*

by a multiplication of the line-of-sight angle measurement by our estimate or measurement of the range from missile to target. The Kalman filter then provides optimal estimates of relative position, relative velocity, and target acceleration. In this model we are using proportional navigation guidance where the guidance command is related to the state estimates according to

$$n_{ck}\Big|_{PN} = \frac{N'}{t_{go}^2}\, \hat{y}_k + \frac{N'}{t_{go}}\, \hat{\dot{y}}_k$$

It is easy to show that this command is mathematically equivalent to the more recognizable form of proportional navigation, or

$$n_{ck}\Big|_{PN} = N'V_c\hat{\lambda}$$

Kalman Gains

In order for the Kalman filter to operate, we need to first compute the filter gains, K_k. These gains are obtained from a set of recursive equations known as the matrix Ricatti equations, which were stated in the first section. The first of the Ricatti equations is

$$M_k = \Phi_k P_{k-1} \Phi_k^T + Q_k$$

where M_k represents the covariance matrix of errors in the estimates after updates. For the three-state system of Fig. 9.2, this matrix can be expanded in scalar form by multiplying out the matrices and by recognizing that M_k is symmetric. Substitution of the necessary matrices yields

$$M = \begin{bmatrix} 1 & T_s & 0.5T_s^2 \\ 0 & 1 & T_s \\ 0 & 0 & 1 \end{bmatrix} \begin{bmatrix} P_{11} & P_{12} & P_{13} \\ P_{12} & P_{22} & P_{23} \\ P_{13} & P_{23} & P_{33} \end{bmatrix} \begin{bmatrix} 1 & 0 & 0 \\ T_s & 1 & 0 \\ 0.5T_s^2 & T_s & 1 \end{bmatrix}$$

$$+ \Phi_s \begin{bmatrix} \dfrac{T_s^5}{20} & \dfrac{T_s^4}{8} & \dfrac{T_s^3}{6} \\[2mm] \dfrac{T_s^4}{8} & \dfrac{T_s^3}{3} & \dfrac{T_s^2}{2} \\[2mm] \dfrac{T_s^3}{6} & \dfrac{T_s^2}{2} & T_s \end{bmatrix}$$

The second Ricatti equation is used to obtain the Kalman gains. It appears that from the second Ricatti equation,

$$K_k = M_k H^T [H M_k H^T + R_k]^{-1}$$

that it is necessary to take a matrix inverse. However, for the model of Fig. 9.1, the R_k matrix is 1×1; hence, we can take the scalar inverse by inspec-

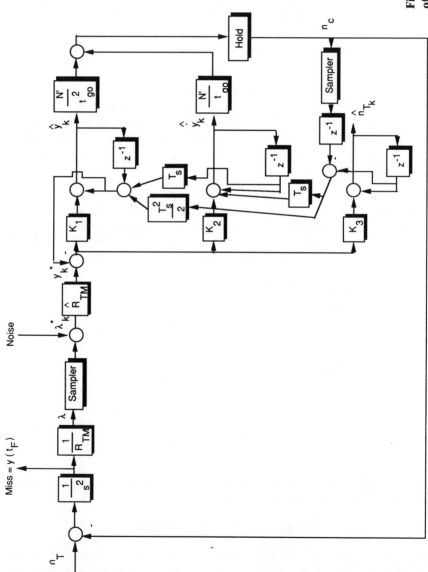

Fig. 9.2 Kalman filter as part of homing loop.

tion and obtain

$$K_1 = \frac{M_{11}}{M_{11} + \sigma_N^2}$$

$$K_2 = \frac{M_{12}}{M_{11} + \sigma_N^2}$$

$$K_3 = \frac{M_{13}}{M_{11} + \sigma_N^2}$$

Finally, the third Ricatti equation is used to obtain the covariance matrix of the errors in the estimates before an update. The third equation,

$$P_k = (I - K_k H) M_k$$

can easily be expanded to

$$P = \begin{bmatrix} (1 - K_1)M_{11} & (1 - K_1)M_{12} & (1 - K_1)M_{13} \\ -K_2 M_{11} + M_{12} & -K_2 M_{12} + M_{22} & -K_2 M_{13} + M_{23} \\ -K_3 M_{11} + M_{13} & -K_3 M_{12} + M_{23} & -K_3 M_{13} + M_{33} \end{bmatrix}$$

Numerical Examples

In order to start the Ricatti equations we need an initial covariance matrix P_0. A particularly useful form for the homing loop model considered is

$$P_0 = \begin{bmatrix} \sigma_{noise}^2 & 0 & 0 \\ 0 & \left[\dfrac{V_M HE}{57.3} \right]^2 & 0 \\ 0 & 0 & n_T^2 \end{bmatrix}$$

where only diagonal elements are used. The initial value of the error in the estimate of position is simply the variance of the measurement noise. The initial guess in the velocity error estimate is related to missile velocity and the expected heading error. Finally, our initial value in the uncertainty in target acceleration is represented by the magnitude of the maximum possible acceleration. This is by no means the only way to initialize the covariance matrix, but it is not bad.

Listing 9.1 presents a FORTRAN listing of a program used to solve the Ricatti equations recursively for the Kalman gains. In this program it is assumed that the angular measurement noise is 1 milliradian (mr). This noise must be converted to a positional noise by the multiplication of range. The process noise model is considered to be a target maneuver of amplitude 3 g, with starting time that is uniformly distributed over the 10-s flight time. We can see from the listing that the Ricatti equations have been expanded to scalar form and that the symmetry property of the Ricatti equations has been exploited.

Listing 9.1   Listing of FORTRAN program to solve Ricatti equations

```
        REAL M11,M12,M13,M22,M23,M33,K1,K2,K3
        VC = 4000.
        XNT = 96.6
        VM = 3000.
        HEDEG = 20.
        SIGRIN = .001
        TS = .1
        TF = 10.
        TS2 = TS*TS
        TS3 = TS2*TS
        TS4 = TS3*TS
        TS5 = TS4*TS
        PHIN = XNT*XNT/TF
        RTM = VC*TF
        SIGNOISE = SQRT(SIGRIN**2 + (SIGGL/RTM)**2)
        SIGPOS = RTM*SIGNOISE
        SIGN2 = SIGPOS**2
        P11 = SIGN2
        P12 = 0.
        P13 = 0.
        P22 = (VM*HEDEG/57.3)**2
        P23 = 0.
        P33 = XNT*XNT
        T = 0.
        H = .01
        S = 0.
10      IF(T > (TF - .0001))GOTO 999
        TGO = TF - T + .000001
        RTM = VC*TGO
        SIGNOISE = SIGRIN
        SIGPOS = RTM*SIGNOISE
        SIGN2 = SIGPOS**2
        M11 = P11 + TS*P12 + .5*TS2*P13 + TS*(P12 + TS*P22 + .5*TS2*P23)
        M11 = M11 + .5*TS2*(P13 + TS*P23 + .5*TS2*P33) + TS5*PHIN/20.
        M12 = P12 + TS*P22 + .5*TS2*P23 + TS*(P13 + TS*P23 + .5*TS2*P33) + TS4*PHIN/8.
        M13 = P13 + TS*P23 + .5*TS2*P33 + PHIN*TS3/6.
        M22 = P22 + TS*P23 + TS*(P23 + TS*P33) + PHIN*TS3/3.
        M23 = P23 + TS*P33 + .5*TS2*PHIN
        M33 = P33 + PHIN*TS
        K1 = M11/(M11 + SIGN2)
        K2 = M12/(M11 + SIGN2)
        K3 = M13/(M11 + SIGN2)
        P11 = (1. - K1)*M11
        P12 = (1. - K1)*M12
        P13 = (1. - K1)*M13
        P22 = - K2*M12 + M22
        P23 = - K2*M13 + M23
        P33 = - K3*M13 + M33
        WRITE(9,*)T,K1,K2,K3
        T = T + TS
        GOTO 10
999     CONTINUE
        WRITE(9,*)T,K1,K2,K3
        PAUSE
        END
```

Figure 9.3 displays the three Kalman gain profiles resulting from solving the Ricatti equations with initial conditions as shown in Listing 9.1. We can see that, unlike the constant-gain digital fading memory filter, the Kalman filter has time-varying gains. After an initial transient period, the gains appear to be monotonically increasing. This means that, after awhile, the filter bandwidth is continually increasing.

In order to see how the filter is performing, we must not only look at the filter gains but must also investigate the accuracy of the various state estimates. The covariance matrix has information on the accuracy of the state estimates if the filter's model of the real world is accurate. If the filter model

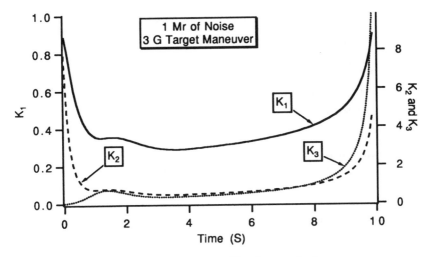

Fig. 9.3   Kalman gain profiles for nominal case.

is not matched to the real world, then the performance projections offered by the covariance matrix are not particularly useful. One way of getting more meaningful performance projections is by placing the three-state Kalman filter in the homing loop.

Listing 9.2 presents an engagement simulation, based on the model of Fig. 9.2, with the three-state Kalman filter included. In the nominal case we are not using the estimate of the target acceleration for guidance purposes. A careful examination of the listing shows that the simulation is divided into a continuous and discrete part. In the continuous section we are integrating the differential equations for the relative velocity and acceleration using the second-order Runge-Kutta numerical integration technique. In the discrete section we are solving the Ricatti equations for the Kalman gains and using the recursive Kalman filter to generate state estimates. We go to the continuous section every integration interval H, and we go to the discrete section every sampling interval T_s. For the simulation to work properly, T_s/H must be an integer.

Figure 9.4 shows that in the nominal case the Kalman filter accurately estimates the 3-g target maneuver after about 3 s. This is consistent with Fig. 9.3, which also shows that it takes about 3 s for the Kalman gains to go through their initial transient period. Note that, after about 5 s, the error in the estimate of target acceleration has been stabilized and is quite small, as shown in Fig. 9.4. The filter's internal prediction of how well it is estimating target acceleration can be found by taking the square root of the third diagonal element in the covariance matrix. Figure 9.5 shows that the single flight errors in the estimate of target acceleration agrees with the covariance matrix predictions in the sense that it is within the theoretical bounds approximately 68% of the time.

Thus far the filter knows the truth about the real world in the sense that it knows the measurement and process noise statistics exactly. In practice, since these statistics are never known a priori, one adjusts the bandwidth of

Listing 9.2　Listing of Kalman filter in homing loop

```
        REAL M11,M12,M13,M22,M23,M33,K1,K2,K3
        VC = 4000.
        XNT = 96.6
        YIC = 0.
        VM = 3000.
        HEDEG = 0.
        HEDEGFIL = 20.
        XNP = 3.
        SIGRIN = .001
        TS = .1
        APN = 0.
        TF = 10.
        Y = YIC
        YD = - VM*HEDEG/57.3
        YDIC = YD
        TS2 = TS*TS
        TS3 = TS2*TS
        TS4 = TS3*TS
        TS5 = TS4*TS
        PHIN = XNT*XNT/TF
        RTM = VC*TF
        SIGNOISE = SIGRIN
        SIGPOS = RTM*SIGNOISE
        SIGN2 = SIGPOS**2
        P11 = SIGN2
        P12 = 0.
        P13 = 0.
        P22 = (VM*HEDEGFIL/57.3)**2
        P23 = 0.
        P33 = XNT*XNT
        T = 0.
        H = .01
        S = 0.
        YH = 0.
        YDH = 0.
        XNTH = 0.
        XNC = 0.
10      IF(T > (TF - .0001))GOTO 999
        YOLD = Y
        YDOLD = YD
        STEP = 1
        GOTO 200
66      STEP = 2
        Y = Y + H*YD
        YD = YD + H*YDD
        T = T + H
        GOTO 200
55      CONTINUE
        Y = .5*(YOLD + Y + H*YD)
        YD = .5*(YDOLD + YD + H*YDD)
        S = S + H
C       COLLECT DATA PERIODICALLY
        IF(S < (TS - .0001))GOTO 10
        S = 0.
        TGO = TF - T + .000001
        RTM = VC*TGO
        SIGNOISE = SIGRIN
        SIGPOS = RTM*SIGNOISE
        SIGN2 = SIGPOS**2
        M11 = P11 + TS*P12 + .5*TS2*P13 + TS*(P12 + TS*P22 + .5*TS2*P23)
        M11 = M11 + .5*TS2*(P13 + TS*P23 + .5*TS2*P33) + TS5*PHIN/20.
        M12 = P12 + TS*P22 + .5*TS2*P23 + TS*(P13 + TS*P23 + .5*TS2*P33) + TS4*PHIN/8.
        M13 = P13 + TS*P23 + .5*TS2*P33 + PHIN*TS3/6.
        M22 = P22 + TS*P23 + TS*(P23 + TS*P33) + PHIN*TS3/3.
        M23 = P23 + TS*P33 + .5*TS2*PHIN
        M33 = P33 + PHIN*TS
        K1 = M11/(M11 + SIGN2)
        K2 = M12/(M11 + SIGN2)
        K3 = M13/(M11 + SIGN2)
        P11 = (1. - K1)*M11
        P12 = (1. - K1)*M12
        P13 = (1. - K1)*M13
        P22 = - K2*M12 + M22
```

(Listing 9.2 continued on next page.)

Listing 9.2 (cont.) Listing of Kalman filter in homing loop

```
          P23 = − K2*M13 + M23
          P33 = − K3*M13 + M33
          CALL GAUSS(XLAMNOISE,SIGNOISE)
          YSTAR = RTM*(XLAM + XLAMNOISE)
          RES = YSTAR − YH − TS*YDH − .5*TS*TS*(XNTH − XNC)
          YH = K1*RES + YH + TS*YDH + .5*TS*TS*(XNTH − XNC)
          YDH = K2*RES + YDH + TS*(XNTH − XNC)
          XNTH = K3*RES + XNTH
          XLAMDH = (YH + YDH*TGO)/(VC*TGO*TGO)
          XNC = XNP*VC*XLAMDH + APN*.5*XNP*XNTH
          ERRNT = XNT − XNTH
          SP33 = SQRT(P33)
          SP33P = − SP33
          WRITE(9,*)T,Y,XNC,XNT,XNTH,ERRNT,SP33,SP33P
          GOTO 10
200       CONTINUE
          TGO = TF − T + .00001
          RTM = VC*TGO
          XLAM = Y/(VC*TGO)
          XLAMD = (RTM*YD + Y*VC)/(RTM**2)
          YDD = XNT − XNC
          IF(STEP − 1)66,66,55
999       CONTINUE
          PAUSE
          END

          SUBROUTINE GAUSS(X,SIG)
          INTEGER RANDOM,SUM
          INTEGER*4 TOOLBX
          PARAMETER (RANDOM = Z'86140000')
          SUM = 0
          DO 14 J = 1,6
          IRAN = TOOLBX(RANDOM)
          SUM = SUM + IRAN
14        CONTINUE
          X = SUM/65536.
          X = 1.414*X*SIG
          RETURN
          END
```

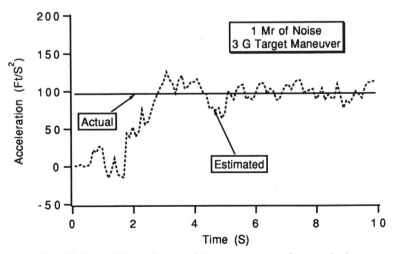

Fig. 9.4 Kalman filter estimate of target maneuver for nominal case.

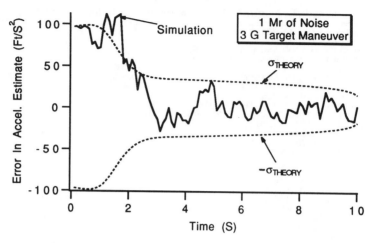

Fig. 9.5   Kalman filter prediciton of performance is excellent.

the filter to a desirable level based on other considerations. For example, if we tell the filter that there is 10 mr of angle noise rather than 1 mr, the first Kalman gain value is approximately halved, as shown in Fig. 9.6. Since the filter gain is decreasing, the filter bandwidth must also be decreasing. This means that, when the filter thinks there is more measurement noise, it does more filtering or slows down (lower bandwidth).

An experiment was conducted to illustrate the impact that filter bandwidth has on the resultant estimate. In this experiment the actual noise level was kept at 1 mr, whereas the filter estimate of the measurement noise statistics was changed from 1 mr (matched case, filter assumption correct) to 10 mr (mismatched case, filter assumption wrong). Figure 9.7 shows that when the filter is matched its estimate of target maneuver becomes very good at about 3 s. If the filter thinks there is 10 mr of measurement noise, it takes about 6 s for the filter estimates to become very good. Thus, telling the filter that there is more measurement noise (even if there is not) is a practical way of making the filter more sluggish or decreasing its bandwidth.

If we tell the filter that there is either 1 mr or 10 mr of measurement noise but actually turn the real measurement noise off, we have a deterministic case. We can then make flight time a parameter for the case in which there is a 3-g target maneuver and evaluate system miss distance caused by the target maneuver. Figure 9.8 shows that the faster system ($\sigma = 1$ mr) has less miss distance induced by target maneuver than the slower system ($\sigma = 10$ mr). However, in both cases we can see that the guidance system time constant must be very small since the miss distance sensitivity to target maneuver is small and rapidly approaches zero.

If we run our simulation with measurement noise only ($\sigma = 1$ mr and no target maneuver), we must operate in the Monte Carlo mode. Fifty-run Monte Carlo sets were made for 20 different values of flight time for a total of 1000 runs. Figure 9.9 shows how the standard deviation of the noise-

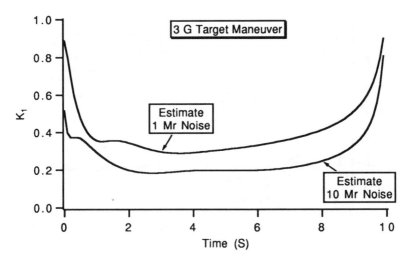

Fig. 9.6   Increasing measurement noise estimate decreases Kalman gain.

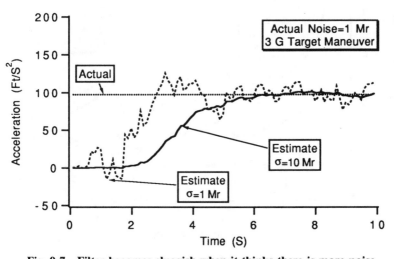

Fig. 9.7   Filter becomes sluggish when it thinks there is more noise.

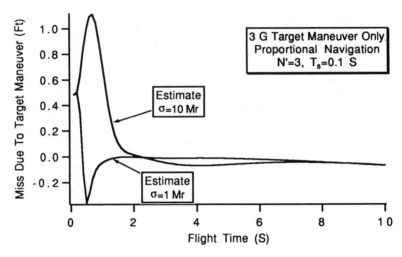

Fig. 9.8   Kalman filter guidance system has small sensitivity to target maneuver.

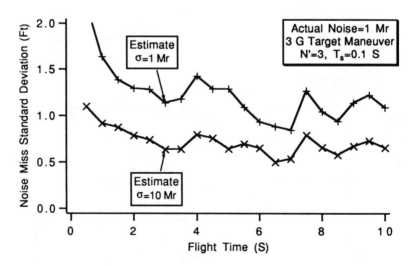

Fig. 9.9   Decreasing filter bandwidth decreases noise-induced miss.

induced miss varies with flight time for a case in which the filter is optimal ($\sigma = 1$ mr) and one in which the filter bandwidth has been intentionally decreased ($\sigma = 10$ mr). We can see from Fig. 9.9 that decreasing the filter bandwidth (telling the filter that there is more measurement noise) decreases the system miss distance due to the actual measurement noise (1 mr). This behavior is opposite to that of the two-state digital fading memory filter (see Fig. 7.19) in which decreasing the filter bandwidth always appeared to increase miss distance! Of course, the constant gain digital fading memory filter bandwidth was fixed, whereas the Kalman filter bandwidth is time-varying. By comparing Figs. 9.8 and 9.9 we can see that the guidance system designer has a juggling act. Increasing the filter bandwidth reduces the miss due to target maneuver while increasing the miss due to noise. The optimal practical filter bandwidth is dependent on the levels of the input disturbances.

The sampling time can also have a profound effect on filtering properties and system performance. Figure 9.10 shows that increasing the sampling time T_s from 0.1 s to 0.5 s (or decreasing sampling rate from 10 Hz to 2 Hz) increases the Kalman gain. We saw from Chapter 7 on digital fading memory filters that decreasing the sampling rate tends to decrease the total system bandwidth. Thus, the Kalman filter is attempting to increase its bandwidth to compensate for the decrease in system bandwidth due to sampling at a lower rate.

Figure 9.11 shows that the filter estimate of target acceleration for both sampling times is about the same. This means that the filter has successfully compensated for the effective decrease in system bandwidth due to a decrease in the sampling rate.

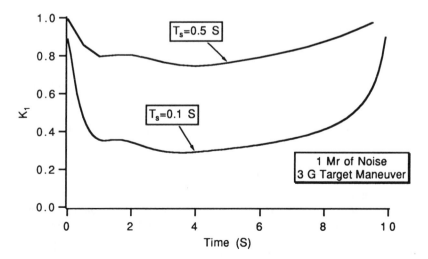

Fig. 9.10   Kalman gain increases with decreasing sampling rate.

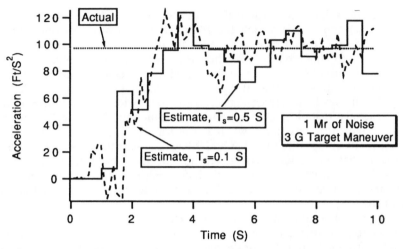

Fig. 9.11   Kalman filter bandwidth appears to be independent of sampling rate.

Although Kalman filter performance appears to be approximately independent of sampling rate, system performance is not! If we remove the actual measurement noise from the simulation and run with target maneuver only for different flight times, we can generate miss distance curves. Figure 9.12 shows how the target-maneuver-induced miss varies with the sampling rate. We can see that the miss for $T_s = 0.5$ s is much greater than the miss for $T_s = 0.1$ s for flight times less than 2 s.

The simulation was also run with measurement noise only in the Monte Carlo mode. Figure 9.13 shows that decreasing the sampling rate also increases the measurement-noise-induced miss. Generally, hardware costs increase with higher sampling rates. Therefore, an important job of the guidance system designer is to set a limit on the sampling rate to get both acceptable cost and adequate performance.

It is important to note that in the preceding experiment the noise standard deviation remained constant when the data rate changed. In many systems the noise spectral density remains constant and so the noise standard deviation must change as the data rate changes. The interested reader is referred to Appendix A for a more complete discussion of this topic.

Experiments With Optimal Guidance[2]

In Chapter 8 we derived an optimal guidance law that attempted to cancel out the guidance system dynamics and, in addition, we relaxed the missile acceleration requirements. In this section we will show how an optimal guidance system might be implemented and provide a numerical example to illustrate how such a system might perform in the presence of measurement noise.

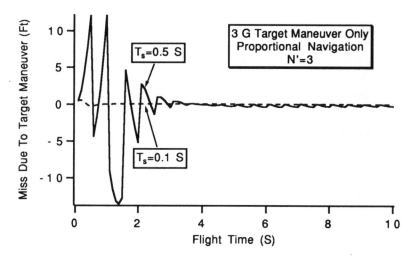

Fig. 9.12   Target maneuver miss increases with decreasing sampling rate.

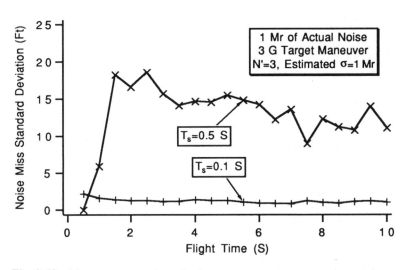

Fig. 9.13   Measurement noise miss increases with decreasing sampling rate.

Listing 9.3   Monte Carlo engagement simulation to test optimal guidance

```
        DIMENSION Z(1000)
        INTEGER RUN,APN
        REAL M11,M12,M13,M22,M23,M33,K1,K2,K3
        VC = 4000.
        XNT = 96.6
        YIC = 0.
        VM = 3000.
        HEDEG = 20.
        XNP = 3.
        SIGNOISE = .001
        TS = .1
        TAU = .5
        NOISE = 1
        RUN = 50
        APN = 0
        XLIM = 999999.
106     CONTINUE
        DO 60 TF = .5,10,.5
        Z1 = 0.
        DO 20 I = 1,RUN
        Y = YIC
        YD = 0.
        YDIC = YD
        TS2 = TS*TS
        TS3 = TS2*TS
        TS4 = TS3*TS
        TS5 = TS4*TS
        PHIN = XNT*XNT/TF
        RTM = VC*TF
        SIGPOS = RTM*SIGNOISE
        SIGN2 = SIGPOS**2
        P11 = SIGN2
        P12 = 0.
        P13 = 0.
        P22 = (VM*HEDEG/57.3)**2
        P23 = 0.
        P33 = XNT*XNT
        T = 0.
        H = .01
        S = 0.
        YH = 0.
        YDH = 0.
        XNTH = 0.
        XNC = 0.
        XNL = 0.
10      IF(T > (TF − .0001))GOTO 999
        YOLD = Y
        YDOLD = YD
        XNLOLD = XNL
        STEP = 1
        GOTO 200
66      STEP = 2
        Y = Y + H*YD
        YD = YD + H*YDD
        XNL = XNL + H*XNLD
        T = T + H
        GOTO 200
55      CONTINUE
        Y = .5*(YOLD + Y + H*YD)
        YD = .5*(YDOLD + YD + H*YDD)
        XNL = .5*(XNLOLD + XNL + H*XNLD)
        S = S + H
        IF(S < (TS − .0001))GOTO 10
        S = 0.
        TGO = TF − T + .000001
        RTM = VC*TGO
        SIGPOS = RTM*SIGNOISE
        SIGN2 = SIGPOS**2
        M11 = P11 + TS*P12 + .5*TS2*P13 + TS*(P12 + TS*P22 + .5*TS2*P23)
        M11 = M11 + .5*TS2*(P13 + TS*P23 + .5*TS2*P33) + TS5*PHIN/20.
        M12 = P12 + TS*P22 + .5*TS2*P23 + TS*(P13 + TS*P23 + .5*TS2*P33) + TS4*PHIN/8.
        M13 = P13 + TS*P23 + .5*TS2*P33 + PHIN*TS3/6.
        M22 = P22 + TS*P23 + TS*(P23 + TS*P33) + PHIN*TS3/3.
```

(Listing 9.3 continued on next page.)

```
          M23 = P23 + TS*P33 + .5*TS2*PHIN
          M33 = P33 + PHIN*TS
          K1 = M11/(M11 + SIGN2)
          K2 = M12/(M11 + SIGN2)
          K3 = M13/(M11 + SIGN2)
          P11 = (1. - K1)*M11
          P12 = (1. - K1)*M12
          P13 = (1. - K1)*M13
          P22 = - K2*M12 + M22
          P23 = - K2*M13 + M23
          P33 = - K3*M13 + M33
          IF(NOISE = 1)THEN
              CALL GAUSS(XLAMNOISE,SIGNOISE)
          ELSE
              XLAMNOISE = 0.
          ENDIF
          YSTAR = RTM*(XLAM + XLAMNOISE)
          RES = YSTAR - YH - TS*YDH - .5*TS*TS*(XNTH - XNL)
          YH = K1*RES + YH + TS*YDH + .5*TS*TS*(XNTH - XNL)
          YDH = K2*RES + YDH + TS*(XNTH - XNL)
          XNTH = K3*RES + XNTH
          XLAMDH = (YH + YDH*TGO)/(VC*TGO*TGO)
          IF(APN = 0)THEN
              XNC = XNP*VC*XLAMDH
          ELSEIF(APN = 1)THEN
              XNC = XNP*VC*XLAMDH + APN*.5*XNP*XNTH
          ELSE
              X = TGO/TAU
              TOP = 6.*X*X*(EXP(- X) - 1. + X)
              BOT1 = 2*X*X*X + 3. + 6.*X - 6.*X*X
              BOT2 = - 12.*X*EXP(- X) - 3.*EXP(- 2.*X)
              XNPP = TOP/(.0001 + BOT1 + BOT2)
              XNEW = XNPP*XNL*(EXP(- X) + X - 1.)/(X*X)
              XNC = XNPP*VC*XLAMDH + .5*XNPP*XNTH - XNEW
          ENDIF
          IF(XNC > XLIM)XNC = XLIM
          IF(XNC < - XLIM)XNC = - XLIM
          GOTO 10
200       CONTINUE
          TGO = TF - T + .00001
          RTM = VC*TGO
          XLAM = Y/(VC*TGO)
          XLAMD = (RTM*YD + Y*VC)/(RTM**2)
          XNLD = (XNC - XNL)/TAU
          YDD = XNT - XNL
          IF(STEP - 1)66,66,55
999       CONTINUE
          Z(I) = Y
          Z1 = Z(I) + Z1
          XMEAN = Z1/I
20        CONTINUE
          SIGMA = 0.
          Z1 = 0.
          DO 50 I = 1,RUN
          Z1 = (Z(I) - XMEAN)**2 + Z1
          IF(I = 1)THEN
              SIGMA = 0.
          ELSE
              SIGMA = SQRT(Z1/(I - 1))
          ENDIF
50        CONTINUE
          WRITE(9,*)TF,SIGMA,XMEAN
60        CONTINUE
          PAUSE
          END
          SUBROUTINE GAUSS(X,SIG)
          INTEGER RANDOM,SUM
          INTEGER*4 TOOLBX
          PARAMETER (RANDOM = Z'86140000')
          SUM = 0
          DO 14 J = 1,6
          IRAN = TOOLBX(RANDOM)
          SUM = SUM + IRAN
14        CONTINUE
          X = SUM/65536.
          X = 1.414*X*SIG
          RETURN
          END
```

Listing 9.3 presents a FORTRAN Monte Carlo simulation of an optimal guidance system with a three-state digital Kalman filter and a single-lag representation of the flight control system. The filter structure is identical to the one shown if Fig. 9.2, except that the achieved missile acceleration n_L rather than the commanded acceleration n_c is fed back into the filter. The filter estimates relative position and velocity, which can be converted into a line-of-sight rate estimate as shown in the listing. In addition, the filter estimates the target maneuver level. The achieved missile acceleration is assumed to be known perfectly. This quantity is fed into the filter and, in addition, is used as part of an optimal guidance law as was discussed in Chapter 8 and can be seen in Listing 9.3.

A 50-run Monte Carlo set was made with the engagement model of Listing 9.3. In the nominal case the flight control system time constant was set to 0.5 s, the effective navigation ratio was 3, and the sampling time was 0.1 s. The nominal error disturbances, as can be seen from Listing 9.3, consist of 1 mr of measurement noise and a constant 3-g target maneuver occurring at the beginning of flight. Figures 9.14 and 9.15 show 50-run Monte Carlo results for the standard deviation and mean miss distances for this case as a function of the flight time. Both figures show results for proportional navigation ($APN = 0$) and an optimal guidance law ($APN = 2$). Since there is one random disturbance and one deterministic disturbance, we can interpret the standard deviation of the miss to be the noise-induced miss and the mean of the miss to be the target-maneuver-induced miss. Both figures clearly show that, for the case in which the guidance time constant is 0.5 s, optimal guidance yields smaller miss distances, even in the presence of measurement noise errors. The differences between the guidance laws is greatest for the smaller flight times. If the ratio of the flight time to the

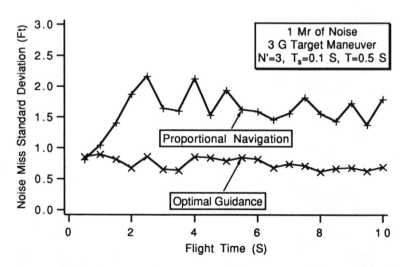

Fig. 9.14 Optimal guidance yields smaller noise-induced miss in presence of large guidance system time constant.

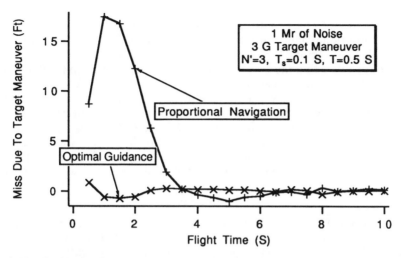

Fig. 9.15 Optimal guidance yields smaller target-maneuver-induced miss in presence of large guidance system time constant.

guidance system time constant is large, proportional navigation is known to be an effective guidance law. Thus, the optimal guidance law, discussed in a deterministic setting in Chapter 8, can be implemented and made to work successfully in a more realistic setting. Optimal guidance is yielding superior performance to proportional navigation because it is attempting to cancel out dynamically the flight control system time constant. We can see from both figures that optimal guidance performance, unlike that of proportional navigation, is approximately independent of flight time.

Another performance advantage of optimal guidance is that it is supposed to relax the missile acceleration requirements. The previous case was rerun

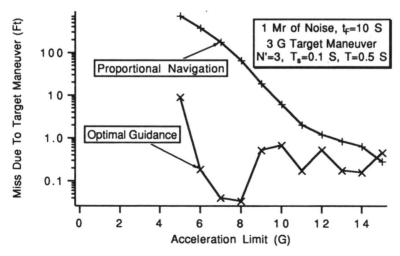

Fig. 9.16 Optimal guidance reduces missile acceleration requirements.

for a 10-s flight. This flight time was chosen because the performance of both proportional navigation and optimal guidance is about the same, from a miss distance point of view, as can be seen from Figs. 9.14 and 9.15. The reason for this is that the 10-s flight time is large compared to the 0.5-s flight control system time constant. However, in the new case to be run the engagement simulation was made nonlinear in the sense that missile acceleration saturation effects were included. The missile commanded acceleration limit was made a parameter in the study. Figure 9.16 displays the mean miss distance vs the acceleration limit for a case in which there was a 3-g target maneuver and 1 mr of measurement noise. We can see from the figure that the acceleration requirements for optimal guidance are clearly relaxed.

Summary

In this chapter we have shown how both Kalman filtering and optimal guidance concepts could be applied to a missile guidance system. It was shown, via a numerical example, that when these concepts were applied there were substantial performance benefits and a relaxing of missile acceleration requirements. However, range and time to go information must be available for Kalman filtering and optimal guidance to work. If the required information is lacking or inaccurate, the performance of this type of guidance system may degrade to the point where its performance is worse than that of a conventional proportional navigation guidance system.[2]

References

[1]Gelb, A., *Applied Optimal Estimation,* MIT Press, Cambridge, MA, 1974.
[2]Nesline, F. W., and Zarchan, P., "A New Look at Classical Versus Modern Homing Guidance," *Journal of Guidance and Control,* Vol. 4, Jan.-Feb. 1981, pp. 78–85.

Chapter 10

Other Forms of Tactical Guidance

Introduction

THUS far we have studied proportional navigation type homing guidance systems. In this type of guidance system the missile seeker provides the information required for guidance by receiving energy reflected from the target (i.e., radar signal). The virtue of homing guidance is that measurement accuracy is continually improving because the missile (and its seeker) is getting closer to the target as the flight progresses.

With command guidance a missile seeker is not required. A source that is external to the missile both transmits and receives the energy (i.e., radar signal). One limitation of command guidance is that, as intercepts take place further away from the energy source, measurement accuracy and hence guidance accuracy degrade. Another limitation of command guidance is that the external energy source must illuminate the target often enough (i.e., high data rate) to make guidance effective. This means that the energy source can only service a few targets simultaneously in a command guidance implementation.

In this chapter we shall discuss three types of command guidance systems: proportional navigation command guidance, beam rider guidance, and command to line-of-sight guidance. The reasons for implementing these systems have more to do with cost, ease of implementation, and lack of susceptibility to countermeasures rather than performance benefits. However, the guidance features of these systems will be compared via numerical examples.

Proportional Navigation Command Guidance[1]

Figure 10.1 shows the basic geometry involved in a proportional navigation command guidance system. The energy source and receiver (a radar application in this example), which are collocated, track both the missile and target. For radar applications we can assume that measurements of both angle and range, with respect to the radar, of both the missile and target are available. In the notation of Fig. 10.1, we have missile measurements of R_M and θ_M and target measurements of R_T and θ_T.

In order to implement proportional navigation guidance in the command guidance system of Fig. 10.1, we must first derive line-of-sight angle λ information from the measurements available. In order to do this we must first recognize that

$$\tan\theta_T = R_{T2}/R_{T1}$$

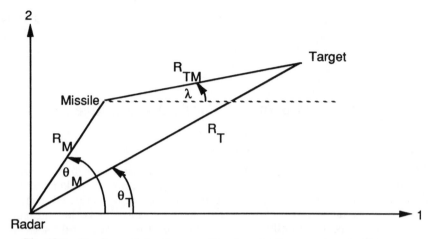

Fig. 10.1   Fundamentals of proportional navigation command guidance.

Since R_T and θ_T are measured, we can express the inertial components of the distance from the radar to the target as

$$R_{T1} = R_T \cos\theta_T$$

$$R_{T2} = R_T \sin\theta_T$$

In a similar way we can express the components of the range from the radar to the missile by first recognizing that

$$\tan\theta_M = R_{M2}/R_{M1}$$

and then expressing the inertial components of the range from the energy source to the missile in terms of the measurements as

$$R_{M1} = R_M \cos\theta_M$$

$$R_{M2} = R_M \sin\theta_M$$

We can now find the relative missile-target range inertial components from

$$R_{TM1} = R_{T1} - R_{M1}$$

$$R_{TM2} = R_{T2} - R_{M2}$$

Finally, the line-of-sight angle can be expressed in terms of the relative range components as

$$\lambda = \tan^{-1}(R_{TM2}/R_{TM1})$$

In order to develop the line-of-sight rate signal required for proportional navigation, we must take the derivative of the line-of-sight angle via a digital filter. In order to illustrate a possible implementation of proportional navigation command guidance, via simulation, a model is postulated. In this hypothetical model the missile states are known perfectly (i.e., retroreflector on missile), and the range from the energy source to the target is also known perfectly. In this example the measurement of the target angle is corrupted by 1 milliradian (mr) of noise.

An effective line-of-sight rate is reconstructed from the angular measurement according to the previously developed relationships in this section in order to derive a pseudomeasurement of the line-of-sight angle. A two-state digital fading memory filter is used to get an estimate of the line-of-sight rate from the pseudomeasurement. The line-of-sight rate estimate is used to implement a proportional navigation guidance law. A FORTRAN command guidance simulation, using the previously discussed concepts, appears in Listing 10.1.

The command guidance simulation was run with 1 mr of noise on the measurement of the target angle. Figure 10.2 presents the line-of-sight rate estimate generated by the digital fading memory filter ($\beta = 0.8$). Superimposed on the figure are homing guidance results for the same example. We can see from Fig. 10.2 that the noise transmission appears to be approximately the same for both command and homing guidance for most of the flight. However, toward the end of the flight there is a dramatic increase in the noise transmission of the command guidance system.

In order to explain why command guidance appears to have excessive noise transmission when compared to homing guidance, it is necessary to develop an analytical model. For analysis and understanding a linearized model of a command guidance system will be developed. The linearization will be accomplished by using small-angle approximations when possible.

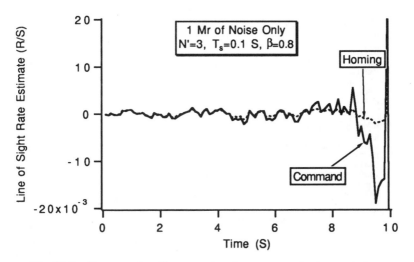

Fig. 10.2   Command guidance system has more noise transmission.

Listing 10.1   Proportional navigation command guidance simulation

```
           VM = 3000.
           VT = 1000.
           XNT = 0.
           RM1IC = 0.
           RM2IC = 10000.
           RT1IC = 40000.
           RT2IC = 10000.
           HEDEG = 0.
           XNP = 3.
           BETA = .8
           TS = .1
           SIGNOISE = .001
           NOISE = 1
           RT1 = RT1IC
           RT2 = RT2IC
           RM1 = RM1IC
           RM2 = RM2IC
           BETAT = 0.
           VT1 = - VT*COS(BETAT)
           VT2 = VT*SIN(BETAT)
           HE = HEDEG/57.3
           GFILTER = 1. - BETA**2
           HFILTER = (1. - BETA)**2
           XLAMH = 0.
           XLAMDH = 0.
           XNC = 0.
           T = 0.
           S = 0.
           RTM1 = RT1 - RM1
           RTM2 = RT2 - RM2
           RTM = SQRT(RTM1**2 + RTM2**2)
           XLAM = ATAN2(RTM2,RTM1)
           XLEAD = ASIN(VT*SIN(BETAT + XLAM)/VM)
           THET = XLAM + XLEAD
           VM1 = VM*COS(THET + HE)
           VM2 = VM*SIN(THET + HE)
           VTM1 = VT1 - VM1
           VTM2 = VT2 - VM2
           VC = - (RTM1*VTM1 + RTM2*VTM2)/RTM
   10      IF(VC<0.)GOTO 999
           IF(RTM<1000.)THEN
               H = .0002
           ELSE
               H = .01
           ENDIF
           BETATOLD = BETAT
           RT1OLD = RT1
           RT2OLD = RT2
           RM1OLD = RM1
           RM2OLD = RM2
           VM1OLD = VM1
           VM2OLD = VM2
           STEP = 1
           GOTO 200
   66      STEP = 2
           BETAT = BETAT + H*BETATD
           RT1 = RT1 + H*VT1
           RT2 = RT2 + H*VT2
           RM1 = RM1 + H*VM1
           RM2 = RM2 + H*VM2
           VM1 = VM1 + H*AM1
           VM2 = VM2 + H*AM2
           T = T + H
           GOTO 200
   55      CONTINUE
           BETAT = .5*(BETATOLD + BETAT + H*BETATD)
           RT1 = .5*(RT1OLD + RT1 + H*VT1)
```

(Listing 10.1 continued on next page.)

Listing 10.1   (cont.) Proportional navigation command guidance simulation

```
        RT2 = .5*(RT2OLD + RT2 + H*VT2)
        RM1 = .5*(RM1OLD + RM1 + H*VM1)
        RM2 = .5*(RM2OLD + RM2 + H*VM2)
        VM1 = .5*(VM1OLD + VM1 + H*AM1)
        VM2 = .5*(VM2OLD + VM2 + H*AM2)
        S = S + H
        IF(S<(TS − .0001))GOTO 10
        S = 0.
        IF(NOISE = 1)THEN
            CALL GAUSS(XLAMNOISE,SIGNOISE)
        ELSE
            THETTNOISE = 0.
        ENDIF
        THETTM = THETT + THETTNOISE
        THETMM = THETM
        RT1M = RT*COS(THETTM)
        RT2M = RT*SIN(THETTM)
        RM1M = RM*COS(THETMM)
        RM2M = RM*SIN(THETMM)
        XLAMM = ATAN2(RT2M − RM2M,RT1M − RM1M)
        RES = XLAMM − (XLAMH + TS*XLAMDH)
        XLAMH = GFILTER*RES + XLAMH + TS*XLAMDH
        XLAMDH = HFILTER*RES/TS + XLAMDH
        XNC = XNP*VC*XLAMDH
        RT1KM = RT1/3280.
        RT2KM = RT2/3280.
        RM1KM = RM1/3280.
        RM2KM = RM2/3280.
        WRITE(9,*)T,XLAMD,XLAMDH,XNC,RTM
        GOTO 10
200     CONTINUE
        THETT = ATAN2(RT2,RT1)
        THETM = ATAN2(RM2,RM1 + .001)
        RT = SQRT(RT1**2 + RT2**2)
        RM = SQRT(RM1**2 + RM2**2)
        RTM1 = RT1 − RM1
        RTM2 = RT2 − RM2
        RTM = SQRT(RTM1**2 + RTM2**2)
        VTM1 = VT1 − VM1
        VTM2 = VT2 − VM2
        VC = − (RTM1*VTM1 + RTM2*VTM2)/RTM
        XLAM = ATAN2(RTM2,RTM1)
        XLAMD = (RTM1*VTM2 − RTM2*VTM1)/(RTM*RTM)
        XNC = XNP*VC* XLAMDH
        AM1 = − XNC*SIN(XLAM)
        AM2 = XNC*COS(XLAM)
        VT1 = − VT*COS(BETAT)
        VT2 = VT*SIN(BETAT)
        BETATD = XNT/VT
        IF(STEP − 1)66,66,55
999     CONTINUE
        WRITE(9,*)T,XLAMD,XLAMDH,XNC,RTM
        PAUSE
        END
        SUBROUTINE GAUSS(X,SIG)
        INTEGER RANDOM,SUM
        INTEGER*4 TOOLBX
        PARAMETER (RANDOM = Z'86140000')
        SUM = 0
        DO 14 J = 1,6
        IRAN = TOOLBX(RANDOM)
        SUM = SUM + IRAN
14      CONTINUE
        X = SUM/65536.
        X = 1.414*X*SIG
        RETURN
        END
```

For convenience let us define new variables:

$$y_T = R_{T2}$$

$$y_M = R_{M2}$$

$$y = R_{T2} - R_{M2}$$

where y_T and y_M are the perpendicular distances from the target and missile to the ground. The relative perpendicular missile-target separation is termed y. Using small-angle approximations leads to the simplified expressions for the target and missile angles

$$\theta_T \approx y_T/R_T$$

$$\theta_M \approx y_M/R_M$$

The line-of-sight angle, as in the homing case, can also be derived using the small-angle approximation, or

$$\lambda \approx y/R_{TM}$$

where R_{TM} is the separation between missile and target. As in the homing case, the miss distance for command guidance is defined as

$$\text{Miss} = y(t_F)$$

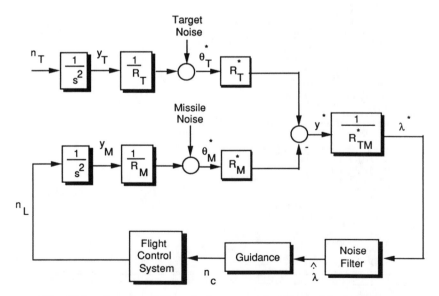

Fig. 10.3   Conceptual linearized command guidance block diagram.

From the linearized equations presented thus far we can draw a block diagram representing a command guidance system. Figure 10.3 presents the command guidance block diagram. Here we can see that target acceleration is integrated twice to yield target position and a division by range produces the target angle θ_T. Thus far this process represents the physics of the command guidance engagement. The target angle measurement is corrupted by noise. An expression for the missile angle θ_M is derived in a similar manner. A measurement of the missile angle is also contaminated by noise. To generate guidance commands, the measured missile and target angles are multiplied by their respective range measurements and subtracted in order to get the measured relative missile-target position y^*. Another division by the measured range from missile to target is required to generate a pseudomeasurement of the line-of-sight angle λ^* required for guidance.

Note that in the command guidance process, unlike the homing process, various range measurements were required (R_T^*, R_M^*, and R_{TM}^*) just to get the pseudomeasurement of the line-of-sight angle. In homing, line-of-sight angle information is available from the seeker, without the need for range measurements. In proportional navigation command guidance, a noise filter, with derivative action, is required to remove the noise and get an estimate of the line-of-sight rate so that a guidance command can be generated. The guidance command is uplinked to the missile, which responds to the command via its flight control system. The resultant missile acceleration n_L completes the command guidance loop of Fig. 10.3.

In order to develop a command guidance model that resembles the homing loop, let us make the assumption that all ranges are known perfectly (we can always change this assumption without making the model nonlinear) and that the missile noise is insignificant compared to the target noise. Since ranges are known perfectly, we can cancel actual and measured ranges and use block diagram manipulation to get an even simpler model. The command guidance system of Fig. 10.3 can now be drawn in a form that

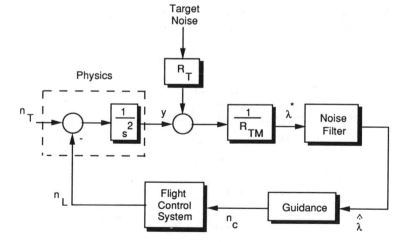

Fig. 10.4 Linearized proportional navigation command guidance loop.

resembles the homing loop. The linearized proportional navigation command guidance loop is shown in Fig. 10.4.

At first glance, the command guidance loop looks identical to the standard homing loop diagram, shown in Fig. 10.5, but there are major differences.

In the homing loop diagram of Fig. 10.5, range is not required, and the geometric line-of-sight angle comes from physics. Angular noise corrupts the measurement, by the seeker, of the line-of-sight angle. In our examples so far, we have considered this noise to be range-independent (constant standard deviation). In the basic command guidance loop shown in Fig. 10.4, only relative position comes from physics, and computation of the line-of-sight angle requires range information. We can see from Fig. 10.4 that the effective noise on the line-of-sight angle is the actual angular measurement noise entering the system multiplied by the range from the energy source to the target R_T and divided by the range from missile to target R_{TM}. Since the range from the missile to target tends toward zero as the flight progresses, the effective noise on the line-of-sight angle will get very large near the end of the flight. This means that command guidance systems will generally have to contend with more noise than homing systems near the end of the flight, thus explaining the experimental results of Fig. 10.2.

Beam Rider Guidance[2]

Beam riding is another form of command guidance. The object of beam riding is to fly the missile along a beam (i.e., radar or laser) that is continuously pointed at the target. Since the missile is attempting to fly along a moving beam, the missile guidance commands must be a function of the angular deviation of the missile from the beam. If the beam is always on the target and the missile is always on the beam, an intercept will result. The beam riding guidance principle is probably one of the first methods used because of its simplicity and ease of implementation.

The beam riding missile-target engagement equations are nearly identical to those of homing guidance. Since the proportional navigation guidance law is not used in beam riding, line-of-sight rate information is not required.

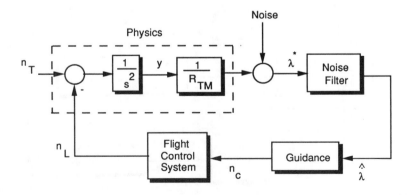

Fig. 10.5   Linearized proportional navigation homing guidance loop.

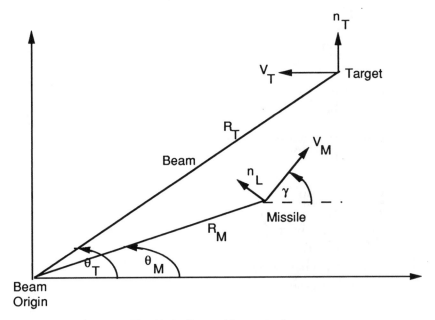

Fig. 10.6   Beam rider geometry.

However, as with proportional navigation command guidance, the missile and target angles with respect to the beam generator, θ_M and θ_T, are important. A typical beam riding geometry is shown in Fig. 10.6, with all important quantities marked. For simplicity we have assumed the beam to be of zero width. In practice we must keep the missile inside the beam for the beam riding principle to work.

From Fig. 10.6 the missile and target angles can be obtained by trigonometry, or

$$\theta_M = \tan^{-1}(R_{M2}/R_{M1})$$

$$\theta_T = \tan^{-1}(R_{T2}/R_{T1})$$

The distance formula can be used to obtain the missile and target ranges from the energy source as

$$R_M = (R_{M1}^2 + R_{M2}^2)^{1/2}$$

$$R_T = (R_{T1}^2 + R_{T2}^2)^{1/2}$$

Again, from Fig. 10.6 we can see that the distance the missile is from the beam, y, is simply given by

$$y = R_M(\theta_T - \theta_M)$$

Listing 10.2   FORTRAN beam rider engagement simulation

```
        VM = 3000.
        VT = 1000.
        XNT = 0.
        RM1IC = 0.
        RM2IC = 1.
        RT1IC = 40000.
        RT2IC = 10000.
        HEDEG = 0.
        XNP = 10.
        TS = .1
        RT1 = RT1IC
        RT2 = RT2IC
        RM1 = RM1IC
        RM2 = RM2IC
        BETAT = 0.
        VT1 = - VT*COS(BETAT)
        VT2 = VT*SIN(BETAT)
        HE = HEDEG/57.3
        XNC = 0.
        T = 0.
        S = 0.
        RTM1 = RT1 - RM1
        RTM2 = RT2 - RM2
        RTM = SQRT(RTM1**2 + RTM2**2)
        THETT = ATAN2(RT2,RT1)
        VM1 = VM*COS(THETT + HE)
        VM2 = VM*SIN(THETT + HE)
        VTM1 = VT1 - VM1
        VTM2 = VT2 - VM2
        VC = - (RTM1*VTM1 + RTM2*VTM2)/RTM
10      IF(VC<0.)GOTO 999
        IF(RTM<1000.)THEN
            H = .0002
        ELSE
            H = .01
        ENDIF
        BETATOLD = BETAT
        RT1OLD = RT1
        RT2OLD = RT2
        RM1OLD = RM1
        RM2OLD = RM2
        VM1OLD = VM1
        VM2OLD = VM2
        STEP = 1
        GOTO 200
66      STEP = 2
        BETAT = BETAT + H*BETATD
        RT1 = RT1 + H*VT1
        RT2 = RT2 + H*VT2
        RM1 = RM1 + H*VM1
        RM2 = RM2 + H*VM2
        VM1 = VM1 + H*AM1
        VM2 = VM2 + H*AM2
        T = T + H
        GOTO 200
55      CONTINUE
        BETAT = .5*(BETATOLD + BETAT + H*BETATD)
        RT1 = .5*(RT1OLD + RT1 + H*VT1)
        RT2 = .5*(RT2OLD + RT2 + H*VT2)
        RM1 = .5*(RM1OLD + RM1 + H*VM1)
        RM2 = .5*(RM2OLD + RM2 + H*VM2)
        VM1 = .5*(VM1OLD + VM1 + H*AM1)
        VM2 = .5*(VM2OLD + VM2 + H*AM2)
        S = S + H
        IF(S<(TS - .0001))GOTO 10
        S = 0.
        RT1K = RT1/1000.
        RT2K = RT2/1000.
        RM1K = RM1/1000.
        RM2K = RM2/1000.
        WRITE(9,*)T,RT1,RT2,RM1,RM2,XNC,RTM
        GOTO 10
200     CONTINUE
        THETT = ATAN2(RT2,RT1)
        THETM = ATAN2(RM2,RM1)
        RT = SQRT(RT1**2 + RT2**2)
```

(Listing 10.2 continued on next page.)

Listing 10.2   (cont.) FORTRAN beam rider engagement simulation

```
        RM = SQRT(RM1**2 + RM2**2)
        RTM1 = RT1 - RM1
        RTM2 = RT2 - RM2
        RTM = SQRT(RTM1**2 + RTM2**2)
        VTM1 = VT1 - VM1
        VTM2 = VT2 - VM2
        VC = -(RTM1*VTM1 + RTM2*VTM2)/RTM
        XLAM = ATAN2(RTM2,RTM1)
        XLAMD = (RTM1*VTM2 - RTM2*VTM1)/(RTM*RTM)
        XNC = XNP*RM*(THETT - THETM)
        AM1 = -XNC*SIN(XLAM)
        AM2 = XNC*COS(XLAM)
        VT1 = -VT*COS(BETAT)
        VT2 = VT*SIN(BETAT)
        BETATD = XNT/VT
        IF(STEP - 1)66,66,55
999     CONTINUE
        WRITE(9,*)T,RT1,RT2,RM1,RM2,XNC,RTM
        PAUSE
        END
```

If the missile is always on the beam ($y = 0$), then the missile will surely hit the target. Therefore, as in the homing and command guidance cases, it is desired to minimize y at the end of flight. Mathematically we are again attempting to null $y(t_F)$, which means we are trying to drive the miss distance to zero. The simplest possible implementation of a guidance law for a beam rider system is to make the missile acceleration command n_c proportional to y, or

$$n_c = Ky = KR_M(\theta_T - \theta_M)$$

Thus, we can see that the guidance command is proportional to the angular displacement off the beam.

A two-dimensional FORTRAN engagement simulation listing for the beam rider loop, utilizing guidance commands that are proportional to the

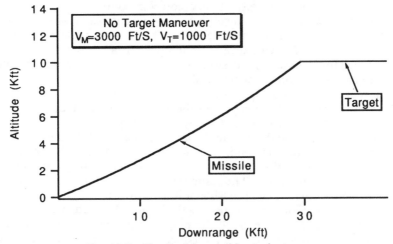

Fig. 10.7   Nominal beam rider trajectory.

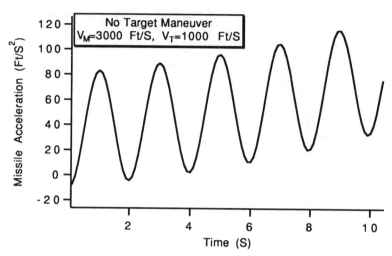

Fig. 10.8   Simple beam rider guidance results in oscillatory missile acceleration profile.

off-axis beam displacement, appears in Listing 10.2. We can see from the listing that the guidance gain, K (XNP in the listing) has a nominal value of 10.

In beam rider guidance the missile is initially fired at the target (i.e., along the line-of-sight that is along the beam), whereas in proportional navigation the missile is fired in a direction to lead the target (i.e., aimed at expected intercept point). Running the engagement simulation of Listing 10.2 yields the trajectory for the nominal beam rider case that appears in Fig. 10.7. The curvature in the beam riding missile trajectory is due solely to the movement of the beam. In the benign case considered there is no target maneuver and the missile is traveling at three times the speed of the target. A proportional navigation trajectory, for this case, would result in a straight-line trajectory since the missile would initially be on a collision course.

Although there does not appear to be anything unusual with the beam rider trajectory, we can see from Fig. 10.8 that the missile acceleration required by beam rider guidance is oscillatory. In addition, the resultant miss distance for this case is 7 ft even though the target is not maneuvering and there are no guidance system lags!

If we reduce the guidance gain K from 10 to 1, the missile acceleration oscillations decrease in frequency, but the miss distance increases from 7 ft to 102 ft, as shown in Fig. 10.9. Clearly something is wrong!

In order to understand why the beam rider guidance system does not appear to work satisfactorily, it is necessary to develop an analytical model. For this purpose we will linearize the beam rider loop using our standard small-angle approximations. The resultant linearized beam rider loop with a perfect flight control system is shown in Fig. 10.10.

The transfer function $G(s)$ represents the beam rider guidance law in Fig. 10.10. We have already attempted the simplest possible implementation of a guidance law for a beam rider missile, which is to make the missile acceleration command n_c proportional to the angular displacement off the

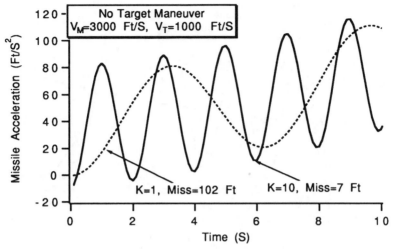

Fig. 10.9   Reducing beam rider gain does not improve system performance.

beam. Since we have already implemented

$$n_c = KR_M(\theta_T - \theta_M) = Ky$$

the guidance law transfer function is simply

$$G(s) = K$$

If we treat the range from the energy source to the missile R_M as a constant, then we can express the transfer function from missile acceleration to target angle as

$$\frac{n_L}{\theta_T}(s) = \frac{KR_M s^2}{s^2 + K}$$

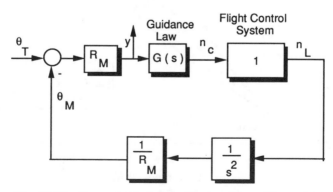

Fig. 10.10   Conceptual model of beam rider guidance loop.

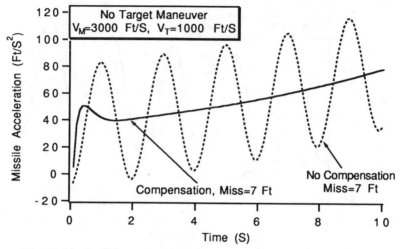

Fig. 10.11 Lead-lag network stabilizes beam rider guidance system.

As was shown in the Laplace transform Table 1.1 of Chapter 1, this transfer function is that of a sinusoid with natural frequency K. Thus, decreasing K will decrease the frequency of oscillation as we saw in the simulation results of Fig. 10.10. One way of stabilizing (eliminating the oscillatory behavior of) the beam rider loop is to add a lead-lag compensation network. For example, one possible compensation network is

$$G(s) = 10\frac{1 + s/2}{1 + s/20}$$

Figure 10.11 shows that the beam rider acceleration commands are completely stabilized when the lead-lag network is added to the beam rider loop.

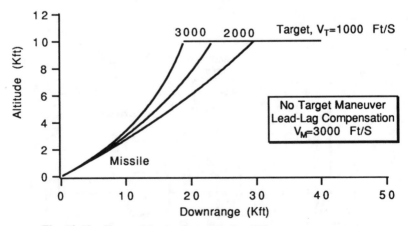

Fig. 10.12 Beam rider trajectories for different target speeds.

The guidance gain K is still 10; hence, the miss distance remains the same, namely, 7 ft. However, since the target is not maneuvering, the beam-rider-induced miss distance is still quite large compared to proportional navigation guidance. In this case, for a zero-lag guidance system, proportional navigation would yield zero miss distance.

Theoretically, one launches a missile, using proportional navigation guidance, on a collision triangle. The missile leads the target so that an intercept will occur if both the target and missile continue to fly in the same direction. As long as the missile can close on the target, proportional navigation performance is essentially independent of geometry. A beam rider missile, on the other hand, must always be near the beam. If the beam generator and missile are initially collocated, one launches a beam rider missile along the line of sight. Since a beam rider missile does not lead the target, it must change the trajectory continuously to catch the target. Figure 10.12 shows beam rider trajectories for cases in which the target speed is made a parameter. The curvature in the missile trajectory becomes more apparent as the target speed increases.

Figure 10.13 shows the corresponding beam rider commanded missile acceleration profiles, along with the resultant miss distances. In each case the beam rider missile had the previously discussed lead-lag compensation network with gain 10. We can see that both miss distance and acceleration increase with increasing target speed. Thus, beam rider performance, unlike proportional navigation performance, is highly dependent on the target speed. For the cases studied, a missile launched on a collision triangle and employing proportional navigation guidance would achieve zero miss distance with zero acceleration requirements!

Figure 10.14 compares the trajectories for beam rider guidance for a 3-g maneuvering target and a target that does not maneuver. In both cases the beam rider guidance system has a lead-lag network with gain 10 and a 3 to 1 missile to target speed advantage.

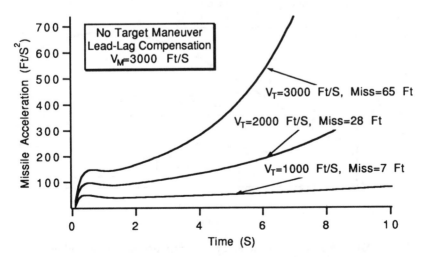

Fig. 10.13   Beam rider system performance is highly dependent on target speed.

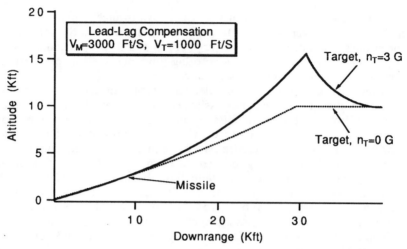

Fig. 10.14 **Beam rider trajectories for maneuvering and nonmaneuvering targets.**

Although beam rider guidance appears to be successful against a maneuvering target, the miss distance increases from 7 ft (nonmaneuvering case) to about 19 ft, as shown in Fig. 10.15. In addition, the missile acceleration requirements increase significantly when the target maneuvers.

Recall that for a zero-lag guidance system proportional navigation achieved zero miss distance against a maneuvering target. Figure 10.16 compares the trajectories of both beam rider guidance and proportional navigation for a case in which the target executes a 3-g target maneuver. We can see that there is less curvature in the proportional navigation trajectory because the missile is initially leading the target.

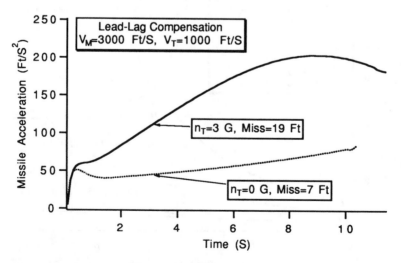

Fig. 10.15 **Maneuvering target increases miss distance and acceleration requirements for beam rider guidance.**

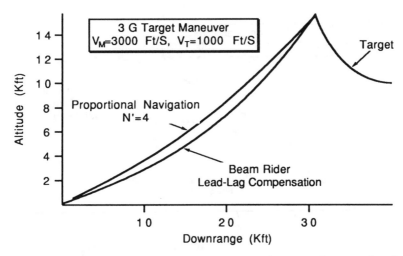

Fig. 10.16   Trajectory comparison of beam rider guidance and proportional navigation.

Figure 10.17 shows what we have already suspected, namely, that proportional navigation yields zero miss distance and much smaller acceleration requirements than a beam rider guidance system when the target is maneuvering.

Command to Line-of-Sight Guidance[2,3]

Beam riding performance can be significantly improved by taking the beam motion into account. This is analogous to homing guidance in which proportional navigation performance is improved by taking target maneuver information into account (augmented proportional navigation). If we recall that the angle of the beam with respect to the target (see Fig. 10.6) is given by

$$\theta_T = \tan^{-1}(R_{T2}/R_{T1})$$

then the angular velocity and acceleration of the beam can be found by taking successive derivatives of the preceding expression, yielding

$$\dot{\theta}_T = \frac{R_{T1}V_{T2} - R_{T2}V_{T1}}{R_T^2}$$

$$\ddot{\theta}_T = \frac{a_{T2}\cos\theta_T - a_{T1}\sin\theta_T - 2\dot{\theta}_T\dot{R}_T}{R_T}$$

where the derivative of the range from the radar to the target can be found from

$$\dot{R}_T = \frac{R_{T1}V_{T1} + R_{T2}V_{T2}}{R_T}$$

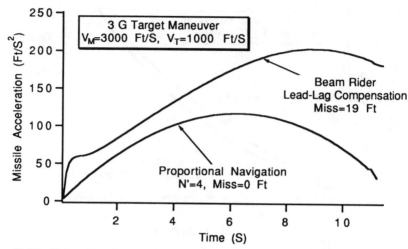

Fig. 10.17 Proportional navigation yields smaller miss distance and lower acceleration requirements than beam rider guidance.

The acceleration perpendicular to the beam a_{TP} can be expressed in terms of the inertial coordinates of target acceleration, or

$$a_{TP} = -a_{T1}\sin\theta_T + a_{T2}\cos\theta_T$$

Therefore, combining terms yields an equivalent expression for the beam acceleration as

$$a_{TP} = R_T\ddot{\theta}_T + 2\dot{R}_T\dot{\theta}_T$$

By analogy, if we want the missile to stay on the beam, we are striving to ensure that

$$\ddot{\theta}_M = \ddot{\theta}_T$$

and

$$\dot{\theta}_M = \dot{\theta}_T$$

If these conditions are met, then the missile acceleration perpendicular to the beam can be found from

$$a_{MP} = R_M\ddot{\theta}_M + 2\dot{R}_M\dot{\theta}_M$$

Substitution yields the final expression for the beam acceleration:

$$a_{MP} = R_M\ddot{\theta}_T + 2\dot{R}_M\dot{\theta}_T$$

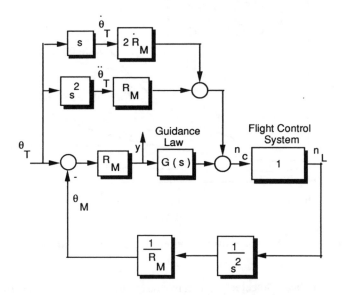

Fig. 10.18   Command to line-of-sight guidance system.

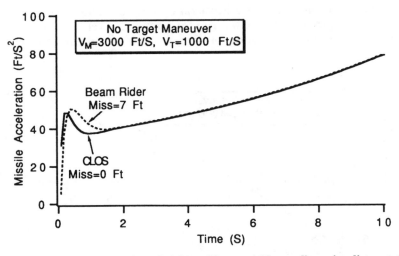

Fig. 10.19   Command to line-of-sight guidance yields smaller miss distance than beam rider guidance.

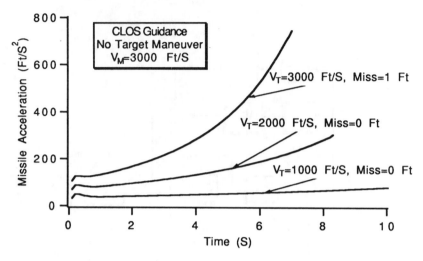

Fig. 10.20 CLOS acceleration requirements are dependent on target speed.

Adding the beam acceleration term a_{MP} to the nominal acceleration generated by the beam rider equations yields command to line-of-sight (CLOS) guidance. A command to line-of-sight guidance loop is shown in Fig. 10.18. Here we can see that the beam rider loop remains unchanged and an extra feedforward path, representing the acceleration of the beam, has been added. The beam rider acceleration command has thus been modified to include an extra term.

In order to see how the extra acceleration term changes system requirements and performance, a case was run for a nonmaneuvering target. Figure 10.19 compares the acceleration profiles of both beam rider and CLOS

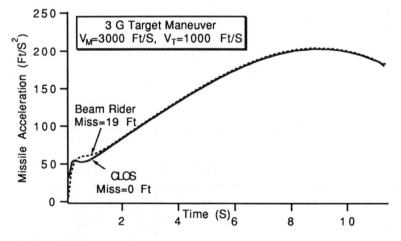

Fig. 10.21 CLOS guidance has smaller miss distance against maneuvering target.

guidance. First, the figure shows that the acceleration requirements at the beginning of the flight are somewhat less for command to line-of-sight guidance than beam rider guidance. The reason for this is that command to line-of-sight guidance is taking into account beam motion. Next, the figure also shows that, although for most of the flight the acceleration requirements for both guidance systems are about the same, the miss distance performance of command to line-of-sight guidance is better.

We saw in the previous section that beam rider performance was highly dependent, in terms of miss distance and acceleration requirements, on target speed. Figure 10.20 shows that, although the acceleration requirements of command to line-of-sight guidance are still dependent on target speed, near zero miss distance can be achieved against a nonmaneuvering target, independent of target speed!

Finally, Fig. 10.21 shows that the acceleration requirements for hitting a maneuvering target with command to line-of-sight guidance and beam rider guidance are about the same. However, command to line-of-sight guidance, in the case examined, had zero miss distance, whereas beam rider guidance yielded a miss distance of 19 ft.

Thus, we can see that taking the beam motion into account improves the performance, if not the acceleration requirements, of a beam rider system.

Summary

In this chapter we studied three different types of command guidance systems: proportional navigation, beam rider, and command to line of sight. We showed that a command proportional navigation guidance system will have to contend with more effective noise on the line of sight than its homing counterpart. It was demonstrated that beam rider guidance required lead-lag compensation in order to guide effectively on the target. Beam rider performance, unlike that of proportional navigation, was shown to be very dependent on target speed and geometry. Finally, it was shown that beam rider performance could be substantially improved by taking beam motion into account.

References

[1]Alpert, J., "Miss Distance Analysis for Command Guided Missiles," *Journal of Guidance, Control, and Dynamics*, Vol. 11, Nov.–Dec. 1988, pp. 481–487.

[2]Garnell, P., and East, D. J., *Guided Weapon Control System*, Pergamon, Oxford, 1977.

[3]Heap, E., "Methodology of Research into Command-Line-of-Sight and Homing Guidance," AGARD Lecture Series No. 52 on Guidance of Tactical Missiles, May 1952.

Chapter 11

Tactical Zones

Introduction

IN the material presented so far it has been assumed that the missile can reach the target and generate sufficient lift to maneuver. For purposes of understanding fundamental guidance issues, we have neglected the fact that the ability of a tactical aerodynamic missile to maneuver is dependent upon its speed, physical characteristics (i.e., wing size), and altitude. In addition, we have also assumed impulsive constant velocity missiles and have not taken into consideration that a missile must burn propellant in order to get up to speed. The resultant missile total weight is directly related to its payload weight and design speed (i.e., propellant weight). Actually, it will soon become obvious that in some tactical missiles most of the weight is the propellant weight. Finally, we have also neglected the fact that while an aerodynamic missile is coasting the missile speed diminishes due to atmospheric drag. In this chapter we shall briefly address previously neglected issues and show how to modify previous computations to account for these important effects.

Velocity Computation

A tactical missile gets up to speed by burning propellant. If the missile is launched from the air, it already has a large initial speed. However, if the missile is launched from the ground, it needs more propellant to reach the same speed since it is starting from rest. In addition, a ground-based missile needs additional propellant since it must travel through more of the denser atmosphere. Figure 11.1 shows a typical weight and thrust profiles for a boost-coast missile. The initial or total weight of the missile is denoted W_T, and its final weight, after the propellant is expended, is the glide weight W_G. The glide weight consists of the missile structure, electronics, and warhead. While propellant is being consumed, the thrust is assumed to be constant, with magnitude T.

We can find the magnitude of the missile velocity after all of the propellant is consumed from basic physics. Applying Newton's second law yields[1,2]

$$F = ma = m \frac{\mathrm{d}V}{\mathrm{d}t} = T$$

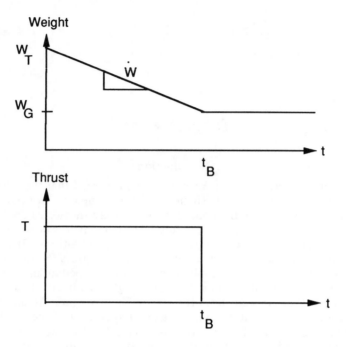

Fig. 11.1   Boost-coast thrust-weight profile.

The change in velocity with respect to time can be expressed in terms of thrust and weight as

$$\frac{\mathrm{d}V}{\mathrm{d}t} = \frac{T}{m} = \frac{Tg}{W}$$

Recognizing that as long as the missile is burning propellant ($0 < t < t_B$) we can express the instantaneous missile weight as

$$W = \dot{W}t + W_T$$

where the derivative of the weight is negative (weight is decreasing). Thus, we can find an expression for the change in velocity due to the burning of propellant by direct integration, or

$$\int_{V_0}^{V_1} \mathrm{d}V = Tg \int_0^{t_B} \frac{\mathrm{d}t}{W}$$

Substitution of the expression for the missile weight into the integral yields

$$V_1 - V_0 = \Delta V = Tg \int_0^{t_B} \frac{\mathrm{d}t}{\dot{W}t + W_T}$$

Evaluation of the integral yields

$$\Delta V = \frac{-Tg}{\dot{W}} \log \frac{W_T}{\dot{W}t_B + W_T}$$

Thus, the change in velocity depends only on the missile total weight, glide weight, thrust magnitude, and rate at which the propellant is burning. The preceding velocity formula, also known as the rocket equation, represents the maximum change in velocity we can impart. Practical effects such as gravity and atmospheric drag will usually work in the direction of decreasing ΔV. The preceding expression can be made more concise and useful by specifying fuel effectiveness in terms of a parameter known as the specific impulse I_{SP}. It is a positive number in units of seconds and is related to the thrust and change in missile weight according to

$$I_{sp} = \frac{-T}{\dot{W}}$$

More fuel-efficient missiles have higher values of specific impulse. Typically, for tactical missiles, the specific impulse has values ranging from 200 s to 300 s. By substituting the specific impulse definition into the velocity change formula, we get

$$\Delta V = I_{sp}\, g \, \log \frac{W_T}{W_G}$$

Now the change in missile velocity during a burn depends only on the total weight, glide weight, and specific impulse. However, the total missile weight is the sum of the glide weight and the propellant weight, or

$$W_T = W_P + W_G$$

The fuel mass fraction mf is defined as the ratio of the missile propellant weight to the total missile weight, or

$$mf = \frac{W_P}{W_T}$$

Because a ground-to-air missile requires more fuel than an air-to-air missile to reach the same speed, it would have a larger fuel mass fraction value. We can now express the change in missile velocity in terms of the specific impulse and fuel mass fraction, or

$$\Delta V = I_{sp}g \, \log \frac{1}{1 - mf}$$

Using the preceding equation, Fig. 11.2 shows how the change in missile velocity varies with fuel mass fraction and specific impulse. We can see from the figure that, if the fuel mass fraction is 0.3 and the specific impulse is 200

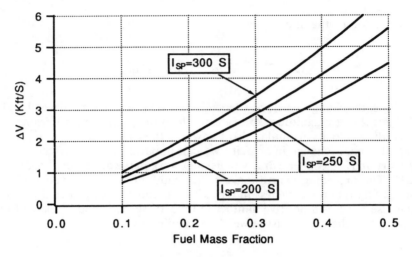

Fig. 11.2   Increasing fuel mass fraction or specific impulse increases missile speed.

s, the change in velocity is about 2300 ft/s. This means that, if the missile were launched from the ground, its final speed, in the absence of drag and gravitational effects, would be 2300 ft/s. If the missile with the same fuel mass fraction were launched from an aircraft traveling at 1000 ft/s, its final speed would be 3300 ft/s.

Drag[3]

Tactical missiles work within the atmosphere. Aerodynamic drag causes the missile to slow down and have less maneuver capability. The drag F_{drag} can be expressed as

$$F_{drag} = QS_{ref}\, C_{D0}$$

where Q is the dynamic pressure, S_{ref} a reference area, and C_{D0} the zero-lift drag. The dynamic pressure is a function of the air density ρ and velocity V and is given by

$$Q = \frac{\rho V^2}{2}$$

In the English system of units used throughout the text, air density is measured in slug per cubic foot (slug/ft³). The reference area is the cross-sectional area of the missile body and is therefore related to the physical characteristics of the missile. The zero-lift drag is a function of the missile speed and aerodynamic shape. Since the air density decreases with altitude, the influence of drag is greatest at the lower altitudes. For analytical reasons it is convenient to use an exponential approximation to the atmosphere. One such approximation below 30,000 ft altitude is given by

$$\rho = 0.002378\, e^{-h/30,000} \qquad (h < 30,000\ \text{ft})$$

whereas above 30,000 ft the exponential approximation becomes

$$\rho = 0.0034 \; e^{-h/22,000} \qquad (h \geq 30,000 \text{ ft})$$

where h is measured in feet.

To check the validity of the exponential approximations, the 1962 U.S. Standard Atmosphere is displayed as a function of altitude in Fig. 11.3. Superimposed on the figure are the exponential approximations. The solid curve represents the actual data points for the standard U.S. atmosphere, whereas the dashed curve represents the preceding exponential approximation. We can see that the exponential approximation is quite accurate.

In the absence of induced drag effects the drag F_{drag} can be expressed in terms of Newton's second law as

$$F = ma = -F_{\text{drag}} = m \frac{\mathrm{d}V}{\mathrm{d}t}$$

Therefore, the rate of change of velocity can be found from

$$\frac{\mathrm{d}V}{\mathrm{d}t} = \frac{-F_{\text{drag}}}{m} = \frac{-QS_{\text{ref}}C_{D0}}{m} = \frac{-0.5\rho V^2 S_{\text{ref}} C_{D0}}{m}$$

Setting up the integral in a useful form for integration, we get

$$\int_{V_0}^{V_1} \frac{\mathrm{d}V}{V^2} = \int_{t_0}^{t_1} \frac{-0.5\rho S_{\text{ref}} C_{D0}}{m} \, \mathrm{d}t$$

If we assume that the air density does not change (constant altitude) and that the zero-lift drag is constant, we can get a closed-form expression for the

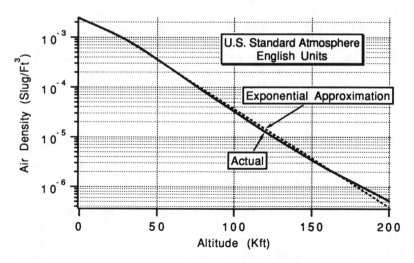

Fig. 11.3 Exponential approximation for air density is very accurate.

new velocity due to drag, or

$$\frac{1}{V_1} = \frac{\rho S_{ref} C_{D0} \Delta t}{2m} + \frac{1}{V_0}$$

where V_0 is the initial velocity, V_1 is the velocity Δt seconds later, and Δt is defined as

$$\Delta t = t_1 - t_0$$

If we define the initial drag deceleration D_0 to be

$$D_0 = \frac{\rho S_{ref} C_{D0} V_0^2}{2m}$$

and a characteristic time T_0 as

$$T_0 = V_0/D_0$$

then we can express the velocity Δt seconds later in the simpler form

$$V_1 = \frac{V_0 T_0}{T_0 + \Delta t}$$

Integrating again yields the total distance R covered in Δt seconds as

$$R = V_0 T_0 \log\left(1 + \frac{\Delta t}{T_0}\right)$$

We now have sufficient information to perform some preliminary calculation concerning the effects of drag on velocity loss and range covered. However, it is first important to see how the magnitude of the drag deceleration is influenced by the zero-lift drag and altitude. Often it is convenient to combine the weight, reference area, and zero-lift drag into an expression known as the ballistic coefficient β, which is defined as

$$\beta = \frac{W}{C_{D0} S_{ref}}$$

where β is in units of pounds per square feet. Figure 11.4 shows how the drag deceleration varies with altitude for different values of ballistic coefficient. We can see that increasing the ballistic coefficient (reducing zero-lift drag) or increasing the altitude reduces the drag deceleration. It is also apparent that, for a velocity of 3000 ft/s, a ballistic coefficient of 500 lb/ft^2 yields a drag deceleration of about 22 g at sea level, 10 g at 25 kft, and 3.5 g at 50 kft. In addition, Fig. 11.4 shows that, as altitude increases, the drag deceleration becomes less dependent on the ballistic coefficient. Eventually, at the higher altitudes, there is no deceleration due to drag.

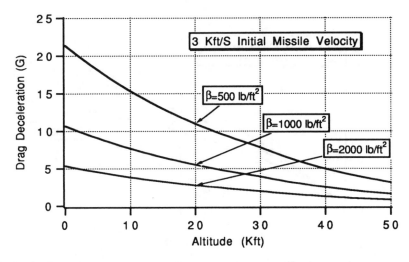

Fig. 11.4   Drag deceleration decreases with increasing altitude and increasing ballistic coefficient.

If we still assume a missile at sea level with an initial velocity of 3000 ft/s, missile speed decreases due to drag as a function of time for different ballistic coefficients, as shown in Fig. 11.5. The velocity drops to about half of its original value in only 4.5 s for $\beta = 500$ lb/ft^2, in about 9 s for $\beta = 1000$ lb/ft^2, and in about 17.5 s for $\beta = 2000$ lb/ft^2.

Figure 11.6 shows the ranges covered for the cases given earlier. At sea level the range covered until the missile velocity drops to half of its value is about 9 kft for $\beta = 500$ lb/ft^2, about 20 kft for $\beta = 1000$ lb/ft^2, and about 35 kft for $\beta = 2000$ lb/ft^2. If the missile is not considered to be effective after it has dropped more than half of its velocity, then we can consider these

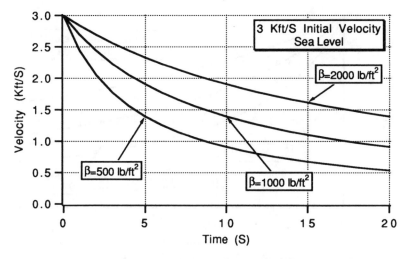

Fig. 11.5   Velocity drops faster with smaller ballistic coefficient.

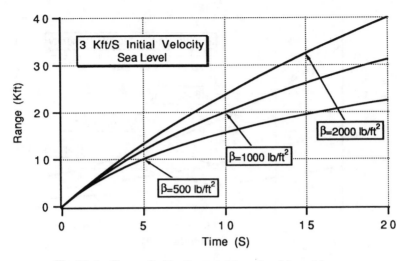

Fig. 11.6   Zone of effectiveness at sea level is not large.

values to be kinematic zones of effectiveness at sea level. The missile will have longer kinematic reach if its ballistic coefficient is higher.

Figure 11.7 shows the velocity loss at 50 kft altitude. We can see that increasing the altitude reduces the missile's velocity loss due to drag and increases the effective range of the missile. We can see from Fig. 11.7 that at 50 kft it takes much longer for the velocity to drop to half of its original value. At 50 kft the velocity drops to about half of its original value in about 30 s (vs 4.5 s at sea level) for $\beta = 500$ lb/ft^2, in about 60 s (vs 9 s at sea level) for $\beta = 1000$ lb/ft^2, and in more than 100 s (vs 17.5 s at sea level) for $\beta = 2000$ lb/ft^2.

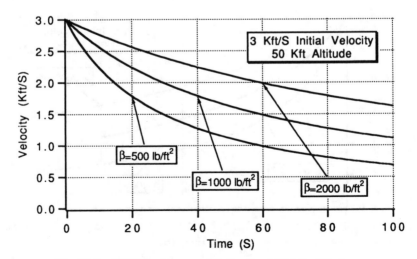

Fig. 11.7   Velocity drops much slower at 50 kft altitude.

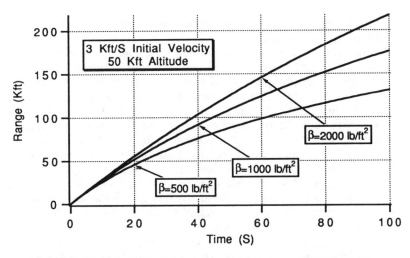

Fig. 11.8   Zone of effectiveness is much greater at 50 kft altitude.

Figure 11.8 shows the range covered as a function of time for missiles with varying ballistic coefficients at an altitude of 50 kft. We can see from the figure that the range covered until the velocity drops to half of its value is about 70 kft (vs 9 kft at sea level) for $\beta = 500$ lb/ft^2, about 125 kft (vs 20 kft at sea level) for $\beta = 1000$ lb/ft^2, and more than 200 kft (vs 35 kft at sea level) for $\beta = 2000$ lb/ft^2.

In summary, increasing the ballistic coefficient (or reducing the zero-lift drag) can have a big payoff in terms of increased zone of effectiveness for aerodynamic missiles that must fly through the more dense atmosphere at low altitudes. Tactical radar homing missiles tend to have a nose with a high fineness ratio in order to make them more aerodynamically efficient. The high fineness-ratio nose also tends to exacerbate parasitic radome effects.[4]

Acceleration[1,2]

Just as there was a drag coefficient to determine slowdown, there is a lift coefficient C_L to determine missile maneuverability. From Newton's second law we can say that

$$F = ma = mn_L = QS_{ref}C_L$$

where n_L represents the missile's acceleration capability. Therefore, the missile acceleration capability, expressed in units of gravity, is given by

$$\frac{n_L}{g} = \frac{0.5\rho V^2 S_{ref} C_L}{W}$$

where W is missile weight in units of pounds. The lift coefficient is a function of the missile aerodynamic shape, speed, angle of attack, and wing size. Larger wings and increasing angle of attack both work in the direction of increasing the lift coefficient.

To demonstrate the sensitivity of the missile acceleration capability to the lift coefficient and altitude, it is best to consider a numerical example. Consider a missile weighing 500 lb with an 0.5-ft^2 reference area and traveling at 3000 ft/s. Figure 11.9 shows how the missile acceleration capability decreases with increasing altitude and decreasing lift coefficient. It is important to note that a missile may have an aerodynamic acceleration capability, at a given altitude, which is far in excess of its structural capability. A loading analysis is required to set practical limits on the maximum allowable commanded missile acceleration. Figure 11.9 shows an example of a missile ($C_L = 4$) which has a 40-g capability at sea level that diminishes to about a 10-g capability at 50 kft altitude. Reducing missile weight or increasing the missile reference area (but keeping weight constant) works in the direction of increasing the missile aerodynamic maneuverability.

Speed also plays an important role in determining missile aerodynamic maneuverability. Figure 11.10 shows that decreasing the missile speed significantly decreases the missile maneuverability. A missile that travels at 3000 ft/s at 20 kft altitude has a maneuverability in excess of 40 g. Halving the missile speed more than halves its maneuverability. We have seen in previous chapters that a missile requires a certain acceleration advantage to effectively engage maneuvering targets. Therefore, for a given altitude and missile configuration, there is a minimum speed at which the missile can effectively engage a responsive threat.

Gravity

Thus far in our analysis we have neglected gravity and assumed a constant-altitude missile. Actually, gravity will eventually cause a coasting mis-

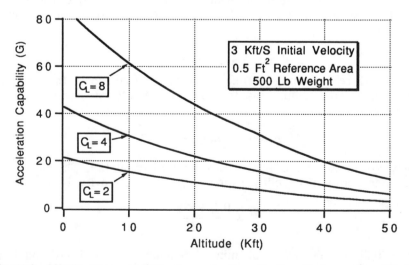

Fig. 11.9   Missile maneuverability decreases dramatically with increasing altitude.

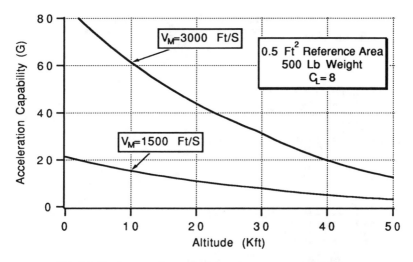

Fig. 11.10   Decreasing speed decreases maneuverability.

sile to crash to the ground. If we neglect the atmosphere and launch an impulsive 3000-ft/s missile at various flight-path angles γ, we will get different range capabilities due to gravity alone, as shown in Fig. 11.11. As expected, the 45-deg launch results in maximum range.

Atmospheric drag will of course prevent the missile from achieving the range capabilities indicated in Fig. 11.11. Listing 11.1 presents a FORTRAN simulation of an impulsive missile launched at a flight-path angle *GAMDEG* missile in the presence of gravity and an atmosphere (zero-lift drag). As in the previous section, the ballistic coefficient is used rather than the zero-lift drag coefficient to account for zero-lift-drag–induced slowdown effects. Lift-induced drag is neglected in this simplified analysis.

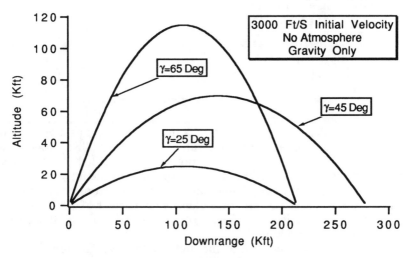

Fig. 11.11   Trajectory profiles for various launch angles.

Listing 11.1   Trajectory simulation

```
        INTEGER STEP
        H = .1
        VM = 3000.
        BETA = 1000.
        T = 0.
        S = 0.
        GAMDEG = 45.
        VM1 = VM*COS(GAMDEG/57.3)
        VM2 = VM*SIN(GAMDEG/57.3)
        RM1 = 0.
        RM2 = 0.
  10    IF(T>0..AND.RM2< = 0.)GOTO 999
        RM1OLD = RM1
        RM2OLD = RM2
        VM1OLD = VM1
        VM2OLD = VM2
        STEP = 1
        GOTO 200
  66    STEP = 2
        RM1 = RM1 + H*VM1
        RM2 = RM2 + H*VM2
        VM1 = VM1 + H*AM1
        VM2 = VM2 + H*AM2
        T = T + H
        GOTO 200
  55    CONTINUE
        RM1 = .5*(RM1OLD + RM1 + H*VM1)
        RM2 = .5*(RM2OLD + RM2 + H*VM2)
        VM1 = .5*(VM1OLD + VM1 + H*AM1)
        VM2 = .5*(VM2OLD + VM2 + H*AM2)
        S = S + H
        IF(S<.99999)GOTO 10
        S = 0.
        RM1K = RM1/1000.
        RM2K = RM2/1000.
        WRITE(9,*)T,RM1K,RM2K
        GOTO 10
 200    CONTINUE
        IF(RM2<30000.)THEN
            RHO = .002378*EXP( - RM2/30000)
        ELSE
            RHO = .0034*EXP( - RM2/22000)
        ENDIF
        VM = SQRT(VM1**2 + VM2**2)
        Q = .5*RHO*VM*VM
        GAM = ATAN2(VM2,VM1)
        DRAG = Q*32.2/BETA
        AM1 = - DRAG*COS(GAM)
        AM2 = - 32.2 - DRAG*SIN(GAM)
        IF(STEP - 1)66,66,55
 999    CONTINUE
        VM = SQRT(VM1**2 + VM2**2)
        RM1K = RM1/1000.
        RM2K = RM2/1000.
        WRITE(9,*)T,RM1K,RM2K
        PAUSE
        END
```

Consider a 45-deg sea-level launch of a missile that attains a velocity of 3000 ft/s instantaneously. Cases were run in which the ballistic coefficient varied from 500 lb/ft^2 to infinity (no drag). Figure 11.12 shows that drag dramatically changes the maximum range capability of the interceptor. The maximum range for a 45-deg launch angle decreases from about 300 kft (no-drag case) to about 100 kft for a ballistic coefficient of 2000 lb/ft^2, to about 55 kft for a ballistic coefficient of 1000 lb/ft^2, and to 30 kft for a ballistic coefficient of 500 lb/ft^2.

Drag becomes less important at the higher altitudes. The previous case was repeated, but the initial launch altitude was increased from sea level to

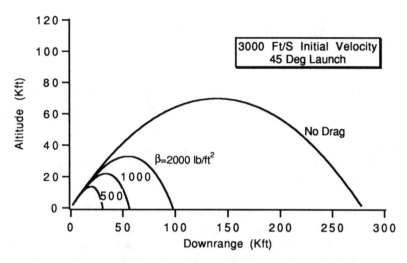

Fig. 11.12   **Drag dramatically reduces range capability of missile.**

50 kft. Figure 11.13 shows that the differences between the drag free trajectory and the one in which the ballistic coefficient is 2000 lb/ft² is much smaller than before. The maximum range without drag in this case is about 350 kft, whereas the maximum range for a ballistic coefficient of 2000 lb/ft² is about 275 kft. For a ballistic coefficient of 500 lb/ft² the maximum range reduces to 175 kft.

Thus, we can see that drag not only plays a role in reducing missile speed so that it has less acceleration capability but it also plays a significant role in determining the kinematic reach of the missile. For long-range ground-launched missiles, trajectory shaping is often used to get the missile to higher

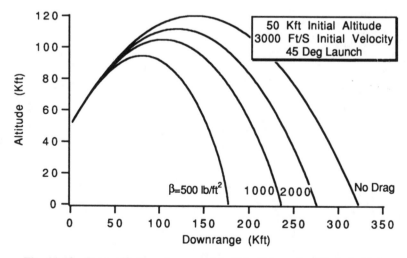

Fig. 11.13   **Drag effects reduce considerably if launch altitude is high.**

altitudes as quickly as possible so that range and velocity losses due to drag can be minimized.

Summary

In this chapter we have considered and shown how to model previously neglected effects. A simple design formula, known as the rocket equation, was derived in order to show the influence of propellant weight on missile speed capability. In addition, we investigated how drag reduces the kinematic reach of the missile and how the atmosphere helps in providing the missile with lift to maneuver. Finally, a numerical example was presented showing how to generate flyout zones.

References

[1]Locke, A. S., *Guidance*, Van Nostrand, Toronto, 1955.
[2]Jerger, J. J., *System Preliminary Design*, Van Nostrand, Princeton, NJ, 1960.
[3]Travers, P., "Interceptor Dynamics," Unpublished Lecture Notes, Raytheon, circa 1971.
[4]Eichblatt, E. (ed.), *Test and Evaluation of the Tactical Missile*, Vol. 119, Progress in Astronautics and Aeronautics, AIAA, Washington, DC, 1989.

Chapter 12

Strategic Considerations

Introduction

IN all of the work presented so far we have based our models on a flat-Earth, constant-gravity model. For tactical interceptor missions, where speeds are less than 5000 ft/s, altitudes under 100 kft, and ranges covered under 100 n.mi., these assumptions are reasonable. In the strategic world where speeds are near-orbital and the distances covered are intercontinental, the flat-Earth constant-gravity assumption is not only inaccurate but can also give misleading results in terms of the size of the zone of effectiveness. However, we shall also see in subsequent chapters that the guidance lessons learned in the tactical world are still valid and give valuable insight into the requirements and effectiveness of strategic interceptors. Before proceeding with the development of models, it is worthwhile to review some of the historical background of strategic ballistic missiles.

Background[1]

Germany's V-2 was the world's first long-range ballistic missile. When a loophole in the Treaty of Versailles was found, the Wehrmacht's Ordinance Department authorized the development of this large long-range rocket and selected Artillery Captain Walter Domberger to supervise the project. After 14 years of testing the V-2 was ready for field use and was finally deployed in the fall of 1944, and it was launched from mobile field battery positions in France and Holland. Each single-stage missile weighed nearly 30,000 lb, reached a burnout velocity of about 6000 ft/s, and had a range of approximately 230 miles. Between September 1944 and March 1945 German field units launched more than 3000 V-2 missiles. Approximately 1900 missiles were launched against Allied targets on the European continent, primarily Antwerp, Belgium. The rest fell on London and southern England.

After the war, the U.S. Army brought German V-2 engineers and enough pieces for about 80 missiles into this country. As part of Project Hermes, more than 70 V-2s were launched by the U.S. during the late 1940s and early 1950s. These rockets formed the basis for U.S. strategic ballistic missile technology and was also essential for subsequent advances in the exploration of space.

Gravitational Model

In the tactical world, in the absence of thrust, drag, and lift, the flat-Earth constant-gravity assumption is easy to understand. In this mathematical model the gravitational acceleration is independent of altitude with value 32.2 ft/s^2, always in a downward direction. The tactical missile inertial coordinate system is fixed to the surface of a flat Earth and is depicted in Fig. 12.1. Here the missile has velocity V and is at a flight-path angle γ with respect to the surface of the Earth. In addition the missile is in a constant-gravity field with acceleration level g. The missile is at an initial location that is distance dr downrange from the origin of the coordinate system and at an altitude alt from the surface of the Earth.

The differential equations acting on the missile are

$$\dot{V}_1 = 0$$

$$\dot{V}_2 = -g$$

$$\dot{R}_1 = V_1$$

$$\dot{R}_2 = V_2$$

where V is velocity and R is range. The down-range component is denoted by 1, and the altitude component is denoted by 2. The initial conditions for velocity and position are given by

$$V_1(0) = V \cos\gamma$$

$$V_2(0) = V \sin\gamma$$

$$R_1(0) = dr$$

$$R_2(0) = alt$$

Since the coordinate system is inertial, we can integrate directly in the down-range and altitude directions to get velocity from acceleration and position from velocity. In this model, the gravitational acceleration is al-

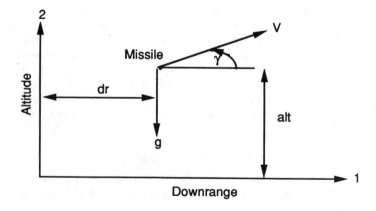

Fig. 12.1   Missile in gravity field using flat-Earth model.

ways 32.2 ft/s² in the negative altitude direction, regardless of altitude. Therefore, we know that this model can only be valid at the lower altitudes, since in actuality the gravitational acceleration decreases with increasing altitudes.

In general, a body in a gravitational field can be depicted in an Earth-centered coordinate system shown in Fig. 12.2. In this system the Earth is nonrotating and the gravitational acceleration acting on the missile is toward the center of the Earth. The missile has velocity V with respect to a reference that is tangent to the Earth and perpendicular to r (line from center of Earth to missile). The radius of the Earth is denoted by a in this figure.

According to Newton's law of universal gravitation, two bodies attract each other with a force that acts along a line connecting the two bodies. The force is proportional to the product of the masses of the two bodies and inversely proportional to the square of the distance between the two bodies. If one of the bodies is the Earth and the mass of the second body is negligible compared to the Earth, Newton's law of universal gravitation can be expressed in vector form as[2,3]

$$\ddot{r} = \frac{-gm\, r}{r^3}$$

where r is a vector from the center of the Earth to the second body, and gm is known as the gravitational parameter with the value

$$gm = 1.4077*10^{16} \text{ ft}^3/\text{s}^2$$

For simulation purposes and to be consistent with the work we have already done with tactical interceptors, it is natural to desire to express Newton's law

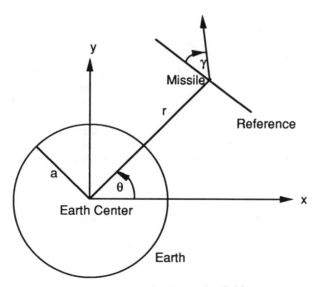

Fig. 12.2 Missile in gravity field.

in Cartesian coordinates. We shall soon see that for analytical purposes it will be more convenient to work in polar coordinates. By substituting

$$r = xi + yj$$

we can express Newton's law of universal gravitation in Earth-centered inertial coordinates (x, y) as

$$\ddot{x} = \frac{-gm\,x}{(x^2 + y^2)^{1.5}}$$

$$\ddot{y} = \frac{-gm\,y}{(x^2 + y^2)^{1.5}}$$

where x and y are component distances from the center of the Earth to the body or missile. From Fig. 12.2 we can see that the initial conditions for the preceding differential equations are

$$x(0) = (a + alt_0)\,\cos\theta_0$$

$$y(0) = (a + alt_0)\,\sin\theta_0$$

$$\dot{x}(0) = V\cos\left(\frac{\pi}{2} - \gamma + \theta_0\right)$$

$$\dot{y}(0) = V\sin\left(\frac{\pi}{2} - \gamma + \theta_0\right)$$

where V is the initial missile velocity, alt_0 the initial missile altitude with respect to the surface of the Earth, γ the angle the velocity vector makes with respect to the reference, and θ_0 the initial angular location of the missile with respect to the x axis. Velocity and position components, with respect to the center of the Earth, can be found from repeated integration of the preceding differential equations. Once we have found the location of the missile with respect to the center of the Earth, it is useful to express the missile location with respect to the surface of the Earth. The instantaneous altitude of the missile can simply be found by finding the distance from the center of the Earth to the missile and then subtracting the Earth's radius, or

$$alt = (x^2 + y^2)^{0.5} - a$$

We can find the distance traveled along the surface of the Earth by referring to Fig. 12.3.

In general, the initial location of the missile can be expressed in vector notation as

$$r_0 = x_0 i + y_0 j$$

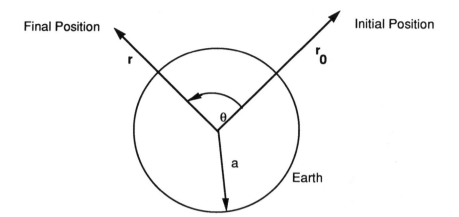

Fig. 12.3   Projecting distance missile travels on surface of Earth.

and the future location of the missile at any arbitrary time can be expressed as

$$r = xi + yj$$

The angle between the two vectors r_0 and r can be found from the definition of the vector dot product, or

$$\theta = \cos^{-1} \frac{r_0 \cdot r}{|r_0||r|}$$

Therefore, the distance traveled, which is projected on the surface of a circular Earth, is given by

$$dist = a\theta$$

For comparative purposes, the equations of motion for a missile in a gravity field were programmed using the flat-Earth constant-gravity model and the Earth-centered coordinate system using Newton's law of universal gravitation. The FORTRAN gravity field simulation appears in Listing 12.1. We can see from the listing that the position and velocity components in the flat-Earth model are denoted $RT1$, $RT2$, $VT1$, and $VT2$, respectively. In the Earth-centered system, the position and velocity components are denoted X, Y, $X1$, and $Y1$, respectively. The differential equations describing the missile in a gravity field for both coordinate systems can be found after statement label 200. In the Earth-centered system, the missile position (x, y) is converted to a downrange and altitude so that a trajectory comparison can be made with answers obtained from the flat-Earth model.

A case was run in which an impulsive missile was launched from the surface of the Earth at a 45-deg angle. The initial missile velocity was 3000

Listing 12.1   Gravity field simulation

```
        INTEGER STEP
        H = 1.
        A = 2.0926E7
        GM = 1.4077E16
        GAM = 45.
        ALTNM = 0.
        V = 3000.
        ALT = ALTNM/6076.
        ANG = 0.
        VRX = V*COS(1.5708 - GAM/57.3 + ANG)
        VRY = V*SIN(1.5708 - GAM/57.3 + ANG)
        G = 32.2
        S = 0.
        SCOUNT = 0.
        RT1 = ALT*COS(ANG)
        RT2 = ALT*SIN(ANG)
        VT1 = VRX
        VT2 = VRY
        X = (A + ALT)*COS(ANG)
        Y = (A + ALT)*SIN(ANG)
        XFIRST = X
        YFIRST = Y
        X1 = VRX
        Y1 = VRY
        T = 0.
10      IF(ALTNM < 0.)GOTO 999
        RT1OLD = RT1
        RT2OLD = RT2
        VT1OLD = VT1
        VT2OLD = VT2
        XOLD = X
        YOLD = Y
        X1OLD = X1
        Y1OLD = Y1
        STEP = 1
        GOTO 200
66      STEP = 2
        RT1 = RT1 + H*RT1D
        RT2 = RT2 + H*RT2D
        VT1 = VT1 + H*VT1D
        VT2 = VT2 + H*VT2D
        X = X + H*XD
        Y = Y + H*YD
        X1 = X1 + H*X1D
        Y1 = Y1 + H*Y1D
        T = T + H
        GOTO 200
55      RT1 = (RT1OLD + RT1)/2. + .5*H*RT1D
        RT2 = (RT2OLD + RT2)/2. + .5*H*RT2D
        VT1 = (VT1OLD + VT1)/2. + .5*H*VT1D
        VT2 = (VT2OLD + VT2)/2. + .5*H*VT2D
        X = (XOLD + X)/2. + .5*H*XD
        Y = (YOLD + Y)/2. + .5*H*YD
        X1 = (X1OLD + X1)/2. + .5*H*X1D
        Y1 = (Y1OLD + Y1)/2. + .5*H*Y1D
        S = S + H
        SCOUNT = SCOUNT + H
        IF(SCOUNT.LT.1.99999)GOTO 10
        SCOUNT = 0.
        RT1NM = RT1/6076.
        RT2NM = RT2/6076.
        ALTNM = (SQRT(X**2 + Y**2) - A)/6076.
        CALL DISTANCE(X,Y,XFIRST,YFIRST,DISTNM)
        WRITE(9,*)T,RT1NM,RT2NM,DISTNM,ALTNM
        GOTO 10
200     CONTINUE
        AT1 = 0.
        AT2 = -G
        RT1D = VT1
        RT2D = VT2
        VT1D = AT1
        VT2D = AT2
        TEMBOT = (X**2 + Y**2)**1.5
```

(Listing 12.1 continued on next page.)

Listing 12.1   (cont.) Gravity field simulation

```
        X1D = - GM*X/TEMBOT
        Y1D = - GM*Y/TEMBOT
        XD = X1
        YD = Y1
        IF(STEP - 1)66,66,55
999     CONTINUE
        PAUSE
        END
        SUBROUTINE DISTANCE(XT,YT,XF,YF,DISTNM)
        SAVE
        R = SQRT(XT**2 + YT**2)
        RF = SQRT(XF**2 + YF**2)
        A = 2.0926E7
        CBETA = (XT*XF + YT*YF)/(R*RF)
        IF(CBETA < 1.)THEN
            BETA = ACOS(CBETA)
            DISTNM = A*BETA/6076.
        ELSE
            DISTNM = (XT - XF)/6076.
        ENDIF
        RETURN
        END
```

ft/s. Figure 12.4 shows that the flat-Earth model (valid for a tactical missile) and the Earth-centered coordinate system model (valid for a strategic missile) yield the same missile trajectories. The total range traveled in both cases is about 47 n.mi., and the maximum altitude is about 12 n.mi.

Figure 12.5 shows that, when the initial speed of the impulsive missile is doubled to 6000 ft/s, we start to see some differences in the resultant missile trajectories. In this case the missile travels about 180 n.mi. and the maximum altitude reached is about 50 n.mi. Remember that the correct answers are the ones given by the Earth-centered coordinate system differential equations. However, even in this case, the flat-Earth approximation (i.e., constant-gravity model) is fairly accurate.

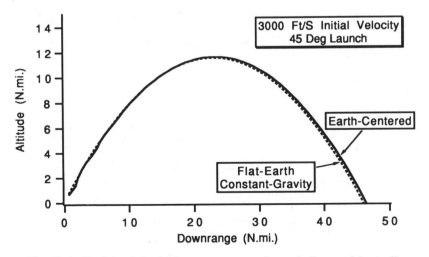

Fig. 12.4   Both models yield same answers when missile speed is small.

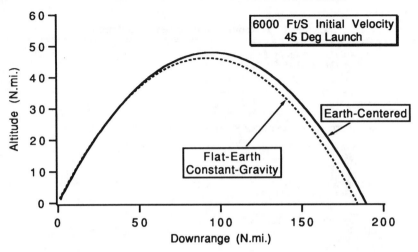

Fig. 12.5   Flat-Earth model is still fairly accurate when missile speed is doubled.

Figure 12.6 shows, that when the impulsive missile speed is again doubled to 12,000 ft/s, the flat-Earth model yields large discrepancies in the resultant missile trajectory. The missile actually travels much farther than the flat-Earth model indicates, since the gravitational acceleration is reduced at the higher altitudes according to Newton's law of universal gravitation. In this case the distance traveled is more than 800 n.mi., and the peak altitude is about 220 n.mi.

Polar Coordinate System[4,5]

In the previous section we have shown how to accurately simulate a missile in a gravity field. The differential equations representing Newton's

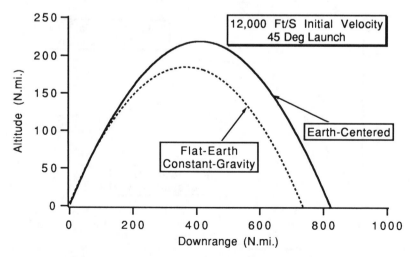

Fig. 12.6   Flat-Earth model is inaccurate when missile speed is again doubled.

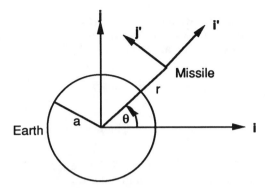

Fig. 12.7   Polar coordinate system with missile in gravity field.

law of universal gravitation were first presented in vector form and then converted for simulation purposes to an Earth-centered Cartesian coordinate system. The Earth-centered coordinate system is extremely useful for simulation work because all integration can be done directly in the inertial frame. However, in order to get insight into the nature of trajectories in a gravity field and to get closed-form solutions, it is more convenient to work analytically in a polar coordinate system whose origin is also at the center of the Earth. Figure 12.7 displays the polar coordinate system from which we proceed with our analysis.

In Fig. 12.7 we have defined a moving coordinate system that has the missile at the origin. The new coordinate system has an i' component along the distance vector and a j' component perpendicular to r. The relationship between the inertial Earth-centered coordinate system and the moving coordinate system is depicted in Fig. 12.8.

The relationship between the fixed and moving coordinate frames can be expressed mathematically as

$$i' = \cos\theta i + \sin\theta j$$

$$j' = -\sin\theta i + \cos\theta j$$

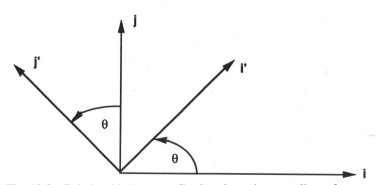

Fig. 12.8   Relationship between fixed and moving coordinate frames.

Since the new coordinate system is moving, we can express its rate of change with respect to the polar angle θ. Differentiating the preceding set of expressions with respect to the polar angle yields

$$\frac{di'}{d\theta} = -\sin\theta i + \cos\theta j = j'$$

$$\frac{dj'}{d\theta} = -\cos\theta i - \sin\theta j = -i'$$

We can now find the rate of change of the new coordinate system as a function of time according to the chain rule, or

$$\frac{di'}{dt} = \frac{d\theta}{dt}\frac{di'}{d\theta} = \dot{\theta}j'$$

$$\frac{dj'}{dt} = \frac{d\theta}{dt}\frac{dj'}{d\theta} = -\dot{\theta}i'$$

We now have sufficient information so that we can take derivatives of vectors. The distance vector r can be expressed in the moving coordinate system as

$$r = ri'$$

Taking the derivative of the preceding expression yields

$$\dot{r} = \dot{r}i' + r\dot{i}'$$

However, we have just shown that

$$\dot{i}' = -\dot{\theta}j'$$

$$\dot{j}' = \dot{\theta}i'$$

Therefore, substitution yields the radial velocity expression

$$\dot{r} = r\dot{\theta}j' + \dot{r}i'$$

Taking the derivative once more yields

$$\ddot{r} = (\ddot{r} - r\dot{\theta}^2)i' + (r\ddot{\theta} + 2\dot{r}\dot{\theta})j'$$

We know that gravitational acceleration is along i', and there is no acceleration along j'. Therefore, the preceding vector differential equation can be expressed as the following two scalar differential equations:

$$\frac{-gm}{r^2} = \ddot{r} - r\dot{\theta}^2$$

$$0 = r\ddot{\theta} + 2\dot{r}\dot{\theta}$$

Since

$$\frac{d}{dt}(r^2\dot\theta) = 2r\dot r\dot\theta + r^2\ddot\theta$$

we can say that

$$\frac{d}{dt}(r^2\dot\theta) = 0$$

Integration yields a constant of integration that must be a moment arm times a tangential velocity, or

$$r^2\dot\theta = (a + alt)V\cos\gamma$$

In summary, the differential equations describing a missile in a gravity field can also be expressed in polar coordinates as

$$\ddot r - r\dot\theta^2 + \frac{gm}{r^2} = 0$$

$$r^2\dot\theta = (a + alt)V\cos\gamma$$

where the initial conditions are

$$r(0) = a + alt$$

$$\theta(0) = 0$$

$$\dot r(0) = V\sin\gamma$$

A FORTRAN simulation was set up to demonstrate that the polar and Cartesian Earth-centered differential equations are equivalent. Listing 12.2 presents the gravity field simulation for both coordinate systems. The position and velocity components in the Cartesian system appear in the listing as X, Y, $X1$, and $Y1$, respectively. The range, its derivative, and the polar angle in the polar coordinate system are denoted by $R0$, $R1$, and PSI in the listing. The differential equations for both the Cartesian and polar coordinate systems appear after label 200 in the listing.

An experiment was run in which a missile with an initial velocity 24,000 ft/s was launched from the surface of the Earth at an angle of 45 deg with respect to the reference. The resultant trajectories for both sets of differential equations appear in Fig. 12.9. We can see that the resultant trajectories are identical for all practical purposes. It is interesting to note that with an initial speed of 24,000 ft/s the impulsive missile traveled nearly 4500 n.mi. and reached an altitude of 1700 n.mi.

Closed-Form Solutions[4,5]

For those readers familiar with the literature on astrodynamics, apologies are offered in advance for the text's unconventional notation. Many other authors use *re* or *Re* rather than *a* for the radius of the Earth and use *a* rather

Listing 12.2   Gravity field simulation with different coordinate systems

```
          INTEGER STEP
          H = 1.
          A = 2.0926E7
          GM = 1.4077E16
          GAM = 45.
          ALTNM = 0.
          V = 24000.
          ANGDEG = 0.
          ANG = ANGDEG/57.3
          VRX = V*COS(1.5708 – GAM/57.3 + ANG)
          VRY = V*SIN(1.5708 – GAM/57.3 + ANG)
          ALT = ALTNM/6076.
          S = 0.
          SCOUNT = 0.
          R0 = A + ALT
          R1 = V*SIN(GAM/57.3)
          PSI = 0.
          X = (A + ALT)*COS(ANG)
          Y = (A + ALT)*SIN(ANG)
          XFIRST = X
          YFIRST = Y
          X1 = VRX
          Y1 = VRY
          T = 0.
  10      IF(ALTNM < 0.)GOTO 999
          R0OLD = R0
          R1OLD = R1
          PSIOLD = PSI
          XOLD = X
          YOLD = Y
          X1OLD = X1
          Y1OLD = Y1
          STEP = 1
          GOTO 200
  66      STEP = 2
          R0 = R0 + H*R0D
          R1 = R1 + H*R1D
          PSI = PSI + H*PSID
          X = X + H*XD
          Y = Y + H*YD
          X1 = X1 + H*X1D
          Y1 = Y1 + H*Y1D
          T = T + H
          GOTO 200
  55      R0 = (R0OLD + R0)/2 + .5*H*R0D
          R1 = (R1OLD + R1)/2 + .5*H*R1D
          PSI = (PSIOLD + PSI)/2 + .5*H*PSID
          X = (XOLD + X)/2 + .5*H*XD
          Y = (YOLD + Y)/2 + .5*H*YD
          X1 = (X1OLD + X1)/2 + .5*H*X1D
          Y1 = (Y1OLD + Y1)/2 + .5*H*Y1D
          S = S + H
          SCOUNT = SCOUNT + H
          IF(SCOUNT.LT.9.99999)GOTO 10
          SCOUNT = 0.
          SPOLARNM = A*PSI/6076.
          ALTPOLARNM = (R0 – A)/6076.
          ALTNM = (SQRT(X**2 + Y**2) – A)/6076.
          CALL DISTANCE(X,Y,XFIRST,YFIRST,DISTNM)
          WRITE(9,*)T,SPOLARNM,ALTPOLARNM,DISTNM,ALTNM
          GOTO 10
 200      CONTINUE
          PSID = (A + ALT)*V*COS(GAM/57.3)/(R0*R0)
          R1D = – GM/(R0*R0) + R0*PSID*PSID
          R0D = R1
          TEMBOT = (X**2 + Y**2)**1.5
          X1D = – GM*X/TEMBOT
          Y1D = – GM*Y/TEMBOT
          XD = X1
          YD = Y1
          IF(STEP – 1)66,66,55
 999      CONTINUE
          PAUSE
```

(Listing 12.2 continued on next page.)

Listing 12.2   (cont.) Gravity field simulation with different coordinate systems

```
END
SUBROUTINE DISTANCE(XT,YT,XF,YF,DISTNM)
SAVE
R = SQRT(XT**2 + YT**2)
RF = SQRT(XF**2 + YF**2)
A = 2.0926E7
CBETA = (XT*XF + YT*YF)/(R*RF)
IF(CBETA<1.)THEN
    BETA = ACOS(CBETA)
    DISTNM = A*BETA/6076.
ELSE
    DISTNM = (XT − XF)/6076.
ENDIF
RETURN
END
```

than a_1 for the semimajor axis of an ellipse. The choice of a for the radius of the Earth was solely historical (i.e., it was used in Ref. 4), whereas the use of a_1 for the semimajor axis of an ellipse was to avoid further confusion. In this section we will solve the previously derived differential equations of Newton's law of universal gravitation expressed in polar coordinates. In other words, we seek to find closed-form solutions of the polar differential equations

$$\ddot{r} - r\dot{\theta}^2 + \frac{gm}{r^2} = 0$$

$$r^2\dot{\theta} = (a + alt)V \cos\gamma$$

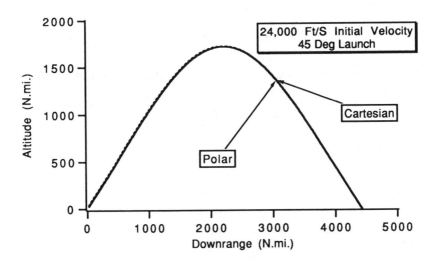

Fig. 12.9 Polar and Earth-centered gravity field equations yield identical trajectories.

For convenience let us define constants r_0 and p such that

$$r_0 = a + alt$$

$$p = (a + alt)V \cos\gamma = r_0 V \cos\gamma$$

In addition, we will define an inverse range to be

$$u = 1/r$$

The goal is to convert both polar differential equations to one second-order differential equation in terms of u. First we know from the chain rule that u varies with time according to

$$\frac{du}{dt} = \frac{d\theta}{dt}\frac{du}{d\theta} = \dot\theta\,\frac{du}{d\theta} = \frac{p}{r^2}\frac{du}{d\theta}$$

An alternate way of seeing how u changes with respect to time is

$$\frac{du}{dt} = \frac{du}{dr}\frac{dr}{dt} = \frac{-1}{r^2}\frac{dr}{dt}$$

Equating both expressions yields

$$\frac{dr}{dt} = -p\,\frac{du}{d\theta}$$

Next we define z to be

$$z = \frac{dr}{dt}$$

Using the chain rule to see how z changes with respect to time yields

$$\frac{dz}{dt} = \frac{d\theta}{dt}\frac{dz}{d\theta} = \frac{p}{r^2}\frac{d}{d\theta}\left[\frac{dr}{dt}\right] = \frac{p}{r^2}\frac{d}{d\theta}\left[-p\,\frac{du}{d\theta}\right]$$

Therefore, we can say that

$$\frac{dz}{dt} = \frac{d^2r}{dt^2} = \frac{-p^2}{r^2}\frac{d^2u}{d\theta^2}$$

Substitution allows us to rewrite the second-order differential equation in range as

$$\ddot{r} - r\dot\theta^2 + \frac{gm}{r^2} = 0 = \frac{-p^2}{r^2}\frac{d^2u}{d\theta^2} - r\frac{p^2}{r^4} + gm\,u^2$$

Simplification yields

$$\frac{d^2u}{d\theta^2} + u = \frac{gm}{p^2}$$

For purposes that will be obvious later we can define a new constant to be

$$\lambda = \frac{r_0 V^2}{gm}$$

We can now summarize the transformed range polar differential equation to be

$$\frac{d^2u}{d\theta^2} + u = \frac{1}{\lambda r_0 \cos^2 \gamma}$$

The original initial conditions on the polar differential equations were

$$r(0) = r_0$$

$$\dot{r}(0) = V \sin\gamma$$

Since we already know that

$$\frac{du}{d\theta} = -\frac{1}{p}\frac{dr}{dt} = \frac{-1}{r_0 V \cos\gamma}\frac{dr}{dt}$$

we can say that

$$\frac{du}{d\theta}(0) = \frac{-\tan\gamma}{r_0}$$

The other initial condition is simply

$$u(0) = \frac{1}{r(0)} = \frac{1}{r_0}$$

The solution to the preceding second-order differential equation is

$$u = A \sin\theta + B \cos\theta + \frac{1}{\lambda r_0 \cos^2 \gamma}$$

where A and B can be found from the initial conditions. After some algebra we obtain the complete solution in terms of u as

$$u = \frac{1 - \cos\theta}{\lambda r_0 \cos^2\gamma} + \frac{1}{r_0}\frac{\cos(\theta + \gamma)}{\cos\gamma}$$

However, since

$$u = 1/r$$

the solution in terms of r becomes

$$\frac{r_0}{r} = \frac{1 - \cos\theta}{\lambda \cos^2\gamma} + \frac{\cos(\theta + \gamma)}{\cos\gamma}$$

or, more conveniently,

$$r = \frac{r_0\lambda \cos^2\gamma}{1 - \cos\theta + \lambda \cos\gamma \cos(\theta + \gamma)} = \frac{r_0\lambda \cos^2\gamma}{1 - \lambda \sin\theta \cos\gamma \sin\gamma - \cos\theta(1 - \lambda \cos^2\gamma)}$$

Thus, given missile altitude (r_0), velocity (λ), and flight-path angle γ, we find the missile location r as a function of the central angle θ. The preceding closed-form solution is also the equation of an ellipse in a polar coordinate system. To prove this interesting fact we must first recognize that the equation for an ellipse in polar coordinates is

$$r = \frac{a_1(1 - e^2)}{1 - e \cos(\theta - \omega)} = \frac{a_1(1 - e^2)}{1 - e \sin\theta \sin\omega - e \cos\theta \cos\omega}$$

where a_1 is the semimajor axis, e the eccentricity, and ω the argument of the apogee. The trajectory equation and the equation for an ellipse are equivalent if

$$e \sin\omega = \lambda \cos\gamma \sin\gamma$$

$$e \cos\omega = 1 - \lambda \cos^2\gamma$$

Squaring and adding the preceding equations yields an expression for the eccentricity in terms of λ, or

$$e = [1 + \lambda (\lambda - 2) \cos^2\gamma]^{0.5}$$

The trajectory equation yields a circle if $e = 0$, an ellipse if $0 < e < 1$, a parabola if $e = 1$, and a hyperbola for $e > 1$. If we set the flight-path angle γ to zero, we can see that we get circular motion if $\lambda = 1$, elliptical motion for $0 < \lambda < 2$, parabolic motion for $\lambda = 2$, and hyperbolic motion for $\lambda > 2$. Since we can express the initial velocity in terms of λ as

$$V = \sqrt{\frac{\lambda g m}{r_0}}$$

we can determine the trajectory shape from the magnitude of the velocity! The Earth-centered trajectory generator was modified so that the initial flight-path angle was zero and the initial velocity expressed in terms of λ

according to the preceding velocity equation. In addition, the outputs, rather than being downrange and altitude, were expressed in the natural x, y units (i.e., distance from the center of the Earth converted to nautical miles). Listing 12.3 presents the resultant FORTRAN orbit generator program. We can see from the listing that the missile is initially at 1000 n.mi. altitude.

A case was run in which λ was set to 1. Figure 12.10 shows that the simulation indicates that the missile trajectory is indeed circular—as theory predicted! Figure 12.11 shows that when λ was set to 1.5 the simulation got an elliptical orbit for the missile—as theory predicted! Values of λ between 0 and 2 should yield elliptical orbital motion, with 1 being circular.

Listing 12.3   FORTRAN orbit generator

```
      INTEGER STEP
      H = 10.
      A = 2.0926E7
      GM = 1.4077E16
      GAM = 0.
      ALTNM = 1000.
      ALT = ALTNM*6076.
      XLAM = 1.
      V = SQRT(GM*XLAM/(A + ALT))
      ANGDEG = 90.
      ANG = ANGDEG/57.3
      VRX = V*COS(1.5708 - GAM/57.3 + ANG)
      VRY = V*SIN(1.5708 - GAM/57.3 + ANG)
      S = 0.
      SCOUNT = 0.
      X = (A + ALT)*COS(ANG)
      Y = (A + ALT)*SIN(ANG)
      XFIRST = X
      YFIRST = Y
      X1 = VRX
      Y1 = VRY
      T = 0.
      TF = 30000.
10    IF(T > TF)GOTO 999
      XOLD = X
      YOLD = Y
      X1OLD = X1
      Y1OLD = Y1
      STEP = 1
      GOTO 200
66    STEP = 2
      X = X + H*XD
      Y = Y + H*YD
      X1 = X1 + H*X1D
      Y1 = Y1 + H*Y1D
      T = T + H
      GOTO 200
55    X = (XOLD + X)/2 + .5*H*XD
      Y = (YOLD + Y)/2 + .5*H*YD
      X1 = (X1OLD + X1)/2 + .5*H*X1D
      Y1 = (Y1OLD + Y1)/2 + .5*H*Y1D
      S = S + H
      SCOUNT = SCOUNT + H
      IF(SCOUNT.LT.49.99999)GOTO 10
      SCOUNT = 0.
      XNM = X/6076.
      YNM = Y/6076.
      WRITE(9,*)T,XNM,YNM
      GOTO 10
200   CONTINUE
      TEMBOT = (X**2 + Y**2)**1.5
      X1D = - GM*X/TEMBOT
      Y1D = - GM*Y/TEMBOT
      XD = X1
      YD = Y1
      IF(STEP - 1)66,66,55
999   CONTINUE
      PAUSE
      END
```

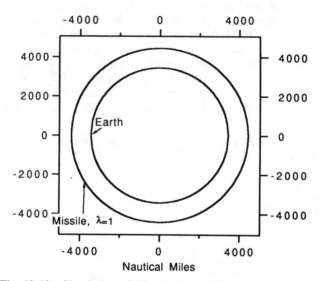

Fig. 12.10 Simulation yields circular orbit when λ is unity.

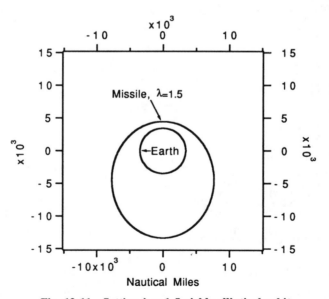

Fig. 12.11 Setting λ = 1.5 yields elliptical orbit.

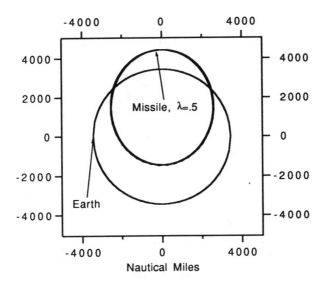

Fig. 12.12   Setting λ too small results in orbit which intersects Earth.

Theory says that if we set $\lambda = 0.5$ we should also get an elliptical orbit. However, Figure 12.12 shows that, although the simulation indicates an elliptical orbit, it is one that intersects the Earth! Therefore, values of λ between 0 and 1 yield suborbital motion. Although this type of trajectory is not appropriate for a satellite, it is appropriate for a ballistic missile! Finally Fig. 12.13 shows that when $\lambda = 2$ we have achieved escape velocity and the missile motion is parabolic. This type of orbit does not intersect the Earth.

Hit Equation[4,5]

We have seen that the previously derived trajectory equation is useful in obtaining closed-form solutions for satellite orbits and ballistic missile trajectories. If we specialize in the ballistic missile case, we can also get closed-form solutions from the trajectory equation, which, given an initial missile flight-path angle, altitude, and distance to be traveled (missile hits the Earth at that distance), will define the magnitude of the missile velocity required.

If we desire for the missile to travel a distance *dist,* then the total central angle traveled ϕ is given by (see Fig. 12.7)

$$\phi = dist/a$$

where a is the radius of the Earth. The missile hits the Earth when $r = a$. Therefore, substituting $r = a$ and $\theta = \phi$ into the trajectory equation solution yields

$$\frac{r_0}{a} = \frac{1 - \cos\phi}{\lambda \cos^2\gamma} + \frac{\cos(\phi + \gamma)}{\cos\gamma}$$

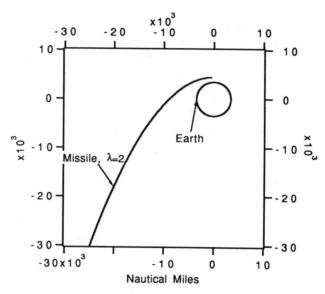

Fig. 12.13   Setting λ = 2 results in parabolic trajectory for missile.

Recognizing that

$$\lambda = \frac{r_0 V^2}{gm}$$

we can solve for the velocity. After some algebra we obtain

$$V = \sqrt{\frac{gm(1 - \cos\phi)}{r_0 \cos\gamma \left[\dfrac{r_0 \cos\gamma}{a} - \cos(\phi + \gamma) \right]}}$$

This equation tells us the velocity required to hit a target a certain distance away from our launch point, given we want to launch with a certain flight-path angle γ. Figure 12.14 displays the velocity formula in graphic form. We can see that, as expected, longer distances require larger missile velocities. If the initial flight-path angle is too large, the ballistic missile will never hit the Earth because the resultant velocity will exceed the escape velocity (λ = 2) and the trajectory will not be elliptical.

Listing 12.4 presents a modified ballistic missile simulation using the preceding velocity formula to derive the desired initial velocity given the desired flight-path angle, initial missile altitude, and distance to be covered. From the listing we can see that the missile is launched from the surface of the Earth with an initial flight-path angle of 23 deg. The target is 6000 n.mi. downrange on the surface of the Earth. Although the velocity formula was derived from solutions in the polar coordinate system, the simulation is based in the Cartesian coordinate system.

Listing 12.4 Simulation to demonstrate validity of velocity formula

```
        INTEGER STEP
        H = 1.
        A = 2.0926E7
        GM = 1.4077E16
        GAMDEG = 23.
        GAM = GAMDEG/57.3
        DISTNM = 6000.
        ANGDEG = 0.
        ANG = ANGDEG/57.3
        PHI = DISTNM*6076./A
        ALTNM = 0.
        ALT = ALTNM*6076.
        R0 = A + ALT
        TOP = GM*(1. – COS(PHI))
        TEMP = R0*COS(GAM)/A – COS(PHI + GAM)
        BOT = R0*COS(GAM)*TEMP
        V = SQRT(TOP/BOT)
        VRX = V*COS(1.5708 – GAM + ANG)
        VRY = V*SIN(1.5708 – GAM + ANG)
        S = 0.
        SCOUNT = 0.
        X = (A + ALT)*COS(ANG)
        Y = (A + ALT)*SIN(ANG)
        XFIRST = X
        YFIRST = Y
        X1 = VRX
        Y1 = VRY
        T = 0.
10      IF(ALT<0.)GOTO 999
        XOLD = X
        YOLD = Y
        X1OLD = X1
        Y1OLD = Y1
        STEP = 1
        GOTO 200
66      STEP = 2
        X = X + H*XD
        Y = Y + H*YD
        X1 = X1 + H*X1D
        Y1 = Y1 + H*Y1D
        T = T + H
        GOTO 200
55      X = (XOLD + X)/2 + .5*H*XD
        Y = (YOLD + Y)/2 + .5*H*YD
        X1 = (X1OLD + X1)/2 + .5*H*X1D
        Y1 = (Y1OLD + Y1)/2 + .5*H*Y1D
        ALT = SQRT(X**2 + Y**2) – A
        S = S + H
        SCOUNT = SCOUNT + H
        IF(SCOUNT.LT.9.99999)GOTO 10
        SCOUNT = 0.
        XNM = X/6076.
        YNM = Y/6076.
        ALTNM = ALT/6076.
        CALL DISTANCE(X,Y,XFIRST,YFIRST,DISTNM)
        WRITE(9,*)T,XNM,YNM,DISTNM,ALTNM
        GOTO 10
200     CONTINUE
        TEMBOT = (X**2 + Y**2)**1.5
        X1D = – GM*X/TEMBOT
        Y1D = – GM*Y/TEMBOT
        XD = X1
        YD = Y1
        IF(STEP – 1)66,66,55
999     CONTINUE
        XNM = X/6076.
        YNM = Y/6076.
        ALTNM = ALT/6076.
        CALL DISTANCE(X,Y,XFIRST,YFIRST,DISTNM)
        WRITE(9,*)T,XNM,YNM,DISTNM,ALTNM
        PAUSE
        END
        SUBROUTINE DISTANCE(XT,YT,XF,YF,DISTNM)
```

(Listing 12.4 continued on next page.)

Listing 12.4   (cont.) Simulation to demonstrate validity of velocity formula

```
SAVE
R = SQRT(XT**2 + YT**2)
RF = SQRT(XF**2 + YF**2)
A = 2.0926E7
CBETA = (XT*XF + YT*YF)/(R*RF)
IF(CBETA<1.)THEN
     BETA = ACOS(CBETA)
     DISTNM = A*BETA/6076.
ELSE
     DISTNM = (XT − XF)/6076.
ENDIF
RETURN
END
```

Figure 12.15 presents simulation results, in the form of an altitude vs down-range plot for the nominal case of Listing 12.4. We can see that the missile indeed travels the desired distance of 6000 n.mi. before hitting the surface of the Earth. The peak altitude for the missile is in excess of 800 n.mi. Figure 12.16 presents the same trajectory information in a way in which the curvature of the Earth is apparent.

Flight Time[4,5]

We have already seen that, given a distance to be covered and initial flight-path angle, it was possible to derive a formula for the required velocity. Also associated with this velocity is the time to reach the target or time of flight, t_F. It is also possible, based on the trajectory equation solution for r, to derive a closed-form solution for the time of flight. From the original gravity field differential equation in polar coordinates we know that

$$r^2 \frac{d\theta}{dt} = r_0 V \cos\gamma$$

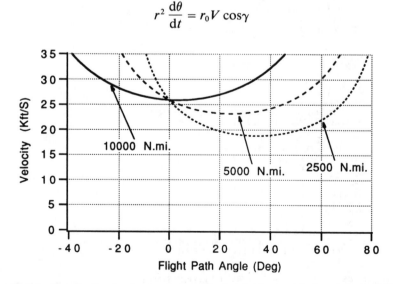

Fig. 12.14   Required velocity depends on range to be traveled and desired flight-path angle.

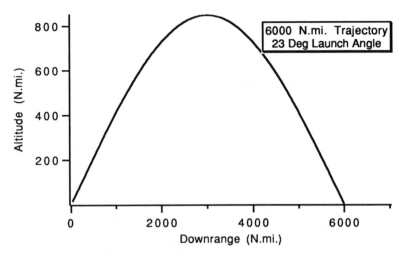

Fig. 12.15   Closed-form solution for velocity is accurate.

We can cross multiply terms to set up the integrals

$$\int_0^\phi r^2 \, d\theta = \int_0^{t_F} r_0 V \cos\gamma \, dt$$

Integration of the right-hand side of the equation and substitution of the trajectory solution into the left-hand side yields the integral

$$t_F = \frac{1}{r_0 V \cos\gamma} \int_0^\phi \frac{r_0^2 \lambda^2 \cos^4\gamma}{[1 - \cos\theta + \lambda \cos\gamma \cos(\theta + \gamma)]^2} \, d\theta$$

After integration and much algebra, the closed-form solution assuming $\lambda < 2$ for the flight time simplifies to

$$t_F = \frac{r_0}{V \cos\gamma} \left\{ \frac{\tan\gamma(1 - \cos\phi) + (1 - \lambda)\sin\phi}{(2 - \lambda)\left[\dfrac{1 - \cos\phi}{\lambda \cos^2\gamma} + \dfrac{\cos(\gamma + \phi)}{\cos\gamma}\right]} \right.$$

$$\left. + \frac{2 \cos\gamma}{\lambda\left(\dfrac{2}{\lambda} - 1\right)^{1.5}} \tan^{-1}\left(\frac{\sqrt{\dfrac{2}{\lambda} - 1}}{\cos\gamma \cot\dfrac{\phi}{2} - \sin\gamma}\right) \right\}$$

Figure 12.17 displays the flight time formula in graphic form. We can see that, as expected, it takes longer for a ballistic missile to travel greater distances. In addition, increasing the flight-path angle tends to increase the time of flight. For example, it takes about 1800 s for a ballistic missile to travel 5000 n.mi. when the flight-path angle is 20 deg. Increasing the flight-

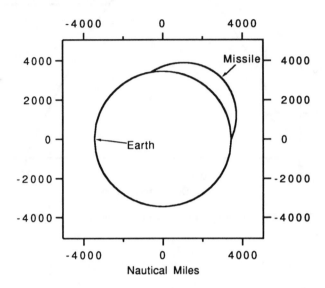

Fig. 12.16   Six thousand nautical miles, 23-deg trajectory.

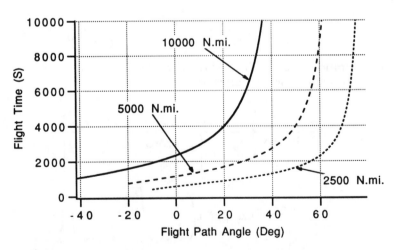

Fig. 12.17   Flight time increases with increasing flight-path angle and increasing distance to be traveled.

path angle to 40 deg increases the flight time to nearly 2800 s. We can also see that flight time increases monotonically and smoothly with increasing values of flight-path angle. We shall make use of this interesting observation later.

Summary

This chapter was our first introduction into the strategic world. We saw that the constant-gravity, flat-Earth model used for tactical interceptors was not correct for strategic interceptors. Simulation models based on Newton's law of universal gravitation were derived from first principles. It was shown that an Earth-centered Cartesian system was useful for simulation and a polar model was more useful for analytical work. A closed-form solution was obtained for a ballistic missile's velocity in terms of flight-path angle and distance to be covered, and another expression was derived relating the flight time to the velocity. Simulation results confirmed the closed-form solutions. We shall make much use of these relationships later.

References

[1] Kennedy, G. P., *Rockets, Missiles and Spacecraft of the National Air and Space Museum*, Smithsonian Institution Press, Washington DC, 1983.

[2] Bate, R. R., Mueller, D. D., and White, J. E., *Fundamentals of Astrodynamics*, Dover, New York, 1971.

[3] Battin, R. H., *An Introduction to the Mathematics and Methods of Astrodynamics*, AIAA Education Series, New York, 1987.

[4] Wheelon, A. D., "Free Flight of a Ballistic Missile," *ARS Journal*, Vol. 29, Dec. 1959, pp. 915-926.

[5] Regan, F., *Re-Entry Vehicle Dynamics*, AIAA Education Series, New York, 1984.

Chapter 13

Boosters

Introduction

WE have seen in Chapter 12 that, in order for a ballistic interceptor to travel long distances or go into orbit, it must attain speeds in excess of 20 kft/s. From the rocket equation we saw in Chapter 11 that, with fuel mass fractions of less than 0.5 (i.e., tactical missiles), it was impossible to reach these speeds. In this chapter we shall investigate preliminary booster designs so that speeds required for strategic travel can be achieved.

Review

In Chapter 11 we saw that the change in velocity is related to specific impulse I_{sp} and fuel mass fraction mf according to the rocket equation, or

$$\Delta V = I_{sp} g \, \log \frac{1}{1 - mf}$$

Figure 13.1 displays the rocket equation in graphic form. From this figure we can see that fuel mass fractions approaching 0.9 are required if we wish to attain speeds in excess of 20 kft/s for fuel specific impulses of less than 300 s. The figure clearly shows that fuel mass fractions of less than 0.5 (i.e., tactical missiles) lead to velocities that are not adequate for a strategic application.

We can think of a strategic interceptor as consisting of two sections: a booster and payload. A single-stage booster (we will consider staging later in this chapter) consists of fuel and structure denoted by weights W_P and W_S, respectively, as shown in Fig. 13.2. Initially we will consider that the sole purpose of the single-stage booster is to get the payload up to speed. The payload, denoted by weight W_{pay}, consists of structure, electronics, a divert engine, and fuel. The purpose of the payload for strategic guided interceptors is to acquire the target and maneuver, using divert fuel, to hit the target.

If it is desired that the interceptor change its velocity by amount ΔV, then the weight of the structure, fuel, and payload must also follow the rocket equation as

$$W_S + W_P + W_{pay} = (W_S + W_{pay}) \exp\left(\frac{\Delta V}{g I_{sp}}\right)$$

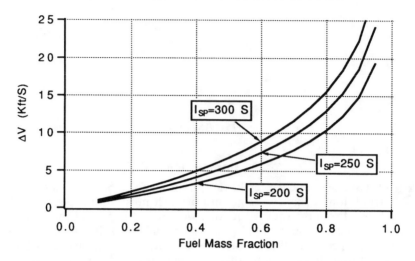

Fig. 13.1   Large fuel mass fractions are required for strategic applications.

where I_{sp} denotes the specific impulse of the booster fuel and is measured in seconds. The fuel mass fraction has been defined as the ratio of the propellant weight to the total weight. In order to simplify computations in this chapter, an approximate fuel mass fraction mf^* is defined as the ratio of the propellant weight to the sum of the propellant weight plus structure or

$$mf^* = \frac{W_P}{W_P + W_S}$$

For small payloads the approximate and actual fuel mass fractions are equivalent. We can express the weight of the booster structure to the propellant weight and fuel approximate mass fraction according to

$$W_S = \frac{W_P(1 - mf^*)}{mf^*}$$

Substitution of the preceding relationship into the rocket equation yields, after some algebra, a formula for the propellant weight in terms of the

Booster	Payload
W_S W_P	W_{PAY}

Fig. 13.2   Single-stage strategic interceptor model.

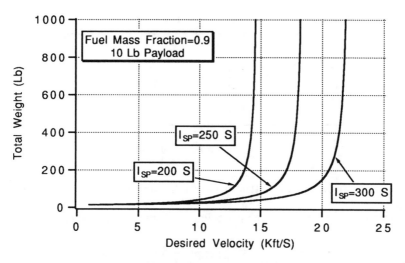

Fig. 13.3   A great deal of weight is required to bring small payloads to strategic speeds.

payload weight, velocity desired, approximate fuel mass fraction, and specific impulse. This relationship can be expressed as

$$W_P = \frac{W_{pay}\left[\exp\left(\dfrac{\Delta V}{gI_{sp}}\right) - 1\right]}{\dfrac{1}{mf^*} - \dfrac{1 - mf^*}{mf^*}\exp\left(\dfrac{\Delta V}{gI_{sp}}\right)}$$

The total interceptor weight W_{tot} consists of the booster fuel and structure plus the payload, or

$$W_{tot} = W_S + W_P + W_{pay}$$

Based on the preceding relationships, Fig. 13.3 displays the total weight vs the desired change in velocity for an approximate fuel mass fraction of 0.9 and payload weight of 10 lb. We can see that, for a booster to reach a desired velocity of 20 kft/s from rest (in the absence of atmospheric drag), with a specific impulse of 300 s, more than 150 lb of total weight is required—just for a 10-lb payload! Doubling the payload weight will double the total weight. Decreasing the specific impulse or decreasing the fuel mass fraction both work in the direction of increasing the total weight.

Staging

We have seen in the previous section that it can take a great deal of total weight to propel small payloads to near-orbital speeds. One way of reducing the total weight for a given approximate fuel mass fraction and specific impulse is to use staging. Figure 13.4 presents a two-stage booster. In this

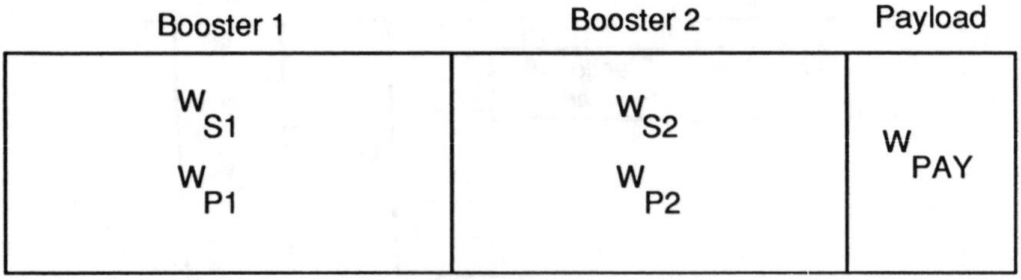

Booster 1	Booster 2	Payload
W_{S1} W_{P1}	W_{S2} W_{P2}	W_{PAY}

Fig. 13.4   Two-stage booster.

figure, the propellant and structural weights are indicated in each of the stages.

Therefore, the second-stage propellant weight can be expressed as

$$W_{P2} = \frac{W_{\text{pay}}\left[\exp\left(\dfrac{\Delta V_2}{gI_{sp2}}\right) - 1\right]}{\dfrac{1}{mf2^*} - \dfrac{1 - mf2^*}{mf2^*}\exp\left(\dfrac{\Delta V_2}{gI_{sp2}}\right)}$$

where ΔV_2 is the desired velocity change attributed to the second stage, $mf2^*$ is the second-stage approximate fuel mass fraction, and I_{sp2} is the second-stage specific impulse. The structural weight of the second stage can then be expressed as

$$W_{S2} = \frac{W_{P2}(1 - mf2^*)}{mf2^*}$$

The weight of the second stage plus payload, W_{tot2}, is simply

$$W_{tot2} = W_{P2} + W_{S2} + W_{\text{pay}}$$

We can now find the propellant weight of the first stage by treating W_{tot2} as an effective payload. The resultant weight is

$$W_{P1} = \frac{W_{tot2}\left[\exp\left(\dfrac{\Delta V_1}{gI_{sp1}}\right) - 1\right]}{\dfrac{1}{mf1^*} - \dfrac{1 - mf1^*}{mf1^*}\exp\left(\dfrac{\Delta V_1}{gI_{sp1}}\right)}$$

where ΔV_1 is the desired velocity change attributed to the first stage, $mf1^*$ is the first-stage approximate fuel mass fraction, and I_{sp1} is the first-stage specific impulse. The structural weight of the first stage can then be expressed as

$$W_{S1} = \frac{W_{P1}(1 - mf1^*)}{mf1^*}$$

Finally, the total interceptor weight (first stage plus rest) is given by

$$W_{tot} = W_{P1} + W_{S1} + W_{tot2}$$

Using the preceding relationships for a two-stage interceptor, the total weight was calculated as a function of desired velocity change for various values of specific impulse. It was assumed that each stage of the interceptor had equal specific impulses and equal approximate fuel mass fractions. In addition, it was also assumed that half of the desired velocity was obtained with the first stage and the second half of the desired velocity was obtained with the second stage. Figure 13.5 shows how the total weight varies. For a desired velocity of 20 kft/s, Fig. 13.5 shows that, for a 300-s specific impulse, approximately 100 lb of total weight are required for a 10-lb payload using a two-stage interceptor. Figure 13.3 shows that for the same case a one-stage interceptor requires more than 150 lb of total weight. Thus, staging appears to be beneficial.

If the approximate fuel mass fraction were unity, the structural weight would be zero. In this case there would be no benefit to staging. In a sense, the unity fuel mass fraction case represents the minimum total weight that can propel a payload to a desired velocity for a given specific impulse. Figure 13.6 presents a comparison of weight requirements for different staging options. In the comparison an approximate fuel mass fraction of 0.9 and specific impulse 250 s were assumed for each of the stages. In addition, it was assumed that each stage contributed an equal fraction to the total desired velocity change. Superimposed on the figure is the infinite stage case (approximate fuel mass fraction equals unity) to represent minimal attainable weight. We can see that three stages gets near-optimal answers for the case in which the approximate fuel mass fraction is 0.9 and specific impulse is 250 s.

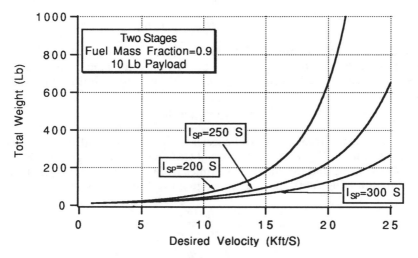

Fig. 13.5   Adding a stage reduces total weight requirements.

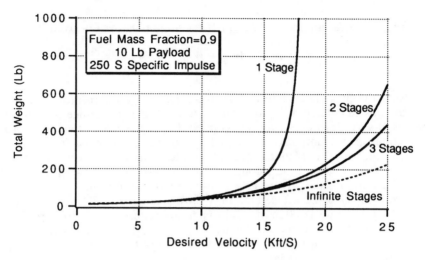

Fig. 13.6   Three stages yields near-minimal weight.

Booster Numerical Example

We now have enough information so that we can begin, to first order, to model the boost phase of a strategic interceptor. In the previous section we derived formulas so that we could calculate weights based on desired velocity, approximate fuel mass fraction, and specific impulse. The maximum axial acceleration will occur right before staging, since that is where the interceptor weight is a minimum. If the maximum axial acceleration for each stage is given, then we have enough information to find the thrust levels for each of the stages. For example, in a two-stage strategic interceptor, the thrust level during stage 1, T_1, is given by

$$T_1 = a_{\text{max}1} (W_{\text{tot}2} + W_{S1})$$

where $a_{\text{max}1}$ is the maximum axial acceleration of the first stage, in units of gravity, and $W_{\text{tot}2} + W_{S1}$ is the weight of the first stage right before staging. The thrust level of the second stage can be found in a similar way and is given by

$$T_2 = a_{\text{max}2}(W_{\text{pay}} + W_{S2})$$

where $a_{\text{max}2}$ is the maximum axial acceleration of the second stage, in units of gravity, and $W_{\text{pay}} + W_{S2}$ is the weight of the second stage right before staging. We can find the thrust burn times from specific impulse and thrust information. The first- and second-stage burn times are given by

$$t_{B1} = \frac{I_{\text{sp}1} W_{P1}}{T_1}$$

$$t_{B2} = \frac{I_{\text{sp}2} W_{P2}}{T_2}$$

We now have enough information so that given sufficient high level information we can compute a hypothetical booster's thrust-weight profiles. Listing 13.1 presents a FORTRAN program in which thrust-weight information is computed to yield a desired velocity change. The program assumes a two-stage booster with a 100-lb payload. The specific impulse for both stages is the same and is 250 s, and the approximate fuel mass fraction for both stages is also the same and is 0.85. The desired change in velocity is 20,000 ft/s with the first stage contributing one-third of the desired ΔV and the second stage contributing the rest. The maximum axial acceleration in both stages is specified to be 10 g. The program also integrates the computed acceleration to check if the desired velocity is reached.

The program was run with the nominal inputs, and the interceptor total weight was computed to be 6169 lb. Table 13.1 summarizes the program's computation of key parameters.

Figure 13.7 presents the information of Table 13.1 in graphic form (but not to scale) as a thrust-weight profile. The sharp weight drops at 32.2 and 138.2 s represent staging events (structural weight dropped). After the interceptor is finished burning propellant at 138.2 s, the total weight is the payload weight of 100 lb, as can be seen from the figure.

The FORTRAN program of Listing 13.1 also had a capability to integrate the one-dimensional equation of motion

$$\dot{V} = \frac{gT}{W}$$

where g is the gravitational acceleration, T the thrust level, and W the interceptor weight. Values for the instantaneous thrust and weight are obtained from Fig. 13.7. Figure 13.8 displays the resultant velocity and acceleration profiles for the nominal case. We can first see that the desired velocity goal of 20 kft/s has been reached by the end of the second-stage burn and that one-third of the velocity was attained at the end of the first-stage burn. We can also see from the acceleration profile that the desired maximum acceleration level of 10 g was also met. However, the axial booster acceleration is not constant and varied between 4 g and 10 g during the first-stage burn and varied between 2 g and 10 g during the second-stage burn.

Gravity Turn[1]

Now that we have a nominal two-stage booster design, we would like to simulate its flight. Since booster steering is beyond the scope of this chapter, we will assume that the booster is launched at an initial flight-path angle γ with respect to the surface of the Earth. For counterclockwise travel Fig. 13.9 indicates the appropriate sign conventions and angle definitions, whereas for clockwise travel Fig. 13.10 is appropriate.

If we attempt to align the thrust vector with the booster velocity vector, we will obtain a gravity turn. The acceleration due to the booster thrusting a_T is given by

$$a_T = \frac{gT}{W}$$

Listing 13.1   FORTRAN thrust-weight computations

```
        INTEGER STEP
        XISP1 = 250.
        XISP2 = 250.
        XMF1 = .85
        XMF2 = .85
        WPAY = 100.
        DELV = 20000.
        DELV1 = .3333*DELV
        DELV2 = .6667*DELV
        AMAX1 = 10.
        AMAX2 = 10.
        TOP2 = WPAY*(EXP(DELV2/(XISP2*32.2)) − 1.)
        BOT2 = 1/XMF2 − ((1. − XMF2)/XMF2)*EXP(DELV2/(XISP2*32.2))
        WP2 = TOP2/BOT2
        WS2 = WP2*(1 − XMF2)/XMF2
        WTOT2 = WP2 + WS2 + WPAY
        TRST2 = AMAX2*(WPAY + WS2)
        TB2 = XISP2*WP2/TRST2
        TOP1 = WTOT2*(EXP(DELV1/(XISP1*32.2)) − 1.)
        BOT1 = 1/XMF1 − ((1. − XMF1)/XMF1)*EXP(DELV1/(XISP1*32.2))
        WP1 = TOP1/BOT1
        WS1 = WP1*(1 − XMF1)/XMF1
        WTOT = WP1 + WS1 + WTOT2
        TRST1 = AMAX1*(WTOT2 + WS1)
        TB1 = XISP1*WP1/TRST1
        DELVK = DELV/1000.
        WRITE(9,*)'TOTAL WEIGHT = ',WTOT
        WRITE(9,*)'WP2 = ',WP2
        WRITE(9,*)'WS2 = ',WS2
        WRITE(9,*)'WP1 = ',WP1
        WRITE(9,*)'WS1 = ',WS1
        WRITE(9,*)'TRST2 = ',TRST2
        WRITE(9,*)'TRST1 = ',TRST1
        WRITE(9,*)'TB2 = ',TB2
        WRITE(9,*)'TB1 = ',TB1
        PAUSE
        H = .1
        T = 0.
        S = 0.
        V = 0.
10      IF(T>(TB1 + TB2))GOTO 999
        VOLD = V
        STEP = 1
        GOTO 200
66      STEP = 2
        V = V + H*A
        T = T + H
        GOTO 200
55      V = (VOLD + V)/2 + .5*H*A
        S = S + H
        IF(S<.99999)GOTO 10
        S = 0.
        AG = A/32.2
        VK = V/1000.
        WRITE(9,*)T,VK,AG
        GOTO 10
200     CONTINUE
        IF(T<TB1)THEN
            WGT = −WP1*T/TB1 + WTOT
            TRST = TRST1
        ELSEIF(T<(TB1 + TB2))THEN
            WGT = −WP2*T/TB2 + WTOT2 + WP2*TB1/TB2
            TRST = TRST2
        ELSE
            WGT = WPAY
            TRST = 0.
        ENDIF
        A = 32.2*TRST/WGT
        IF(STEP − 1)66,66,55
999     CONTINUE
        AG = A/32.2
        VK = V/1000.
        WRITE(9,*)T,VK,AG
        PAUSE
        END
```

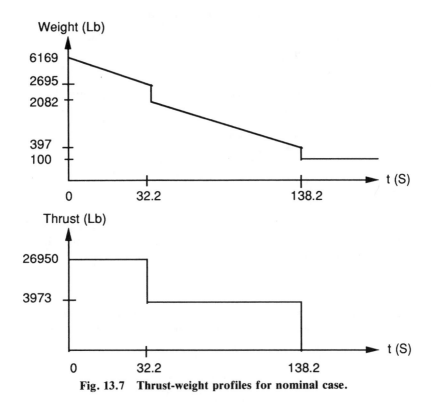

Fig. 13.7 Thrust-weight profiles for nominal case.

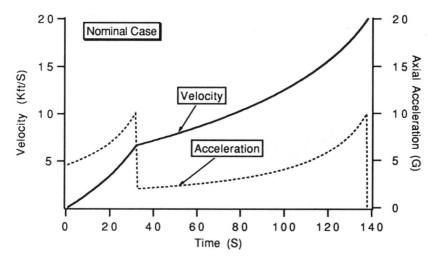

Fig. 13.8 Velocity and acceleration goals met with nominal design.

Table 13.1   Simulation outputs

Symbol	Definition	Value
W_{tot}	Total interceptor weight	6169 lb
W_{P1}	First-stage propellant weight	3474 lb
W_{S1}	First-stage structural weight	613 lb
W_{P2}	Second-stage propellant weight	1685 lb
W_{S2}	Second-stage structural weight	297 lb
T_1	Thrust level of first stage	26,950 lb
t_{B1}	Thrust burn time of first stage	32.2 s
T_2	Thrust level of second stage	3973 lb
t_{B2}	Thrust burn time of second stage	106 s

where T is the thrust magnitude in pounds, W the missile weight, and g is 32.2 ft/s². The booster velocity V at any time could be found from the velocity components as

$$V = (\dot{x}^2 + \dot{y}^2)^{0.5}$$

Therefore, during a gravity turn at any time the components of acceleration acting on the booster in our Earth-centered coordinate system are given by

$$\ddot{x} = \frac{-gm\,x}{(x^2 + y^2)^{1.5}} + \frac{a_T \dot{x}}{V}$$

$$\ddot{y} = \frac{-gm\,y}{(x^2 + y^2)^{1.5}} + \frac{a_T \dot{y}}{V}$$

where the initial conditions on velocity are related to the initial flight-path angle and location. For counterclockwise travel, the velocity initial condi-

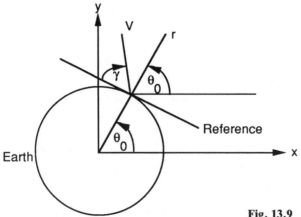

Fig. 13.9   Counterclockwise travel.

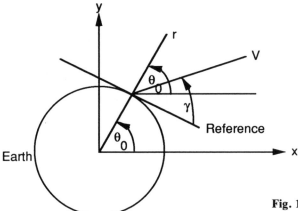

Fig. 13.10   Clockwise travel.

tions are

$$\dot{x}(0) = V(0) \cos\left(\frac{\pi}{2} - \gamma_0 + \theta_0\right)$$

$$\dot{y}(0) = V(0) \sin\left(\frac{\pi}{2} - \gamma_0 + \theta_0\right)$$

whereas for clockwise travel the appropriate velocity initial conditions are

$$\dot{x}(0) = V(0) \cos\left(-\frac{\pi}{2} + \gamma_0 + \theta_0\right)$$

$$\dot{y}(0) = V(0) \sin\left(-\frac{\pi}{2} + \gamma_0 + \theta_0\right)$$

The initial components of the booster location are given by

$$x(0) = (a + alt)\cos\theta_0$$

$$y(0) = (a + alt)\sin\theta_0$$

Listing 13.2 presents a FORTRAN program that, given some booster design parameters, finds the appropriate thrust-weight profiles and, in addition, flies the booster through a gravity turn. We can see from the listing that the nominal booster design is the default case and that the initial flight-path angle of the booster during the gravity turn is 85 deg. During the trajectory the flight-path angle will start from 85 deg and gradually reduce to smaller values.

Cases were run with the nominal design, and the initial flight-path angle was made a parameter. The resultant trajectories, shown in Fig. 13.11, indicate that large flight-path angles are required just to get a trajectory for a gravity turn! If the flight-path angle is less than 75 deg, the booster will

Listing 13.2   Gravity turn simulation

```
        INTEGER STEP
        LOGICAL LEFT
        LEFT = .TRUE.
        XISP1 = 250.
        XISP2 = 250.
        XMF1 = .85
        XMF2 = .85
        WPAY = 100.
        DELV = 20000.
        DELV1 = .3333*DELV
        DELV2 = .6667*DELV
        AMAX1 = 10.
        AMAX2 = 10.
        GAMDEG = 85.
        TOP2 = WPAY*(EXP(DELV2/(XISP2*32.2)) − 1.)
        BOT2 = 1/XMF2 − ((1. − XMF2)/XMF2)*EXP(DELV2/(XISP2*32.2))
        WP2 = TOP2/BOT2
        WS2 = WP2*(1 − XMF2)/XMF2
        WTOT2 = WP2 + WS2 + WPAY
        TRST2 = AMAX2*(WPAY + WS2)
        TB2 = XISP2*WP2/TRST2
        TOP1 = WTOT2*(EXP(DELV1/(XISP1*32.2)) − 1.)
        BOT1 = 1/XMF1 − ((1. − XMF1)/XMF1)*EXP(DELV1/(XISP1*32.2))
        WP1 = TOP1/BOT1
        WS1 = WP1*(1 − XMF1)/XMF1
        WTOT = WP1 + WS1 + WTOT2
        TRST1 = AMAX1*(WTOT2 + WS1)
        TB1 = XISP1*WP1/TRST1
        DELVK = DELV/1000.
        WRITE(9,*)'TOTAL WEIGHT = ',WTOT
        WRITE(9,*)'WP2 = ',WP2
        WRITE(9,*)'WS2 = ',WS2
        WRITE(9,*)'WP1 = ',WP1
        WRITE(9,*)'WS1 = ',WS1
        WRITE(9,*)'TRST2 = ',TRST2
        WRITE(9,*)'TRST1 = ',TRST1
        WRITE(9,*)'TB2 = ',TB2
        WRITE(9,*)'TB1 = ',TB1
        PAUSE
        H = .1
        T = 0.
        S = 0.
        A = 2.0926E7
        GM = 1.4077E16
        ALTNM = 0.
        ALT = ALTNM*6076.
        ANGDEG = 90.
        ANG = ANGDEG/57.3
        IF(LEFT)THEN
            VRX = COS(1.5708 − GAMDEG/57.3 + ANG)
            VRY = SIN(1.5708 − GAMDEG/57.3 + ANG)
        ELSE
            VRX = COS(− 1.5708 + GAMDEG/57.3 + ANG)
            VRY = SIN(− 1.5708 + GAMDEG/57.3 + ANG)
        ENDIF
        X = (A + ALT)*COS(ANG)
        Y = (A + ALT)*SIN(ANG)
        ALT = SQRT(X**2 + Y**2) − A
        XFIRST = X
        YFIRST = Y
        X1 = VRX
        Y1 = VRY
10      IF(ALT<0..AND.T>10.)GOTO 999
        XOLD = X
        YOLD = Y
        X1OLD = X1
        Y1OLD = Y1
        STEP = 1
        GOTO 200
```

(Listing 13.2 continued on next page.)

Listing 13.2   (cont.) Gravity turn simulation

```
66     STEP = 2
       X = X + H*XD
       Y = Y + H*YD
       X1 = X1 + H*X1D
       Y1 = Y1 + H*Y1D
       T = T + H
       GOTO 200
55     CONTINUE
       X = (XOLD + X)/2 + .5*H*XD
       Y = (YOLD + Y)/2 + .5*H*YD
       X1 = (X1OLD + X1)/2 + .5*H*X1D
       Y1 = (Y1OLD + Y1)/2 + .5*H*Y1D
       ALT = SQRT(X**2 + Y**2) - A
       S = S + H
       IF(S < 9.99999)GOTO 10
       S = 0.
       CALL DISTANCE(X,Y,XFIRST,YFIRST,DISTNM)
       ALTNM = (SQRT(X**2 + Y**2) - A)/6076.
       XNM = X/6076.
       YNM = Y/6076.
       WRITE(9,*)T,DISTNM,ALTNM,XNM,YNM
       GOTO 10
200    CONTINUE
       IF(T < TB1)THEN
           WGT = - WP1*T/TB1 + WTOT
           TRST = TRST1
       ELSEIF(T < (TB1 + TB2))THEN
           WGT = - WP2*T/TB2 + WTOT2 + WP2*TB1/TB2
           TRST = TRST2
       ELSE
           WGT = WPAY
           TRST = 0.
       ENDIF
       AT = 32.2*TRST/WGT
       VEL = SQRT(X1**2 + Y1**2)
       AXT = AT*X1/VEL
       AYT = AT*Y1/VEL
       TEMBOT = (X**2 + Y**2)**1.5
       X1D = - GM*X/TEMBOT + AXT
       Y1D = - GM*Y/TEMBOT + AYT
       XD = X1
       YD = Y1
       IF(STEP - 1)66,66,55
999    CONTINUE
       CALL DISTANCE(X,Y,XFIRST,YFIRST,DISTNM)
       ALTNM = (SQRT(X**2 + Y**2) - A)/6076.
       XNM = X/6076.
       YNM = Y/6076.
       WRITE(9,*)T,DISTNM,ALTNM,XNM,YNM
       PAUSE
       END
       SUBROUTINE DISTANCE(XT,YT,XF,YF,DISTNM)
       SAVE
       R = SQRT(XT**2 + YT**2)
       A = 2.0926E7
       CBETA = (XT*XF + YT*YF)/(R*A)
       IF(CBETA < 1.)THEN
           BETA = ACOS(CBETA)
           DISTNM = A*BETA/6076.
       ELSE
           DISTNM = (XF - XT)/6076.
       ENDIF
       RETURN
       END
```

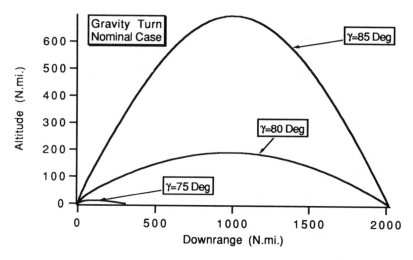

Fig. 13.11   Large flight-path angles are required for initial booster design.

immediately crash into the Earth. As the booster thrusts, the flight-path angle rapidly decreases due to the small booster acceleration (about 4 g at the beginning). Eventually the flight-path angle decreases to the point where the component of the booster acceleration perpendicular to the surface of the Earth is not sufficient to overcome gravity.

To remedy the situation so that we could get smaller flight-path angles to yield longer-range trajectories, the maximum axial booster acceleration during each stage was increased from 10 g to 20 g. The resultant velocity and acceleration profiles due to this change appear in Fig. 13.12. We can see that the booster still reaches a velocity of 20 kft/s, but in half the time of the nominal design.

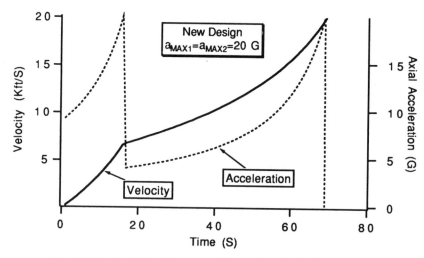

Fig. 13.12   Doubling booster axial acceleration halves burn time.

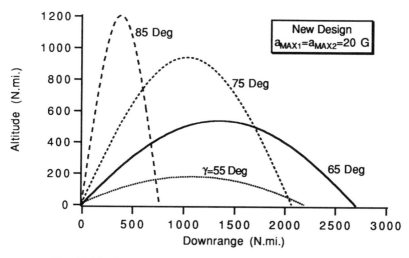

Fig. 13.13   New booster design yields longer flyout ranges.

Gravity turns were performed, via the simulation, for the new booster design, and the results for different flight-path angles appear in Fig. 13.13. We can see that the larger axial booster acceleration allowed the booster to experience lower flight-path angles (without crashing into the ground), which increased the booster range. With the nominal design, the maximum range achieved with a flight-path angle of 85 deg was about 2000 n.mi. The new design, which permitted a lower flight-path angle of 65 deg, increased the maximum range about 2700 n.mi.

Summary

In this chapter we have attempted to show that it takes a great deal of booster weight to bring a small payload to near-orbital speeds. High-level formulas were developed and presented so that booster parameters could be specified from fundamental rocket equation relationships. The impact of a key booster parameter on a simple gravity turn trajectory was demonstrated via a simple numerical example.

Reference

[1]Regan, F., *Re-Entry Vehicle Dynamics,* AIAA Education Series, New York, 1984.

Chapter 14

Lambert Guidance

Introduction

A PARTICULAR problem, known as the problem of Lambert, has intrigued mathematicians for centuries. The solution to this problem is important for navigating spacecraft and for putting strategic missiles on a collision triangle. Elegant numerical solutions exist for the Lambert problem that are based on the known properties of a body in a gravity field.[1] The best of these solutions are numerically very efficient and accurate and, in fact, currently serve as fundamental algorithms in steering both spacecraft and ballistic missiles. Unfortunately, these elegant solutions are extremely difficult to understand because they involve subtle points in conic sections and a detailed understanding of hypergeometric series. In this chapter we shall use an easy to understand but numerically inefficient algorithm for solving Lambert's problem. It will then be shown how to speed up the algorithm by two orders of magnitude using a simple numerical technique. We shall then show how this solution can be used to steer a strategic boosting missile on a collision triangle with a threat.

Statement of Lambert's Problem

A body in a gravity field satisfies Newton's law of universal gravitation, or

$$\ddot{x} = \frac{-gm\,x}{(x^2 + y^2)^{1.5}}$$

$$\ddot{y} = \frac{-gm\,y}{(x^2 + y^2)^{1.5}}$$

Assume that the initial location of a body in the gravity field is given by

$$x(0) = x_0$$

$$y(0) = y_0$$

and it is desired that t_F seconds later the body be at location

$$x(t_F) = x_F$$

$$y(t_F) = y_F$$

Lambert's problem is to find the initial velocity orientation of the body in the gravity field so that the preceding initial conditions and boundary values are satisfied, or

$$\dot{x}(0) = ?$$

$$\dot{y}(0) = ?$$

Solution to Lambert's Problem

We showed in Chapter 12 that, given an initial flight-path angle and distance to be traveled, the initial missile velocity required to hit an object on the surface of the Earth is given by

$$V = \sqrt{\frac{gm(1-\cos\phi)}{r_0 \cos\gamma\left[\dfrac{r_0 \cos\gamma}{a} - \cos(\phi+\gamma)\right]}}$$

where ϕ is the central angle separating the initial location of the missile and its intended target, γ the initial flight-path angle of the missile, a the radius of the Earth, and r_0 the initial distance from the center of the Earth to the missile, which can be expressed as

$$r_0 = a + alt$$

where alt is the initial altitude of the missile with respect to the surface of the Earth. Although the velocity equation was derived for hitting an object on the surface of the Earth, it can be made more general. If we desire to hit a target at any location r_F the preceding velocity equation can be modified to

$$V = \sqrt{\frac{gm(1-\cos\phi)}{r_0 \cos\gamma\left[\dfrac{r_0 \cos\gamma}{r_F} - \cos(\phi+\gamma)\right]}}$$

In this new formula r_F is defined as

$$r_F = a + alt_F$$

where alt_F is the altitude of the intended target.

If the velocity vector is oriented for counterclockwise travel as shown in Fig. 14.1, then, given the preceding solution for the total required velocity, we can find the initial conditions on the velocity components in the Earth-centered system by trigonometry as

$$\dot{x}(0) = V \cos\left(\frac{\pi}{2} - \gamma + \theta_0\right)$$

$$\dot{y}(0) = V \sin\left(\frac{\pi}{2} - \gamma + \theta_0\right)$$

where γ is the orientation of the missile velocity with respect to a reference that is tangent to the Earth and perpendicular to the vector from the center of the Earth to the initial location of the missile. We can see from Fig. 14.1 that θ_0 is the initial angular location of the missile with respect to the x axis of the Earth-centered Cartesian coordinate system.

On the other hand, if the velocity vector is intended to travel clockwise as shown in Fig. 14.2, then the initial conditions on the velocity components in the Earth-centered system can easily be shown to be

$$\dot{x}(0) = V \cos\left(\gamma - \frac{\pi}{2} + \theta_0\right)$$

$$\dot{y}(0) = V \sin\left(\gamma - \frac{\pi}{2} + \theta_0\right)$$

In Chapter 12 we also derived a formula for the time required for the missile to reach its intended target (t_F). The formula, which is valid for elliptical travel $(\lambda < 2)$, does not require the target to be on the surface of the Earth and is given by

$$t_F = \frac{r_0}{V \cos\gamma} \left\{ \frac{\tan\gamma(1 - \cos\phi) + (1 - \lambda)\sin\phi}{(2 - \lambda)\left[\frac{1 - \cos\phi}{\lambda \cos^2\gamma} + \frac{\cos(\gamma + \phi)}{\cos\gamma}\right]} \right.$$

$$\left. + \frac{2\cos\gamma}{\lambda[(2/\lambda) - 1]^{1.5}} \tan^{-1}\left(\frac{\sqrt{\frac{2}{\lambda} - 1}}{\cos\gamma \cot(\phi/2) - \sin\gamma}\right) \right\}$$

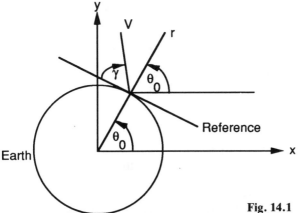

Fig. 14.1   Counterclockwise travel.

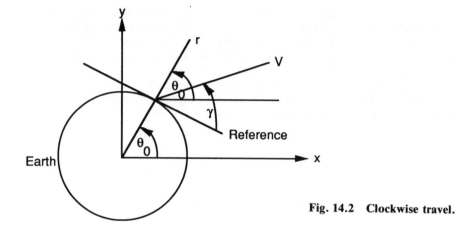

Fig. 14.2   Clockwise travel.

where V is the required velocity to hit the object, and λ was defined in Chapter 12 as

$$\lambda = \frac{r_0 V^2}{gm}$$

and ϕ is the angular distance to be traveled.

To find the angular distance to be traveled, consider the geometry of Fig. 14.3, in which the initial and final position of an object in a gravity field are shown. In this figure r_0 denotes a vector from the center of the Earth to the initial location of the object, and r_F denotes a vector from the center of the Earth to the final location of the object. The angle between the vectors is the central angle ϕ.

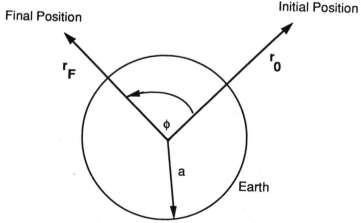

Fig. 14.3   Central angle between initial and final position.

The central angle can be found from the definition of the vector dot product, or

$$\phi = \cos^{-1} \frac{r_0 \cdot r_F}{|r_0| \, |r_F|}$$

Believe it or not, we now have sufficient information to numerically solve Lambert's problem!

If we know the initial and final destination of the target, we have just shown that we can find the central angle ϕ. With a central angle, r_0, r_F, and a flight-path angle γ, sufficient information is available to find the required velocity from our closed-form solution. The resultant velocity can then be used to solve for the flight time from our other closed-form solution. It is important to note that the flight time and velocity obtained are *exact* solutions for the flight-path angle used. Stated mathematically, we can say that given γ, r_0, and r_F we can use the following relationships, which are based on exact closed-form solutions:

$$\phi = f(r_0, r_F)$$

$$V = f(r_0, r_F, \phi, \gamma)$$

$$t_F = f(V, \phi, \gamma)$$

Recall that in Lambert's problem we are given r_0, r_F, and t_F and seek to find V and γ. If we use the preceding relationships, we do not know how to choose γ, nor are we guaranteed that a particular value of γ will yield the desired flight time t_F.

We can solve the problem by the method of brute force. That is, we work out all solutions until we find the one that satisfies the constraints of the problem. For example, we start with $\gamma = -90$ deg, solve for the velocity, and then solve for the time of flight. If the flight time is less than the desired flight time, we repeat the procedure with a slightly larger value of γ. We stop the loop when the computed flight time is greater than the desired flight time. If the flight-path angle that satisfies the preceding procedure is negative, we know that the solution must be rejected since it requires the missile to travel through the Earth. This numerical method converges because we saw in Fig. 12.17 that flight time is smooth and monotonically increasing with increasing flight-path angle.

Numerical Example

Listing 14.1 presents sample FORTRAN code, using double-precision arithmetic, for finding the Lambert solution, based on the procedure developed in the previous section. In the notation of Listing 14.1 we can say that, given an initial angle and altitude for the missile (*XLONGMDEG*, *ALT-NMM*), an initial angle and altitude for the target (*XLONGTDEG*, *ALT-NMT*), and a desired flight time (*TF*), the program iterates on the flight-path angle (*GAMDEG*) until a solution is found. From the listing we can see that the program consists of two loops. The first loop iterates on the

Listing 14.1   Lambert routine using brute force approach

```
        IMPLICIT REAL*8 (A – H)
        IMPLICIT REAL*8 (O – Z)
        XLONGMDEG = 45.
        XLONGTDEG = 90.
        ALTNMT = 0.
        ALTNMM = 0.
        TF = 1000.
        PI = 3.14159
        DEGRAD = 360./(2.*PI)
        A = 2.0926E7
        GM = 1.4077E16
        ALTT = ALTNMT*6076.
        ALTM = ALTNMM*6076.
        XLONGM = XLONGMDEG/DEGRAD
        XLONGT = XLONGTDEG/DEGRAD
        XM = (A + ALTM)*COS(XLONGM)
        YM = (A + ALTM)*SIN(XLONGM)
        XT = (A + ALTT)*COS(XLONGT)
        YT = (A + ALTT)*SIN(XLONGT)
        CALL LAMBERT(XM,YM,TF,XT,YT,VRXM,VRYM,XLONGM,XLONGT)
        WRITE(9,*)TF,VRXM,VRYM
        PAUSE
        END
        SUBROUTINE LAMBERT(XIC,YIC,TFDES,XF,YF,VRX,VRY,XLONGM,XLONGT)
        IMPLICIT REAL*8 (A – H)
        IMPLICIT REAL*8 (O – Z)
        A = 2.0926E7
        GM = 1.4077E16
        RIC = SQRT(XIC**2 + YIC**2)
        RF = SQRT(XF**2 + YF**2)
        CPHI = (XIC*XF + YIC*YF)/(RIC*RF)
        PHI = ACOS(CPHI)
        R0 = RIC
        PI = 3.14159
        DEGRAD = 360./(2.*PI)
        ICOUNT = 0
        DO 10 GAMDEG = – 90.,90.,.1
           GAM = GAMDEG/DEGRAD
           TOP = GM*(1. – COS(PHI))
           TEMP = R0*COS(GAM)/RF – COS(PHI + GAM)
           BOT = R0*COS(GAM)*TEMP
           IF(TOP<0..OR.BOT<0.)GOTO 10
           V = SQRT(TOP/BOT)
           IF (XLONGT>XLONGM) THEN
              VRX = V*COS(PI/2. – GAM + XLONGM)
              VRY = V*SIN(PI/2. – GAM + XLONGM)
           ELSE
              VRX = V*COS( – PI/2. + GAM + XLONGM)
              VRY = V*SIN( – PI/2. + GAM + XLONGM)
           END IF
           XLAM = R0*V*V/GM
           TOP1 = TAN(GAM)*(1 – COS(PHI)) + (1 – XLAM)*SIN(PHI)
           BOT1P = (1 – COS(PHI))/(XLAM*COS(GAM)*COS(GAM))
           BOT1 = (2 – XLAM)*(BOT1P + COS(GAM + PHI)/COS(GAM))
           TOP2 = 2*COS(GAM)
           IF((2/XLAM – 1)<0.)GOTO 10
           BOT2 = XLAM*((2/XLAM – 1)**1.5)
           TOP3 = SQRT(2/XLAM – 1)
           BOT3 = COS(GAM)/TAN(PHI/2) – SIN(GAM)
           TEMP = (TOP2/BOT2)*ATAN2(TOP3,BOT3)
           TF = R0*(TOP1/BOT1 + TEMP)/(V*COS(GAM))
           IF(TF>TFDES)THEN
              EXIT
           ENDIF
10      CONTINUE
        GAMDEGNEW = GAMDEG – .15
        GAMDEGFIN = GAMDEG + 1.
        DO 20 GAMDEG = GAMDEGNEW,GAMDEGFIN,.0001
           GAM = GAMDEG/DEGRAD
           TOP = GM*(1. – COS(PHI))
           TEMP = R0*COS(GAM)/RF – COS(PHI + GAM)
           BOT = R0*COS(GAM)*TEMP
           IF(TOP<0..OR.BOT<0.)GOTO 20
```

(Listing 14.1 continued on next page.)

Listing 14.1   (cont.) Lambert routine using brute force approach

```
            V = SQRT(TOP/BOT)
            IF (XLONGT>XLONGM) THEN
                VRX = V*COS(PI/2. - GAM + XLONGM)
                VRY = V*SIN(PI/2. - GAM + XLONGM)
            ELSE
                VRX = V*COS( - PI/2. + GAM + XLONGM)
                VRY = V*SIN( - PI/2. + GAM + XLONGM)
            END IF
            XLAM = R0*V*V/GM
            TOP1 = TAN(GAM)*(1 - COS(PHI)) + (1 - XLAM)*SIN(PHI)
            BOT1P = (1 - COS(PHI))/(XLAM*COS(GAM)*COS(GAM))
            BOT1 = (2 - XLAM)*(BOT1P + COS(GAM + PHI)/COS(GAM))
            TOP2 = 2*COS(GAM)
            IF((2/XLAM - 1)<0.)GOTO 20
            BOT2 = XLAM*((2/XLAM - 1)**1.5)
            TOP3 = SQRT(2/XLAM - 1)
            BOT3 = COS(GAM)/TAN(PHI/2) - SIN(GAM)
            TEMP = (TOP2/BOT2)*ATAN2(TOP3,BOT3)
            TF = R0*(TOP1/BOT1 + TEMP)/(V*COS(GAM))
            IF(TF>TFDES)THEN
                EXIT
            ENDIF
    20      CONTINUE
            RETURN
            END
```

flight-path angle in units of 0.1 deg. When a flight time is found that exceeds the desired flight time, we exit the loop for another loop that increments the flight-path angle (after decreasing the last flight-path angle by 0.15 deg) in very fine units of 0.0001 deg. This loop is required to get extremely precise answers. When the desired flight time is achieved, we exit the loop and the routine. For most cases the program takes about 1.5 s to execute on a 16 MHz, 32-bit microcomputer with a math coprocessor. The routine, as written, is about 100 times slower than more elegant Lambert routines.[1] We shall show in the next section that by performing a more intelligent search it is possible to find the correct solution to Lambert's problem in less than ten iterations, thus making this approach very competitive with more elegant Lambert routines. However, the goal in this section is to develop a routine that simply works and is easy to understand.

In order to demonstrate how the routine works, the nominal case, shown in the listing, was run. In this case the missile is on the surface of the Earth 45 deg away from the target. It is desired to find the velocity orientation of the missile (VRX, VRY) so that the missile will hit the target in exactly 1000 s. Figure 14.4 shows that the solution converges to the exact value in 1084 iterations. However, the solution appears to be approximately correct after 335 iterations.

In order to investigate the tradeoff between accuracy vs number of iterations required, a simple experiment was conducted. First the second loop of Listing 14.1 was removed from the Lambert subroutine so that the flight-path angle was only incremented in steps of 0.1 deg. Table 14.1 shows that the number of iterations required were reduced from 1084 to 335 and the resultant velocity accuracy (VRX, VRY) appears to be reduced slightly. Actually, the velocities are exact for a 1001-s flight but approximate for a Lambert solution requiring a 1000-s flight. Next, the first loop was modified so that the flight-path angle was incremented in steps of 1 deg (increased from 0.1 deg steps). Table 14.1 shows that the number of iterations

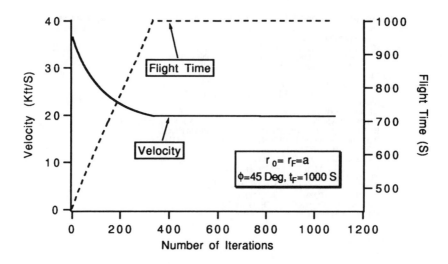

Fig. 14.4   It takes 1084 iterations to get exact solution.

was reduced to only 34, but the accuracy loss was more significant if the desired flight time is truly 1000 s. These answers are exact in the sense a hit will result in 1014 s but inaccurate for the Lambert solution requiring exactly 1000 s.

Speeding Up Lambert Routine

The routine for numerically solving Lambert's problem, presented in the previous section, can be speeded up by more than two orders of magnitude! We have already demonstrated that the brute force search on all possible flight-path angles results in many iterations. We can considerably restrict the brute force search and eliminate many iterations by recalling that the velocity formula was shown in Chapter 12 to be

$$V = \sqrt{\frac{gm(1 - \cos\phi)}{r_0 \cos\gamma \left[\dfrac{r_0 \cos\gamma}{r_F} - \cos(\phi + \gamma)\right]}}$$

Table 14.1   Accuracy experiments

Condition	V_{RX}	V_{RY}	t_F	Iterations
Nominal	−7696	18,329	1000	1084
Remove second loop	−7668	18,332	1001	335
One-degree increments	−7418	18,360	1014	34

Since in this text we are only interested in trajectories for ballistic missiles we can immediately rule out cases that lead to escape velocity ($\lambda = 2$) or

$$\lambda = 2 = \frac{V^2 r_0}{gm}$$

Substitution of the escape velocity condition into the velocity formula yields

$$2 = \frac{(1 - \cos \phi)}{\cos \gamma \left[\dfrac{r_0 \cos \gamma}{r_F} - \cos(\phi + \gamma) \right]}$$

We can solve the preceding equation for the flight-path angle γ. After much algebra we get two solutions corresponding to the minimum and maximum flight-path angles as

$$\gamma_{\min} = \tan^{-1} \left[\frac{\sin \phi - \sqrt{\dfrac{2r_0}{r_F} (1 - \cos \phi)}}{1 - \cos \phi} \right]$$

$$\gamma_{\max} = \tan^{-1} \left[\frac{\sin \phi + \sqrt{\dfrac{2r_0}{r_F} (1 - \cos \phi)}}{1 - \cos \phi} \right]$$

It should not be surprising that there are two solutions for the flight-path angle since we have already observed this phenomenon in Fig. 12.14. We also noticed in Figs. 12.14 and 12.17 that the solution for the velocity and time of flight were smooth, well-behaved functions of the flight-path angle. Based on the nonpathological nature of these solutions and the fact that the flight-path angle is well bounded, we do not have to evaluate each flight-path angle but can instead perform a more efficient search in finding the flight-path angle that corresponds to the desired flight time. For example, we can use an algorithm known as the secant method[3] to perform the search or

$$\gamma_{n+1} = \gamma_n + \frac{(\gamma_n - \gamma_{n-1})(t_{\text{FDES}} - t_{F_n})}{t_{F_n} - t_{F_{n-1}}}$$

We can see from the preceding equation that the new flight-path angle γ_{n+1} is related to previous values γ_n, γ_{n-1}. At each iteration the new computed value of flight-path angle is limited to the minimum and maximum possible values of the flight-path angle derived from the escape velocity condition. The search is terminated when the computed flight time t_{F_n} *is sufficiently close to the desired flight time* t_{FDES}.

Listing 14.2 is identical to the test program of Listing 14.1, except this time the Lambert routine is more efficient. We can see from the new Lambert routine that our initial guess of the flight-path angle is simply the

Listing 14.2   More efficient Lambert routine

```
IMPLICIT REAL*8 (A-H)
IMPLICIT REAL*8 (O-Z)
OPEN(1,STATUS = 'NEW',FILE = 'DATFIL')
XLONGMDEG = 45.
XLONGTDEG = 90.
ALTNMT = 0.
ALTNMM = 0.
TF = 1000.
PI = 3.14159
DEGRAD = 360./(2.*PI)
A = 2.0926E7
GM = 1.4077E16
ALTT = ALTNMT*6076.
ALTM = ALTNMM*6076.
XLONGM = XLONGMDEG/DEGRAD
XLONGT = XLONGTDEG/DEGRAD
XM = (A + ALTM)*COS(XLONGM)
YM = (A + ALTM)*SIN(XLONGM)
XT = (A + ALTT)*COS(XLONGT)
YT = (A + ALTT)*SIN(XLONGT)
CALL LAMBERT(XM,YM,TF,XT,YT,VRXM,VRYM,XLONGM,XLONGT)
PAUSE
CLOSE(1)
END

SUBROUTINE LAMBERT(XIC,YIC,TFDES,XF,YF,VRX,VRY,XLONGM,XLONGT)
IMPLICIT REAL*8 (A-H)
IMPLICIT REAL*8 (O-Z)
A = 2.0926E7
GM = 1.4077E16
RIC = SQRT(XIC**2 + YIC**2)
RF = SQRT(XF**2 + YF**2)
CPHI = (XIC*XF + YIC*YF)/(RIC*RF)
PHI = ACOS(CPHI)
SPHI = SIN(PHI)
R0 = RIC
PI = 3.14159
DEGRAD = 360./(2.*PI)
ICOUNT = 0
GMIN = ATAN2((SPHI-SQRT(2.*R0*(1.-CPHI)/RF)),(1-CPHI))
GMAX = ATAN2((SPHI + SQRT(2.*R0*(1.-CPHI)/RF)),(1-CPHI))
GAM = (GMIN + GMAX)/2.
DO
     TOP = GM*(1.-COS(PHI))
     TEMP = R0*COS(GAM)/RF-COS(PHI + GAM)
     BOT = R0*COS(GAM)*TEMP
     V = SQRT(TOP/BOT)
     IF (XLONGT>XLONGM) THEN
          VRX = V*COS(PI/2.-GAM + XLONGM)
          VRY = V*SIN(PI/2.-GAM + XLONGM)
     ELSE
          VRX = V*COS(-PI/2. + GAM + XLONGM)
          VRY = V*SIN(-PI/2. + GAM + XLONGM)
     END IF
     XLAM = R0*V*V/GM
     TOP1 = TAN(GAM)*(1-COS(PHI)) + (1-XLAM)*SIN(PHI)
     BOT1P = (1-COS(PHI))/(XLAM*COS(GAM)*COS(GAM))
     BOT1 = (2-XLAM)*(BOT1P + COS(GAM + PHI)/COS(GAM))
     TOP2 = 2*COS(GAM)
     BOT2 = XLAM*((2/XLAM-1)**1.5)
     TOP3 = SQRT(2/XLAM-1)
     BOT3 = COS(GAM)/TAN(PHI/2)-SIN(GAM)
     TEMP = (TOP2/BOT2)*ATAN2(TOP3,BOT3)
     TF = R0*(TOP1/BOT1 + TEMP)/(V*COS(GAM))
     ICOUNT = ICOUNT + 1
     WRITE(9,300)ICOUNT,57.3*GAM,VRX,VRY,TF
     WRITE(1,300)ICOUNT,57.3*GAM,VRX,VRY,TF
300  FORMAT(I4,1X,F12.7,1X,F12.5,1X,F12.5,1X,F12.5)
     IF((ABS(TFDES-TF)< = .00000001*TFDES).OR.ICOUNT>100)THEN
          EXIT
     ENDIF
     IF(TF>TFDES)THEN
          GMAX = GAM
```

(Listing 14.2 continued on next page.)

Listing 14.2   (cont.) More efficient Lambert routine

```
        ELSE
            GMIN = GAM
        ENDIF
        IF(ICOUNT = 1)THEN
            XNEXT = (GMAX + GMIN)/2.
        ELSE
            XNEXT = GAM + (GAM-GOLD)*(TFDES-TF)/(TF-TOLD)
            IF(XNEXT > GMAX.OR.XNEXT < GMIN)THEN
                XNEXT = (GMAX + GMIN)/2.
            ENDIF
        ENDIF
        GOLD = GAM
        TOLD = TF
        GAM = XNEXT
    REPEAT
    RETURN
    END
```

average of the minimum and maximum flight-path angles derived from the escape velocity condition.

The nominal case of the previous section was rerun and detailed results for the number of iterations required appears in Table 14.2. We can see that very accurate Lambert solutions are obtained after only four iterations and that after seven iterations we are obtaining a degree of accuracy that is better than obtained with 1084 iterations in the previous section using the brute force approach. *The new Lambert routine is not only more accurate than the one in the previous section but it is also more than two orders of magnitude faster!*

Reference 4 makes extensive tests on this efficient numerical solution to Lambert's problem and shows that it is competitive with the best numerical approaches. In addition, Ref. 4 also shows how this efficient solution to Lambert's problem can be extended to parabolic and hyperbolic trajectories.

Booster Steering

Thus far we have seen that, given that we know where we are and where we want to go and given an arrival time, the Lambert subroutine will tell us the orientation of the velocity vector for an impulsive missile to satisfy the

Table 14.2   Number of iterations are dramatically reduced

Iteration	Flight-path angle, deg	V_{RX}, ft/s	V_{RY}, ft/s	Flight time, s
1	33.7524947	− 3764.57976	18926.02426	1239.37545
2	11.2508376	− 12075.71473	18072.66484	813.53185
3	21.1038504	− 8103.20444	18287.99279	979.68031
4	22.3088581	− 7665.88409	18332.46792	1001.50708
5	22.2256555	− 7695.84063	18329.28399	999.98566
6	22.2264396	− 7695.55815	18329.31392	999.99999
7	22.2264402	− 7695.55795	18329.31394	1000.00000

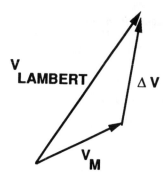

Fig. 14.5 Basis of Lambert guidance.

problem. Since we do not have impulsive missiles (missiles that get up to speed immediately), it is desirable to find out if the Lambert subroutine could be of use in enabling a nonimpulsive missile or booster to reach its target. If we neglect the atmosphere, the solution to the problem is quite simple and is known as Lambert guidance.[1]

Consider the vector diagram shown in Fig. 14.5. All that has to be done at small time increments, while the missile is boosting, is to find the desired velocity from the Lambert subroutine V_{Lambert} and subtract the current missile velocity V_M. The difference in velocities is known as the velocity to be gained, ΔV. If the boosting missile thrust vector is aligned with the velocity to be gained vector, then the desired velocity will be obtained in a feedback fashion. When the desired velocity is achieved, the engine is cut off and the missile flies ballistically to the intended target.

Mathematically, we are saying that the components of the velocity to be gained are

$$\Delta V_x = V_{\text{Lambert}x} - V_{Mx}$$

$$\Delta V_y = V_{\text{Lambert}y} - V_{My}$$

Therefore, the total velocity to be gained is simply

$$\Delta V = (\Delta V_x^2 + \Delta V_y^2)^{0.5}$$

If the magnitude of the current thrust acceleration is given by a_T, then the direction of the thrust acceleration at each instant of time should be aligned with the velocity to be gained vector, or

$$a_{Tx} = a_T \Delta V_x / \Delta V$$

$$a_{Ty} = a_T \Delta V_y / \Delta V$$

Listing 14.3 presents a FORTRAN simulation of a two-stage booster using Lambert guidance during the boost phase. Actually, the scenario is unrealistic because g loading and range safety considerations have been ignored,[2] but it is useful for demonstrating how Lambert guidance works.

Listing 14.3   Booster simulation with Lambert guidance

```
       IMPLICIT REAL*8 (A-H)
       IMPLICIT REAL*8 (O-Z)
       INTEGER STEP,SWITCH
       LOGICAL LEFT,QBOOST
       LEFT = .TRUE.
       QBOOST = .TRUE.
       OPEN(1,STATUS = 'NEW',FILE = 'DATFIL')
       OPEN(2,STATUS = 'NEW',FILE = 'LAMFIL')
       XISP1 = 300.
       XISP2 = 300.
       XMF1 = .90
       XMF2 = .90
       WPAY = 100.
       DELV = 20000.
       DELV1 = .3333*DELV
       DELV2 = .6667*DELV
       AMAX1 = 20.
       AMAX2 = 20.
       TOP2 = WPAY*(EXP(DELV2/(XISP2*32.2))-1.)
       BOT2 = 1/XMF2-((1.-XMF2)/XMF2)*EXP(DELV2/(XISP2*32.2))
       WP2 = TOP2/BOT2
       WS2 = WP2*(1-XMF2)/XMF2
       WTOT2 = WP2 + WS2 + WPAY
       TRST2 = AMAX2*(WPAY + WS2)
       TB2 = XISP2*WP2/TRST2
       TOP1 = WTOT2*(EXP(DELV1/(XISP1*32.2))-1.)
       BOT1 = 1/XMF1-((1.-XMF1)/XMF1)*EXP(DELV1/(XISP1*32.2))
       WP1 = TOP1/BOT1
       WS1 = WP1*(1-XMF1)/XMF1
       WTOT = WP1 + WS1 + WTOT2
       TRST1 = AMAX1*(WTOT2 + WS1)
       TB1 = XISP1*WP1/TRST1
       DELVK = DELV/1000.
       H = 1.
       T = 0.
       S = 0.
       A = 2.0926E7
       GM = 1.4077E16
       ALTNM = 0.
       ALT = ALTNM*6076.
       ANGDEG = 30.
       ANG = ANGDEG/57.3
       XLONGM = ANG
       X = (A + ALT)*COS(ANG)
       Y = (A + ALT)*SIN(ANG)
       ALT = SQRT(X**2 + Y**2)-A
       XFIRST = X
       YFIRST = Y
       X1 = 0.
       Y1 = 0.
       AXT = 0.
       AYT = 0.
       XLONGTDEG = 45.
       XLONGT = XLONGTDEG/57.3
       XF = A*COS(XLONGT)
       YF = A*SIN(XLONGT)
       TF = 500.
10     IF(ALT
       0..AND.T
       10.)GOTO 999
       XOLD = X
       YOLD = Y
       X1OLD = X1
       Y1OLD = Y1
       STEP = 1
       GOTO 200
66     STEP = 2
       X = X + H*XD
       Y = Y + H*YD
       X1 = X1 + H*X1D
       Y1 = Y1 + H*Y1D
       T = T + H
       GOTO 200
```

(Listing 14.3 continued on next page.)

Listing 14.3   (cont.) Booster simulation with Lambert guidance

```
55      CONTINUE
        X = (XOLD + X)/2 + .5*H*XD
        Y = (YOLD + Y)/2 + .5*H*YD
        X1 = (X1OLD + X1)/2 + .5*H*X1D
        Y1 = (Y1OLD + Y1)/2 + .5*H*Y1D
        ALT = SQRT(X**2 + Y**2)-A
        S = S + H
        IF(QBOOST)THEN
             TGOLAM = TF-T
             XLONGM = ATAN2(Y,X)
1            CALL LAMBERT(X,Y,TGOLAM,XF,YF,VRX,VRY,XLONGM,XLONGT,ICOUNT)
             DELX = VRX-X1
             DELY = VRY-Y1
             DEL = SQRT(DELX**2 + DELY**2)
             WRITE(2,*)T,VRX,X1,VRY,Y1
             IF(TRST>0..AND.DEL>500.)THEN
                  AXT = AT*DELX/DEL
                  AYT = AT*DELY/DEL
             ELSEIF(DEL<500.)THEN
                  TRST = 0.
                  QBOOST = .FALSE.
                  AXT = 0.
                  AYT = 0.
                  X1 = VRX
                  Y1 = VRY
                  X1OLD = X1
                  Y1OLD = Y1
             ELSE
                  QBOOST = .FALSE.
                  AXT = 0.
                  AYT = 0.
             ENDIF
        ENDIF
        IF(S.LT.9.99999)GOTO 10
        S = 0.
        CALL DISTANCE(X,Y,XFIRST,YFIRST,DISTNM)
        ALTNM = (SQRT(X**2 + Y**2)-A)/6076.
        VELK = SQRT(X1**2 + Y1**2)/1000.
        GAMDEG = 57.3*ATAN2(Y1,X1)
        XNM = X/6076.
        YNM = Y/6076.
        WRITE(9,*)T,DISTNM,ALTNM
        WRITE(1,*)T,DISTNM,ALTNM
        GOTO 10
200     CONTINUE
        IF(T<TB1)THEN
             WGT = -WP1*T/TB1 + WTOT
             TRST = TRST1
        ELSEIF(T<(TB1 + TB2))THEN
             WGT = -WP2*T/TB2 + WTOT2 + WP2*TB1/TB2
             TRST = TRST2
        ELSE
             WGT = WPAY
             TRST = 0.
        ENDIF
        AT = 32.2*TRST/WGT
        XD = X1
        YD = Y1
        TEMBOT = (X**2 + Y**2)**1.5
        X1D = -GM*X/TEMBOT + AXT
        Y1D = -GM*Y/TEMBOT + AYT
        IF(STEP-1)66,66,55
999     CONTINUE
        CALL DISTANCE(X,Y,XFIRST,YFIRST,DISTNM)
        ALTNM = (SQRT(X**2 + Y**2)-A)/6076.
        VELK = SQRT(X1**2 + Y1**2)/1000.
        WRITE(9,*)T,DISTNM,ALTNM,VELK
        WRITE(1,*)T,DISTNM,ALTNM
        PAUSE
        CLOSE(1)
        CLOSE(2)
        END
```

(Listing 14.3 continued on next page.)

Listing 14.3   (cont.) Booster simulation with Lambert guidance

```
SUBROUTINE DISTANCE(XT,YT,XF,YF,DISTNM)
IMPLICIT REAL*8 (A-H)
IMPLICIT REAL*8 (O-Z)
SAVE
R = SQRT(XT**2 + YT**2)
A = 2.0926E7
CBETA = (XT*XF + YT*YF)/(R*A)
IF(CBETA<1.)THEN
    BETA = ACOS(CBETA)
    DISTNM = A*BETA/6076.
ELSE
    DISTNM = (XF-XT)/6076.
ENDIF
RETURN
END
SUBROUTINE LAMBERT(XIC,YIC,TFDES,XF,YF,VRX,VRY,
1    XLONGM,XLONGT,ICOUNT)
IMPLICIT REAL*8 (A-H)
IMPLICIT REAL*8 (O-Z)
A = 2.0926E7
GM = 1.4077E16
RIC = SQRT(XIC**2 + YIC**2)
RF = SQRT(XF**2 + YF**2)
CPHI = (XIC*XF + YIC*YF)/(RIC*RF)
PHI = ACOS(CPHI)
SPHI = SIN(PHI)
R0 = RIC
PI = 3.14159
DEGRAD = 360./(2.*PI)
ICOUNT = 1
GMIN = ATAN2((SPHI-SQRT(2.*R0*(1.-CPHI)/RF)),(1-CPHI))
GMAX = ATAN2((SPHI + SQRT(2.*R0*(1.-CPHI)/RF)),(1-CPHI))
GAM = (GMIN + GMAX)/2.
DO
    TOP = GM*(1.-COS(PHI))
    TEMP = R0*COS(GAM)/RF-COS(PHI + GAM)
    BOT = R0*COS(GAM)*TEMP
    V = SQRT(TOP/BOT)
    IF (XLONGT>XLONGM) THEN
        VRX = V*COS(PI/2.-GAM + XLONGM)
        VRY = V*SIN(PI/2.-GAM + XLONGM)
    ELSE
        VRX = V*COS(-PI/2. + GAM + XLONGM)
        VRY = V*SIN(-PI/2. + GAM + XLONGM)
    END IF
XLAM = R0*V*V/GM
TOP1 = TAN(GAM)*(1-COS(PHI)) + (1-XLAM)*SIN(PHI)
BOT1P = (1-COS(PHI))/(XLAM*COS(GAM)*COS(GAM))
BOT1 = (2-XLAM)*(BOT1P + COS(GAM + PHI)/COS(GAM))
TOP2 = 2*COS(GAM)
BOT2 = XLAM*((2/XLAM-1)**1.5)
TOP3 = SQRT(2/XLAM-1)
BOT3 = COS(GAM)/TAN(PHI/2)-SIN(GAM)
TEMP = (TOP2/BOT2)*ATAN2(TOP3,BOT3)
TF = R0*(TOP1/BOT1 + TEMP)/(V*COS(GAM))
IF((ABS(TFDES-TF)< = .00000001*TFDES).OR.ICOUNT
100)THEN
    EXIT
ENDIF
IF(TF>FDES)THEN
    GMAX = GAM
ELSE
    GMIN = GAM
ENDIF
IF(ICOUNT = 1)THEN
    XNEXT = (GMAX + GMIN)/2.
ELSE
    XNEXT = GAM + (GAM-GOLD)*(TFDES-TF)/(TF-TOLD)
    IF(XNEXT>GMAX.OR.XNEXT<GMIN)THEN
        XNEXT = (GMAX + GMIN)/2.
    ENDIF
ENDIF
GOLD = GAM
TOLD = TF
GAM = XNEXT
ICOUNT = ICOUNT + 1
REPEAT
RETURN
END
```

The booster considered in this example has a capability of reaching a velocity of 20,000 ft/s. The booster is assumed to have two stages, each of which has a fuel mass fraction of 0.9 and specific impulse of 300 s. The maximum acceleration in each stage is 20 g. One-third of the speed will be attained in the first stage, and the rest of the speed will be attained in the second stage. Burnout of the second stage will be completed at about 60 s. It is desired that the booster, which is initially at angular location $\theta_0 = 30$ deg ($ANGDEG = 30$), reach a target at 45 deg ($XLONGTDEG = 45$) in 500 s ($TF = 500$).

The Lambert feedback loop is at the end of the integration routine and is called every integration interval. When the difference between the desired velocity and the attained velocity is less than 500 ft/s, the simulation automatically sets the actual velocity to the desired velocity to avoid making the integration interval very small in the simulation. At this time the booster cuts off and coasts. The logic in the simulation is self-explanatory.

The nominal case was run where the inputs were previously explained. Figure 14.6 displays the x component of the achieved velocity along with the desired or Lambert velocity. We can see that the two velocities converge at about 48 s. Figure 14.7 presents the y components of the achieved and desired velocities. We can see that this component is much larger than the x component. The discontinuity in the y component at about 15 s is due to staging, and the slight discontinuity near the end of the display is due to setting the achieved velocity to the desired velocity when the velocity to be gained was less than 500 ft/s.

Finally, Fig. 14.8 shows the resultant trajectory. The missile reaches the target at exactly 500 s. We can see from the figure that the trajectory is smooth during the boost phase of flight when Lambert guidance is used.

It is interesting to note that the Lambert solution was reached in about 48 s, even though the missile was capable of burning fuel for nearly 60 s.

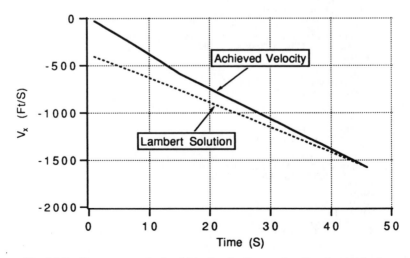

Fig. 14.6 X component of achieved velocity reaches Lambert solution.

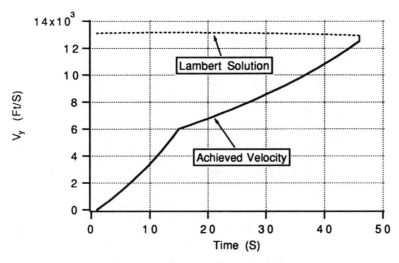

Fig. 14.7 *Y component of achieved velocity reaches Lambert solution.*

Thus, we can see that Lambert guidance can be used to steer a strategic missile with a thrust termination system in the absence of atmospheric effects. The Lambert guidance principle can be used for interceptors that fly ballistically to hit stationary targets. Lambert guidance can also be used for guided interceptors that must hit moving and accelerating targets. In this case, the purpose of Lambert guidance is to place the interceptor on a collision triangle at the end of the boost phase.

General Energy Management (GEM) Steering[2,5]

We have seen in the previous section how it was possible to steer a boosting strategic interceptor to a desired intercept point using Lambert

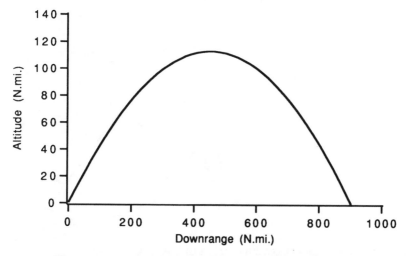

Fig. 14.8 Booster reaches target with Lambert guidance.

guidance. In the example presented in the last section, the thrust had to be terminated before the end of burn in order to achieve the desired Lambert solution. Often there is a restriction, in the absence of a thrust termination system, that all the booster fuel must be consumed. In this case a method other than Lambert guidance must be employed to waste some of the booster's excess energy. A popular energy wasting technique is known as general energy management (GEM) steering.

In order to explain the concept of energy wasting, consider the simplified geometry of Fig. 14.9. In this figure we have the arc of a circle whose length is denoted V_{cap}. This arc represents the velocity capability of the booster. The radius of the circle forming the arc is denoted r, and the central angle is denoted 2θ. A chord is drawn connecting both ends of the arc. The chord length represents the velocity to be gained (subtraction of achieved velocity from Lambert solution velocity) and is denoted ΔV. If the thrust vector is drawn tangent to the chord at the beginning of the arc, it is easy to show from geometry that the thrust vector is at an angle of θ with respect to the chord. Finally, a perpendicular is dropped from the chord to the center of the circle. It is also easy to show that the perpendicular bisects the chord and the central angle.

From Fig. 14.9 we can see that the arc length is related to the central angle according to

$$V_{cap} = 2\theta r$$

Since the perpendicular bisects the central angle, we can also say that

$$\Delta V = 2r\,\sin\theta$$

Therefore, we can ratio the two velocity expressions, yielding

$$\frac{\Delta V}{V_{cap}} = \frac{2r\,\sin\theta}{2r\theta} = \frac{\sin\theta}{\theta}$$

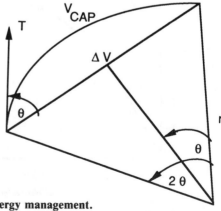

Fig. 14.9 Basic angles in general energy management.

Expanding the sine term into a two-term Taylor series leads to

$$\frac{\Delta V}{V_{cap}} = \left(\theta - \frac{\theta^3}{6}\right)\Big/\theta = 1 - \frac{\theta^2}{6}$$

Solving for the angle yields

$$\theta = \sqrt{6\left(1 - \frac{\Delta V}{V_{cap}}\right)}$$

The formula suggests that if, at each instant of time, we ensure that the thrust vector is at an angle of θ with respect to the velocity to be gained vector, then we can still achieve the Lambert solution at the end of burn and hit the target.

Figure 14.10 shows the proper relationship between the thrust and velocity to be gained vectors relative to the inertial Earth-centered coordinate system. We can see that for counterclockwise travel the components of the thrust acceleration are given by

$$a_{XT} = a_T \cos(\phi - \theta)$$

$$a_{YT} = a_T \sin(\phi - \theta)$$

where θ is the angle between the thrust vector and the velocity to be gained vector, and ϕ is the angle between the velocity to be gained vector and the x axis. For clockwise travel the thrust acceleration components become

$$a_{XT} = a_T \cos(\phi + \theta)$$

$$a_{YT} = a_T \sin(\phi + \theta)$$

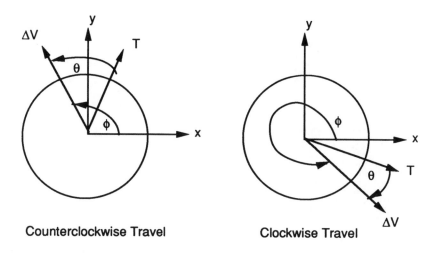

Counterclockwise Travel   Clockwise Travel

Fig. 14.10   Sign conventions for GEM.

Listing 14.4   General energy management simulation

```
      IMPLICIT REAL*8 (A-H)
      IMPLICIT REAL*8 (O-Z)
      INTEGER STEP
      LOGICAL LEFT,QBOOST,QZERO
      OPEN(1,STATUS = 'NEW',FILE = 'DATFIL')
      OPEN(2,STATUS = 'NEW',FILE = 'SPECFIL')
      LEFT = .TRUE.
      QBOOST = .TRUE.
      QZERO = .FALSE.
      XISP1 = 300.
      XISP2 = 300.
      XMF1 = .90
      XMF2 = .90
      WPAY = 100.
      DELV = 20000.
      DELV1 = .3333*DELV
      DELV2 = .6667*DELV
      AMAX1 = 20.
      AMAX2 = 20.
      TOP2 = WPAY*(EXP(DELV2/(XISP2*32.2))-1.)
      BOT2 = 1/XMF2-((1.-XMF2)/XMF2)*EXP(DELV2/(XISP2*32.2))
      WP2 = TOP2/BOT2
      WS2 = WP2*(1-XMF2)/XMF2
      WTOT2 = WP2 + WS2 + WPAY
      TRST2 = AMAX2*(WPAY + WS2)
      TB2 = XISP2*WP2/TRST2
      TOP1 = WTOT2*(EXP(DELV1/(XISP1*32.2))-1.)
      BOT1 = 1/XMF1-((1.-XMF1)/XMF1)*EXP(DELV1/(XISP1*32.2))
      WP1 = TOP1/BOT1
      WS1 = WP1*(1-XMF1)/XMF1
      WTOT = WP1 + WS1 + WTOT2
      TRST1 = AMAX1*(WTOT2 + WS1)
      TB1 = XISP1*WP1/TRST1
      DELVK = DELV/1000.
      WRITE(9,*)'TOTAL WEIGHT = ',WTOT
      WRITE(9,*)'WP2 = ',WP2
      WRITE(9,*)'WS2 = ',WS2
      WRITE(9,*)'WP1 = ',WP1
      WRITE(9,*)'WS1 = ',WS1
      WRITE(9,*)'TRST2 = ',TRST2
      WRITE(9,*)'TRST1 = ',TRST1
      WRITE(9,*)'TB2 = ',TB2
      WRITE(9,*)'TB1 = ',TB1
      H = .1
      T = 0.
      S = 0.
      A = 2.0926E7
      GM = 1.4077E16
      ALTNM = 0.
      ALT = ALTNM*6076.
      ANGDEG = 30.
      ANG = ANGDEG/57.3
      XLONGM = ANG
      X = (A + ALT)*COS(ANG)
      Y = (A + ALT)*SIN(ANG)
      ALT = SQRT(X**2 + Y**2)-A
      X1 = 0.
      Y1 = 0.
      AXT = 0.
      AYT = 0.
      XLONGTDEG = 45.
      XLONGT = XLONGTDEG/57.3
      XF = A*COS(XLONGT)
      YF = A*SIN(XLONGT)
      XFIRST = XF
      YFIRST = YF
      CALL DISTANCE(X,Y,XFIRST,YFIRST,DISTINITNM)
      TF = 500.
      DVCAP = DELV
10    IF(ALT<0..AND.T>10.)GOTO 999
      XOLD = X
      YOLD = Y
      X1OLD = X1
```

(Listing 14.4 continued on next page.)

Listing 14.4   (cont.) Listing 14.4 General energy management simulation

```
            Y1OLD = Y1
            STEP = 1
            GOTO 200
66          STEP = 2
            X = X + H*XD
            Y = Y + H*YD
            X1 = X1 + H*X1D
            Y1 = Y1 + H*Y1D
            T = T + H
            GOTO 200
55          CONTINUE
            X = (XOLD + X)/2 + .5*H*XD
            Y = (YOLD + Y)/2 + .5*H*YD
            X1 = (X1OLD + X1)/2 + .5*H*X1D
            Y1 = (Y1OLD + Y1)/2 + .5*H*Y1D
            ALT = SQRT(X**2 + Y**2)-A
            S = S + H
            TGOLAM = TF-T
            DVCAP = DVCAP-H*AT
            IF(QBOOST.AND.DVCAP > 50.)THEN
                XLONGM = ATAN2(Y,X)
1           CALL LAMBERT(X,Y,TGOLAM,XF,YF,VRX,VRY,XLONGM,XLONGT1,ICOUNT)
                DELX = VRX-X1
                DELY = VRY-Y1
                DEL = SQRT(DELX**2 + DELY**2)
                IF(.NOT.QZERO.AND.DVCAP > DEL)THEN
                    THET = SQRT(6.*(1.-DEL/DVCAP))
                    DEGTHET = 57.3*THET
                ELSE
                    QZERO = .TRUE.
                ENDIF
                PHI = ATAN2(DELY,DELX)
                DEGPHI = 57.3*PHI
                IF(XLONGT > XLONGM)THEN
                    AXT = AT*COS(PHI-THET)
                    AYT = AT*SIN(PHI-THET)
                ELSE
                    AXT = AT*COS(PHI + THET)
                    AYT = AT*SIN(PHI + THET)
                ENDIF
                CALL DISTANCE(X,Y,XFIRST,YFIRST,DISTNM)
                DISTNM = DISTINITNM-DISTNM
                ALTNM = (SQRT(X**2 + Y**2)-A)/6076.
                WRITE(2,*)T,DISTNM,ALTNM,THET*57.3,DVCAP
            ELSEIF(QBOOST)THEN
                CALL LAMBERT(X,Y,TGOLAM,XF,YF,VRX,VRY,XLONGM,
1               XLONGT,ICOUNT)
                TRST = 0.
                QBOOST = .FALSE.
                AXT = 0.
                AYT = 0.
                X1 = VRX
                Y1 = VRY
                X1OLD = X1
                Y1OLD = Y1
                CALL DISTANCE(X,Y,XFIRST,YFIRST,DISTNM)
                DISTNM = DISTINITNM-DISTNM
                ALTNM = (SQRT(X**2 + Y**2)-A)/6076.
                WRITE(2,*)T,DISTNM,ALTNM,THET*57.3,DVCAP
            ELSE
                QBOOST = .FALSE.
                AXT = 0.
                AYT = 0.
            ENDIF
            IF(S.LT.9.99999)GOTO 10
            S = 0.
            CALL DISTANCE(X,Y,XFIRST,YFIRST,DISTNM)
            DISTNM = DISTINITNM-DISTNM
            ALTNM = (SQRT(X**2 + Y**2)-A)/6076.
            VELK = SQRT(X1**2 + Y1**2)/1000.
            XNM = X/6076.
            YNM = Y/6076.
```

(Listing 14.4 continued on next page.)

Listing 14.4　(cont.) Listing 14.4 General energy management simulation

```
         WRITE(9,*)T,DISTNM,ALTNM
         WRITE(1,*)T,DISTNM,ALTNM
         GOTO 10
200      CONTINUE
         IF(T<TB1)THEN
             WGT = -WP1*T/TB1 + WTOT
             TRST = TRST1
         ELSEIF(T<(TB1 + TB2))THEN
             WGT = -WP2*T/TB2 + WTOT2 + WP2*TB1/TB2
             TRST = TRST2
         ELSE
             WGT = WPAY
             TRST = 0.
         ENDIF
         AT = 32.2*TRST/WGT
         XD = X1
         YD = Y1
         TEMBOT = (X**2 + Y**2)**1.5
         X1D = -GM*X/TEMBOT + AXT
         Y1D = -GM*Y/TEMBOT + AYT
         IF(STEP-1)66,66,55
999      CONTINUE
         CALL DISTANCE(X,Y,XFIRST,YFIRST,DISTNM)
         DISTNM = DISTINITNM-DISTNM
         ALTNM = (SQRT(X**2 + Y**2)-A)/6076.
         VELK = SQRT(X1**2 + Y1**2)/1000.
         WRITE(9,*)T,DISTNM,ALTNM,VELK
         WRITE(1,*)T,DISTNM,ALTNM
         PAUSE
         CLOSE(1)
         END
         SUBROUTINE DISTANCE(XT,YT,XF,YF,DISTNM)
         IMPLICIT REAL*8 (A-H)
         IMPLICIT REAL*8 (O-Z)
         SAVE
         R = SQRT(XT**2 + YT**2)
         A = 2.0926E7
         CBETA = (XT*XF + YT*YF)/(R*A)
         IF(CBETA<1.)THEN
             BETA = ACOS(CBETA)
             DISTNM = A*BETA/6076.
         ELSE
             DISTNM = (XF-XT)/6076.
         ENDIF
         RETURN
         END
         SUBROUTINE LAMBERT(XIC,YIC,TFDES,XF,YF,VRX,VRY,XLONGM,XLONGT,ICOUNT)
         IMPLICIT REAL*8 (A-H)
         IMPLICIT REAL*8 (O-Z)
         A = 2.0926E7
         GM = 1.4077E16
         RIC = SQRT(XIC**2 + YIC**2)
         RF = SQRT(XF**2 + YF**2)
         CPHI = (XIC*XF + YIC*YF)/(RIC*RF)
         PHI = ACOS(CPHI)
         SPHI = SIN(PHI)
         R0 = RIC
         PI = 3.14159
         DEGRAD = 360./(2.*PI)
         ICOUNT = 1
         GMIN = ATAN2((SPHI-SQRT(2.*R0*(1.-CPHI)/RF)),(1-CPHI))
         GMAX = ATAN2((SPHI + SQRT(2.*R0*(1.-CPHI)/RF)),(1-CPHI))
         GAM = (GMIN + GMAX)/2.
         DO
             TOP = GM*(1.-COS(PHI))
             TEMP = R0*COS(GAM)/RF-COS(PHI + GAM)
             BOT = R0*COS(GAM)*TEMP
             V = SQRT(TOP/BOT)
             IF (XLONGT>XLONGM) THEN
                 VRX = V*COS(PI/2.-GAM + XLONGM)
                 VRY = V*SIN(PI/2.-GAM + XLONGM)
             ELSE
```

(**Listing 14.4 continued on next page.**)

Listing 14.4   (cont.) Listing 14.4 General energy management simulation

```
            VRX = V*COS(-PI/2. + GAM + XLONGM)
            VRY = V*SIN(-PI/2. + GAM + XLONGM)
        END IF
        XLAM = R0*V*V/GM
        TOP1 = TAN(GAM)*(1-COS(PHI)) + (1-XLAM)*SIN(PHI)
        BOT1P = (1-COS(PHI))/(XLAM*COS(GAM)*COS(GAM))
        BOT1 = (2-XLAM)*(BOT1P + COS(GAM + PHI)/COS(GAM))
        TOP2 = 2*COS(GAM)
        BOT2 = XLAM*((2/XLAM-1)**1.5)
        TOP3 = SQRT(2/XLAM-1)
        BOT3 = COS(GAM)/TAN(PHI/2)-SIN(GAM)
        TEMP = (TOP2/BOT2)*ATAN2(TOP3,BOT3)
        TF = R0*(TOP1/BOT1 + TEMP)/(V*COS(GAM))
        IF((ABS(TFDES-TF)< = .00000001*TFDES).OR.ICOUNT > 100)THEN
            EXIT
        ENDIF
        IF(TF > TFDES)THEN
            GMAX = GAM
        ELSE
            GMIN = GAM
        ENDIF
        IF(ICOUNT = 1)THEN
            XNEXT = (GMAX + GMIN)/2.
        ELSE
            XNEXT = GAM + (GAM-GOLD)*(TFDES-TF)/(TF-TOLD)
            IF(XNEXT > GMAX.OR.XNEXT < GMIN)THEN
                XNEXT = (GMAX + GMIN)/2.
            ENDIF
        ENDIF
        GOLD = GAM
        TOLD = TF
        GAM = XNEXT
        ICOUNT = ICOUNT + 1
    REPEAT
    RETURN
    END
```

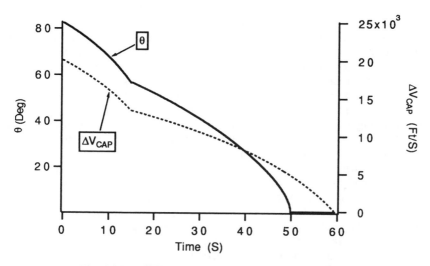

Fig. 14.11   GEM angle reaches steady state quickly.

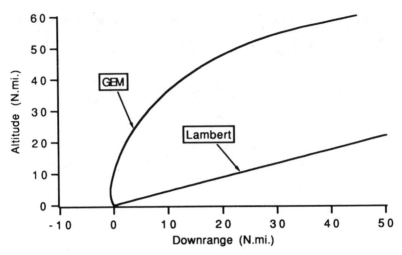

Fig. 14.12   Lambert and GEM trajectories during boost phase are vastly different.

Listing 14.4 presents a simulation of a booster intercepting a ground target using general energy management guidance. This simulation and the nominal operating conditions are identical to that of Listing 14.3, except for the GEM logic after the integration routine. We can see from the listing that the axial acceleration capability of the booster is continually being computed according to

$$\Delta V_{cap} = \Delta V_{cap} - H a_T$$

where H is the integration step size and a_T the instantaneous axial acceleration of the booster. In order to avoid numerical problems, the GEM logic is terminated when the velocity to be gained drops below 50 ft/s. In order to get accurate answers with the GEM logic, it was also necessary to reduce the integration step size from 1 s, as in Listing 14.3, to 0.1 s. We can see from the listing that it is still necessary to use the Lambert subroutine in order to implement the general energy management guidance technique.

A nominal case was run to see how the GEM guidance logic performed. We can see from Fig. 14.11 that, although the booster burn lasts for nearly 60 s, the angle the thrust vector makes with respect to the velocity to be gained vector approaches steady state in slightly over 50 s. Also shown in Fig. 14.11 is a plot of how the velocity capability of the booster diminishes during the burn. The discontinuity in that curve is due to staging.

Figure 14.12 displays the GEM trajectory during the boost phase. It appears from the figure that the booster will never hit the target because it initially appears to be heading in the wrong direction. However, after wasting energy, the GEM-guided booster heads in the right direction. Superimposed on the figure is the Lambert guidance trajectory during boost for the same case. We can see that both trajectories are vastly different during the boost phase.

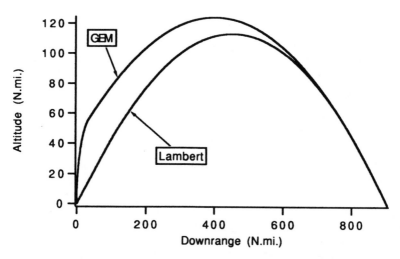

Fig. 14.13 **Both Lambert and GEM trajectories hit target at the same time.**

Figure 14.13 displays the GEM and Lambert trajectories for the entire flight (boost and coast phases). We can see from the figure that, although both trajectories are vastly different during the boost phase, they eventually converge, and both hit the target at the same time.

Summary

In this chapter the Lambert problem was explained, and a novel numerical technique for solving the problem, based on the closed-form solutions of Chapter 12, was introduced. Two techniques were presented showing how the solution to Lambert's problem was fundamental to steering boosters. Numerical examples were presented illustrating the implementation and effectiveness of the booster steering techniques.

References

[1]Battin, R. H., *An Introduction to the Mathematics and Methods of Astrodynamics*, AIAA Education Series, New York, 1987.

[2]Regan, F., *Re-Entry Vehicle Dynamics*, AIAA Education Series, New York, 1984.

[3]Acton, F. S., *Numerical Methods That Work,* Harper and Row, New York, 1970.

[4]Nelson, S. L., and Zarchan, P., "Alternative Approach to the Solution of Lambert's Problem," *Journal of Guidance, Control, and Dynamics,* Vol. 15, July–Aug. 1992, pp. 1003–1009.

[5]Brand, T. J., "A New Approach to Lambert Guidance," Charles Stark Draper Lab., Cambridge, MA, Rept. R-694, June 1971.

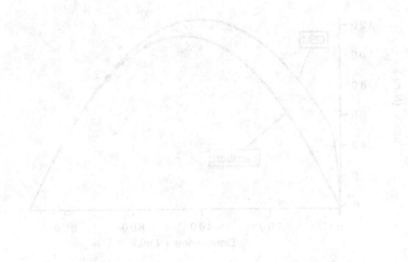

Chapter 15

Strategic Intercepts

Introduction

GUIDANCE concepts for tactical homing missiles were introduced, explained, and demonstrated in Chapters 2, 6, and 8. Strategic missiles travel much faster and farther than tactical missiles. We have shown that the coordinate system and gravity models in our tactical simulations had to be modified to handle the new speed and range regimes of strategic missiles. More specifically, we had to shift our coordinate system from the surface of a flat Earth to the center of a round Earth and use a more general formulation for gravitational acceleration (i.e., Newton's law of universal gravitation).

Since tactical missiles operate within the atmosphere, they can generate lift by moving control surfaces in order to execute guidance commands. Speed, altitude, and structural considerations limit maximum achievable acceleration levels with tactical missiles. Missile slowdown due to drag limits the tactical missile's range and maneuver capability. Strategic missiles, on the other hand, operate outside the atmosphere and must burn fuel (i.e., lateral thrusters) to respond to guidance commands. Achievable engine thrust-to-weight ratios limit maximum strategic lateral acceleration levels. In addition, when the maneuver or divert fuel is exhausted, the strategic missile cannot maneuver at all. Care must be taken to ensure that a strategic missile has sufficient divert fuel so that it can meet system objectives.

Although there are major differences between strategic and tactical missiles, there are also similarities. This chapter will show that tactical guidance laws may be suitable for strategic missiles. Useful design relationships, developed previously in the text for tactical missiles, will be modified and shown to be applicable for strategic missiles as well.

Guidance Review

In Chapter 2 we saw the effectiveness of the proportional navigation guidance law for tactical missiles. A closed-form solution for the required missile acceleration to hit a target, in the presence of heading error, was derived for a zero-lag guidance system. The required missile acceleration was shown to be

$$n_c = \frac{-V_M HE \, N'}{t_F}\left(1 - \frac{t}{t_F}\right)^{N'-2}$$

where V_M is the missile velocity, HE is the angular heading error, N' is the effective navigation ratio, t_F is the flight time, and t is instantaneous time.

With strategic missiles it is often more convenient to talk in terms of prediction error rather than heading error. A prelaunch calculation or prediction must be made of where the target will be at intercept. This location is known as the predicted intercept point. If the calculation is imperfect, a prediction error results, and the missile will not be fired on a perfect collision triangle. The prediction error and heading error are related by

$$Pred\ Err = -V_M HE t_F$$

where *Pred Err* is the prediction error in units of feet. Therefore, substitution of the preceding relationship into the closed-form solution indicates that the missile acceleration required by the proportional navigation guidance law to take out an initial prediction error is given by

$$n_c = \frac{Pred\ Err\ N'}{t_F^2}\left(1 - \frac{t}{t_F}\right)^{N'-2}$$

As was mentioned previously, strategic missiles burn fuel to maneuver. The amount of lateral divert or ΔV required is related to the missile acceleration according to

$$\Delta V = \int_0^{t_F} |n_c|\ dt$$

The strategic interceptor ΔV requirements are related to the total interceptor weight by the rocket equation. Increasing a missile's divert requirements can increase the total weight requirements dramatically. We can find a closed-form solution for the required divert to take out a prediction error by substituting the closed-form solution for the missile acceleration into the preceding integral. After some algebra we obtain

$$\Delta V = \frac{Pred\ Err\ N'}{(N'-1)t_F}$$

Thus, increasing the effective navigation ratio or increasing the flight time (or guidance time) will tend to reduce the lateral divert requirements of the interceptor. The preceding formula for the required lateral divert is plotted in Fig. 15.1 for the case in which the prediction error is 100 kft. We can see that, for an effective navigation ratio of 3, it takes more than 10,000 ft/s of divert to remove the error in 10 s, about 1050 ft/s of divert to remove the error in 100 s, and only about 300 ft/s of divert to remove the error in 500 s. Therefore, larger missile acquisition ranges result in larger guided flight times, which in turn can reduce the lateral divert requirements for a given prediction error. Increasing the effective navigation ratio to 5 only slightly reduces the lateral divert requirements. Doubling the prediction error will double the divert requirements.

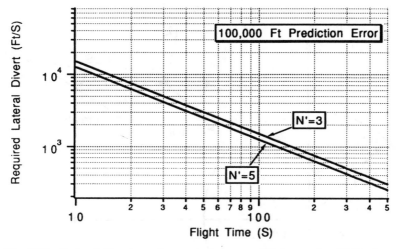

Fig. 15.1 Lateral divert requirements decrease with increasing flight time.

Ballistic Engagement Simulation[1]

We can develop a strategic ballistic missile-target engagement simulation by using an Earth-centered coordinate system as shown in Fig. 15.2. In this figure both the missile and target are in a gravity field as described by Newton's law of universal gravitation. The acceleration differential equations acting on a ballistic target was shown in Chapter 12 to be

$$\ddot{x}_T = \frac{-gm\,x_T}{(x_T^2 + y_T^2)^{1.5}}$$

$$\ddot{y}_T = \frac{-gm\,y_T}{(x_T^2 + y_T^2)^{1.5}}$$

where gm is the gravitational parameter. These differential equations are in an inertial coordinate system whose origin is at the center of the Earth. Therefore, they can be integrated directly to yield the velocity and position of the target with respect to the center of the Earth. The components of the relative position between the missile and target can be expressed as

$$R_{TM1} = x_T - x_M$$

$$R_{TM2} = y_T - y_M$$

and the components of the relative velocity are given by

$$V_{TM1} = \dot{x}_T - \dot{x}_M$$

$$V_{TM2} = \dot{y}_T - \dot{y}_M$$

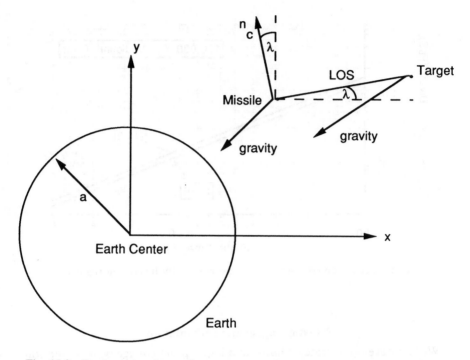

Fig. 15.2   Earth-centered coordinate system and relative engagement geometry.

Application of the distance formula shows that the relative separation between the missile and target can be found from

$$R_{TM} = (R_{TM1}^2 + R_{TM2}^2)^{0.5}$$

The closing velocity, which is defined as the negative rate of change of separation between missile and target, can be obtained by taking the negative derivative of the preceding expression, yielding

$$V_c = \frac{-(R_{TM1}V_{TM1} + R_{TM2}V_{TM2})}{R_{TM}}$$

The line-of-sight angle can be found by trigonometry from Fig. 15.2 as

$$\lambda = \tan^{-1}\frac{R_{TM2}}{R_{TM1}}$$

Therefore, the instantaneous value of the line-of-sight rate can be found by taking the derivative of the preceding expression, using the quotient rule, yielding

$$\dot{\lambda} = \frac{R_{TM1}V_{TM2} - R_{TM2}V_{TM1}}{R_{TM}^2}$$

We now have sufficient information to guide a strategic interceptor. The proportional navigation guidance command is proportional to the line-of-sight rate according to

$$n_c = N' V_c \dot\lambda$$

where N' is the effective navigation ratio and V_c the closing velocity. This guidance command is perpendicular to the line of sight. From Fig. 15.2 we can see that the components of the guidance command in the Earth-centered coordinate system can be found by trigonometry and are given by

$$a_{XM} = -n_c \sin\lambda$$

$$a_{YM} = n_c \cos\lambda$$

Therefore, the acceleration differential equations describing the missile consist of two parts: the gravitational term and the guidance command term. The components of the missile differential equations in Earth-centered coordinates are

$$\ddot{x}_M = \frac{-gm\, x_M}{(x_M^2 + y_M^2)^{1.5}} + a_{XM}$$

$$\ddot{y}_M = \frac{-gm\, y_M}{(x_M^2 + y_M^2)^{1.5}} + a_{YM}$$

where a_{XM} and a_{YM} have already been defined.

Listing 15.1 presents a FORTRAN simulation of an engagement between an impulsive missile and a ballistic target. The simulation, which is based on the differential equations derived in this section, is similar to the tactical engagement simulations presented in the text, except that the coordinate system is Earth-centered and calculations now have to be performed using double-precision arithmetic (i.e., REAL*8). The reason for double-precision arithmetic is that distances are now very large since they are referenced with respect to the center of the Earth. Relative quantities, which are required for guidance command and miss distance computation, involve the subtraction of large numbers. Near the end of the flight the large numbers are nearly equal and single-precision arithmetic does not offer sufficient accuracy.

The program includes a prediction routine (subroutine PREDICT) to determine where the target will be at the intercept time t_F. Before the main simulation begins, this routine integrates the ballistic target equations forward in time to determine the location of the target at time t_F (i.e., predicted intercept point). The Lambert routine (subroutine LAMBERT) determines the velocity components of an impulsive strategic interceptor ($VRXM$ and $VRYM$) so that it will be on a collision triangle with the ballistic target. In other words, given an initial location, a final location, and an arrival time, the Lambert subroutine determines the correct missile velocity components so that it will collide with the target at time t_F. If the predicted intercept

Listing 15.1   Engagement simulation with ballistic target

```
        IMPLICIT REAL*8 (A – H)
        IMPLICIT REAL*8 (O – Z)
        INTEGER STEP
        XLONGMDEG = 45.
        XLONGTDEG = 90.
        ALTNMTIC = 0.
        ALTNMMIC = 0.
        TF = 500.
        GAMDEGT = 23.
        H = 1.
        A = 2.0926E7
        GM = 1.4077E16
        PI = 3.14159
        DEGRAD = 360./(2.*PI)
        XNP = 3.
        PREDERR = 0.
        GAMT = GAMDEGT/57.3
        DISTNMT = 6000.
        PHIT = DISTNMT*6076./A
        ALTT = ALTNMTIC*6076.
        ALTM = ALTNMMIC*6076.
        R0T = A + ALTT
        TOP = GM*(1. – COS(PHIT))
        TEMP = R0T*COS(GAMT)/A – COS(PHIT + GAMT)
        BOT = R0T*COS(GAMT)*TEMP
        VT = SQRT(TOP/BOT)
        XLONGM = XLONGMDEG/DEGRAD
        XLONGT = XLONGTDEG/DEGRAD
        IF (XLONGM > XLONGT) THEN
            X1T = VT*COS(PI/2. – GAMT + XLONGT)
            Y1T = VT*SIN(PI/2. – GAMT + XLONGT)
        ELSE
            X1T = VT*COS( – PI/2. + GAMT + XLONGT)
            Y1T = VT*SIN( – PI/2. + GAMT + XLONGT)
        END IF
        S = 0.
        SCOUNT = 0.
        XLONGM = XLONGMDEG/DEGRAD
        XLONGT = XLONGTDEG/DEGRAD
        XM = (A + ALTM)*COS(XLONGM)
        YM = (A + ALTM)*SIN(XLONGM)
        XT = (A + ALTT)*COS(XLONGT)
        YT = (A + ALTT)*SIN(XLONGT)
        XFIRSTT = XT
        YFIRSTT = YT
        T = 0.
        CALL PREDICT (TF,XT,YT,X1T,Y1T,XTF,YTF)
        YTF = YTF + PREDERR
        CALL LAMBERT(XM,YM,TF,XTF,YTF,VRXM,VRYM,XLONGM,XLONGT,ICOUNT)
        X1M = VRXM
        Y1M = VRYM
        RTM1 = XT – XM
        RTM2 = YT – YM
        RTM = SQRT(RTM1**2 + RTM2**2)
        VTM1 = X1T – X1M
        VTM2 = Y1T – Y1M
        VC = – (RTM1*VTM1 + RTM2*VTM2)/RTM
        DELV = 0.
10      IF(VC<0.)GOTO 999
        TGO = RTM/VC
        IF(TGO>10.)THEN
            H = 1.
        ELSEIF(TGO > .1)THEN
            H = .01
        ELSE
            H = .0001
        ENDIF
        XOLDT = XT
        YOLDT = YT
        X1OLDT = X1T
        Y1OLDT = Y1T
        XOLDM = XM
        YOLDM = YM
```

(Listing 15.1 continued on next page.)

Listing 15.1 (cont.) Engagement simulation with ballistic target

```
          X1OLDM = X1M
          Y1OLDM = Y1M
          DELVOLD = DELV
          STEP = 1
          GOTO 200
  66      STEP = 2
          XT = XT + H*XDT
          YT = YT + H*YDT
          X1T = X1T + H*X1DT
          Y1T = Y1T + H*Y1DT
          XM = XM + H*XDM
          YM = YM + H*YDM
          X1M = X1M + H*X1DM
          Y1M = Y1M + H*Y1DM
          DELV = DELV + H*DELVD
          T = T + H
          GOTO 200
  55      XT = (XOLDT + XT)/2 + .5*H*XDT
          YT = (YOLDT + YT)/2 + .5*H*YDT
          X1T = (X1OLDT + X1T)/2 + .5*H*X1DT
          Y1T = (Y1OLDT + Y1T)/2 + .5*H*Y1DT
          XM = (XOLDM + XM)/2 + .5*H*XDM
          YM = (YOLDM + YM)/2 + .5*H*YDM
          X1M = (X1OLDM + X1M)/2 + .5*H*X1DM
          Y1M = (Y1OLDM + Y1M)/2 + .5*H*Y1DM
          DELV = (DELVOLD + DELV)/2. + .5*H*DELVD
          ALTT = SQRT(XT**2 + YT**2) - A
          ALTM = SQRT(XM**2 + YM**2) - A
          S = S + H
          SCOUNT = SCOUNT + H
          IF(SCOUNT.LT.9.99999)GOTO 10
          SCOUNT = 0.
          XNMT = XT/6076.
          YNMT = YT/6076.
          XNMM = XM/6076.
          YNMM = YM/6076.
          ALTNMT = ALTT/6076.
          CALL DISTANCE(XT,YT,XFIRSTT,YFIRSTT,DISTNMT)
          ALTNMM = ALTM/6076.
          CALL DISTANCE(XM,YM,XFIRSTT,YFIRSTT,DISTNMM)
          WRITE(9,*)T,DISTNMT,ALTNMT,DISTNMM,ALTNMM,XNC,DELV
  200     CONTINUE
          TEMBOTT = (XT**2 + YT**2)**1.5
          X1DT = - GM*XT/TEMBOTT
          Y1DT = - GM*YT/TEMBOTT
          XDT = X1T
          YDT = Y1T
          RTM1 = XT - XM
          RTM2 = YT - YM
          RTM = SQRT(RTM1**2 + RTM2**2)
          VTM1 = X1T - X1M
          VTM2 = Y1T - Y1M
          VC = - (RTM1*VTM1 + RTM2*VTM2)/RTM
          TGO = RTM/VC
          XLAM = ATAN2(RTM2,RTM1)
          XLAMD = (RTM1*VTM2 - RTM2*VTM1)/(RTM*RTM)
          XNC = XNP*VC*XLAMD
          DELVD = ABS(XNC)
          AM1 = - XNC*SIN(XLAM)
          AM2 = XNC*COS(XLAM)
          TEMBOTM = (XM**2 + YM**2)**1.5
          X1DM = - GM*XM/TEMBOTM + AM1
          Y1DM = - GM*YM/TEMBOTM + AM2
          XDM = X1M
          YDM = Y1M
          IF(STEP - 1)66,66,55
  999     CONTINUE
          XNMT = XT/6076.
          YNMT = YT/6076.
          XNMM = XM/6076.
```

(Listing 15.1 continued on next page.)

Listing 15.1   (cont.) Engagement simulation with ballistic target

```
      YNMM = YM/6076.
      ALTNMT = ALTT/6076.
      CALL DISTANCE(XT,YT,XFIRSTT,YFIRSTT,DISTNMT)
      ALTNMM = ALTM/6076.
      CALL DISTANCE(XM,YM,XFIRSTT,YFIRSTT,DISTNMM)
      WRITE(9,*)T,DISTNMT,ALTNMT,DISTNMM,ALTNMM,XNC,DELV
      WRITE(9,*)T,RTM,DELV
      PAUSE
      END

      SUBROUTINE DISTANCE(XT,YT,XF,YF,DISTNM)
      SAVE
      IMPLICIT REAL*8 (A – H)
      IMPLICIT REAL*8 (O – Z)
      R = SQRT(XT**2 + YT**2)
      RF = SQRT(XF**2 + YF**2)
      A = 2.0926E7
      CBETA = (XT*XF + YT*YF)/(R*RF)
      IF(CBETA < 1.)THEN
            BETA = ACOS(CBETA)
            DISTNM = A*BETA/6076.
      ELSE
            DISTNM = (XT – XF)/6076.
      ENDIF
      RETURN
      END

      SUBROUTINE PREDICT (TF,XDUM,YDUM,X1DUM,Y1DUM,XTF,YTF)
      IMPLICIT REAL*8 (A – H)
      IMPLICIT REAL*8 (O – Z)
      INTEGER STEP
      SAVE
      H = 1.
      A = 2.0926E7
      GM = 1.4077E16
      T = 0.
      X = XDUM
      Y = YDUM
      X1 = X1DUM
      Y1 = Y1DUM


10    IF(T > (TF – .00001))GOTO 999
      XOLD = X
      YOLD = Y
      X1OLD = X1
      Y1OLD = Y1
      STEP = 1
      GOTO 200
66    STEP = 2
      X = X + H*XD
      Y = Y + H*YD
      X1 = X1 + H*X1D
      Y1 = Y1 + H*Y1D
      T = T + H
      GOTO 200
55    X = (XOLD + X)/2 + .5*H*XD
      Y = (YOLD + Y)/2 + .5*H*YD
      X1 = (X1OLD + X1)/2 + .5*H*X1D
      Y1 = (Y1OLD + Y1)/2 + .5*H*Y1D
      GOTO 10
200   CONTINUE
      TEMBOT = (X**2 + Y**2)**1.5
      X1D = – GM*X/TEMBOT
      Y1D = – GM*Y/TEMBOT
      XD = X1
      YD = Y1
      IF(STEP – 1)66,66,55
```

(Listing 15.1 continued on next page.)

Listing 15.1   (cont.) Engagement simulation with ballistic target

```
999     CONTINUE
        XTF = X
        YTF = Y
        RETURN
        END

        SUBROUTINE LAMBERT(XIC,YIC,TFDES,XF,YF,VRX,VRY,XLONGM,XLONGT)
1        ,ICOUNT)
        IMPLICIT REAL*8 (A – H)
        IMPLICIT REAL*8 (O – Z)
        A = 2.0926E7
        GM = 1.4077E16
        RIC = SQRT(XIC**2 + YIC**2)
        RF = SQRT(XF**2 + YF**2)
        CPHI = (XIC*XF + YIC*YF)/(RIC*RF)
        PHI = ACOS(CPHI)
        SPHI = SIN(PHI)
        R0 = RIC
        PI = 3.14159
        DEGRAD = 360./(2.*PI)
        ICOUNT = 1
        GMIN = ATAN2(SPHI – SQRT(2.*RO*(1.–CPHI)/RF)),(1-CPHI))
        GMAX = ATAN2(SPHI + SQRT(2.*RO*(1.–CPHI)/RF)),(1–CPHI))
        GAM = (GMIN + GMAX)/2.
        DO
          TOP = GM*(1. – COS(PHI))
          TEMP = R0*COS(GAM)/RF – COS(PHI + GAM)
          BOT = R0*COS(GAM)*TEMP
          V = SQRT(TOP/BOT)
          IF (XLONGT > XLONGM) THEN
            VRX = V*COS(PI/2. – GAM + XLONGM)
            VRY = V*SIN(PI/2. – GAM + XLONGM)
          ELSE
            VRX = V*COS( – PI/2. + GAM + XLONGM)
            VRY = V*SIN( – PI/2. + GAM + XLONGM)
          END IF
          XLAM = R0*V*V/GM
          TOP1 = TAN(GAM)*(1 – COS(PHI)) + (1 – XLAM)*SIN(PHI)
          BOT1P = (1 – COS(PHI))/(XLAM*COS(GAM)*COS(GAM))
          BOT1 = (2 – XLAM)*(BOT1P + COS(GAM + PHI)/COS(GAM))
          TOP2 = 2*COS(GAM)
          BOT2 = XLAM*((2/XLAM – 1)**1.5)
          TOP3 = SQRT(2/XLAM – 1)
          BOT3 = COS(GAM)/TAN(PHI/2) – SIN(GAM)
          TEMP = (TOP2/BOT2)*ATAN2(TOP3,BOT3)
          TF = R0*(TOP1/BOT1 + TEMP)/(V*COS(GAM))
          IF(ABS(FFCES – TF) < = .00000001*TFDES).OR.ICOUNT > 100)THEN
              EXIT
          ENDIF
          IF(TF > TFDES)THEN
              GMAX = GAM
          ELSE
              GMIN = GAM
          ENDIF
          IF(ICOUNT = 1) THEN
            XNEXT = (GMAX + GMIN)/2.
          ELSE
            XNET = GAM + (GAM – GOLD)*(TFDES – TF)/TF – TOLD)
            IF(XNEXT > GMAX.OR.XNEXT < GMIN) THEN
            XNEXT = (GMAX + GMIN)/2.
            ENDIF
          ENDIF
          GOLD = GAM
          TOLD = TF
          GAM = XNEXT
          ICOUNT = – ICOUNT + 1
        REPEAT
        RETURN
```

point is correct, then no guidance system is required for the strategic interceptor to collide with the target.

We can see from the listing that the guidance equations are virtually identical to those of the two-dimensional tactical simulation of Chapter 2. This is not surprising since the proportional navigation guidance law operates on relative quantities that should be independent of coordinate system. The differential equations for the missile and target and the guidance equations appear after statement label 200.

A nominal case was run in which the guidance system was turned off ($XNC = 0$). The resultant trajectory for the 500-s flight is shown in Fig. 15.3. In this case the missile hit the target. This means that our knowledge of the intercept point was perfect (from the prediction subroutine) and that the missile was placed on the correct collision triangle (from Lambert subroutine). The slight curvature in both missile and target trajectories is due to the fact that both objects are in a gravity field for 500 s.

The same nominal case was rerun, except this time the proportional navigation guidance system was turned on. The resultant commanded acceleration profile, which resulted in a successful intercept, along with the missile lateral divert requirements appear in Fig. 15.4. We can see from the figure that, even though the missile was initially on a collision triangle, the proportional navigation guidance system issued acceleration commands. In this case it appears that proportional navigation is behaving in a counterintuitive way since we could have hit the target without any acceleration commands at all!

In order to understand why guidance commands were required of a missile on a collision triangle, let us review some basics. Consider the case of a constant-velocity missile and constant-velocity target on a collision triangle as shown in Fig. 15.5. If we connect lines between the missile and target at different times during the flight, we have a measure of how the line-of-sight

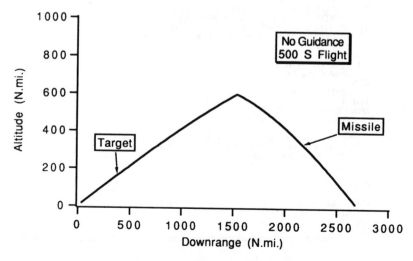

Fig. 15.3 Collision triangle geometry for nominal case.

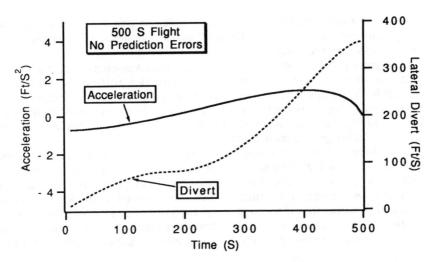

Fig. 15.4 Some divert required with proportional navigation guidance even though missile is on collision triangle.

rate changes with time. We can see from Fig. 15.5 that, when both the missile and target are traveling at constant velocities, the line-of-sight lines are parallel. In other words, the *line-of-sight rate is zero!* Since acceleration commands are proportional to the line-of-sight rate in a proportional navigation system, there will be no commands for a constant velocity missile and target on a collision triangle.

Figure 15.6 also shows a missile and target on a collision triangle. However, this time the missile is traveling at a constant velocity while the target velocity is nonconstant. In this case we can see that the line-of-sight lines are not parallel. Thus, we have a line-of-sight rate generated even though the

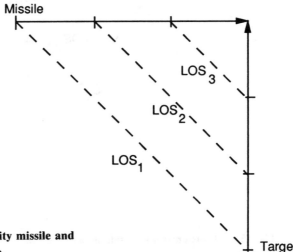

Fig. 15.5 Constant-velocity missile and target on collision triangle.

missile and target are on a collision triangle. In this case a proportional navigation guidance system will generate acceleration commands, even though none are required!

In a gravity field, both the missile and target velocities vary with time. Thus, as shown in Fig. 15.6, the line-of-sight rate will not be zero, even though both the missile and target are on a collision triangle. Proportional navigation will waste some fuel in responding to the small line-of-sight rates. In our nominal case about 350 ft/s of lateral divert was required by the missile to intercept the ballistic target.

A guidance system is required since we cannot always be on a collision triangle. There will always be errors in predicting the location of the intercept point. Consider a case for a proportional navigation guidance system with an effective navigation ratio of 3 in which there is a 100-kft prediction error. This means that if we turned off the guidance system we would miss the target by 100 kft. Based on the formula derived at the beginning of this chapter, theory predicts that the required missile lateral divert should be

$$\Delta V = \frac{Pred\ Err\ N'}{(N' - 1)t_F} = \frac{100,000*3}{2*500} = 300 \text{ ft/s}$$

Figure 15.7 shows the resultant commanded acceleration and lateral divert profiles due to the 100-kft prediction error for a proportional navigation guidance system with an effective navigation ratio of 3. We can see that

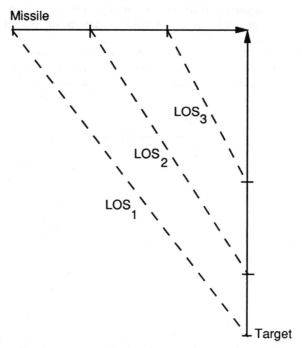

Fig. 15.6   Constant-velocity missile and variable-velocity target on collision triangle.

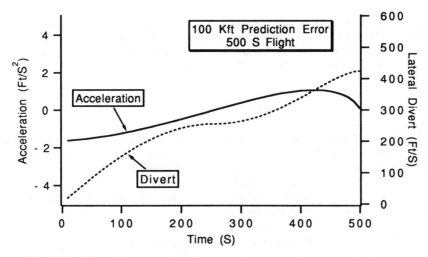

Fig. 15.7   Divert due to prediction error is close to theoretical prediction.

the missile acceleration requirements are small (less than 2 ft/s²) for the flight. However, even at small acceleration levels, about 420 ft/s of lateral divert was required for a successful intercept. This value is somewhat larger than the theoretically predicted value of 300 ft/s because, as we previously saw, the gravity field also adds to the divert requirements.

Theory tells us that, for a fixed prediction error, the divert requirements will increase if the flight time is decreased. Figure 15.8 presents the engagement geometry for a 100-s flight. In this case both the missile and target are initially on a collision triangle.

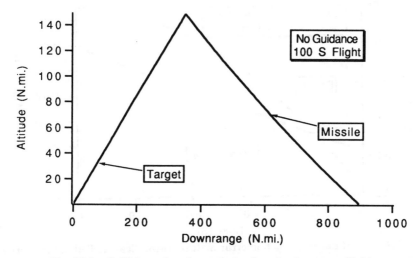

Fig. 15.8   Collision triangle geometry for shorter-range flight.

If we introduce a 100-kft prediction error into the short-range example, theory tells us that the lateral divert requirements should increase substantially. According to the previously presented lateral divert formula, the divert requirements for a 100-s flight should be

$$\Delta V = \frac{Pred\ Err\ N'}{(N'-1)t_F} = \frac{100,000*3}{2*100} = 1500\ ft/s$$

Figure 15.9 displays the commanded acceleration and actual divert requirements obtained by running the engagement simulation. We can see from the figure that the required lateral divert required is indeed nearly 1500 ft/s. Thus, we have demonstrated with nonlinear engagement simulation results that the theoretical formula is a useful and accurate indicator of divert requirements for prediction error.

Boosting Target Considerations[1]

Although a booster does not execute evasive maneuvers, any longitudinal booster acceleration that is perpendicular to the line of sight will appear as a target maneuver to the missile. In Chapter 2 we saw that the closed-form solution for the acceleration required by a missile utilizing proportional navigation guidance was given by

$$n_c\bigg|_{PN} = \frac{N'}{N'-2}\left[1 - \left(1 - \frac{t}{t_F}\right)^{N'-2}\right]n_T$$

where N' is the effective navigation ratio, t is time, t_F the flight time, and n_T the magnitude of the apparent target maneuver. From the definition of

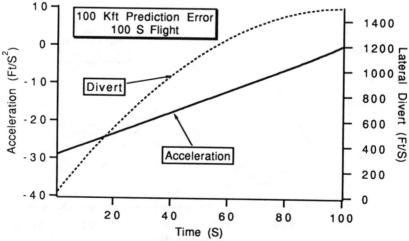

Fig. 15.9   Divert due to prediction error matches theoretical prediction for shorter flight.

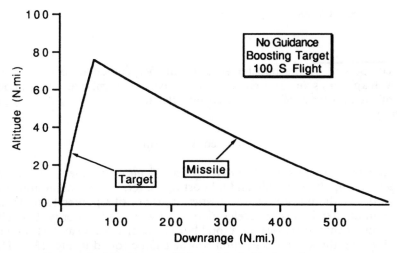

Fig. 15.10 Missile on collision triangle for boosting target.

lateral divert,

$$\Delta V = \int_0^{t_F} |n_c| \, dt$$

we can derive an expression for the lateral divert required to hit a maneuvering target as

$$\Delta V \bigg|_{PN} = \frac{N'}{N' - 1} \, n_T t_F$$

Thus, the lateral divert due to a maneuvering target increases with increasing flight time and decreases with increasing effective navigation ratio.

We can develop an engagement simulation in which the target is a booster. In Chapter 13 we saw how to model a booster performing a gravity turn. We can express the longitudinal acceleration of the booster as

$$a_T = \frac{32.2T}{W}$$

where T is the booster thrust and W the booster weight. In a gravity turn the thrust and velocity vectors are aligned so that the acceleration differential equations for the booster in a gravity field become

$$\ddot{x}_T = \frac{-gm \, x_T}{(x_T^2 + y_T^2)^{1.5}} + \frac{a_T \dot{x}_T}{V_T}$$

$$\ddot{y}_T = \frac{-gm \, y_T}{(x_T^2 + y_T^2)^{1.5}} + \frac{a_T \dot{y}_T}{V_T}$$

where the target velocity V_T is given by

$$V_T = (\dot{x}_T^2 + \dot{y}_T^2)^{0.5}$$

Any component of the booster acceleration perpendicular to the line of sight will appear as an apparent target maneuver to the missile. The component of the booster acceleration perpendicular to the line of sight, a_{PLOS}, is given by

$$a_{PLOS} = \ddot{y}_T \cos\lambda - \ddot{x}_T \sin\lambda$$

Listing 15.2 presents a FORTRAN listing of an engagement simulation between an impulsive missile and a boosting target. The nominal numbers used to derive the booster characteristics are those of Chapter 13 in which the maximum axial booster acceleration of a two-stage booster is 10 g. The thrust-weight characteristics for a total burn time of 138.2 s can be found in Fig. 13.7, and the axial acceleration profile can be found in Fig. 13.8. The simulation is identical to that of Listing 15.1, except for the fact that the target is a booster executing a gravity turn and a 10-g limit has been placed on the commanded acceleration.

A nominal case was run with the guidance system turned off to ensure that the missile and booster were on a collision triangle. Figure 15.10 shows the missile hitting the target in the nominal 100-s flight in which the booster is accelerating the entire time.

The same nominal case was rerun with the proportional navigation guidance system turned on. Figure 15.11 displays the booster acceleration perpendicular to the line of sight for this engagement along with the resultant lateral divert requirements. We can see from the figure that the magnitude of the booster acceleration perpendicular to the line of sight is approximately 100 ft/s² on the average. This means that the booster appears to the missile to be a target executing a 3-g maneuver. The missile lateral divert requirements for this case can be seen from the figure to be approximately 12,000 ft/s.

For this case theory says that the divert requirements should be

$$\Delta V = \Big|_{PN} = \frac{N'}{N'-1} n_T t_F = \frac{3*100*100}{2} = 15,000 \text{ ft/s}$$

In other words, theory and simulation are in close agreement.

We saw that, with tactical missiles, the augmented proportional navigation guidance law reduced the interceptor acceleration requirements. The closed-form solution for the acceleration required to hit a maneuvering target with the augmented proportional navigation guidance law was shown to be given by

$$n_c \Big|_{APN} = 0.5\, n_T N' \left(1 - \frac{t}{t_F}\right)^{N'-2}$$

Listing 15.2   Engagement simulation for boosting target

```
        IMPLICIT REAL*8 (A-H)
        IMPLICIT REAL*8 (O-Z)
        INTEGER STEP
        LOGICAL LEFT
        LEFT = .FALSE.
        XNCLIM = 322.
        H = 1.
        A = 2.0926E7
        GM = 1.4077E16
        PI = 3.14159
        DEGRAD = 360./(2.*PI)
        XNP = 3.
        PREDERR = 0.
        XISP1 = 250.
        XISP2 = 250.
        XMF1 = .85
        XMF2 = .85
        WPAY = 100.
        DELV = 20000.
        DELV1 = .3333*DELV
        DELV2 = .6667*DELV
        AMAX1 = 10.
        AMAX2 = 10.
        XKICKDEG = 80.
        TOP2 = WPAY*(EXP(DELV2/(XISP2*32.2)) – 1.)
        BOT2 = 1/XMF2 – ((1. – XMF2)/XMF2)*EXP(DELV2/(XISP2*32.2))
        WP2 = TOP2/BOT2
        WS2 = WP2*(1 – XMF2)/XMF2
        WTOT2 = WP2 + WS2 + WPAY
        TRST2 = AMAX2*(WPAY + WS2)
        TB2 = XISP2*WP2/TRST2
        TOP1 = WTOT2*(EXP(DELV1/(XISP1*32.2)) – 1.)
        BOT1 = 1/XMF1 – ((1. – XMF1)/XMF1)*EXP(DELV1/(XISP1*32.2))
        WP1 = TOP1/BOT1
        WS1 = WP1*(1 – XMF1)/XMF1
        WTOT = WP1 + WS1 + WTOT2
        TRST1 = AMAX1*(WTOT2 + WS1)
        TB1 = XISP1*WP1/TRST1
        XLONGMDEG = 80.
        XLONGTDEG = 90.
        ALTNMTIC = 0.
        ALTNMMIC = 0.
        XKICKDEG = 80.
        TF = 100.
        ALTT = ALTNMTIC*6076.
        ALTM = ALTNMMIC*6076.
        S = 0.
        SCOUNT = 0.
        XLONGM = XLONGMDEG/DEGRAD
        XLONGT = XLONGTDEG/DEGRAD
        XM = (A + ALTM)*COS(XLONGM)
        YM = (A + ALTM)*SIN(XLONGM)
        XT = (A + ALTT)*COS(XLONGT)
        YT = (A + ALTT)*SIN(XLONGT)
        XFIRSTT = XT
        IF (LEFT) THEN
          X1T = COS(PI/2. – XKICKDEG/DEGRAD + XLONGT)
          Y1T = SIN(PI/2. – XKICKDEG/DEGRAD + XLONGT)
        ELSE
          X1T = COS(– PI/2. + XKICKDEG/DEGRAD + XLONGT)
          Y1T = SIN(– PI/2. + XKICKDEG/DEGRAD + XLONGT)
        END IF
        XFIRSTT = XT
        YFIRSTT = YT
        T = 0.
        TF = 100.
        CALL PREDICT (TF,XT,YT,X1T,Y1T,XTF,YTF
  1           ,WP1,WTOT,TB1,TRST1,TB2,WP2,WTOT2,TRST2,WPAY)
        YTF = YTF + PREDERR
        CALL LAMBERT(XM,YM,TF,XTF,YTF,VRXM,VRYM,XLONGM,
              XLONGT,ICOUNT)
```

(Listing 15.2 continued on next page.)

Listing 15.2   (cont.) Engagement simulation for boosting target

```
            X1M = VRXM
            Y1M = VRYM
            RTM1 = XT – XM
            RTM2 = YT – YM
            RTM = SQRT(RTM1**2 + RTM2**2)
            VTM1 = X1T – X1M
            VTM2 = Y1T – Y1M
            VC = – (RTM1*VTM1 + RTM2*VTM2)/RTM
            DELV = 0.
    10      IF(VC < 0.)GOTO 999
            TGO = RTM/VC
            IF(TGO > 10.)THEN
                H = 1.
            ELSEIF(TGO > .1)THEN
                H = .01
            ELSE
                H = .0001
            ENDIF
            XOLDT = XT
            YOLDT = YT
            X1OLDT = X1T
            Y1OLDT = Y1T
            XOLDM = XM
            YOLDM = YM
            X1OLDM = X1M
            Y1OLDM = Y1M
            DELVOLD = DELV
            STEP = 1
            GOTO 200
    66      STEP = 2
            XT = XT + H*XDT
            YT = YT + H*YDT
            X1T = X1T + H*X1DT
            Y1T = Y1T + H*Y1DT
            XM = XM + H*XDM
            YM = YM + H*YDM
            X1M = X1M + H*X1DM
            Y1M = Y1M + H*Y1DM
            DELV = DELV + H*DELVD
            T = T + H
            GOTO 200
    55      XT = (XOLDT + XT)/2 + .5*H*XDT
            YT = (YOLDT + YT)/2 + .5*H*YDT
            X1T = (X1OLDT + X1T)/2 + .5*H*X1DT
            Y1T = (Y1OLDT + Y1T)/2 + .5*H*Y1DT
            XM = (XOLDM + XM)/2 + .5*H*XDM
            YM = (YOLDM + YM)/2 + .5*H*YDM
            X1M = (X1OLDM + X1M)/2 + .5*H*X1DM
            Y1M = (Y1OLDM + Y1M)/2 + .5*H*Y1DM
            DELV = (DELVOLD + DELV)/2. + .5*H*DELVD
            ALTT = SQRT(XT**2 + YT**2) – A
            ALTM = SQRT(XM**2 + YM**2) – A
            S = S + H
            SCOUNT = SCOUNT + H
            IF(SCOUNT.LT..99999)GOTO 10
            SCOUNT = 0.
            XNMT = XT/6076.
            YNMT = YT/6076.
            XNMM = XM/6076.
            YNMM = YM/6076.
            ALTNMT = ALTT/6076.
            CALL DISTANCE(XT,YT,XFIRSTT,YFIRSTT,DISTNMT)
            ALTNMM = ALTM/6076.
            CALL DISTANCE(XM,YM,XFIRSTT,YFIRSTT,DISTNMM)
            WRITE(9,*)T,DISTNMT,ALTNMT,DISTNMM,ALTNMM,XNC,DELV,ATPLOS
            GOTO 10
    200     CONTINUE
            IF(T < TB1)THEN
                WGT = – WP1*T/TB1 + WTOT
                TRST = TRST1
```

(Listing 15.2 continued on next page.)

Listing 15.2   (cont.) Engagement simulation for boosting target

```
        ELSEIF(T < (TB1 + TB2))THEN
            WGT = - WP2*T/TB2 + WTOT2 + WP2*TB1/TB2
            TRST = TRST2
        ELSE
            WGT = WPAY
            TRST = 0.
        ENDIF
        AT = 32.2*TRST/WGT
        VEL = SQRT(X1T**2 + Y1T**2)
        AXT = AT*X1T/VEL
        AYT = AT*Y1T/VEL
        TEMBOTT = (XT**2 + YT**2)**1.5
        X1DT = - GM*XT/TEMBOTT + AXT
        Y1DT = - GM*YT/TEMBOTT + AYT
        ATPLOS = Y1DT*COS(XLAM) - X1DT*SIN(XLAM)
        XDT = X1T
        YDT = Y1T
        RTM1 = XT - XM
        RTM2 = YT - YM
        RTM = SQRT(RTM1**2 + RTM2**2)
        VTM1 = X1T - X1M
        VTM2 = Y1T - Y1M
        VC = - (RTM1*VTM1 + RTM2*VTM2)/RTM
        TGO = RTM/VC
        XLAM = ATAN2(RTM2,RTM1)
        XLAMD = (RTM1*VTM2 - RTM2*VTM1)/(RTM*RTM)
        XNC = XNP*VC*XLAMD
        IF(XNC > XNCLIM)XNC = XNCLIM
        IF(XNC < - XNCLIM)XNC = - XNCLIM
        DELVD = ABS(XNC)
        AM1 = - XNC*SIN(XLAM)
        AM2 = XNC*COS(XLAM)
        TEMBOTM = (XM**2 + YM**2)**1.5
        X1DM = - GM*XM/TEMBOTM + AM1
        Y1DM = - GM*YM/TEMBOTM + AM2
        XDM = X1M
        YDM = Y1M
        IF(STEP - 1)66,66,55
999     CONTINUE
        XNMT = XT/6076.
        YNMT = YT/6076.
        XNMM = XM/6076.
        YNMM = YM/6076.
        ALTNMT = ALTT/6076.
        CALL DISTANCE(XT,YT,XFIRSTT,YFIRSTT,DISTNMT)
        ALTNMM = ALTM/6076.
        CALL DISTANCE(XM,YM,XFIRSTT,YFIRSTT,DISTNMM)
        WRITE(9,*)T,DISTNMT,ALTNMT,DISTNMM,ALTNMM,XNC,DELV,ATPLOS
        WRITE(9,*)T,RTM,DELV
        PAUSE
        END

        SUBROUTINE DISTANCE(XT,YT,XF,YF,DISTNM)
        SAVE
        IMPLICIT REAL*8 (A-H)
        IMPLICIT REAL*8 (O-Z)
        R = SQRT(XT**2 + YT**2)
        RF = SQRT(XF**2 + YF**2)
        A = 2.0926E7
        CBETA = (XT*XF + YT*YF)/(R*RF)
        IF(CBETA < 1.)THEN
            BETA = ACOS(CBETA)
            DISTNM = A*BETA/6076.
        ELSE
            DISTNM = (XT - XF)/6076.
        ENDIF
        RETURN
        END
```

(Listing 15.2 continued on next page.)

Listing 15.2   (cont.) Engagement simulation for boosting target

```
        SUBROUTINE PREDICT (TF,XDUM,YDUM,X1DUM,Y1DUM,XTF,YTF
    1       ,WP1,WTOT,TB1,TRST1,TB2,WP2,WTOT2,TRST2,WPAY)
        IMPLICIT REAL*8 (A-H)
        IMPLICIT REAL*8 (O-Z)
        INTEGER STEP
        SAVE
        H = 1.
        A = 2.0926E7
        GM = 1.4077E16
        T = 0.
        X = XDUM
        Y = YDUM
        X1 = X1DUM
        Y1 = Y1DUM
   10   IF(T > (TF - .00001))GOTO 999
        XOLD = X
        YOLD = Y
        X1OLD = X1
        Y1OLD = Y1
        STEP = 1
        GOTO 200
   66   STEP = 2
        X = X + H*XD
        Y = Y + H*YD
        X1 = X1 + H*X1D
        Y1 = Y1 + H*Y1D
        T = T + H
        GOTO 200
   55   X = (XOLD + X)/2 + .5*H*XD
        Y = (YOLD + Y)/2 + .5*H*YD
        X1 = (X1OLD + X1)/2 + .5*H*X1D
        Y1 = (Y1OLD + Y1)/2 + .5*H*Y1D
        GOTO 10
  200   CONTINUE
        IF(T < TB1)THEN
            WGT = - WP1*T/TB1 + WTOT
            TRST = TRST1
        ELSEIF(T < (TB1 + TB2))THEN
            WGT = - WP2*T/TB2 + WTOT2 + WP2*TB1/TB2
            TRST = TRST2
        ELSE
            WGT = WPAY
            TRST = 0.
        ENDIF
        AT = 32.2*TRST/WGT
        VEL = SQRT(X1**2 + Y1**2)
        AXT = AT*X1/VEL
        AYT = AT*Y1/VEL
        TEMBOTT = (X**2 + Y**2)**1.5
        X1D = - GM*X/TEMBOTT + AXT
        Y1D = - GM*Y/TEMBOTT + AYT
        XD = X1
        YD = Y1
        IF(STEP - 1)66,66,55
  999   CONTINUE
        XTF = X
        YTF = Y
        RETURN
        END

        SUBROUTINE LAMBERT(XIC,YIC,TFDES,XF,YF,VRX,VRY,XLONGM,XLONGT
    1       ,ICOUNT)
        IMPLICIT REAL*8 (A-H)
        IMPLICIT REAL*8 (O-Z)
        A = 2.0926E7
        GM = 1.4077E16
        RIC = SQRT(XIC**2 + YIC**2)
        RF = SQRT(XF**2 + YF**2)
        CPHI = (XIC*XF + YIC*YF)/(RIC*RF)
        PHI = ACOS(CPHI)
```

(Listing 15.2 continued on next page.)

Listing 15.2   (cont.) Engagement simulation for boosting target

```
SPHI = SIN(PHI)
R0 = RIC
PI = 3.14159
DEGRAD = 360./(2.*PI)
ICOUNT = 1
GMIN = ATAN2((SPHI – SQRT(2.*R0*(1. – CPHI)/RF)),(1 – CPHI))
GMAX = ATAN2((SPHI + SQRT(2.*R0*(1. – CPHI)/RF)),(1 – CPHI))
GAM = (GMIN + GMAX)/2.
DO
    TOP = GM*(1. – COS(PHI))
    TEMP = R0*COS(GAM)/RF – COS(PHI + GAM)
    BOT = R0*COS(GAM)*TEMP
    V = SQRT(TOP/BOT)
    IF (XLONGT > XLONGM) THEN
       VRX = V*COS(PI/2. – GAM + XLONGM)
       VRY = V*SIN(PI/2. – GAM + XLONGM)
    ELSE
       VRX = V*COS( – PI/2. + GAM + XLONGM)
       VRY = V*SIN( – PI/2. + GAM + XLONGM)
    END IF
    XLAM = R0*V*V/GM
    TOP1 = TAN(GAM)*(1 – COS(PHI)) + (1 – XLAM)*SIN(PHI)
    BOT1P = (1 – COS(PHI))/(XLAM*COS(GAM)*COS(GAM))
    BOT1 = (2 – XLAM)*(BOT1P + COS(GAM + PHI)/COS(GAM))
    TOP2 = 2*COS(GAM)
    BOT2 = XLAM*((2/XLAM – 1)**1.5)
    TOP3 = SQRT(2/XLAM – 1)
    BOT3 = COS(GAM)/TAN(PHI/2) – SIN(GAM)
    TEMP = (TOP2/BOT2)*ATAN2(TOP3,BOT3)
    TF = R0*(TOP1/BOT1 + TEMP)/(V*COS(GAM))
    IF((ABS(TFDES – TF) < = .00000001*TFDES).OR.ICOUNT > 100)THEN
       EXIT
    ENDIF
    IF(TF > TFDES)THEN
       GMAX = GAM
    ELSE
       GMIN = GAM
    ENDIF
    IF(ICOUNT = 1)THEN
       XNEXT = (GMAX + GMIN)/2.
    ELSE
       XNEXT = GAM + (GAM – GOLD)*(TFDES – TF)/(TF – TOLD)
       IF(XNEXT > GMAX.OR.XNEXT < GMIN)THEN
          XNEXT = (GMAX + GMIN)/2.
       ENDIF
    ENDIF
    GOLD = GAM
    TOLD = TF
    GAM = XNEXT
    ICOUNT = ICOUNT + 1
REPEAT
RETURN
END
```

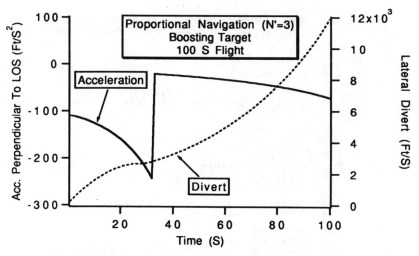

Fig. 15.11   Divert due to apparent maneuver agrees with theory.

Using the fact that the lateral divert is the integral of the absolute value of the acceleration, it is easy to show that

$$\Delta V \bigg|_{APN} = 0.5 \frac{N'}{N'-1} n_T t_F = 0.5 \ \Delta V \bigg|_{PN}$$

In other words, theory says that the divert requirements for an augmented proportional navigation guidance system are half the divert requirements of a proportional navigation guidance system.

In order to implement augmented proportional navigation guidance in the engagement simulation, it is necessary to modify the guidance command to

$$n_c \bigg|_{APN} = N' V_c \dot{\lambda} + \frac{N'}{2} a_{PLOS}$$

where a_{PLOS} is the booster acceleration perpendicular to the line of sight. The nominal simulation case was rerun, except this time the augmented proportional navigation guidance law was used. Figure 15.12 shows that the missile lateral divert requirements were dramatically reduced to about 6700 ft/s (down from about 12,000 ft/s in the proportional navigation case).

Theory says the divert requirements for the augmented proportional navigation guidance law should be

$$\Delta V \bigg|_{APN} = 0.5 \frac{N'}{N'-1} n_T t_F = \frac{0.5*3*100*100}{2} = 7500 \ \text{ft/s}$$

which is in close agreement with the simulation results.

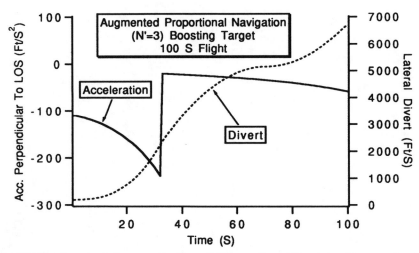

Fig. 15.12 Augmented proportional navigation reduces divert requirements due to boosting target.

Summary

In this chapter we have shown that the guidance concepts developed for the tactical world are applicable to the strategic world. In fact, closed-form solutions for the required missile acceleration to hit targets can be converted to lateral divert formulas. Nonlinear engagement simulation results indicate that the divert requirement formulas for prediction error, apparent target acceleration, and guidance law are not only useful but are in fact accurate indicators of strategic interceptor requirements.

Reference

[1]Zarchan, P., "Space Based Interceptor Engagement Simulation and Analysis," Charles Stark Draper Lab., Cambridge, MA, Rept. R-2025, Dec. 1987.

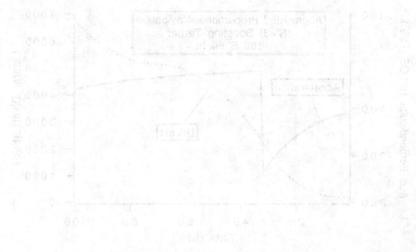

Chapter 16

Miscellaneous Topics

Introduction

IN this chapter we shall cover some important topics that have not yet been discussed. First we shall show how lateral divert requirements can be reduced if we add an extra term to the proportional navigation guidance law to account for gravity. Next we will demonstrate that, if complete information on all the target states is available, the ultimate guidance law, predictive guidance, can be used to relax system divert requirements. A section will be devoted to showing how all the booster states can be estimated given that range and angle measurements are available. Finally, a new guidance law, known as pulsed guidance, is developed for those situations in which an interceptor does not have throttleable divert engines.

Gravity Compensation

We saw in Chapter 15 that, in the absence of prediction errors, lateral divert fuel was still required to hit a ballistic target. Changes in the missile and target velocities due to gravity caused the line of sight to rotate. The proportional navigation guidance law responded to the apparent line-of-sight rate with acceleration commands. If we have knowledge of gravitational acceleration, it seems reasonable that it might be possible to compensate for unnecessary accelerations via the guidance law.

Consider the ballistic missile-target model of Fig. 16.1. In this case the only accelerations acting on the missile and target is gravity. However, since the missile and target are in different locations and since gravitational acceleration is always toward the center of the Earth, the gravitational vectors for the missile and target will have different magnitudes and directions. The missile and target gravitational vectors can be expressed as

$$grav_M = gravx_M i + gravy_M j$$

$$grav_T = gravx_T i + gravy_T j$$

where the gravitational components for the missile and target can be found from

$$gravx_M = \frac{-gm \, x_M}{(x_M^2 + y_M^2)^{1.5}}$$

$$grav y_M = \frac{-gm\, y_M}{(x_M^2 + y_M^2)^{1.5}}$$

$$grav x_T = \frac{-gm\, x_T}{(x_T^2 + y_T^2)^{1.5}}$$

$$grav y_T = \frac{-gm\, y_T}{(x_T^2 + y_T^2)^{1.5}}$$

From Fig. 16.1 we can see that the component of gravity perpendicular to the line of sight for both the missile and target can be found by trigonometry and is given by

$$grav_{MPLOS} = -grav x_M \sin\lambda + grav y_M \cos\lambda$$

$$grav_{TPLOS} = -grav x_T \sin\lambda + grav y_T \cos\lambda$$

The gravitational acceleration difference between the target and missile can be treated as an additional term in the zero effort miss. Therefore, we can modify the proportional navigation guidance law to account for gravity. The resultant law, which is similar to augmented proportional navigation, is

$$n_c = N' V_c \dot{\lambda} + \frac{N'}{2}(grav_{TPLOS} - grav_{MPLOS})$$

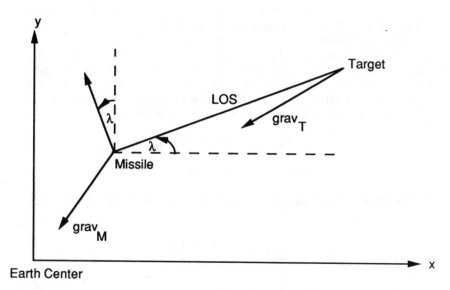

Fig. 16.1   Model for understanding gravity compensation.

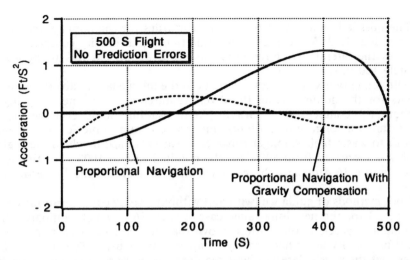

Fig. 16.2   Gravity compensation results in smaller acceleration levels for nominal case.

The similarity of proportional navigation with gravity compensation and augmented proportional navigation is due to the fact that the gravitational components of the missile and target are treated as an apparent residual target acceleration.

The nominal 500-s ballistic case of Chapter 15 was repeated in which the missile and target are on a collision triangle (see Figs. 15.3 and 15.4). In this case there are zero prediction errors. Figure 16.2 compares the acceleration profiles of proportional navigation, for this case, when gravity compensation is both included and excluded. We can see that in both cases the acceleration levels are low, but the gravity compensation results in even smaller acceleration levels.

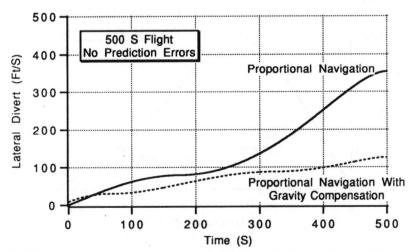

Fig. 16.3   Gravity compensation reduces divert requirements for nominal case.

The missile lateral divert requirement profiles for the nominal case appear in Fig. 16.3. We can see from this figure that gravity compensation reduces the lateral divert requirements from about 350 ft/s to approximately 120 ft/s.

Although gravity compensation reduced the missile lateral divert requirements for the nominal case, the divert requirements were not very high without the compensation. Gravity compensation should even be more important for longer-range flights since there is more time for a strategic missile to waste fuel. A longer-range case was examined in which the flight time was increased from 500 s for the nominal case to 1000 s for the new case. Figure 16.4 depicts the engagement geometry for the longer-range case.

Both methods of guidance (with and without gravity compensation) were compared for the new long-range case. Figure 16.5, which compares the commanded acceleration profiles, shows that the acceleration requirements are substantially less when gravity compensation is used. The figure indicates that the missile lateral divert requirements were reduced from nearly 4000 ft/s to about 1200 ft/s when gravity compensation was used. In this case there would be a dramatic advantage in terms of fuel and weight savings in using gravity compensation.

The gravity compensation guidance law assumes that the required gravitational components of both the missile and target can be measured or estimated precisely. Errors in estimating the gravitational components will of course degrade the effectiveness of this type of compensation, perhaps to the point where its performance is the same or worse than that of proportional navigation.

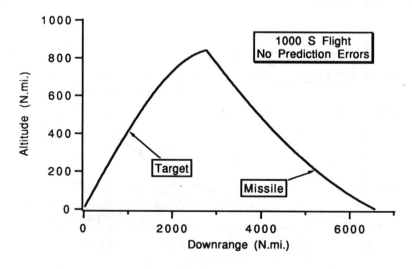

Fig. 16.4 Engagement geometry for longer-range case.

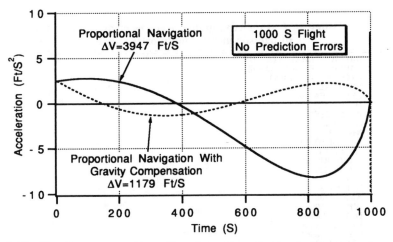

Fig. 16.5   Gravity compensation offers dramatic reduction in divert requirements for long-range case.

Predictive Guidance

We have seen how interceptor lateral divert requirements can be reduced when extra information, if it exists, is incorporated into the guidance law. If an exact model of the target and missile dynamics were available, one could achieve the best performance with predictive guidance. The principle behind predictive guidance is quite simple. We take our dynamic models of the target and missile and numerically integrate them forward until the desired intercept time. In other words, we are predicting the future location of the missile and target. The difference between the predicted missile and target position at the intercept time is the zero effort miss. If the predicted coordinates of the missile at intercept in the Earth-centered system is given by (x_{MF}, y_{MF}) and the coordinates of the target are given by coordinates of the target (x_{TF}, y_{TF}), then the Earth-centered components of the zero effort miss are given by

$$ZEM_x = x_{TF} - x_{MF}$$

$$ZEM_y = y_{TF} - y_{MF}$$

We can find the component of the zero effort miss perpendicular to the line of sight by trigonometry in Fig. 16.1. The zero effort miss perpendicular to the line of sight is given by

$$ZEM_{PLOS} = -ZEM_x \sin\lambda + ZEM_y \cos\lambda$$

We saw from our discussion of optimal guidance that the acceleration guidance command should be proportional to the zero effort miss and inversely proportional to the square of time to go until intercept, or

$$n_c = \frac{N' ZEM_{PLOS}}{t_{go}^2}$$

**Listing 16.1   Predictive guidance engagement simulation
of ballistic missile and booster target**

```
IMPLICIT REAL*8 (A – H)
IMPLICIT REAL*8 (O – Z)
INTEGER STEP,BOOST
LOGICAL LEFT
LEFT = .FALSE.
H = 1.
A = 2.0926E7
GM = 1.4077E16
XNP = 3.
AXMGUID = 0.
AYMGUID = 0.
PREDERR = 0.
XISP1 = 250.
XISP2 = 250.
XMF1 = .85
XMF2 = .85
WPAY = 100.
DELV = 20000.
DELV1 = .3333*DELV
DELV2 = .6667*DELV
AMAX1 = 10.
AMAX2 = 10.
XKICKDEG = 80.
TOP2 = WPAY*(EXP(DELV2/(XISP2*32.2)) – 1.)
BOT2 = 1/XMF2 – ((1. – XMF2)/XMF2)*EXP(DELV2/(XISP2*32.2))
WP2 = TOP2/BOT2
WS2 = WP2*(1 – XMF2)/XMF2
WTOT2 = WP2 + WS2 + WPAY
TRST2 = AMAX2*(WPAY + WS2)
TB2 = XISP2*WP2/TRST2
TOP1 = WTOT2*(EXP(DELV1/(XISP1*32.2)) – 1.)
BOT1 = 1/XMF1 – ((1. – XMF1)/XMF1)*EXP(DELV1/(XISP1*32.2))
WP1 = TOP1/BOT1
WS1 = WP1*(1 – XMF1)/XMF1
WTOT = WP1 + WS1 + WTOT2
TRST1 = AMAX1*(WTOT2 + WS1)
TB1 = XISP1*WP1/TRST1
ALTNMT = 0.
ALTNMM = 0.
ALTT = ALTNMT*6076.
ALTM = ALTNMM*6076.
PI = 3.14159
DEGRAD = 360./(2.*PI)
S = 0.
SCOUNT = 0.
XLONGMDEG = 80.
XLONGTDEG = 90.
XLONGM = XLONGMDEG/DEGRAD
XLONGT = XLONGTDEG/DEGRAD
XM = (A + ALTM)*COS(XLONGM)
YM = (A + ALTM)*SIN(XLONGM)
XT = (A + ALTT)*COS(XLONGT)
YT = (A + ALTT)*SIN(XLONGT)
XFIRSTT = XT
YFIRSTT = YT
IF (LEFT) THEN
     X1T = COS(PI/2. – XKICKDEG/DEGRAD + XLONGT)
     Y1T = SIN(PI/2. – XKICKDEG/DEGRAD + XLONGT)
ELSE
     X1T = COS( – PI/2. + XKICKDEG/DEGRAD + XLONGT)
     Y1T = SIN( – PI/2. + XKICKDEG/DEGRAD + XLONGT)
END IF
T = 0.
TF = 100.
TGO = TF – T
CALL PREDICT (T,TF,XT,YT,X1T,Y1T,XTF,YTF
1    ,WP1,WTOT,TB1,TRST1,TB2,WP2,WTOT2,TRST2,WPAY
2    ,XM,YM,X1M,Y1M,ZEM1,ZEM2,TGO)
YTF = YTF + PREDERR
CALL LAMBERT(XM,YM,TF,XTF,YTF,VRXM,VRYM,XLONGM,XLONGT)
```

(Listing 16.1 continued on next page.)

Listing 16.1 (cont.) Predictive guidance engagement simulation of ballistic missile and booster target

```
        X1M = VRXM
        Y1M = VRYM
        RTM1 = XT − XM
        RTM2 = YT − YM
        RTM = SQRT(RTM1**2 + RTM2**2)
        VTM1 = X1T − X1M
        VTM2 = Y1T − Y1M
        VC = − (RTM1*VTM1 + RTM2*VTM2)/RTM
        DELV = 0.
10      IF(VC < 0.)GOTO 999
        TGO = RTM/VC
        IF(TGO > 10.)THEN
            H = 1.
        ELSEIF(TGO > .1)THEN
            H = .01
        ELSE
            H = .0001
        ENDIF
        XOLDT = XT
        YOLDT = YT
        X1OLDT = X1T
        Y1OLDT = Y1T
        XOLDM = XM
        YOLDM = YM
        X1OLDM = X1M
        Y1OLDM = Y1M
        DELVOLD = DELV
        STEP = 1
        GOTO 200
66      STEP = 2
        XT = XT + H*XDT
        YT = YT + H*YDT
        X1T = X1T + H*X1DT
        Y1T = Y1T + H*Y1DT
        XM = XM + H*XDM
        YM = YM + H*YDM
        X1M = X1M + H*X1DM
        Y1M = Y1M + H*Y1DM
        DELV = DELV + H*DELVD
        T = T + H
        GOTO 200
55      XT = (XOLDT + XT)/2 + .5*H*XDT
        YT = (YOLDT + YT)/2 + .5*H*YDT
        X1T = (X1OLDT + X1T)/2 + .5*H*X1DT
        Y1T = (Y1OLDT + Y1T)/2 + .5*H*Y1DT
        XM = (XOLDM + XM)/2 + .5*H*XDM
        YM = (YOLDM + YM)/2 + .5*H*YDM
        X1M = (X1OLDM + X1M)/2 + .5*H*X1DM
        Y1M = (Y1OLDM + Y1M)/2 + .5*H*Y1DM
        DELV = (DELVOLD + DELV)/2. + .5*H*DELVD
        ALTT = SQRT(XT**2 + YT**2) − A
        ALTM = SQRT(XM**2 + YM**2) − A
        S = S + H
        SCOUNT = SCOUNT + H
        IF(SCOUNT.LT..99999)GOTO 10
        SCOUNT = 0.
        CALL PREDICT (T,TF,XT,YT,X1T,Y1T,XTF,YTF
     1      ,WP1,WTOT,TB1,TRST1,TB2,WP2,WTOT2,TRST2,WPAY
     2      ,XM,YM,X1M,Y1M,ZEM1,ZEM2,TGO)
        ZEMPLOS = − ZEM1*SIN(XLAM) + ZEM2*COS(XLAM)
        XNC = XNP*ZEMPLOS/(TGO*TGO)
        XNMT = XT/6076.
        YNMT = YT/6076.
        XNMM = XM/6076.
        YNMM = YM/6076.
        ALTNMT = ALTT/6076.
        CALL DISTANCE(XT,YT,XFIRSTT,YFIRSTT,DISTNMT)
        ALTNMM = ALTM/6076.
        CALL DISTANCE(XM,YM,XFIRSTT,YFIRSTT,DISTNMM)
        WRITE(9,*)T,DISTNMT,ALTNMT,DISTNMM,ALTNMM,XNC,DELV,ATPLOS
        GOTO 10
```

(Listing 16.1 continued on next page.)

Listing 16.1   (cont.) Predictive guidance engagement simulation of ballistic missile and booster target

```
200     CONTINUE
        IF(T<TB1)THEN
                WGT = - WP1*T/TB1 + WTOT
                TRST = TRST1
        ELSEIF(T<(TB1 + TB2))THEN
                WGT = - WP2*T/TB2 + WTOT2 + WP2*TB1/TB2
                TRST = TRST2
        ELSE
                WGT = WPAY
                TRST = 0.
        ENDIF
        AT = 32.2*TRST/WGT
        VEL = SQRT(X1T**2 + Y1T**2)
        AXT = AT*X1T/VEL
        AYT = AT*Y1T/VEL
        ATPLOS = AYT*COS(XLAM) - AXT*SIN(XLAM)
        TEMBOTT = (XT**2 + YT**2)**1.5
        X1DT = - GM*XT/TEMBOTT + AXT
        Y1DT = - GM*YT/TEMBOTT + AYT
        XDT = X1T
        YDT = Y1T
        RTM1 = XT - XM
        RTM2 = YT - YM
        RTM = SQRT(RTM1**2 + RTM2**2)
        VTM1 = X1T - X1M
        VTM2 = Y1T - Y1M
        VC = - (RTM1*VTM1 + RTM2*VTM2)/RTM
        TGO = RTM/VC
        XLAM = ATAN2(RTM2,RTM1)
        XLAMD = (RTM1*VTM2 - RTM2*VTM1)/(RTM*RTM)
        AXMGUID = - XNC*SIN(XLAM)
        AYMGUID = XNC*COS(XLAM)
        DELVD = ABS(XNC)
        TEMBOTM = (XM**2 + YM**2)**1.5
        X1DM = - GM*XM/TEMBOTM + AXMGUID
        Y1DM = - GM*YM/TEMBOTM + AYMGUID
        XDM = X1M
        YDM = Y1M
        IF(STEP - 1)66,66,55
999     CONTINUE
        XNMT = XT/6076.
        YNMT = YT/6076.
        XNMM = XM/6076.
        YNMM = YM/6076.
        ALTNMT = ALTT/6076.
        CALL DISTANCE(XT,YT,XFIRSTT,YFIRSTT,DISTNMT)
        ALTNMM = ALTM/6076.
        CALL DISTANCE(XM,YM,XFIRSTT,YFIRSTT,DISTNMM)
        WRITE(9,*)T,DISTNMT,ALTNMT,DISTNMM,ALTNMM,XNC,DELV,ATPLOS
        WRITE(9,*)T,RTM,DELV
        PAUSE
        END

        SUBROUTINE DISTANCE(XT,YT,XF,YF,DISTNM)
        IMPLICIT REAL*8 (A - H)
        IMPLICIT REAL*8 (O - Z)
        SAVE
        R = SQRT(XT**2 + YT**2)
        RF = SQRT(XF**2 + YF**2)
        A = 2.0926E7
        CBETA = (XT*XF + YT*YF)/(R*RF)
        IF(CBETA<1.)THEN
                BETA = ACOS(CBETA)
                DISTNM = A*BETA/6076.
        ELSE
                DISTNM = (XT - XF)/6076.
        ENDIF
        RETURN
        END
```

(Listing 16.1 continued on next page.)

```
       SUBROUTINE PREDICT (TDUM,TF,XDUM,YDUM,X1DUM,Y1DUM,XTF,YTF
    1    ,WP1,WTOT,TB1,TRST1,TB2,WP2,WTOT2,TRST2,WPAY
    2    ,XMDUM,YMDUM,X1MDUM,Y1MDUM,ZEM1,ZEM2,TGO)
       IMPLICIT REAL*8 (A - H)
       IMPLICIT REAL*8 (O - Z)
       INTEGER STEP
       SAVE
       IF(TGO > 1)THEN
             H = 1.
       ELSE
             H = TGO
       ENDIF
       A = 2.0926E7
       GM = 1.4077E16
       T = TDUM
       X = XDUM
       Y = YDUM
       X1 = X1DUM
       Y1 = Y1DUM
       XM = XMDUM
       YM = YMDUM
       X1M = X1MDUM
       Y1M = Y1MDUM
10     IF(T > (TF - .00001))GOTO 999
       XOLD = X
       YOLD = Y
       X1OLD = X1
       Y1OLD = Y1
       XOLDM = XM
       YOLDM = YM
       X1OLDM = X1M
       Y1OLDM = Y1M
       STEP = 1
       GOTO 200
66     STEP = 2
       X = X + H*XD
       Y = Y + H*YD
       X1 = X1 + H*X1D
       Y1 = Y1 + H*Y1D
       XM = XM + H*XDM
       YM = YM + H*YDM
       X1M = X1M + H*X1DM
       Y1M = Y1M + H*Y1DM
       T = T + H
       GOTO 200
55     X = (XOLD + X)/2 + .5*H*XD
       Y = (YOLD + Y)/2 + .5*H*YD
       X1 = (X1OLD + X1)/2 + .5*H*X1D
       Y1 = (Y1OLD + Y1)/2 + .5*H*Y1D
       XM = (XOLDM + XM)/2 + .5*H*XDM
       YM = (YOLDM + YM)/2 + .5*H*YDM
       X1M = (X1OLDM + X1M)/2 + .5*H*X1DM
       Y1M = (Y1OLDM + Y1M)/2 + .5*H*Y1DM
       GOTO 10
200    CONTINUE
       IF(T < TB1)THEN
             WGT = - WP1*T/TB1 + WTOT
             TRST = TRST1
       ELSEIF(T < (TB1 + TB2))THEN
             WGT = - WP2*T/TB2 + WTOT2 + WP2*TB1/TB2
             TRST = TRST2
       ELSE
             WGT = WPAY
             TRST = 0.
       ENDIF
       AT = 32.2*TRST/WGT
       VEL = SQRT(X1**2 + Y1**2)
       AXT = AT*X1/VEL
       AYT = AT*Y1/VEL
       TEMBOTT = (X**2 + Y**2)**1.5
       X1D = - GM*X/TEMBOTT + AXT
       Y1D = - GM*Y/TEMBOTT + AYT
       XD = X1
       YD = Y1
       TEMBOTM = (XM**2 + YM**2)**1.5
       X1DM = - GM*XM/TEMBOTM
```

(Listing 16.1 continued on next page.)

```
        Y1DM = - GM*YM/TEMBOTM
        XDM = X1M
        YDM = Y1M
        IF(STEP - 1)66,66,55
999     CONTINUE
        XTF = X
        YTF = Y
        ZEM1 = X - XM
        ZEM2 = Y - YM
        RETURN
        END

        SUBROUTINE LAMBERT(XIC,YIC,TFDES,XF,YF,VRX,VRY,XLONGM,XLONGT)

        IMPLICIT REAL*8 (A - H)
        IMPLICIT REAL*8 (O - Z)
        A = 2.0926E7
        GM = 1.4077E16
        RIC = SQRT(XIC**2 + YIC**2)
        RF = SQRT(XF**2 + YF**2)
        CPHI = (XIC*XF + YIC*YF)/(RIC*RF)
        PHI = ACOS(CPHI)
        SPHI = SIN(PHI)
        R0 = RIC
        PI = 3.14159
        DEGRAD = 360./(2.*PI)
        ICOUNT = 1
        GMIN = ATAN2((SPHI - SQRT(2.*RO*(1. - CPHI)/RF)),(1 - CPHI))
        GMAX = ATAN2((SPHI - SQRT(2.*RO*(1. - CPHI)/RF)),(1 - CPHI))
        GAM = (GMIN + GMAX)/2.
        DO
           TOP = GM*(1. - COS(PHI))
           TEMP = R0*COS(GAM)/RF - COS(PHI + GAM)
           BOT = R0*COS(GAM)*TEMP
           V = SQRT(TOP/BOT)
           IF (XLONGT > XLONGM) THEN
             VRX = V*COS(PI/2. - GAM + XLONGM)
             VRY = V*SIN(PI/2. - GAM + XLONGM)
           ELSE
             VRX = V*COS( - PI/2. + GAM + XLONGM)
             VRY = V*SIN( - PI/2. + GAM + XLONGM)
           END IF
           XLAM = R0*V*V/GM
           TOP1 = TAN(GAM)*(1 - COS(PHI)) + (1 - XLAM)*SIN(PHI)
           BOT1P = (1 - COS(PHI))/(XLAM*COS(GAM)*COS(GAM))
           BOT1 = (2 - XLAM)*(BOT1P + COS(GAM + PHI)/COS(GAM))
           TOP2 = 2*COS(GAM)
           BOT2 = XLAM*((2/XLAM - 1)**1.5)
           TOP3 = SQRT(2/XLAM - 1)
           BOT3 = COS(GAM)/TAN(PHI/2) - SIN(GAM)
           TEMP = (TOP2/BOT2)*ATAN2(TOP3,BOT3)
           TF = R0*(TOP1/BOT1 + TEMP)/(V*COS(GAM))
           IF(TF > TFDES)THEN
              EXIT
           ENDIF
           IF(TF > TFDES)THEN
             GMAX = GAM
           ELSE
             GMIN = GAM
           ENDIF
           IF(ICOUNT = 1)THEN
             XNEXT = (GMAX + GMIN)/2,
           ELSE
             XNEXT = GAM + (GAM - GOLD)*(TFDES - TF)/(TF - TOLD)
             IF(XNEXT > GMAX.OR.XNEXT < GMIN) THEN
               XNEXT = (GMAX + GMIN)/2.
             ENDIF
           ENDIF
           GOLD = GAM
           TOLD = TF
           GAM = XNEXT
           ICOUNT = ICOUNT + 1
        REPEAT
        RETURN
        END
```

Proportional navigation, augmented proportional navigation, and our previously derived optimal guidance law can all be expressed in the preceding form. In these guidance laws we have closed-form expressions for the zero effort miss. In other words, an integration of simple dynamics (assumed to be a polynomial in time) was conducted to get a closed-form expression. In predictive guidance, we ignore closed-form solutions of approximate processes and obtain the exact solution for the zero effort miss at each guidance update by numerical integration. The resultant accuracy of the computed zero effort miss depends on the size of the integration interval. Small integration intervals yield accurate answers but may take too long to be obtained in flight. Of course, the accuracy also depends on the equations used. Having inaccurate models of the target will lead to erroneous predictions of the zero effort miss, and in this case the performance of predictive guidance may be substantially worse than that of proportional navigation.

Listing 16.1 presents an engagement simulation of a ballistic missile and a boosting target. This simulation is identical to the one of Listing 15.2, except that the guidance law has changed from proportional navigation to predictive guidance. We can see from the listing that subroutine PREDICT is not only used to establish the initial estimate of the intercept point but also is now used at each guidance update to compute the zero effort miss. An examination of the prediction subroutine shows that the equations of the target and missile have been perfectly modeled. Even the integration step size is an exact match. We can see from the listing that guidance commands, based on predictive guidance, are calculated at each guidance update throughout the flight.

The nominal 100-s boosting target case of the previous chapter (see Figs. 15.9 and 15.10) was repeated to see the effectiveness of the new

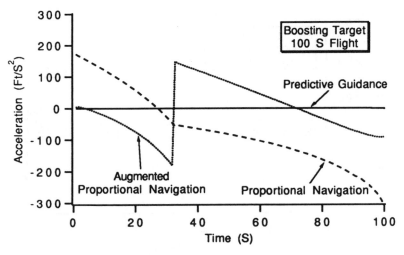

Fig. 16.6 Acceleration requirements for predictive guidance can be very small.

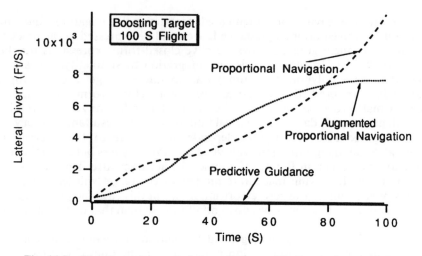

Fig. 16.7 Divert requirements for predictive guidance can be miniscule.

guidance law. Figure 16.6 compares the commanded missile acceleration requirements for proportional navigation, augmented proportional navigation, and predictive guidance. We can see that, as expected, augmented proportional navigation requires much less acceleration than proportional navigation. The required acceleration is large because, as we saw in the previous chapter, much of the longitudinal booster acceleration was perpendicular to the line of sight (on average about 100 ft/s²) and thus appeared as a target maneuver to the missile. However, we can also see that predictive guidance virtually requires zero acceleration to intercept the boosting target. The reason for this is that the missile is initially on a

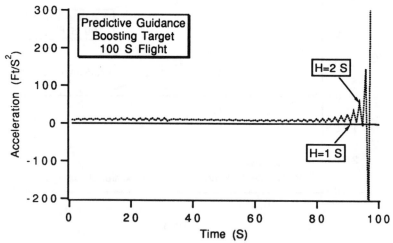

Fig. 16.8 Predictive guidance performance is sensitive to numerical integration step size.

collision triangle with the target. Therefore, no commands are really necessary for a successful intercept.

Figure 16.7 presents the missile lateral divert requirement profiles for the same case. Here we can see that proportional navigation required about 12,000 ft/s of lateral divert, augmented proportional navigation required about 6700 ft/s of lateral divert, and predictive guidance only required 2 ft/s of lateral divert!

The divert requirements for predictive guidance are quite small because the prediction is perfect. In other words, we have a perfect model of the missile and target and a perfect numerical integration technique. The integration is perfect because the same method (second-order Runge-Kutta) and step size are used in the simulation and prediction portion of the program. In a practical application of predictive guidance a larger integration step size, H, might have to be used to satisfy flight computer throughput requirements. Figure 16.8 shows what happens to the acceleration profile when the integration step size used in the prediction subroutine is increased from 1 s to 2 s (simulation portion of program uses 1-s integration step size). We can see that the acceleration profile develops an oscillation and will be unable to hit the target.

Booster Estimation With Range and Angle Measurements

Thus far, except for Chapters 7 and 9, we have assumed that information concerning all the target states was available. These states were used in all the guidance concepts used in the text. In this section we shall show a simple, if not optimal, way of estimating the booster states required for predictive guidance given that a range and angle measurement are available. Consider the model of Fig. 16.9, in which it is assumed that the missile location (x_M, y_M) is known and that range from the missile to the target R_{TM} and the line-of-sight angle λ are measured. Estimating the location, velocity, and acceleration of the target is desired. From Fig. 16.9 we can see that

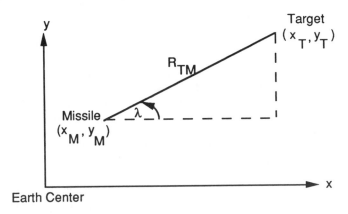

Fig. 16.9   Model for estimating booster states given range and angle information.

the location of the target can be expressed as

$$x_T = x_M + R_{TM} \cos\lambda$$

$$y_T = y_M + R_{TM} \sin\lambda$$

If we assume that range is measured perfectly and that the line-of-sight angle measurement is contaminated with noise, λ_{noise}, then the measurements of target location x_T^* and y_T^* are given by

$$x_T^* = x_M + R_{TM} \cos(\lambda + \lambda_{noise})$$

$$y_T^* = y_M + R_{TM} \sin(\lambda + \lambda_{noise})$$

The preceding measurement equations are not in a suitable form for an optimal linear Kalman filter, since the measurement is not a linear function of the states. However, we will ignore that fact and use the simple polynomial Kalman filter, one for x_T^* and the other for y_T^*, which was derived in Chapter 9. Both filters were incorporated into the booster engagement simulation of Listing 15.2, and the resultant simulation is shown in Listing 16.2. In this simulation augmented proportional navigation guidance makes use of the actual states. The filter is only in the simulation to see how well the target states can be estimated.

The quality of the estimates from the Kalman filter depends on the measurement noise level. Although the filter adjusts its bandwidth to accommodate different noise intensities, in general, estimation accuracy will degrade as the measurement noise level increases. In addition, it is more difficult to estimate higher-order states. In other words, it is more difficult to estimate velocity than it is to estimate position, and it is more difficult to estimate acceleration than to estimate velocity.

For our example the most difficult estimate is that of booster acceleration. Figure 16.10 shows how the filter estimate of acceleration in the x coordinate of the Earth-centered coordinate system compares to the x component of the actual acceleration for varying amounts of noise intensity. For only 0.1 milliradians (mr) of noise the filter estimate closely follows the actual acceleration. Even though the filter is not optimal, it appears to be good enough. As the noise level increases through two orders of magnitude, the filter estimate degrades substantially in the sense that the estimate lags the actual value by as much as 20 s. This would cause problems if the filtering and guidance were connected in the simulation.

Other factors such as inaccurate range measurements would also cause filter performance to degrade. In each application, filter performance must be evaluated with appropriate noise levels to determine if the estimates are of sufficient quality to be used with more advanced guidance techniques. If the estimates are of poor quality, the proportional navigation guidance law, which does not need acceleration information, may yield the best overall system performance.

Listing 16.2   Booster engagement simulation with Kalman filter based on range and angle measurement

```
IMPLICIT REAL*8 (A – H)
IMPLICIT REAL*8 (O – Z)
REAL*8 M11,M12,M13,M22,M23,M33,K1,K2,K3
INTEGER STEP,BOOST,SWITCH
LOGICAL QCONV
SWITCH = 0
H = 1.
A = 2.0926E7
GM = 1.4077E16
XNP = 3.
TS = 1.
XLONGTDEG = 90.
XLONGMDEG = 80.
DEGRAD = 57.3
SIGLAM = .001
PREDERR = 0.
XISP1 = 250.
XISP2 = 250.
XMF1 = .85
XMF2 = .85
WPAY = 100.
DELV = 20000.
DELV1 = .3333*DELV
DELV2 = .6667*DELV
AMAX1 = 10.
AMAX2 = 10.
XKICKDEG = 80.
TOP2 = WPAY*(EXP(DELV2/(XISP2*32.2)) – 1.)
BOT2 = 1/XMF2 – ((1. – XMF2)/XMF2)*EXP(DELV2/(XISP2*32.2))
WP2 = TOP2/BOT2
WS2 = WP2*(1 – XMF2)/XMF2
WTOT2 = WP2 + WS2 + WPAY
TRST2 = AMAX2*(WPAY + WS2)
TB2 = XISP2*WP2/TRST2
TOP1 = WTOT2*(EXP(DELV1/(XISP1*32.2)) – 1.)
BOT1 = 1/XMF1 – ((1. – XMF1)/XMF1)*EXP(DELV1/(XISP1*32.2))
WP1 = TOP1/BOT1
WS1 = WP1*(1 – XMF1)/XMF1
WTOT = WP1 + WS1 + WTOT2
TRST1 = AMAX1*(WTOT2 + WS1)
TB1 = XISP1*WP1/TRST1
ALTNMT = 0.
ALTNMM = 0.
ALTT = ALTNMT*6076.
ALTM = ALTNMM*6076.
S = 0.
SCOUNT = 0.
XLONGM = XLONGMDEG/DEGRAD
XLONGT = XLONGTDEG/DEGRAD
XM = A*COS(XLONGM)
YM = A*SIN(XLONGM)
XT = (A + ALTT)*COS(XLONGT)
YT = (A + ALTT)*SIN(XLONGT)
XFIRSTT = XT
YFIRSTT = YT
X1T = COS(XKICKDEG/57.3)
Y1T = SIN(XKICKDEG/57.3)
K1 = 0.
K2 = 0.
K3 = 0.
XTH = XT
XTDH = X1T
XTDDH = 0.
YTH = YT
YTDH = Y1T
YTDDH = 0.
T = 0.
TF = 100.
PHIN = 100*100/TF
CALL PREDICT (TF,XT,YT,X1T,Y1T,XTF,YTF
```

(Listing 16.2 continued on next page.)

Listing 16.2 (cont.) Booster engagement simulation with Kalman filter based on range and angle measurement

```
    1     ,WP1,WTOT,TB1,TRST1,TB2,WP2,WTOT2,TRST2,WPAY)
          YTF = YTF + PREDERR
          CALL LAMBERT(XM,YM,TF,XTF,YTF,VRXM,VRYM,XLONGM,XLONGT)
              ,ICOUNT)
          X1M = VRXM
          Y1M = VRYM
          RTM1 = XT – XM
          RTM2 = YT – YM
          RTM = SQRT(RTM1**2 + RTM2**2)
          SIGPOS = SIGLAM*RTM
          P11 = SIGPOS*SIGPOS
          P12 = 0.
          P13 = 0.
          P22 = 0.
          P23 = 0.
          P33 = 100*100
          VTM1 = X1T – X1M
          VTM2 = Y1T – Y1M
          VC = – (RTM1*VTM1 + RTM2*VTM2)/RTM
          DELV = 0.
   10     IF(VC < 0.)GOTO 999
          TGO = RTM/VC
          IF(TGO > 10.)THEN
                 H = 1.
          ELSEIF(TGO > .1)THEN
                 H = .01
          ELSE
                 H = .0001
          ENDIF
          XOLDT = XT
          YOLDT = YT
          X1OLDT = X1T
          Y1OLDT = Y1T
          XOLDM = XM
          YOLDM = YM
          X1OLDM = X1M
          Y1OLDM = Y1M
          DELVOLD = DELV
          STEP = 1
          GOTO 200
   66     STEP = 2
          XT = XT + H*XDT
          YT = YT + H*YDT
          X1T = X1T + H*X1DT
          Y1T = Y1T + H*Y1DT
          XM = XM + H*XDM
          YM = YM + H*YDM
          X1M = X1M + H*X1DM
          Y1M = Y1M + H*Y1DM
          DELV = DELV + H*DELVD
          T = T + H
          GOTO 200
   55     XT = (XOLDT + XT)/2 + .5*H*XDT
          YT = (YOLDT + YT)/2 + .5*H*YDT
          X1T = (X1OLDT + X1T)/2 + .5*H*X1DT
          Y1T = (Y1OLDT + Y1T)/2 + .5*H*Y1DT
          XM = (XOLDM + XM)/2 + .5*H*XDM
          YM = (YOLDM + YM)/2 + .5*H*YDM
          X1M = (X1OLDM + X1M)/2 + .5*H*X1DM
          Y1M = (Y1OLDM + Y1M)/2 + .5*H*Y1DM
          DELV = (DELVOLD + DELV)/2. + .5*H*DELVD
          ALTT = SQRT(XT**2 + YT**2) – A
          ALTM = SQRT(XM**2 + YM**2) – A
          S = S + H
          SCOUNT = SCOUNT + H
          IF(SCOUNT.LT.(TS – .00001))GOTO 10
          SCOUNT = 0.
          TS2 = TS*TS
          TS3 = TS2*TS
          TS4 = TS3*TS
          TS5 = TS4*TS
```

(Listing 16.2 continued on next page.)

Listing 16.2   (cont.) Booster engagement simulation with Kalman filter based on range and angle measurement

```
          SIGN2 = SIGPOS*SIGPOS
          M11 = P11 + TS*P12 + .5*TS2*P13 + TS*(P12 + TS*P22 + .5*TS2*P23)
          M11 = M11 + .5*TS2*(P13 + TS*P23 + .5*TS2*P33) + TS5*PHIN/20.
          M12 = P12 + TS*P22 + .5*TS2*P23 + TS*(P13 + TS*P23 + .5*TS2*P33) + TS4*PHIN/8.
          M13 = P13 + TS*P23 + .5*TS2*P33 + PHIN*TS3/6.
          M22 = P22 + TS*P23 + TS*(P23 + TS*P33) + PHIN*TS3/3.
          M23 = P23 + TS*P33 + .5*TS2*PHIN
          M33 = P33 + PHIN*TS
          BOT = M11 + SIGN2
          K1 = M11/BOT
          K2 = M12/BOT
          K3 = M13/BOT
          FACT = 1. – K1
          P11 = FACT*M11
          P12 = FACT*M12
          P13 = FACT*M13
          P22 = – K2*M12 + M22
          P23 = – K2*M13 + M23
          P33 = – K3*M13 + M33
          CALL GAUSS(XLAMNOISE,SIGLAM)
          YTMEAS = YM + RTM*SIN(XLAM + XLAMNOISE)
          XTMEAS = XM + RTM*COS(XLAM + XLAMNOISE)
          RESX = XTMEAS – XTH – TS*XTDH – .5*TS2*XTDDH
          XTH = K1*RESX + XTH + TS*XTDH + .5*TS2*XTDDH
          XTDH = K2*RESX + XTDH + TS*XTDDH
          XTDDH = K3*RESX + XTDDH
          RESY = YTMEAS – YTH – TS*YTDH – .5*TS2*YTDDH
          YTH = K1*RESY + YTH + TS*YTDH + .5*TS2*YTDDH
          YTDH = K2*RESY + YTDH + TS*YTDDH
          YTDDH = K3*RESY + YTDDH
          XNMT = XT/6076.
          YNMT = YT/6076.
          XNMM = XM/6076.
          YNMM = YM/6076.
          ALTNMT = ALTT/6076.
          CALL DISTANCE(XT,YT,XFIRSTT,YFIRSTT,DISTNMT)
          ALTNMM = ALTM/6076.
          CALL DISTANCE(XM,YM,XFIRSTT,YFIRSTT,DISTNMM)
          WRITE(9,*)T,X1DT,XTDDH
          GOTO 10
200       CONTINUE
          IF(T < TB1)THEN
                  WGT = – WP1*T/TB1 + WTOT
                  TRST = TRST1
          ELSEIF(T < (TB1 + TB2))THEN
                  WGT = – WP2*T/TB2 + WTOT2 + WP2*TB1/TB2
                  TRST = TRST2
          ELSE
                  WGT = WPAY
                  TRST = 0.
          ENDIF
          AT = 32.2*TRST/WGT
          VEL = SQRT(X1T**2 + Y1T**2)
          AXT = AT*X1T/VEL
          AYT = AT*Y1T/VEL
          TEMBOTT = (XT**2 + YT**2)**1.5
          X1DT = – GM*XT/TEMBOTT + AXT
          Y1DT = – GM*YT/TEMBOTT + AYT
          ATPLOS = Y1DT*COS(XLAM) – X1DT*SIN(XLAM)
          XDT = X1T
          YDT = Y1T
          RTM1 = XT – XM
          RTM2 = YT – YM
          RTM = SQRT(RTM1**2 + RTM2**2)
          VTM1 = X1T – X1M
          VTM2 = Y1T – Y1M
          VC = – (RTM1*VTM1 + RTM2*VTM2)/RTM
          TGO = RTM/VC
          XLAM = ATAN2(RTM2,RTM1)
          XLAMD = (RTM1*VTM2 – RTM2*VTM1)/(RTM*RTM)
          XNC = XNP*VC*XLAMD + .5*XNP*ATPLOS
```

(Listing 16.2 continued on next page.)

348 TACTICAL AND STRATEGIC MISSILE GUIDANCE

Listing 16.2   (cont.) Booster engagement simulation with Kalman filter based on range and angle measurement

```
         DELVD = ABS(XNC)
         AM1 = - XNC*SIN(XLAM)
         AM2 = XNC*COS(XLAM)
         TEMBOTM = (XM**2 + YM**2)**1.5
         X1DM = - GM*XM/TEMBOTM + AM1
         Y1DM = - GM*YM/TEMBOTM + AM2
         XDM = X1M
         YDM = Y1M
         IF(STEP - 1)66,66,55
999      CONTINUE
         XNMT = XT/6076.
         YNMT = YT/6076.
         XNMM = XM/6076.
         YNMM = YM/6076.
         ALTNMT = ALTT/6076.
         CALL DISTANCE(XT,YT,XFIRSTT,YFIRSTT,DISTNMT)
         ALTNMM = ALTM/6076.
         CALL DISTANCE(XM,YM,XFIRSTT,YFIRSTT,DISTNMM)
         WRITE(9,*)T,X1DT,XTDDH
         WRITE(9,*)T,RTM,DELV
         PAUSE
         END

         SUBROUTINE DISTANCE(XT,YT,XF,YF,DISTNM)
         IMPLICIT REAL*8 (A – H)
         IMPLICIT REAL*8 (O – Z)
         SAVE
         R = SQRT(XT**2 + YT**2)
         RF = SQRT(XF**2 + YF**2)
         A = 2.0926E7
         CBETA = (XT*XF + YT*YF)/(R*RF)
         IF(CBETA < 1.)THEN
             BETA = ACOS(CBETA)
             DISTNM = A*BETA/6076.
         ELSE
             DISTNM = (XT – XF)/6076.
         ENDIF
         RETURN
         END

         SUBROUTINE PREDICT (TF,XDUM,YDUM,X1DUM,Y1DUM,XTF,YTF
1        ,WP1,WTOT,TB1,TRST1,TB2,WP2,WTOT2,TRST2,WPAY)
         IMPLICIT REAL*8 (A – H)
         IMPLICIT REAL*8 (O – Z)
         INTEGER STEP
         SAVE
         H = 1.
         A = 2.0926E7
         GM = 1.4077E16
         T = 0.
         X = XDUM
         Y = YDUM
         X1 = X1DUM
         Y1 = Y1DUM
10       IF(T > (TF - .00001))GOTO 999
         XOLD = X
         YOLD = Y
         X1OLD = X1
         Y1OLD = Y1
         STEP = 1
         GOTO 200
66       STEP = 2
         X = X + H*XD
         Y = Y + H*YD
         X1 = X1 + H*X1D
         Y1 = Y1 + H*Y1D
         T = T + H
         GOTO 200
55       X = (XOLD + X)/2 + .5*H*XD
         Y = (YOLD + Y)/2 + .5*H*YD
         X1 = (X1OLD + X1)/2 + .5*H*X1D
         Y1 = (Y1OLD + Y1)/2 + .5*H*Y1D
         GOTO 10
```

(Listing 16.2 continued on next page.)

**Listing 16.2   (cont.) Booster engagement simulation with Kalman filter based
on range and angle measurement**

```
200    CONTINUE
       IF(T < TB1)THEN
                WGT = - WP1*T/TB1 + WTOT
                TRST = TRST1
       ELSEIF(T < (TB1 + TB2))THEN
                WGT = - WP2*T/TB2 + WTOT2 + WP2*TB1/TB2
                TRST = TRST2
       ELSE
                WGT = WPAY
                TRST = 0.
       ENDIF
       AT = 32.2*TRST/WGT
       VEL = SQRT(X1**2 + Y1**2)
       AXT = AT*X1/VEL
       AYT = AT*Y1/VEL
       TEMBOTT = (X**2 + Y**2)**1.5
       X1D = - GM*X/TEMBOTT + AXT
       Y1D = - GM*Y/TEMBOTT + AYT
       XD = X1
       YD = Y1
       IF(STEP - 1)66,66,55
999    CONTINUE
       XTF = X
       YTF = Y
       RETURN
       END

       SUBROUTINE LAMBERT(XIC,YIC,TFDES,XF,YF,VRX,VRY,XLONGM,XLONGT)
  1       ,ICOUNT)
       IMPLICIT REAL*8 (A - H)
       IMPLICIT REAL*8 (O - Z)
       A = 2.0926E7
       GM = 1.4077E16
       RIC = SQRT(XIC**2 + YIC**2)
       RF = SQRT(XF**2 + YF**2)
       CPHI = (XIC*XF + YIC**YF)/(RIC*RF)
       PHI = ACOS(CPHI)
       SPHI = SIN(PHI)
       R0 = RIC
       PI = 3.14159
       DEGRAD = 360./(2.*PI)
       ICOUNT = 1
       GMIN = ATAN2((SPHI - SQRT(2.*RO*(1. - CPHI)/RF)),(1 - CPHI))
       GMAX = ATAN2((SPHI - SQRT(2.*RO*(1. - CPHI)/RF)),(1 - CPHI))
       GAM = (GMIN + GMAX)/2.
       DO
           TOP = GM*(1. - COS(PHI))
           TEMP = R0*COS(GAM)/RF - COS(PHI + GAM)
           BOT = R0*COS(GAM)*TEMP
           V = SQRT(TOP/BOT)
           IF (XLONGT > XLONGM) THEN
               VRX = V*COS(PI/2. - GAM + XLONGM)
               VRY = V*SIN(PI/2. - GAM + XLONGM)
           ELSE
               VRX = V*COS( - PI/2. + GAM + XLONGM)
               VRY = V*SIN( - PI/2. + GAM + XLONGM)
           END IF
           XLAM = R0*V*V/GM
           TOP1 = TAN(GAM)*(1 - COS(PHI)) + (1 - XLAM)*SIN(PHI)
           BOT1P = (1 - COS(PHI))/(XLAM*COS(GAM)*COS(GAM))
           BOT1 = (2 - XLAM)*(BOT1P + COS(GAM + PHI)/COS(GAM))
           TOP2 = 2*COS(GAM)
           BOT2 = XLAM*((2/XLAM - 1)**1.5)
           TOP3 = SQRT(2/XLAM - 1)
           BOT3 = COS(GAM)/TAN(PHI/2) - SIN(GAM)
           TEMP = (TOP2/BOT2)*ATAN2(TOP3,BOT3)
           TF = R0*(TOP1/BOT1 + TEMP)/(V*COS(GAM))
           IF(ABS(TFDES - TF) < = .00000001*TFDES).OR.ICOUNT > 100)THEN
               EXIT
           ENDIF
           IF(TF > TFDES)THEN
               GMAX = GAM
```

(Listing 16.2 continued on next page.)

Listing 16.2 (cont.) Booster engagement simulation with Kalman filter based on range and angle measurement

```
          ELSE
            GMIN = GAM
          ENDIF
          IF(ICOUNT = 1)THEN
            XNEXT = (GMAX + GMIN)/2,
          ELSE
            XNEXT = GAM + (GAM − GOLD)*(TFDES − TF)/(TF − TOLD)
            IF(XNEXT > GMAX.OR.XNEXT < GMIN) THEN
              XNEXT = (GMAX + GMIN)/2.
          ENDIF
          GOLD = GAM
          TOLD = TF
          GAM = XNEXT
          ICOUNT = ICOUNT + 1
        REPEAT
        RETURN
        END

        SUBROUTINE GAUSS(X,SIG)
        IMPLICIT REAL*8 (A − H)
        IMPLICIT REAL*8 (O − Z)
        INTEGER RANDOM,SUM
        INTEGER*4 TOOLBX
        PARAMETER (RANDOM = Z'86140000')
        SUM = 0
        DO 14 J = 1,6
        IRAN = TOOLBX(RANDOM)
        SUM = SUM + IRAN
14      CONTINUE
        X = SUM/65536.
        X = 1.414*X*SIG
        RETURN
        END
```

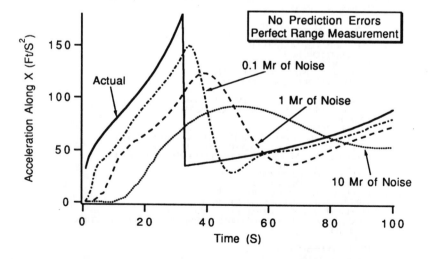

Fig. 16.10   Filter performance degrades with increasing measurement noise intensity.

Pulsed Guidance

A strategic interceptor maneuvers with divert engines. Sometimes the engines are effectively throttleable. This means that, by issuing divert commands in opposite directions, any effective acceleration level (within engine thrust-to-weight ratio constraints) can be reached. This is ideal for the implementation of proportional navigation type guidance laws. However, sometimes it is only possible to issue guidance commands of fixed amplitude when the engine is on. In this case we can only influence the duration of the guidance pulse by turning the engine off. In this situation it is not obvious how a guidance law can be implemented or if proportional navigation is appropriate.

Consider the acceleration diagram in Fig. 16.11. Here we have a guidance pulse of magnitude a feet per square seconds lasting for Δt seconds. Implicit in the diagram is the approximation that the acceleration level is constant for the duration of the pulse. Actually, the acceleration level would be increasing for a constant thrust level because of the expenditure of fuel. We wish to derive a guidance law whose output for a given acceleration magnitude a contains information concerning the duration of the guidance pulse Δt.

We have previously seen how proportional navigation is related to the zero effort miss ZEM. In proportional navigation type guidance, we take the entire guided portion of the flight to remove the zero effort miss. If we have a single pulse, as shown in Fig. 16.11, we must remove the zero effort miss in Δt seconds. For a pulse of amplitude a and duration Δt we can integrate the acceleration twice as shown in Fig. 16.11 and say that

$$ZEM = 0.5 \, a\Delta t^2 + a\Delta t \, (t_{go} - \Delta t)$$

However, we also know that the proportional navigation guidance law can be expressed as

$$n_c = N' V_c \dot{\lambda} = \frac{N' ZEM}{t_{go}^2}$$

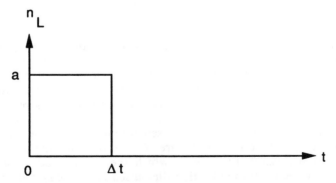

Fig. 16.11   Conceptual diagram for pulsed guidance law.

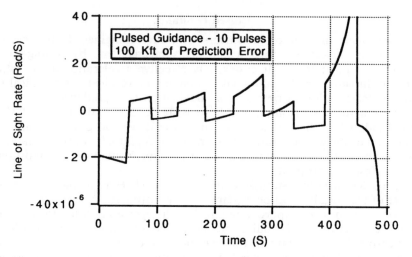

Fig. 16.12   Pulsed guidance attempts to drive line-of-sight rate to zero with each pulse.

Therefore, the zero effort miss can be expressed in terms of the line-of-sight rate as

$$ZEM = V_c t_{go}^2 \dot{\lambda}$$

Equating the expressions for the proportional navigation zero effort miss with the one for the pulse of fixed duration, we get

$$V_c t_{go}^2 \dot{\lambda} = 0.5 \ a \Delta t^2 + a \Delta t \ (t_{go} - \Delta t)$$

This is a quadratic equation in terms of Δt. Using the quadratic formula and eliminating the unrealistic root, we obtain a closed-form expression for the pulse duration time as

$$\Delta t = t_{go} \left(1 - \sqrt{1 - \frac{2V_c}{a} \dot{\lambda}} \right)$$

In order to implement a pulse guidance scheme we must know in advance the number of pulses to be used. For simplicity, let us assume that the pulses are equally distributed throughout the flight. If it is time for a pulse to commence, we calculate the pulse duration from the preceding formula. An engagement simulation with a pulsed guidance system is presented in Listing 16.3.

A nominal case was run with the pulsed guidance system in which there was 100 kft of prediction error. Figure 16.12 shows the line-of-sight rate profile for a successful intercept in which the missile had 10 guidance pulses. We can see from the plot that the pulsed guidance system is always trying to drive the line-of-sight rate to zero after each pulse is issued. This

Listing 16.3   Pulsed guidance simulation

```
       IMPLICIT REAL*8 (A – H)
       IMPLICIT REAL*8 (O – Z)
       INTEGER STEP
       LOGICAL PULSE_ON,ACQUIRE
       XLONGMDEG = 45.
       XLONGTDEG = 90.
       ALTNMTIC = 0.
       ALTNMMIC = 0.
       TF = 500.
       GAMDEGT = 23.
       AMAG = 64.4
       PULSES = 10.
       PREDERR = – 100000.
       PULSE_ON = .FALSE.
       ACQUIRE = .TRUE.
       PULSE_NUM = PULSES – 1.
       H = 1.
       A = 2.0926E7
       GM = 1.4077E16
       PI = 3.14159
       DEGRAD = 360./(2.*PI)
       XNC = 0.
       GAMT = GAMDEGT/57.3
       DISTNMT = 6000.
       PHIT = DISTNMT*6076./A
       ALTT = ALTNMTIC*6076.
       ALTM = ALTNMMIC*6076.
       R0T = A + ALTT
       TOP = GM*(1. – COS(PHIT))
       TEMP = R0T*COS(GAMT)/A – COS(PHIT + GAMT)
       BOT = R0T*COS(GAMT)*TEMP
       VT = SQRT(TOP/BOT)
       XLONGM = XLONGMDEG/DEGRAD
       XLONGT = XLONGTDEG/DEGRAD
       IF (XLONGM > XLONGT) THEN
           X1T = VT*COS(PI/2. – GAMT + XLONGT)
           Y1T = VT*SIN(PI/2. – GAMT + XLONGT)
       ELSE
           X1T = VT*COS( – PI/2. + GAMT + XLONGT)
           Y1T = VT*SIN( – PI/2. + GAMT + XLONGT)
       END IF
       S = 0.
       SCOUNT = 0.
       XLONGM = XLONGMDEG/DEGRAD
       XLONGT = XLONGTDEG/DEGRAD
       XM = (A + ALTM)*COS(XLONGM)
       YM = (A + ALTM)*SIN(XLONGM)
       XT = (A + ALTT)*COS(XLONGT)
       YT = (A + ALTT)*SIN(XLONGT)
       XFIRSTT = XT
       YFIRSTT = YT
       T = 0.
       CALL PREDICT (TF,XT,YT,X1T,Y1T,XTF,YTF)
       YTF = YTF + PREDERR
       CALL LAMBERT(XM,YM,TF,XTF,YTF,VRXM,VRYM,XLONGM,XLONGT)
  1       ,ICOUNT)
       X1M = VRXM
       Y1M = VRYM
       RTM1 = XT – XM
       RTM2 = YT – YM
       RTM = SQRT(RTM1**2 + RTM2**2)
       VTM1 = X1T – X1M
       VTM2 = Y1T – Y1M
       VC = – (RTM1*VTM1 + RTM2*VTM2)/RTM
       DELV = 0.
  10   IF(VC < 0.)GOTO 999
       TGO = RTM/VC
       IF(TGO > 10.)THEN
           H = 1.
       ELSEIF(TGO > .1)THEN
           H = .01
       ELSE
           H = .0001
```

(Listing 16.3 continued on next page.)

Listing 16.3   (cont.) Pulsed guidance simulation

```
        ENDIF
        XOLDT = XT
        YOLDT = YT
        X1OLDT = X1T
        Y1OLDT = Y1T
        XOLDM = XM
        YOLDM = YM
        X1OLDM = X1M
        Y1OLDM = Y1M
        DELVOLD = DELV
        STEP = 1
        GOTO 200
66      STEP = 2
        XT = XT + H*XDT
        YT = YT + H*YDT
        X1T = X1T + H*X1DT
        Y1T = Y1T + H*Y1DT
        XM = XM + H*XDM
        YM = YM + H*YDM
        X1M = X1M + H*X1DM
        Y1M = Y1M + H*Y1DM
        DELV = DELV + H*DELVD
        T = T + H
        GOTO 200
55      XT = (XOLDT + XT)/2 + .5*H*XDT
        YT = (YOLDT + YT)/2 + .5*H*YDT
        X1T = (X1OLDT + X1T)/2 + .5*H*X1DT
        Y1T = (Y1OLDT + Y1T)/2 + .5*H*Y1DT
        XM = (XOLDM + XM)/2 + .5*H*XDM
        YM = (YOLDM + YM)/2 + .5*H*YDM
        X1M = (X1OLDM + X1M)/2 + .5*H*X1DM
        Y1M = (Y1OLDM + Y1M)/2 + .5*H*Y1DM
        DELV = (DELVOLD + DELV)/2. + .5*H*DELVD
        ALTT = SQRT(XT**2 + YT**2) - A
        ALTM = SQRT(XM**2 + YM**2) - A
        IF(PULSE_ON)THEN
            IF(T > TOFF)THEN
                PULSE_ON = .FALSE.
                XNC = 0.
            ENDIF
        ENDIF
        IF(PULSE_NUM > 0.)THEN
            IF(TGO < = (TF - 0.)*PULSE_NUM/(PULSES - 1.)) THEN
                PULSE_NUM = PULSE_NUM - 1.
                PULSE_ON = .TRUE.
                DISC = 1. - 2.*VC*ABS(XLAMD)/AMAG
                IF(DISC > 0.)THEN
                    TPULSE = TGO*(1. - SQRT(DISC))
                    IF(XLAMD > 0.)THEN
                        XNC = AMAG
                    ELSE
                        XNC = - AMAG
                    ENDIF
                ELSE
                    TPULSE = 0.
                ENDIF
                IF(TGO < TPULSE)THEN
                    TOFF = 9999999.
                ELSE
                    TOFF = T + TPULSE
                ENDIF
            ENDIF
        ELSE
            DISC = 1. - 2.*VC*ABS(XLAMD)/AMAG
            IF(DISC > 0.)THEN
                TPULSE = TGO*(1. - SQRT(DISC))
            ELSE
                TPULSE = 999999.
            ENDIF
            IF (TGO < = TPULSE) THEN
                IF(XLAMD > 0.)THEN
                    XNC = AMAG
```

(Listing 16.3 continued on next page.)

Listing 16.3   (cont.) Pulsed guidance simulation

```
                  ELSE
                      XNC = − AMAG
                  ENDIF
                  PULSE_ON = .TRUE.
                  TOFF = 999999.
              END IF
          END IF
      S = S + H
      SCOUNT = SCOUNT + H
      IF(SCOUNT.LT..99999)GOTO 10
      SCOUNT = 0.
      XNMT = XT/6076.
      YNMT = YT/6076.
      XNMM = XM/6076.
      YNMM = YM/6076.
      ALTNMT = ALTT/6076.
      CALL DISTANCE(XT,YT,XFIRSTT,YFIRSTT,DISTNMT)
      ALTNMM = ALTM/6076.
      CALL DISTANCE(XM,YM,XFIRSTT,YFIRSTT,DISTNMM)
      WRITE(9,*)T,XNC,XLAMD,DELV
      GOTO 10
200   CONTINUE
      TEMBOTT = (XT**2 + YT**2)**1.5
      X1DT = − GM*XT/TEMBOTT
      Y1DT = − GM*YT/TEMBOTT
      XDT = X1T
      YDT = Y1T
      RTM1 = XT − XM
      RTM2 = YT − YM
      RTM = SQRT(RTM1**2 + RTM2**2)
      VTM1 = X1T − X1M
      VTM2 = Y1T − Y1M
      VC = − (RTM1*VTM1 + RTM2*VTM2)/RTM
      TGO = RTM/VC
      XLAM = ATAN2(RTM2,RTM1)
      XLAMD = (RTM1*VTM2 − RTM2*VTM1)/(RTM*RTM)
      DELVD = ABS(XNC)
      AM1 = − XNC*SIN(XLAM)
      AM2 = XNC*COS(XLAM)
      TEMBOTM = (XM**2 + YM**2)**1.5
      X1DM = − GM*XM/TEMBOTM + AM1
      Y1DM = − GM*YM/TEMBOTM + AM2
      XDM = X1M
      YDM = Y1M
      IF(STEP − 1)66,66,55
999   CONTINUE
      XNMT = XT/6076.
      YNMT = YT/6076.
      XNMM = XM/6076.
      YNMM = YM/6076.
      ALTNMT = ALTT/6076.
      CALL DISTANCE(XT,YT,XFIRSTT,YFIRSTT,DISTNMT)
      ALTNMM = ALTM/6076.
      CALL DISTANCE(XM,YM,XFIRSTT,YFIRSTT,DISTNMM)
      WRITE(9,*)T,XNC,XLAMD,DELV
      WRITE(9,*)T,RTM,DELV
      PAUSE
      END

      SUBROUTINE DISTANCE(XT,YT,XF,YF,DISTNM)
      IMPLICIT REAL*8 (A − H)
      IMPLICIT REAL*8 (O − Z)
      SAVE
      R = SQRT(XT**2 + YT**2)
      RF = SQRT(XF**2 + YF**2)
      A = 2.0926E7
      CBETA = (XT*XF + YT*YF)/(R*RF)
      IF(CBETA < 1.)THEN
          BETA = ACOS(CBETA)
          DISTNM = A*BETA/6076.
      ELSE
          DISTNM = (XT − XF)/6076.
      ENDIF
      RETURN
      END
```

(Listing 16.3 continued on next page.)

Listing 16.3   (cont.) Pulsed guidance simulation

```
        SUBROUTINE PREDICT (TF,XDUM,YDUM,X1DUM,Y1DUM,XTF,YTF)
        IMPLICIT REAL*8 (A – H)
        IMPLICIT REAL*8 (O – Z)
        INTEGER STEP
        SAVE
        H = 1.
        A = 2.0926E7
        GM = 1.4077E16
        T = 0.
        X = XDUM
        Y = YDUM
        X1 = X1DUM
        Y1 = Y1DUM
   10   IF(T > (TF – .00001))GOTO 999
        XOLD = X
        YOLD = Y
        X1OLD = X1
        Y1OLD = Y1
        STEP = 1
        GOTO 200
   66   STEP = 2
        X = X + H*XD
        Y = Y + H*YD
        X1 = X1 + H*X1D
        Y1 = Y1 + H*Y1D
        T = T + H
        GOTO 200
   55   X = (XOLD + X)/2 + .5*H*XD
        Y = (YOLD + Y)/2 + .5*H*YD
        X1 = (X1OLD + X1)/2 + .5*H*X1D
        Y1 = (Y1OLD + Y1)/2 + .5*H*Y1D
        GOTO 10
  200   CONTINUE
        TEMBOT = (X**2 + Y**2)**1.5
        X1D = – GM*X/TEMBOT
        Y1D = – GM*Y/TEMBOT
        XD = X1
        YD = Y1
        IF(STEP – 1)66,66,55
  999   CONTINUE
        XTF = X
        YTF = Y
        RETURN
        END

        SUBROUTINE LAMBERT(XIC,YIC,TFDES,XF,YF,VRX,VRY,XLONGM,XLONGT)
    1   ,ICOUNT)
        IMPLICIT REAL*8 (A – H)
        IMPLICIT REAL*8 (O – Z)
        A = 2.0926E7
        GM = 1.4077E16
        RIC = SQRT(XIC**2 + YIC**2)
        RF = SQRT(XF**2 + YF**2)
        CPHI = (XIC*XF + YIC*YF)/(RIC*RF)
        PHI = ACOS(CPHI)
        SPHI = SIN(PHI)
        R0 = RIC
        PI = 3.14159
        DEGRAD = 360./(2.*PI)
        ICOUNT = 1
        GMIN = ATAN2((SPHI – SQRT(2.*R0*(1. – CPHI)/RF)),(1 – CPHI))
        GMAX = ATAN2((SPHI – SQRT(2.*R0*(1. – CPHI)/RF)),(1 – CPHI))
        GAM = (GMIN + GMAX)/2.
        DO
          TOP = GM*(1. – COS(PHI))
          TEMP = R0*COS(GAM)/RF – COS(PHI + GAM)
          BOT = R0*COS(GAM)*TEMP
          V = SQRT(TOP/BOT)
          IF (XLONGT > XLONGM) THEN
            VRX = V*COS(PI/2. – GAM + XLONGM)
            VRY = V*SIN(PI/2. – GAM + XLONGM)
          ELSE
            VRX = V*COS(– PI/2. + GAM + XLONGM)
```

(Listing 16.3 continued on next page.)

Listing 16.3 (cont.) Pulsed guidance simulation

```
      VRY = V*SIN(- PI/2. + GAM + XLONGM)
   END IF
   XLAM = R0*V*V/GM
   TOP1 = TAN(GAM)*(1 - COS(PHI)) + (1 - XLAM)*SIN(PHI)
   BOT1P = (1 - COS(PHI))/(XLAM*COS(GAM)*COS(GAM))
   BOT1 = (2 - XLAM)*(BOT1P + COS(GAM + PHI)/COS(GAM))
   TOP2 = 2*COS(GAM)
   BOT2 = XLAM*((2/XLAM - 1)**1.5)
   TOP3 = SQRT(2/XLAM - 1)
   BOT3 = COS(GAM)/TAN(PHI/2) - SIN(GAM)
   TEMP = (TOP2/BOT2)*ATAN2(TOP3,BOT3)
   TF = R0*(TOP1/BOT1 + TEMP)/(V*COS(GAM))
   IF((ABS(TFDES - TF) < .00000001*TFDES).OR.ICOUNT > 100)THEN
      EXIT
   ENDIF
   IF(TF > TFDES)THEN
      GMAX = GAM
   ELSE
      GMIN = GAM
   ENDIF
   IF(ICOUNT = 1)THEN
      XNEXT = (GMAX + GMIN)/2,
   ELSE
      XNEXT = GAM + (GAM - GOLD)*(TFDES - TF)/(TF - TOLD)
      IF(XNEXT > GMAX.OR.XNEXT < GMIN) THEN
         XNEXT = (GMAX + GMIN)/2.
      ENDIF
   ENDIF
   GOLD = GAM
   TOLD = TF
   GAM = XNEXT
   ICOUNT = ICOUNT + 1
REPEAT
RETURN
END
```

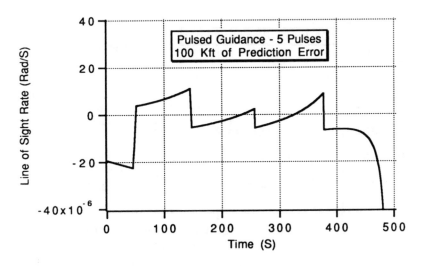

Fig. 16.13 Pulsed guidance works with fewer pulses.

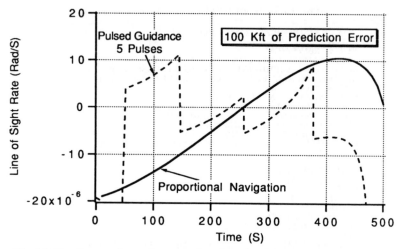

Fig. 16.14   Comparison of proportional navigation and pulsed guidance.

is not surprising, since the pulsed guidance law was derived with this concept in mind.

Figure 16.13 shows a similar case, except only five guidance pulses are used. We can see that the pulsed guidance law is still attempting to drive the line-of-sight rate to zero after each pulse is issued. However, since there are fewer pulses, the line-of-sight rate builds up to larger values in between pulses.

The line-of-sight rate profiles for the five pulse case are overlaid with the proportional navigation results for the identical case and are shown in Fig. 16.14. We can see that proportional navigation drives the line-of-sight rate to zero at the end of the flight only.

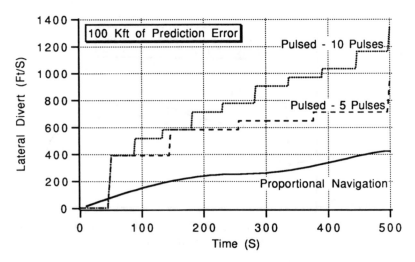

Fig. 16.15   Pulsed guidance does not reduce lateral divert requirements.

Although each of the cases studied so far resulted in successful intercepts, the divert requirements for each guidance concept are different. Figure 16.15 displays the required lateral divert profiles for each of the cases. We can see that proportional navigation has the smallest divert requirements. Increasing the number of pulses in a pulsed guidance system appears to increase the lateral divert requirements.

We use pulsed guidance when the divert engine characteristics make it infeasible to use proportional navigation. The price paid is somewhat higher lateral divert requirements.

Chapter 17

Ballistic Target Properties

Introduction[1,2]

ALTHOUGH surface-to-surface missiles were used as terror weapons during World War II and the Iran-Iraq War, most of the world became familiar with the ballistic missile threat during the 1991 Persian Gulf War. Hundreds of millions of TV viewers will never forget the wail of sirens and images of Scud missiles glowing in the night-time skies over Tel Aviv and Dhahran as they decelerated through the atmosphere toward their civilian targets after having traveled hundreds of miles from their launch sites in Iraq. Viewers, regardless of nationality, were riveted by the drama of the almost nightly duels between the Patriot interceptor and its intended prey—the Scud ballistic target.

In the chapters pertaining to tactical guidance the interceptor's intended target was considered to be an aircraft, whereas in the chapters pertaining to strategic guidance the engagement threat was either considered to be a booster or an exoatmospheric ballistic target. In the remaining chapters of the text we will consider the special problems encountered in intercepting an endoatmospheric ballistic target.

Ballistic Target Model

When a ballistic target re-enters the atmosphere after having traveled a long distance, its speed is high and the remaining time to ground impact is relatively short. The small distances traveled by ballistic targets after they re-enter the atmosphere enable us to accurately model these threats using the flat-Earth, constant gravity approximation as was done in modeling tactical interceptors. This simplification is important because it will lead to useful closed-form solutions for ballistic targets.

Figure 17.1 presents the flat-Earth, constant gravity model for the ballistic endoatmospheric threat. In this model only drag and gravity act on the ballistic target.[3] We can see from Fig. 17.1 that the target has velocity V_T and is initially at re-entry angle γ_T. Note that drag F_{drag} acts in a direction opposite to the velocity vector and gravity g always acts downward in the flat-Earth model. Therefore, if the effect of drag is greater than that of gravity, the target will slow up or decelerate. Since we will eventually consider the ballistic target as an interceptor threat, the magnitude of the target deceleration will be of interest to us.

From Fig. 17.1 we can see that the target re-entry angle γ_T can be computed, using trigonometry, from the two inertial components of the

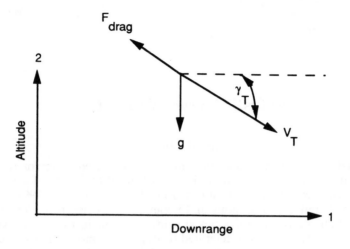

Fig. 17.1   Ballistic target geometry.

target velocity as

$$\gamma_T = \tan^{-1}\frac{-V_{T2}}{V_{T1}}$$

The acceleration components of the ballistic target in the inertial downrange and altitude directions of Fig. 17.1 can either be expressed in terms of the target weight W, reference area S_{ref}, zero lift drag C_{D0}, and gravity g or more simply in terms of the ballistic coefficient β (defined in Chapter 11) according to

$$\frac{\mathrm{d}V_{T1}}{\mathrm{d}t} = \frac{-F_{\mathrm{drag}}}{m}\cos\gamma_T = \frac{-QS_{\mathrm{ref}}C_{D0}g}{W}\cos\gamma_T = \frac{-Qg}{\beta}\cos\gamma_T$$

$$\frac{\mathrm{d}V_{T2}}{\mathrm{d}t} = \frac{F_{\mathrm{drag}}}{m}\sin\gamma_T - g = \frac{QS_{\mathrm{ref}}C_{D0}g}{W}\sin\gamma_T - g = \frac{Qg}{\beta}\sin\gamma_T - g$$

where Q is the dynamic pressure. Recall that the dynamic pressure has been previously defined as

$$Q = 0.5\rho V_T^2$$

where V_T is the total target velocity which can be expressed in terms of component velocities as

$$V_T = \sqrt{V_{T1}^2 + V_{T2}^2}$$

and ρ is the air density measured in slug/ft^3 and was shown to be accurately approximated exponentially in Chapter 11 as

$$\rho = 0.0034e^{\frac{-R_{T2}}{22,000}}$$

above 30,000 ft and

$$\rho = 0.002378e^{\frac{-R_{T2}}{30,000}}$$

below 30,000 ft. The target altitude R_{T2} is measured in feet. Since the acceleration equations are in a fixed or inertial frame, they can be integrated directly to yield velocity and position.

Ballistic Target Experiments

A simulation of a ballistic target, based on the acceleration differential equations of the previous section, appears in Listing 17.1. The ballistic target acceleration differential equations appear after statement label 200, and the initial conditions, required for the integration of the differential equations, appear at the beginning of the simulation (before statement label 5). We can see that the program is initialized with a target altitude of 100 kft, a target velocity of 6000 ft/s, and a re-entry angle of 45 deg. The nominal ballistic coefficient for the target is 500 lb/ft^2. From statement label 5 we can see that the simulation stops when the ballistic threat hits the ground ($R_{T2} < 0$). Every tenth of a second the target location is printed in kft, acceleration in g, and velocity in ft/s. The simulation integration step size of 0.01 s ($H = 0.01$) is sufficiently small to get accurate answers with the second-order Runge-Kutta numerical integration technique.

The nominal case of Listing 17.1 was run and Fig. 17.2 presents the resultant trajectory of the ballistic target. We can see from the figure that the target trajectory is approximately a straight line (we shall exploit this

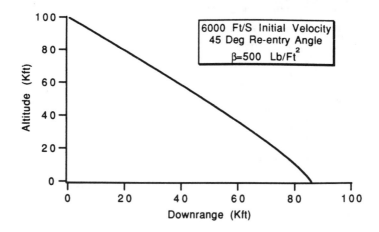

Fig. 17.2 Nominal ballistic target trajectory is approximately a straight line.

Listing 17.1   Ballistic target simulation

```
      INTEGER STEP
      RT1 = 0.
      RT2 = 100000.
      VT = 6000.
      GAMTDEG = 45.
      BETA = 500.
      VT1 = VT*COS(GAMTDEG/57.3)
      VT2 = - VT*SIN(GAMTDEG/57.3)
      T = 0.
      H = .01
      S = 0.
   5  IF(RT2<0.)GOTO 999
      S = S + H
      RT1OLD = RT1
      RT2OLD = RT2
      VT1OLD = VT1
      VT2OLD = VT2
      STEP = 1
      GOTO 200
  66  STEP = 2
      RT1 = RT1 + H*VT1
      RT2 = RT2 + H*VT2
      VT1 = VT1 + H*AT1
      VT2 = VT2 + H*AT2
      T = T + H
      GOTO 200 55
      CONTINUE
      RT1 = .5*(RT1OLD + RT1 + H*VT1)
      RT2 = .5*(RT2OLD + RT2 + H*VT2)
      VT1 = .5*(VT1OLD + VT1 + H*AT1)
      VT2 = .5*(VT2OLD + VT2 + H*AT2)
      IF(S.GE..09999)THEN
        S = 0.
        ATG = SQRT(AT1**2 + AT2**2)/32.2
        RT1K = RT1/1000.
        RT2K = RT2/1000.
        VT = SQRT(VT1**2 + VT2**2)
        ATG = SQRT(AT1**2 + AT2**2)/32.2
        WRITE(9,*)T,RT1K,RT2K,ATG,VT
      END IF
      GOTO 5
 200  CONTINUE
      IF(RT2.LE.30000.)THEN
        RHO = .002378*EXP(- RT2/30000.)
      ELSE
        RHO = .0034*EXP(- RT2/22000.)
      ENDIF
      VT = SQRT(VT1**2 + VT2**2)
      Q = .5*RHO*VT**2
      GAMT = ATAN2(- VT2,VT1)
      AT1 = - 32.2*Q*COS(GAMT)/BETA
      AT2 = - 32.2 + 32.2*Q*SIN(GAMT)/BETA
      IF(STEP-1)66,66,55
 999  CONTINUE
      ATG = SQRT(AT1**2 + AT2**2)/32.2
      RT1K = RT1/1000.
      RT2K = RT2/1000.
      VT = SQRT(VT1**2 + VT2**2)
      ATG = SQRT(AT1**2 + AT2**2)/32.2
      WRITE(9,*)T,RT1K,RT2K,ATG,VT
      PAUSE
      END
```

observation later). At the lower altitudes there is slight curvature in the trajectory due to both drag and gravity.

Figure 17.3 displays the deceleration and velocity of the nominal target as a function of altitude. At 100-kft altitude the target has an initial velocity of 6000 ft/s and there is 1 g of acceleration due to gravity (there is too little atmosphere at 100 kft to cause substantial drag). The drag deceleration increases and target velocity decreases as the target descends in altitude. At approximately 40 kft altitude the target deceleration peaks and is nearly 8 g. At this altitude of maximum deceleration the target speed is approximately 63% of its original value (i.e., 3800 = 0.63*6000).

The simulation of Listing 17.1 was rerun and this time the initial target velocity at 100-kft altitude was made a parameter. We can see from the simulation results, displayed in Fig. 17.4, that target deceleration increases as the target speed increases. This should not be surprising since the acceleration differential equations tell us that deceleration is proportional to the dynamic pressure (i.e., target velocity squared). Therefore very fast ballistic threats can cause enormous decelerations. Surprisingly, the simulation results of in Fig. 17.4 also indicate that the altitude of maximum target deceleration appears to be approximately independent of the target speed!

The simulation of Listing 17.1 was again rerun and this time the target ballistic coefficient was made a parameter. Simulation results, displayed in Fig. 17.5, appear to indicate that the peak target deceleration is approximately independent of ballistic coefficient. This is surprising since there is more drag with lower ballistic coefficients. However, these simulation results also indicate that the altitude at which the peak target deceleration occurs decreases with increasing ballistic coefficient.

Another experiment was conducted using Listing 17.1. This time the initial target velocity and ballistic coefficient were fixed and the re-entry angle was made a parameter. Simulation results, displayed in Fig. 17.6, indicate that the peak target deceleration increases with increasing re-entry

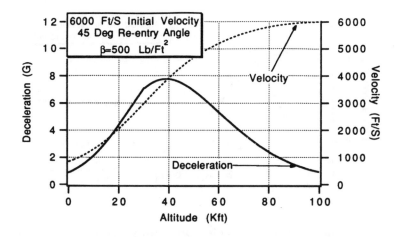

Fig. 17.3 Peak target deceleration occurs at 40 kft.

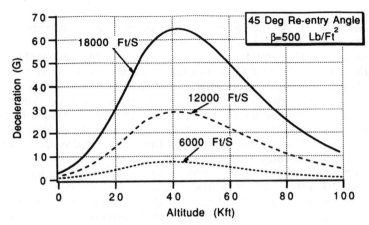

Fig. 17.4   Peak target deceleration increases with increasing target speed.

angle. This is reasonable because as the re-entry angle increases the resultant target trajectory tends to become more vertical and more drag is experienced. In addition, Fig. 17.6 shows that the altitude at which the peak target deceleration occurs decreases with increasing re-entry angle.

Closed-Form Solutions for Ballistic Targets

In this section we will derive some useful closed-form solutions for ballistic targets and compare the theoretical solutions to the simulation results of the previous section. If we neglect gravity, Newton's second law says that we can express the drag force acting on a ballistic target in terms of the dynamic pressure, reference area, and zero lift drag according to

$$F_{\text{drag}} = m\frac{\mathrm{d}V_T}{\mathrm{d}t} = -QS_{\text{ref}}C_{D0}$$

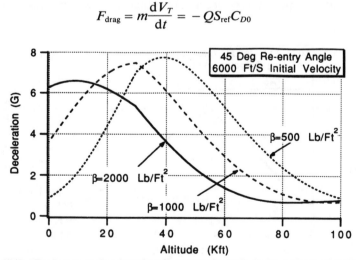

Fig. 17.5   Peak target deceleration is approximately independent of ballistic coefficient.

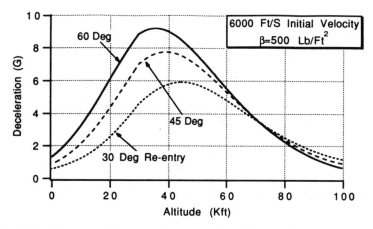

Fig. 17.6   Peak target deceleration increases with increasing re-entry angle.

Using definitions of dynamic pressure and ballistic coefficient we can rewrite the preceding differential equation as

$$\frac{dV_T}{dt} = \frac{-\rho g V_T^2}{2\beta}$$

If we assume that the target trajectory is always a straight line (as appeared to be the case in Fig. 17.2) then the re-entry angle γ_T is a constant. Figure 17.1 indicates that for the constant re-entry angle assumption, the altitude component of velocity can be expressed in terms of the total velocity as

$$V_{T2} = \frac{dR_{T2}}{dt} = -V_T \sin \gamma_T$$

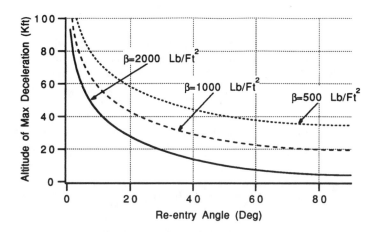

Fig. 17.7   Theory indicates that altitude at which maximum deceleration occurs is independent of velocity.

According to the chain rule we can express the rate of change of the total velocity as

$$\frac{dV_T}{dt} = \frac{dV_T}{dR_{T2}}\frac{dR_{T2}}{dt} = -\frac{dV_T}{dR_{T2}}V_T\sin\gamma_T$$

Substitution of the expression for the rate of change of the total velocity into the preceding equation yields

$$\frac{-\rho g V_T^2}{2\beta} = -\frac{dV_T}{dR_{T2}}V_T\sin\gamma_T$$

Assuming that the exponential approximation for air density

$$\rho = 0.0034e^{-\frac{R_{T2}}{22,000}}$$

applies everywhere (actually another approximation is better below 30,000 ft and is indicated in the previous section) we can rearrange the preceding differential equation so that velocity terms are on one side and altitude terms are on the other side. Rewriting the resultant differential equation with integrals yields

$$\int_{V_{T_{IC}}}^{V_T}\frac{dV_T}{V_T} = \frac{0.0034g}{2\beta\sin\gamma_T}\int_{R_{T2_{IC}}}^{R_{T2}}e^{-\frac{R_{T2}}{22,000}}dR_{T2}$$

where gravity, the ballistic coefficient, and the re-entry angle have been brought outside the integral since they are considered to be constants. Integrating the preceding expression yields the velocity formula where the target velocity is a function of its initial velocity, re-entry angle, ballistic coefficient, and altitude (or air density) according to

$$V_T = V_{T_{IC}}e^{-\frac{22,000g\rho}{2\beta\sin\gamma_T}}$$

The maximum deceleration experienced by the target will occur at an altitude in which the dynamic pressure is a maximum. Substituting the velocity formula into the definition of dynamic pressure yields

$$Q = 0.5\rho V_T^2 = 0.5\rho V_{T_{IC}}^2 e^{-\frac{22,000g\rho}{\beta\sin\gamma_T}}$$

We can find when the dynamic pressure is a maximum by taking its derivative with respect to the air density and setting the resultant expression to zero or

$$\frac{dQ}{d\rho} = 0 = 0.5V_{T_{IC}}^2 e^{-\frac{2,000g\rho}{\beta\sin\gamma_T}} - 0.5\rho V_{T_{IC}}^2\frac{22,000g}{\beta\sin\gamma_T}e^{-\frac{22,000g\rho}{\beta\sin\gamma_T}}$$

After some algebra we find that the maximum dynamic pressure condition is

$$\beta\sin\gamma_T = 22,000\rho g$$

The velocity of the target at the maximum dynamic pressure condition can be found by substituting the preceding expression into the velocity formula yielding

$$V_T \bigg|_{\text{max } Q} \quad V_{T_{\text{IC}}} e^{-\frac{22,000 g \rho}{2\beta \sin \gamma_T}} = V_{T_{\text{IC}}} e^{-0.5} = 0.606 V_{T_{\text{IC}}}$$

In other words the velocity of the target is always 61% of its initial value when the dynamic pressure is a maximum! This important result was also observed empirically in the simulation results of Fig. 17.3.

To find the altitude at which maximum target deceleration occurs we must first find the altitude or air density at which the dynamic pressure is greatest. The air density at maximum dynamic pressure can be found from the maximum dynamic pressure condition to be

$$\rho_{\text{max } Q} = \frac{\beta \sin \gamma_T}{22,000 g}$$

Since the the altitude at maximum dynamic pressure is related to the air density at maximum dynamic pressure according to

$$\rho_{\text{max } Q} = 0.0034 e^{-\frac{R_{T2\text{max } Q}}{22,000}}$$

we can solve for the altitude at this important flight condition. After some algebra we obtain

$$R_{T2\text{max } Q} = 22,000 \, \ell n \, \frac{0.0034 * 22,000 g}{\beta \sin \gamma_T} = 22,000 \, \ell n \, \frac{2409}{\beta \sin \gamma_T}$$

where the altitude at which maximum target deceleration occurs is expressed in units of feet. From the preceding relationship we can see that the altitude of maximum target deceleration does not depend on target velocity but only on the ballistic coefficient and re-entry angle! This observation is in agreement with the simulation results of Fig. 17.4.

The closed-form solution for the altitude of maximum target deceleration is displayed as a function of the re-entry angle in Fig. 17.7. Here we can see that the altitude of maximum target deceleration increases with decreasing re-entry angle and decreasing ballistic coefficient. The theoretical results of Fig. 17.7, which neglects gravity and approximates the atmosphere below 30,000 ft, are in excellent agreement with the simulation results of Figs. 17.4–17.6.

Since the maximum target deceleration, expressed in units of g, is proportional to the maximum dynamic pressure and inversely proportional to the target ballistic coefficient, we obtain

$$\frac{a}{g} \bigg|_{\text{max}} = \frac{-Q_{\text{max}}}{\beta} = \frac{-0.5 \rho_{\text{max } Q} V_T^2 \big|_{\text{max } Q}}{\beta} = \frac{-0.5 \beta \sin \gamma_T}{22,000 g \beta} 0.606^2 V_{T_{\text{IC}}}^2$$

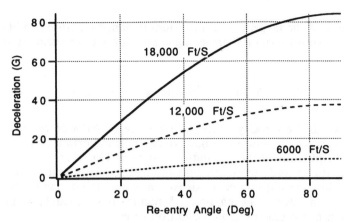

Fig. 17.8   Theory tells us that maximum deceleration is independent of ballistic coefficient.

where the negative sign indicates target deceleration rather than target acceleration. Simplification of the preceding formula yields

$$\left.\frac{a}{g}\right|_{max} = -2.6*10^{-7}V_{T_{IC}}^2 \sin \gamma_T$$

Thus we can see that maximum deceleration does not depend on the target ballistic coefficient but only on the velocity and re-entry angle as was also observed empirically in the simulation results displayed in Fig. 17.5! The maximum deceleration formula is displayed as a function of the re-entry angle in Fig. 17.8. We can see that the maximum target deceleration increases with increasing target velocity (actually as the square of target velocity) and increasing re-entry angle. The theoretical results of Fig. 17.8, which neglects gravity and approximates the atmosphere below 30,000 ft, are also in excellent agreement with the simulation results of Figs. 17.4–17.6.

Missile Aerodynamics

We have just observed the deceleration properties of a ballistic target as a function of its ballistic coefficient, velocity, altitude, and re-entry angle. In this section we want to get an idea of the generic acceleration capability of a pursuing interceptor so that we can better understand ballistic target engagements. In order to get a first-order estimate of the aerodynamic capability of a missile we shall treat the interceptor as a cylinder with length L and diameter D.

Basic aerodynamic theory tells us that the lift coefficient C_L for a cylinder is[4]

$$C_L = 2\alpha + \frac{1.5S_{plan}\alpha^2}{S_{ref}}$$

where α is the angle of attack or the angle between the missile body and its velocity vector. The planform area S_{plan} and reference area S_{ref} are related to the geometry of a cylinder according to

$$S_{\text{plan}} \approx LD$$

$$S_{\text{ref}} = \frac{\pi D^2}{4}$$

From Chapter 11 we know that the relationship between acceleration and the lift coefficient is given by

$$F = ma = \frac{Wn_L}{g} = QS_{\text{ref}}C_L$$

where W is the missile weight, n_L the lateral missile acceleration, g the acceleration of gravity, and Q the dynamic pressure or

$$Q = 0.5\rho V_M^2$$

The air density ρ can be found from the exponential approximation discussed in both this chapter and Chapter 11. Substitution of the lift coefficient and dynamic pressure into Newton's second law yields the formula for the acceleration capability in units of g of a flying telephone pole (or cylinder) as a function of missile velocity, angle of attack, and altitude (or air density) for a given missile length, diameter, and weight.

$$\frac{n_L}{g} = \frac{QS_{\text{ref}}C_L}{W} = \frac{0.5\rho V_M^2 S_{\text{ref}}}{W}\left[2\alpha + \frac{1.5 S_{\text{plan}}\alpha^2}{S_{\text{ref}}}\right]$$

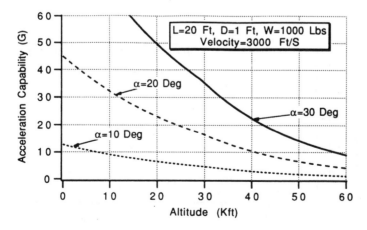

Fig. 17.9 Missile acceleration capability decreases with increasing altitude and decreasing angle of attack.

To get a better understanding of the preceding acceleration equation let us consider a numerical example in which the missile weighs 1000 lb, and is 20 ft long and 1 ft in diameter. Figure 17.9 displays the resultant acceleration capability of a cylindrical missile without wings and tails, using the preceding equation, with velocity 3000 ft/s and three different angles of attack as a function of altitude. We can see that interceptor acceleration capability decreases as altitude increases and as angle of attack decreases. This is why interceptors have a reduced acceleration capability at the higher altitudes and is also why they must operate at higher angles of attack at the higher altitudes in order to maintain the same acceleration capability they had at the lower altitudes. We can see that for this example, the missile has only a 7-g capability at 50-kft altitude if its maximum angle of attack is limited to 20 deg. Increasing the maximum angle of attack capability to 30 deg will double the acceleration capability of the interceptor at 50-kft altitude while reducing the maximum angle of attack by 10 deg halves the acceleration capability at that altitude.

Figure 17.10 shows that the interceptor acceleration capability increases as missile velocity increases. Increasing the missile velocity by 1000 ft/s at 50-kft altitude nearly doubles the interceptor acceleration capability. Reducing the interceptor velocity by 1000 ft/s approximately halves the acceleration capability of the interceptor at that altitude.

We can compare the lateral acceleration capability of our generic interceptor (or flying telephone pole) to the deceleration levels of the ballistic target. Figure 17.11 compares a 3000-ft/s cylindrical interceptor with a maximum angle-of-attack capability of 20 deg to a 6000-ft/s ballistic target with a 500-lb/ft^2 ballistic coefficient and a 45-deg re-entry angle. We can see that the interceptor acceleration capability increases with decreasing altitude whereas the target deceleration capability increases with decreasing altitude until it peaks at 40 kft. At 50-kft altitude the interceptor acceleration capability and target deceleration characteristics are matched at approximately 7 g. From an interceptor acceleration capability point of view,

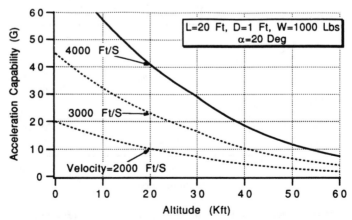

Fig. 17.10   Missile acceleration capability increases with increasing missile velocity.

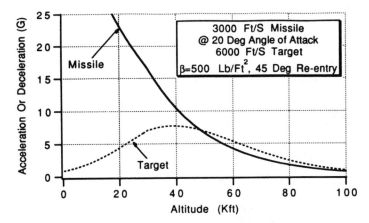

Fig. 17.11 Cylindrical interceptor acceleration capability matches target deceleration characteristics at 50-kft altitude.

the ideal intercept should take place at very low altitude where the interceptor has enormous capability and a considerable acceleration advantage over the target. In fact, from a missile point of view, the ideal intercept altitude is near sea level where the interceptor acceleration capability is largest and target deceleration capability smallest. However, practical considerations may require the interceptor to engage the ballistic target at much higher altitudes.

Intercepting a Ballistic Target

In this chapter we have spent considerable time simulating and understanding the properties of ballistic targets. We have seen that fast ballistic targets can go through tremendous deceleration levels as they re-enter the atmosphere. The component of target deceleration perpendicular to the line of sight appears as a target maneuver to a pursuing interceptor. In this section we will investigate some of the difficulties and potential solutions associated with an interceptor trying to engage a ballistic target within the atmosphere.

Listing 17.2 presents the FORTRAN source code for an engagement simulation involving a constant speed interceptor and decelerating ballistic target. At the beginning of the simulation the target is defined as having a 6000-ft/s initial velocity at 200-kft altitude with a re-entry angle of 45 deg and ballistic coefficient of 500 lb/ft^2. It is desired to fire an interceptor immediately and have the intercept take place at 50-kft altitude ($RT2DES = 50,000$).

Subroutine INITIAL is called to predict the location of the target at intercept ($RT1F$, $RT2F$) and to compute the time $TFDES$ it will take the target to reach the intercept altitude. Essentially subroutine INITIAL is a mini-simulation of the target. Note that we must tell this subroutine the estimated ballistic coefficient $BETEST$ of the target. If the estimated ballistic coefficient is in error, interceptor launch errors will result. From the

Listing 17.2   Ballistic target engagement simulation

```
        INTEGER STEP,APN
        APN = 0
        XNP = 3.
        RT1 = 0.
        RT2 = 200000.
        RM1 = 170000.
        RM2 = 0.
        VT = 6000.
        RT2DES = 50000.
        GAMTDEG = 45.
        BETA = 500.
        BETEST = 500.
        XNCLIMG = 999999.
        XNCLIM = XNCLIMG*32.2
        VT1 = VT*COS(GAMTDEG/57.3)
        VT2 = - VT*SIN(GAMTDEG/57.3)
        CALL INITIAL(RT2DES,RT1,RT2,VT1,VT2,BETEST,RT1F,RT2F,TFDES)
        RTM1F = RT1F - RM1
        RTM2F = RT2F - RM2
        GAMMDEG = 57.3*ATAN2(RTM2F,RTM1F)
        RTMF = SQRT(RTM1F**2 + RTM2F**2)
        VM = RTMF/TFDES
        WRITE(9,*)VM
        VM1 = VM*COS(GAMMDEG/57.3)
        VM2 = VM*SIN(GAMMDEG/57.3)
        RTM1 = RT1 - RM1
        RTM2 = RT2 - RM2
        RTM = SQRT(RTM1**2 + RTM2**2)
        VTM1 = VT1 - VM1
        VTM2 = VT2 - VM2
        VC = - (RTM1*VTM1 + RTM2*VTM2)/RTM
        T = 0.
        H = .01
        S = 0.
        XNC = 0.
        ZEMPLOS = 0.
        ZEM1 = 0.
        ZEM2 = 0.
5       IF(VC < 0.)GOTO 999
        IF(RTM < 1000.)THEN
          H = .0002
        ELSE
          H = .01
        ENDIF
        S = S + H
        RT1OLD = RT1
        RT2OLD = RT2
        VT1OLD = VT1
        VT2OLD = VT2
        RM1OLD = RM1
        RM2OLD = RM2
        VM1OLD = VM1
        VM2OLD = VM2
        STEP = 1
        GOTO 200
66      STEP = 2
        RT1 = RT1 + H*VT1
        RT2 = RT2 + H*VT2
        VT1 = VT1 + H*AT1
        VT2 = VT2 + H*AT2
        RM1 = RM1 + H*VM1
        RM2 = RM2 + H*VM2
        VM1 = VM1 + H*AM1
        VM2 = VM2 + H*AM2
        T = T + H
        GOTO 200
55      CONTINUE
        RT1 = .5*(RT1OLD + RT1 + H*VT1)
        RT2 = .5*(RT2OLD + RT2 + H*VT2)
        VT1 = .5*(VT1OLD + VT1 + H*AT1)
        VT2 = .5*(VT2OLD + VT2 + H*AT2)
        RM1 = .5*(RM1OLD + RM1 + H*VM1)
        RM2 = .5*(RM2OLD + RM2 + H*VM2)
        VM1 = .5*(VM1OLD + VM1 + H*AM1)
        VM2 = .5*(VM2OLD + VM2 + H*AM2)
        IF(S.GE..09999)THEN
          S = 0.
```

(Listing 17.2 continued on next page.)

Listing 17.2 (cont.) Ballistic target engagement simulation

```
            ATG = SQRT(AT1**2 + AT2**2)/32.2
            RT1K = RT1/1000.
            RT2K = RT2/1000.
            RM1K = RM1/1000.
            RM2K = RM2/1000.
            XNCG = XNC/32.2
            ATPLOSG = ATPLOS/32.2
            VM = SQRT(VM1**2 + VM2**2)
            CADEG = 180. − 57.3*ACOS((VT1*VM1 + VT2*VM2)/(VT*VM))
            WRITE(9,*)T,RT1K,RT2K,RM1K,RM2K,ATG,XNCG,ATPLOSG
          END IF
          GOTO 5
200       CONTINUE
          IF(RT2.LE.30000.)THEN
            RHO = .002378*EXP( − RT2/30000.)
          ELSE
            RHO = .0034*EXP( − RT2/22000.)
          ENDIF
          VT = SQRT(VT1**2 + VT2**2)
          Q = .5*RHO*VT**2
          GAMT = ATAN2( − VT2,VT1)
          AT1 = − 32.2*Q*COS(GAMT)/BETA
          AT2 = − 32.2 + 32.2*Q*SIN(GAMT)/BETA
          RTM1 = RT1 − RM1
          RTM2 = RT2 − RM2
          RTM = SQRT(RTM1**2 + RTM2**2)
          VTM1 = VT1 − VM1
          VTM2 = VT2 − VM2
          VC = − (RTM1*VTM1 + RTM2*VTM2)/RTM
          XLAM = ATAN2(RTM2,RTM1)
          XLAMD = (RTM1*VTM2 − RTM2*VTM1)/(RTM*RTM)
          ATPLOS = − AT1*SIN(XLAM) + AT2*COS(XLAM)
          IF(APN = 2)THEN
            CALL PREDICT(T,TFDES,RT1,RT2,VT1,VT2,RM1,RM2,VM1,
      1        VM2,BETEST,ZEM1,ZEM2)
            TGO = RTM/VC
            ZEMPLOS = − ZEM1*SIN(XLAM) + ZEM2*COS(XLAM)
            XNC = XNP*ZEMPLOS/TGO**2
          ELSEIF(APN = 1)THEN
            XNC = XNP*VC*XLAMD + .5*XNP*ATPLOS
          ELSE
            XNC = XNP*VC*XLAMD
          ENDIF
          IF(XNC > XNCLIM)XNC = XNCLIM
          IF(XNC < − XNCLIM)XNC = − XNCLIM
          AM1 = − XNC*SIN(XLAM)
          AM2 = XNC*COS(XLAM)
          IF(STEP − 1)66,66,55
999       CONTINUE
          ATG = SQRT(AT1**2 + AT2**2)/32.2
          RT1K = RT1/1000.
          RT2K = RT2/1000.
          RM1K = RM1/1000.
          RM2K = RM2/1000.
          XNCG = XNC/32.2
          ATPLOSG = ATPLOS/32.2
          VM = SQRT(VM1**2 + VM2**2)
          CADEG = 180. − 57.3*ACOS((VT1*VM1 + VT2*VM2)/(VT*VM))
          WRITE(9,*)T,RT1K,RT2K,RM1K,RM2K,ATG,XNCG,ATPLOSG
          WRITE(9,*)RTM
          PAUSE
          END

          SUBROUTINE INITIAL(RT2DES,RT1IC,RT2IC,VT1IC,VT2IC,BETA,
      1      RT1F,RT2F,TFDES)
          SAVE
          INTEGER STEP
          RT1 = RT1IC
          RT2 = RT2IC
          VT1 = VT1IC
          VT2 = VT2IC
          T = 0.
          H = .01
```

(Listing 17.2 continued on next page.)

Listing 17.2   (cont.) Ballistic target engagement simulation

```
   5   IF(RT2< = RT2DES)GOTO 999
       RT1OLD = RT1
       RT2OLD = RT2
       VT1OLD = VT1
       VT2OLD = VT2
       STEP = 1
       GOTO 200
  66   STEP = 2
       RT1 = RT1 + H*VT1
       RT2 = RT2 + H*VT2
       VT1 = VT1 + H*AT1
       VT2 = VT2 + H*AT2
       T = T + H
       GOTO 200
  55   CONTINUE
       RT1 = .5*(RT1OLD + RT1 + H*VT1)
       RT2 = .5*(RT2OLD + RT2 + H*VT2)
       VT1 = .5*(VT1OLD + VT1 + H*AT1)
       VT2 = .5*(VT2OLD + VT2 + H*AT2)
       GOTO 5
 200   CONTINUE
       IF(RT2.LE.30000.)THEN
          RHO = .002378*EXP( - RT2/30000.)
       ELSE
          RHO = .0034*EXP( - RT2/22000.)
       ENDIF
       VT = SQRT(VT1**2 + VT2**2)
       Q = .5*RHO*VT**2
       GAMT = ATAN2( - VT2,VT1)
       AT1 = - 32.2*Q*COS(GAMT)/BETA
       AT2 = - 32.2 + 32.2*Q*SIN(GAMT)/BETA
       IF(STEP - 1)66,66,55
 999   CONTINUE
       RT1F = RT1
       RT2F = RT2
       TFDES = T
       RETURN
       END

       SUBROUTINE PREDICT(TIC,TFDES,RT1IC,RT2IC,VT1IC,VT2IC,RM1IC
   1   ,RM2IC,VM1IC,VM2IC,BETA,ZEM1,ZEM2)
       SAVE
       INTEGER STEP
       RT1 = RT1IC
       RT2 = RT2IC
       VT1 = VT1IC
       VT2 = VT2IC
       RM1 = RM1IC
       RM2 = RM2IC
       VM1 = VM1IC
       VM2 = VM2IC
       T = TIC
       H = .1
       RTM1 = RT1 - RM1
       RTM2 = RT2 - RM2
       RTM = SQRT(RTM1**2 + RTM2**2)
       VTM1 = VT1 - VM1
       VTM2 = VT2 - VM2
       VC = - (RTM1*VTM1 + RTM2*VTM2)/RTM
   5   IF(T > = (TFDES - .00001))GOTO 999
       TGO = RTM/VC
       IF(TGO>1.)THEN
          H = .5
       ELSE
          H = .01
       ENDIF
       RT1OLD = RT1
       RT2OLD = RT2
       VT1OLD = VT1
       VT2OLD = VT2
       RM1OLD = RM1
```

(Listing 17.2 continued on next page.)

Listing 17.2   (cont.) Ballistic target engagement simulation

```
        RM2OLD = RM2
        VM1OLD = VM1
        VM2OLD = VM2
        STEP = 1
        GOTO 200
 66     STEP = 2
        RT1 = RT1 + H*VT1
        RT2 = RT2 + H*VT2
        VT1 = VT1 + H*AT1
        VT2 = VT2 + H*AT2
        RM1 = RM1 + H*VM1
        RM2 = RM2 + H*VM2
        VM1 = VM1 + H*AM1
        VM2 = VM2 + H*AM2
        T = T + H
        GOTO 200
 55     CONTINUE
        RT1 = .5*(RT1OLD + RT1 + H*VT1)
        RT2 = .5*(RT2OLD + RT2 + H*VT2)
        VT1 = .5*(VT1OLD + VT1 + H*AT1)
        VT2 = .5*(VT2OLD + VT2 + H*AT2)
        RM1 = .5*(RM1OLD + RM1 + H*VM1)
        RM2 = .5*(RM2OLD + RM2 + H*VM2)
        VM1 = .5*(VM1OLD + VM1 + H*AM1)
        VM2 = .5*(VM2OLD + VM2 + H*AM2)
        GOTO 5
200     CONTINUE
        IF(RT2.LE.30000.)THEN
           RHO = .002378*EXP(-RT2/30000.)
        ELSE
           RHO = .0034*EXP(-RT2/22000.)
        ENDIF
        VT = SQRT(VT1**2 + VT2**2)
        Q = .5*RHO*VT**2
        GAMT = ATAN2(-VT2,VT1)
        AT1 = -32.2*Q*COS(GAMT)/BETA
        AT2 = -32.2 + 32.2*Q*SIN(GAMT)/BETA
        AM1 = 0.
        AM2 = 0.
        RTM1 = RT1 - RM1
        RTM2 = RT2 - RM2
        RTM = SQRT(RTM1**2 + RTM2**2)
        VTM1 = VT1 - VM1
        VTM2 = VT2 - VM2
        VC = -(RTM1*VTM1 + RTM2*VTM2)/RTM
        IF(STEP - 1)66,66,55
999     CONTINUE
        ZEM1 = RT1 - RM1
        ZEM2 = RT2 - RM2
        RETURN
        END
```

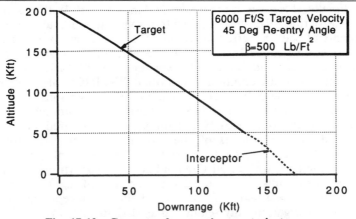

Fig. 17.12   Geometry for near inverse trajectory.

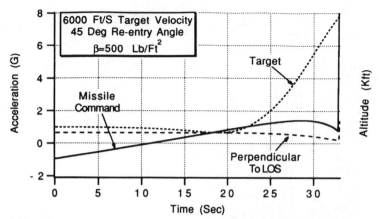

Fig. 17.13 Missile guidance commands are small because very little of target deceleration is perpendicular to line of sight.

outputs of subroutine INITIAL the interceptor launch angle *GAMMDEG* and total velocity *VM* are computed so that the interceptor will be on a perfect collision course with the target (assuming missile is fired when target is at 200-kft altitude). For simplicity, gravity and drag effects are not included on the interceptor.

The missile and target differential equations appear after statement label 200. The ballistic target differential equations are identical to those that have already been modeled in this chapter. The constant speed interceptor differential equations are identical to those found in Chapter 2. Three interceptor guidance options appear. The parameter *APN* determines which guidance law is used and *XNCLIMG* determines the interceptor acceleration capability (nominally set to infinity). If *APN* is 0 we get the proportional navigation guidance law, and if *APN* is 1 we get augmented proportional navigation where the augmented term includes the component of target acceleration (or deceleration) perpendicular to the line-of-sight *AT-PLOS*. Finally, if *APN* is 2, predictive guidance is used. With this guidance option, subroutine PREDICT is called to provide an estimate of the inertial components of the zero effort miss (*ZEM*1, *ZEM*2) given the target and missile states (*RT*1, *RT*2, *VT*1, *VT*2, *RM*1, *RM*2, *VM*1, *VM*2), the current time *T*, and the desired intercept time *TFDES* (derived from subroutine INITIAL). In addition, subroutine PREDICT also requires an estimate of the target ballistic coefficient *BETEST*. Subroutine PREDICT is a mini-engagement simulation in which the missile cannot maneuver (i.e., zero effort). Subroutine PREDICT terminates at the desired intercept time *TFDES* and the components of the miss distance or zero effort miss (*ZEM*1, *ZEM*2) are passed back to the main program. The resultant guidance command, with predictive guidance, is proportional to the computed zero effort miss perpendicular to the line of sight and inversely proportional to the square of time to go until intercept. In summary, proportional navigation only requires line-of-sight rate information, augmented proportional navigation requires range information in order to derive instantaneous target deceleration information, and predictive guidance requires both range information and an estimate of the target ballistic coefficient.

A nominal case was run in which a proportional navigation interceptor guides on a ballistic target as shown in Fig. 17.12. The geometry is considered near head-on and is also known as an inverse trajectory. The target trajectory is much longer than the missile trajectory since the target is traveling at a much higher velocity.

Figure 17.13 displays the important accelerations for the nominal case. We can see that the target deceleration is approximately 8 g at intercept (or 50 kft). This is in accordance with the ballistic target simulation results of Fig. 17.4 and the theoretical results of Fig. 17.8. We can see that since the engagement geometry is near inverse, there is no target deceleration perpendicular to the line of sight. From a missile point of view, the target does not appear to be maneuvering. Since the missile is initially on a collision course and there is no apparent target maneuver, very little acceleration is required by an interceptor using proportional navigation to hit the target.

A more stressing geometry was considered in which the interceptor is initially at 50 kft downrange ($RM1 = 50,000$). The engagement geometry, shown in Fig. 17.14, is no longer inverse. The intercept still takes place at 50-kft altitude and the missile has a speed of 3000 ft/s in order to be on a collision course. It is assumed that the interceptor has a maximum angle of attack limit of 20 deg yielding a maximum acceleration capability of 7 g ($XNCLIMG = 7$) at the intercept altitude based on the results of the previous section for our flying telephone pole ($W = 1000$ lb, $L = 20$ ft, $D = 1$ ft).

Figure 17.15 shows that the target deceleration is unchanged for this new engagement geometry and approaches 8 g near intercept. However, the component of target deceleration perpendicular to the line of sight is much larger than it was for the inverse trajectory case and that the peak value is in excess of 3 g. Therefore it is not surprising that the interceptor requires more than 7 g (missile acceleration limit) to hit the apparent 3-g target maneuver. Acceleration saturation follows causing a large miss distance.

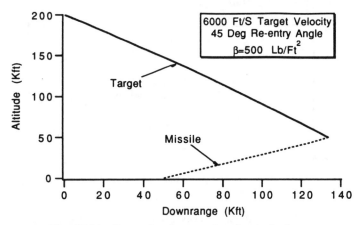

Fig. 17.14   Example of more stressing trajectory.

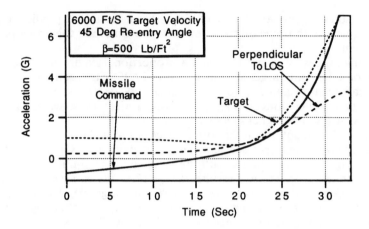

Fig. 17.15 More missile acceleration is required in stressing trajectory because more target deceleration is perpendicular to line of sight.

Augmented proportional navigation and predictive guidance can be used to relax the acceleration requirements of the interceptor under this stressing engagement geometry. Figure 17.16 shows that the previously unsuccessful intercept can be made successful with either advanced guidance law. However, both guidance laws require more information than does proportional navigation in order to operate successfully.

Summary

We have seen that ballistic targets can go through enormous decelerations as they re-enter the atmosphere. The magnitude of the target deceleration

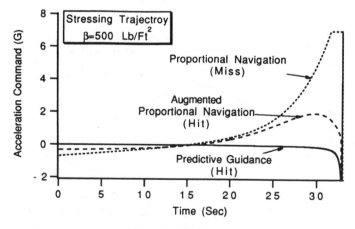

Fig. 17.16 More advanced guidance laws offer significant benefits for stressing trajectory.

increases with increasing target speed and increasing target re-entry angle. Any target deceleration that is perpendicular to the line of sight will appear as a target maneuver to the interceptor. It is best for a pursuing interceptor to engage the target on an inverse trajectory where little of the target deceleration is perpendicular to the line of sight.[5] If for practical reasons the target must be engaged under stressing conditions, the interceptor must be sized to have adequate acceleration capability if proportional navigation guidance is used. Advanced guidance laws such as predictive guidance can significantly relax the interceptor acceleration requirements if missile-target range information is available and if the target ballistic coefficient is either known or can be estimated accurately.

References

[1]Riezenman, M., "Revising The Script After Patriot," *IEEE Spectrum*, Sept. 1991, pp. 49–52.

[2]Canavan, G., "Strategic Defense In Past And Future Conflicts," *The Journal of Practical Applications In Space*, Vol. 2, No. 3, Spring 1991, pp. 1–42.

[3]Regan, F., *Re-Entry Vehicle Dynamics*, AIAA Education Series, AIAA, New York, 1984.

[4]Jerger, J. J., *System Preliminary Design*, Van Nostrand, Princeton, NJ, 1960.

[5]Lin, C. F., *Modern Navigation, Guidance, and Control Processing*, Prentice-Hall, Englewood Cliffs, NJ, 1991.

Chapter 18

Extended Kalman Filtering and Ballistic Coefficient Estimation

Introduction

WE have seen in the previous chapter that knowledge of the target ballistic coefficient could be used in advanced guidance laws such as predictive guidance to relax the interceptor acceleration requirements in stressing engagement geometries. In addition, knowledge of the target ballistic coefficient is required for fire control due to the importance of accurate intercept point predictions in launching the interceptor on a collision course. Therefore the accurate estimation of the ballistic coefficient of a target re-entering the atmosphere is very important for both guidance and fire control purposes. In this chapter we shall show, in detail, how extended Kalman filtering concepts can be applied to ballistic coefficient estimation.

Theoretical Equations[1]

In order to apply extended Kalman filtering techniques it is first necessary to describe the real world by a set of nonlinear differential equations. One standard dynamical model of the system or real world is given by

$$\dot{x} = f(x) + w$$

where x is a vector of the system states, $f(x)$ is a nonlinear function of those states, and w is a random zero mean process. The process noise matrix describing the random process w for the preceding model is given by

$$Q = E(ww^T)$$

Finally, the measurement equation, required for the application of an extended Kalman filter, is considered a nonlinear function of the states according to

$$z = h(x) + v$$

where v is a random zero mean process described by the measurement noise matrix R which is defined as

$$R = E(vv^T)$$

For systems in which the measurements are discrete we can rewrite the measurement equation as

$$z_k = h(x_k) + v_k$$

The discrete measurement noise matrix R_k consists of measurement noise source variances. Since the system and measurement equations are nonlinear, a first-order approximation is used in the Ricatti equations for the systems dynamic matrix F and measurement matrix H. The matrices are related to the system and measurement equations according to

$$F = \left. \frac{\partial f(x)}{\partial x} \right|_{x = \hat{x}}$$

$$H = \left. \frac{\partial h(x)}{\partial x} \right|_{x = \hat{x}}$$

The fundamental matrix, also required for the Ricatti equations, is usually approximated by the first two terms of the Taylor series expansion $\exp(FT_s)$ and is given by

$$\Phi_k \approx I + FT_s$$

where T_s is the sampling time and I is the identity matrix. Note that the approximations to the systems dynamics matrix, measurement matrix, and fundamental matrix are time-varying and nonlinear because they depend on the system state estimates. The Ricatti equations, needed for the computation of the Kalman gains, are still given by the matrix difference equations of Chapter 9 and are repeated for convenience as

$$M_k = \Phi_k P_{k-1} \Phi_k{}^T + Q_k$$

$$K_k = M_k H^T [HM_k H^T + R_k]^{-1}$$

$$P_k = (I - K_k H)M_k$$

where P_k is a covariance matrix representing errors in the state estimates before an update and M_k is the covariance matrix representing errors in the state estimates after an update. Since Φ_k and H are nonlinear functions of the state estimates, the Kalman gains can not be computed off line as is possible with a linear Kalman filter. The discrete process noise matrix Q_k can still be found from the continuous process noise matrix Q and the fundamental matrix according to

$$Q_k = \int_0^{T_s} \Phi(\tau) Q \Phi^T(\tau) d\tau$$

If the dynamical model of a linear Kalman filter is matched to the real world, the covariance matrix P_k can not only be used to calculate Kalman gains but can also provide exact predictions of the errors in the state estimates. The extended Kalman filter offers no such guarantees and in fact the Ricatti equation covariance matrix may indicate excellent performance projections when the filter is performing poorly or is even broken.

The preceding approximations only have to be used in the computation of Kalman gains. The actual extended Kalman filtering equations do not have to use those approximations but instead can be written in terms of the nonlinear measurement equation where the new estimate is the old estimate plus a gain times a residual or

$$\hat{x}_{k+1} = \hat{x}_k + K_k[z_k - h(\hat{x}_k)]$$

In the preceding equation the residual is the difference between the actual measurement and the nonlinear measurement equation. The new state estimates do not have to be propagated forward from the old estimate with the fundamental matrix but instead can be obtained directly by integrating the actual nonlinear differential equations at each sampling interval. For example, Euler integration (see Appendix A) can be applied to the nonlinear system differential equations yielding

$$\hat{\dot{x}} = f(\hat{x}_{k-1})$$

$$\hat{x}_k = \hat{x}_{k-1} + \hat{\dot{x}}T_s$$

where state estimates are used instead of the actual states and the sampling time T_s is used as an integration step size.

Differential Equation for One-Dimensional Ballistic Target

To illustrate how extended Kalman filtering concepts can be applied let us consider the one-dimensional tracking problem originally considered by Gelb[1] and illustrated in Fig. 18.1. In this example a ballistic target is falling on a straight line path directly toward a surface-based tracking radar. Only drag and gravity act on the ballistic target. This is equivalent to the case in the previous chapter in which the target re-entry angle is 90 deg. In this problem the tracking radar measures the distance from the radar to the target every T_s s. In addition, the tracking radar has the incentive of working well in this application because it is directly in the path of the ballistic target.

We can see from Fig. 18.1 that drag acts upward whereas gravity acts downward. The total acceleration acting on the ballistic target can be expressed in terms of a zero lift drag C_{D0} or a ballistic coefficient β as

$$\frac{\mathrm{d}V_{T2}}{\mathrm{d}t} = \frac{F_{\text{drag}}}{m} - g = \frac{QS_{\text{ref}}C_{D0}\,g}{W} - g = \frac{Qg}{\beta} - g$$

where g is the acceleration of gravity and Q is the dynamic pressure. The dynamic pressure can be expressed in terms of the air density ρ and the

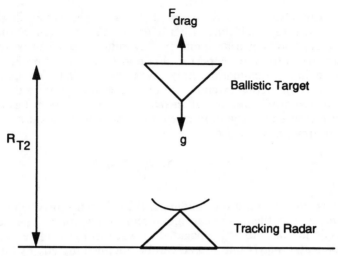

Fig. 18.1 Forces acting on a one-dimensional ballistic target.

ballistic target velocity V_{T2} as

$$Q = 0.5\rho V_{T2}^2$$

For purposes of simplicity we can assume that the air density is measured in slug/ft³ and is exponentially related to altitude R_{T2} measured in feet according to

$$\rho = 0.0034e^{-\frac{R_{T2}}{22,000}}$$

and ignore the fact that the coefficients of the exponential approximation change below 30,000 ft. If we assume that the ballistic coefficient of the target is a constant, its derivative must be zero. Therefore the three differential equations which govern the one-dimensional ballistic target can be summarized as

$$\dot{R}_{T2} = V_{T2}$$

$$\dot{V}_{T2} = \frac{0.0034e^{-\frac{R_{T2}}{22,000}}g V_{T2}^2}{2\beta} - g$$

$$\dot{\beta} = 0$$

If we want to account for the fact that there may be a large uncertainty in the ballistic coefficient or that it might actually change with time we could modify the third state equation to be

$$\dot{\beta} = u_s$$

where u_s is white process noise with spectral density Φ_s.

Extended Kalman Filter for One-Dimensional Ballistic Target

In the previous section we showed that the differential equations governing the one-dimensional ballistic target could be expressed in terms of position R_{T2}, velocity V_{T2}, and ballistic coefficient β. Therefore a plausible candidate for the system state vector is

$$x = \begin{bmatrix} R_{T2} \\ V_{T2} \\ \beta \end{bmatrix}$$

In the Gelb example the tracking radar measures position directly. Therefore the measurement equation in this example is a linear function of the states or

$$R_{T2}^* = R_{T2} + v_k = \underbrace{[1\ 0\ 0]}_{H} \begin{bmatrix} R_{T2} \\ V_{T2} \\ \beta \end{bmatrix} + v_k$$

where the uncertainty in the position measurement is simply the scalar variance or

$$R_k = E(v_k v_k^T) = \sigma_k^2$$

The systems dynamics matrix can be obtained from the three differential equations describing the target according to the definition of the theoretical section as

$$F = \left.\frac{\partial f(x)}{\partial x}\right|_{x=\hat{x}} = \begin{bmatrix} \dfrac{\partial \dot{R}_{T2}}{\partial R_{T2}} & \dfrac{\partial \dot{R}_{T2}}{\partial V_{T2}} & \dfrac{\partial \dot{R}_{T2}}{\partial \beta} \\[2mm] \dfrac{\partial \dot{V}_{T2}}{\partial R_{T2}} & \dfrac{\partial \dot{V}_{T2}}{\partial V_{T2}} & \dfrac{\partial \dot{V}_{T2}}{\partial \beta} \\[2mm] \dfrac{\partial \dot{\beta}}{\partial R_{T2}} & \dfrac{\partial \dot{\beta}}{\partial V_{T2}} & \dfrac{\partial \dot{\beta}}{\partial \beta} \end{bmatrix}_{x=\hat{x}}$$

After taking partial derivatives of the three system differential equations we obtain

$$F = \begin{bmatrix} 0 & 1 & 0 \\[2mm] \dfrac{-\hat{\rho} g \hat{V}_{T2}^2}{44{,}000\hat{\beta}} & \dfrac{\hat{\rho} g \hat{V}_{T2}}{\hat{\beta}} & \dfrac{-\hat{\rho} g \hat{V}_{T2}^2}{2\hat{\beta}} \\[2mm] 0 & 0 & 0 \end{bmatrix}$$

where the estimated air density is given by

$$\hat{\rho} = 0.0034 e^{-\frac{\hat{R}_{T2}}{22,000}}$$

The fundamental matrix can be obtained from the systems dynamics matrix as

$$\mathbf{\Phi}_k \approx \mathbf{I} + \mathbf{F}T_s = \begin{bmatrix} 1 & T_s & 0 \\ \dfrac{-\hat{\rho}g\hat{V}_{T2}^2 T_s}{44,000\hat{\beta}} & 1 + \dfrac{\hat{\rho}g\hat{V}_{T2}T_s}{\hat{\beta}} & \dfrac{-\hat{\rho}g\hat{V}_{T2}^2 T_s}{2\hat{\beta}} \\ 0 & 0 & 1 \end{bmatrix}$$

whereas the continuous process noise matrix can be found from

$$\mathbf{Q} = \begin{bmatrix} 0 & 0 & 0 \\ 0 & 0 & 0 \\ 0 & 0 & \Phi_s \end{bmatrix}$$

where Φ_s is the spectral density of the process noise. The discrete process noise matrix can be obtained from the continuous process noise matrix according to the relationship

$$\mathbf{Q}_k = \int_0^{T_s} \mathbf{\Phi}(\tau)\mathbf{Q}\mathbf{\Phi}^T(\tau)\mathrm{d}\tau$$

If we substitute τ for T_s in the previous fundamental matrix approximation we get

$$\mathbf{\Phi}(\tau) = \begin{bmatrix} 0 & \tau & 0 \\ f_{21}\tau & 1 + f_{22}\tau & f_{23}\tau \\ 0 & 0 & 1 \end{bmatrix}$$

where f_{21}, f_{22}, and f_{23} are defined in terms of the state estimates as

$$f_{21} = \frac{-\hat{\rho}g\hat{V}_{T2}^2}{44,000\hat{\beta}}$$

$$f_{22} = \frac{\hat{\rho}g\hat{V}_{T2}}{\hat{\beta}}$$

$$f_{23} = \frac{-\hat{\rho}g\hat{V}_{T2}^2}{2\hat{\beta}}$$

Assuming that f_{21}, f_{22}, and f_{23} are approximately constant over the sampling interval we can integrate with respect to τ and obtain the discrete process noise matrix as

$$Q_k = \Phi_s \begin{bmatrix} 0 & 0 & 0 \\ 0 & f_{23}^2 \dfrac{T_s^3}{3} & f_{23}\dfrac{T_s^2}{2} \\ 0 & f_{23}\dfrac{T_s^2}{2} & T_s \end{bmatrix}$$

If we want to neglect process noise in our model then Φ_s is set to zero.

Since the measurement noise matrix R_k is a scalar in this three-state system, there will only be three Kalman gains at each update (i.e., K_1, K_2, and K_3). The Kalman gains will also depend on the state estimates because the fundamental matrix depends on the system state estimates. As was mentioned previously, the new extended Kalman filter states will simply be the old states propagated forward by Euler integration, plus a gain times a residual, or

$$\text{Residual} = R_{T2}^* - \hat{R}_{T2_{k-1}} - \overline{R_{T2}}T_s$$

$$\hat{R}_{T2_k} = \hat{R}_{T2_{k-1}} + \overline{R_{T2}}T_s + K_1^*\text{Residual}$$

$$\hat{V}_{T2_k} = \hat{V}_{T2_{k-1}} + \overline{V_{T2}}T_s + K_2^*\text{Residual}$$

$$\hat{\beta}_k = \hat{\beta}_{k-1} + K_3^*\text{Residual}$$

The barred quantities in the preceding set of difference equations represent the derivatives required by Euler integration and are obtained directly from the nonlinear system equations as

$$\overline{R_{T2}} = \hat{V}_{T2_{k-1}}$$

$$\overline{V_{T2}} = \frac{0.0034e^{-\frac{\hat{R}T2_{k-1}}{22,000}}\, g\hat{V}_{T2_{k-1}}^2}{2\hat{\beta}_{k-1}} - g$$

We now have all of the equations necessary to simulate an extended Kalman filter for the one-dimensional tracking problem.

Numerical Example

The same numerical example considered by Gelb[1] is presented here in which a target with ballistic coefficient 500 lb/ft^2 is initially at 100-kft altitude and is traveling downward at a speed of 6000 ft/s. A surface-based radar measures the range from the radar to the target (i.e., altitude in this example) every 0.05 s with measurement variance 500 ft^2. The initial estimate of position is 100,025 ft (25-ft error), of velocity is 6150 ft/s (150-ft/s error), and of the ballistic coefficient is 800 lb/ft^2 (300-lb/ft^2 error). Uncertainties in the initial state estimates are also reflected in the initial covariance matrix. The first diagonal element of the initial covariance matrix represents the variance of the error in the initial estimate of position and is taken to be the variance of the measurement noise or 500 ft². The second diagonal element of the initial covariance matrix represents the variance of the error in the initial estimate of velocity and is taken to be 20,000 ft²/s² (slightly less than 150²). The third diagonal element of the initial covariance matrix represents the variance of the error in the initial estimate of ballistic coefficient and is taken to the square of the initial error in estimating the ballistic coefficient or 90,000 lb²/ft⁴ (or 300²). The off-diagonal elements of the initial covariance matrix are set to zero and it is assumed that there is no process noise.

Listing 18.1 presents the resultant one-dimensional extended Kalman filter for ballistic coefficient estimation derived in the previous section. Matrix subroutines[2] are included for the solution of the discrete Ricatti equations so that we do not have to manually perform all matrix operations as was done in Chapter 9. In addition, double-precision arithmetic is used to ensure the accuracy of the results. The initial conditions for the actual ballistic target, filter state estimates, and initial covariance matrix reflect the nominal case. Since $Q33$ (or Φ_s) is set to zero there is no process noise. The second-order Runge-Kutta numerical integration technique is used for solving the actual nonlinear differential equations representing the ballistic target with integration step size of 0.001 s. The exponential approximation for the air density, used in calculating the drag on the actual ballistic target, matches the assumption made in the extended Kalman filter derivation. The actual ballistic coefficient and its estimate are printed every sampling interval. In addition, the actual errors in the estimate of the ballistic coefficient are computed and compared to the square root of the third diagonal element of the covariance matrix. This diagonal element represents the extended Kalman filter's internal prediction of the error in the estimate of the ballistic coefficient.

The nominal case of Listing 18.1 was run and the estimated and actual ballistic coefficients are displayed versus altitude in Fig. 18.2. At 100-kft

Listing 18.1   One-dimensional extended Kalman filter for ballistic coefficient estimation

```
IMPLICIT REAL*8 (A–H)
IMPLICIT REAL*8 (O–Z)
REAL*8 PHI(3,3),P(3,3),M(3,3),PHIP(3,3),PHIPPHIT(3,3),GAIN(3,1)
REAL*8 Q(3,3),HMAT(1,3),HM(1,3),MHT(3,1)
REAL*8 PHIT(3,3)
REAL*8 PHTHPR(3,3),HMHT(1,1),HT(3,1),KH(3,3),IDN(3,3),IKH(3,3)
INTEGER ORDER,STEP
RT2 = 100000.
VT2 = —6000.
BETA = 500.
RT2H = 100025.
VT2H = —6150.
BETAH = 800.
OPEN(2,STATUS = 'NEW',FILE = 'COVFIL')
OPEN(1,STATUS = 'NEW',FILE = 'DATFIL')
ORDER = 3
```

(Listing 18.1 continued on next page.)

```
                TS = .05
                TF = 30.
                Q33 = 0./TF
                T = 0.
                S = 0.
                H = .001
                SIGNOISE = SQRT(500.)
                DO 1000 I = 1,ORDER
                DO 1000 J = 1,ORDER
                  PHI(I,J) = 0.
                  P(I,J) = 0.
                  Q(I,J) = 0.
                  IDN(I,J) = 0.
     1000       CONTINUE
                IDN(1,1) = 1.
                IDN(2,2) = 1.
                IDN(3,3) = 1.
                P(1,1) = SIGNOISE*SIGNOISE
                P(2,2) = 20000.
                P(3,3) = 300.**2
                DO 1100 I = 1,ORDER
                HMAT(1,I) = 0.
                HT(I,1) = 0.
     1100       CONTINUE
                HMAT(1,1) = 1.
                HT(1,1) = 1.
       10       IF(RT2 < 0.)GOTO 999
                RT2OLD = RT2
                VT2OLD = VT2
                STEP = 1
                GOTO 200
       66       STEP = 2
                RT2 = RT2 + H*RT2D
                VT2 = VT2 + H*VT2D
                T = T + H
                GOTO 200
       55       CONTINUE
                RT2 = .5*(RT2OLD + RT2 + H*RT2D)
                VT2 = .5*(VT2OLD + VT2 + H*VT2D)
                S = S + H
                IF(S.LE.(TS—.00001))GOTO 10
                S = 0.
                RHOH = .0034*EXP(—RT2H/22000.)
                F21 = —32.2*RHOH*VT2H*VT2H/(2.*22000.*BETAH)
                F22 = RHOH*32.2*VT2H/BETAH
                F23 = —RHOH*32.2*VT2H*VT2H/(2.*BETAH*BETAH)
                PHI(1,1) = 1.
                PHI(1,2) = TS
                PHI(2,1) = F21*TS
                PHI(2,2) = 1. + F22*TS
                PHI(2,3) = F23*TS
                PHI(3,3) = 1.
                Q(2,2) = F23*F23*Q33*TS*TS*TS/3.
                Q(2,3) = F23*Q33*TS*TS/2.
                Q(3,2) = Q(2,3)
                Q(3,3) = Q33*TS
                CALL MATTRN(PHI,ORDER,ORDER,PHIT)
                CALL MATMUL(PHI,ORDER,ORDER,P,ORDER,ORDER,PHIP)
                CALL MATMUL(PHIP,ORDER,ORDER,PHIT,ORDER,ORDER,PHIPPHIT)
                CALL MATADD(PHIPPHIT,ORDER,ORDER,Q,M)
                CALL MATMUL(HMAT,1,ORDER,M,ORDER,ORDER,HM)
                CALL MATMUL(HM,1,ORDER,HT,ORDER,1,HMHT)
                HMHTR = HMHT(1,1) + SIGNOISE*SIGNOISE
                HMHTRINV = 1./HMHTR
                CALL MATMUL(M,ORDER,ORDER,HT,ORDER,1,MHT)
                DO 150 I = 1,ORDER
                GAIN(I,1) = MHT(I,1)*HMHTRINV
      150       CONTINUE
                CALL MATMUL(GAIN,ORDER,1,HMAT,1,ORDER,KH)
                CALL MATSUB(IDN,ORDER,ORDER,KH,IKH)
                CALL MATMUL(IKH,ORDER,ORDER,M,ORDER,ORDER,P)
                XNOISE = GAUSS(SIGNOISE)
                RT2DB = VT2H
                VT2DB = .0034*32.2*VT2H*VT2H*EXP(—RT2H/22000.)/(2.*BETAH)—32.2
                RES = RT2 + XNOISE—(RT2H + RT2DB*TS)
                RT2H = RT2H + RT2DB*TS + GAIN(1,1)*RES
                VT2H = VT2H + VT2DB*TS + GAIN(2,1)*RES
                BETAH = BETAH + GAIN(3,1)*RES
```

(Listing 18.1 continued on next page.)

```
            ERRY = RT2—RT2H
            SP11 = SQRT(P(1,1))
            ERRV = VT2—VT2H
            SP22 = SQRT(P(2,2))
            ERRBETA = BETA—BETAH
            SP33 = SQRT(P(3,3))
            RT2K = RT2/1000.
            WRITE(9,*)T,RT2K,RT2,RT2H,VT2,VT2H,BETA,BETAH
            WRITE(1,*)T,RT2K,RT2,RT2H,VT2,VT2H,BETA,BETAH
            WRITE(2,*)T,RT2K,ERRY,SP11,—SP11,ERRV,SP22,—SP22,ERRBETA,SP33,
      1     —SP33
            GOTO 10
      200   CONTINUE
            RT2D = VT2
            VT2D = .0034*32.2*VT2*VT2*EXP(—RT2/22000.)/(2.*BETA)—32.2
            IF(STEP—1)66,66,55
      999   CONTINUE
            PAUSE
            END

            REAL*8 FUNCTION GAUSS(SIGMA)
            IMPLICIT REAL*8(A–H)
            IMPLICIT REAL*8(O–Z)
            INTEGER TOOLBX
            INTEGER RANDOM
            PARAMETER (RANDOM = Z'86140000')
            DATA YNORM/ 2.1579186E—5/
            IACUM   = 0
            DO 100 I = 1,2
            IX   = TOOLBX(RANDOM)
            IY   = TOOLBX(RANDOM)
      100   IACUM   = IACUM + IX + IY + TOOLBX(RANDOM)
            GAUSS   = IACUM*YNORM*SIGMA
            RETURN
            END

            SUBROUTINE MATTRN(A,IROW,ICOL,AT)
            IMPLICIT REAL*8 (A–H)
            IMPLICIT REAL*8 (O–Z)
            REAL*8 A(IROW,ICOL),AT(ICOL,IROW)
            DO 105 I = 1,IROW
            DO 105 J = 1,ICOL
            AT(J,I) = A(I,J)
      105   CONTINUE
            RETURN
            END

            SUBROUTINE MATMUL(A,IROW,ICOL,B,JROW,JCOL,C)
            IMPLICIT REAL*8 (A–H)
            IMPLICIT REAL*8 (O–Z)
            REAL*8 A(IROW,ICOL),B(JROW,JCOL),C(IROW,JCOL)
            DO 110 I = 1,IROW
            DO 110 J = 1,JCOL
              C(I,J) = 0.
              DO 110 K = 1,ICOL
                C(I,J) = C(I,J) + A(I,K)*B(K,J)
      110   CONTINUE
            RETURN
            END

            SUBROUTINE MATADD(A,IROW,ICOL,B,C)
            IMPLICIT REAL*8 (A–H)
            IMPLICIT REAL*8 (O–Z)
            REAL*8 A(IROW,ICOL),B(IROW,ICOL),C(IROW,ICOL)
            DO 120 I = 1,IROW
            DO 120 J = 1,ICOL
              C(I,J) = A(I,J) + B(I,J)
      120   CONTINUE
            RETURN
            END

            SUBROUTINE MATSUB(A,IROW,ICOL,B,C)
            IMPLICIT REAL*8 (A–H)
            IMPLICIT REAL*8 (O–Z)
            REAL*8 A(IROW,ICOL),B(IROW,ICOL),C(IROW,ICOL)
            DO 120 I = 1,IROW
            DO 120 J = 1,ICOL
              C(I,J) = A(I,J)—B(I,J)
      120   CONTINUE
            RETURN
            END
```

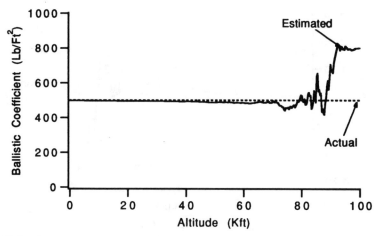

Fig. 18.2   After a while extended Kalman filter is able to estimate ballistic coefficient.

altitude (i.e., beginning of the estimation process) the initial estimate of the ballistic coefficient is on the high side by 300 lb/ft^2. As the target descends in altitude, the filter's estimate of the ballistic coefficient appears to be continually improving. Below 60-kft altitude, the extended Kalman filter has an excellent estimate of the target's ballistic coefficient.

Figure 18.3 compares single flight results for the actual error in the estimate of the ballistic coefficient (labeled simulation) with the theoretical predictions of the covariance matrix (labeled σ_{THEORY}). Note that the covariance matrix thinks that as the ballistic target descends in altitude and more measurements are taken, the estimates continually improve (or the error in the estimate of the ballistic coefficient goes to zero). Therefore it appears

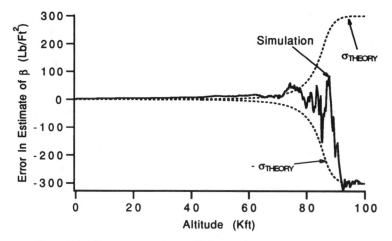

Fig. 18.3   Theory and single flight results appear to agree.

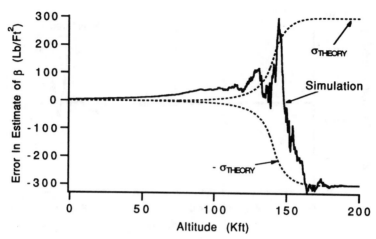

Fig. 18.4   Extended Kalman filter unable to estimate ballistic coefficient above 150 kft.

that the single flight results agree with the covariance matrix predictions in this example.

We can rerun the nominal case but start at 200-kft altitude rather than 100-kft altitude. Figure 18.4 indicates that both the theoretical and actual errors in the estimate of the ballistic coefficient do not improve from the initial guess until the ballistic target descends below 150-kft altitude. The lack of estimation capability is due to the absence of drag in the high altitude regime. In other words, at the higher altitudes the ballistic coefficient is not observable from just position measurements. This result can be very important if we must predict the future location of the ballistic target in the atmosphere based on estimates of the ballistic coefficient at very high altitudes.

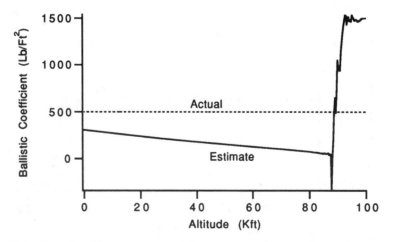

Fig. 18.5   Extended Kalman filter breaks if we severely overestimate ballistic coefficient.

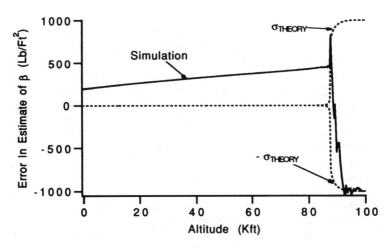

Fig. 18.6   Extended Kalman filter does not even realize it is broken.

Another case was run where the ballistic target started at the nominal altitude of 100 kft. However, this time the initial estimate of the ballistic coefficient was 1500 lb/ft^2 (i.e., 1000-lb/ft^2 error) rather than 800 lb/ft^2 (i.e., 300-lb/ft^2 error). The third diagonal element of the initial covariance matrix was increased to 1000^2 to reflect the larger initial uncertainty in the ballistic coefficient. Figure 18.5 shows that under these circumstances, the extended Kalman filter is unable to estimate the ballistic coefficient before the ballistic target hits the tracking radar. Unlike a linear Kalman filter, the extended Kalman filter's performance is highly dependent on initial conditions!

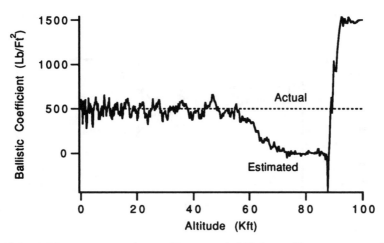

Fig. 18.7   Adding process noise enables extended Kalman filter to recover from overestimating ballistic coefficient.

Figure 18.6 shows that even though the extended Kalman filter is not able to estimate the ballistic coefficient when we initially severely overestimate the ballistic coefficient by 1000 lb/ft^2, the filter's covariance matrix predictions indicate that the errors in the estimate of the ballistic coefficient are near zero. Apparently this filter does not even realize when it is broken! Therefore we can see that although the covariance matrix is required for Kalman gain computation, its theoretical predictions are not always useful!

In the preceding example the filter is not able to recover when we initially overestimate the ballistic coefficient by a large amount. The filter's lack of robustness is due to a zero process noise matrix (i.e., $Q_k = 0$). When the process noise is zero the filter thinks it is very smart (i.e., it must have a terrific dynamical model) and eventually stops looking at the measurements. Under these circumstances the filter changes from an extended Kalman filter to an arrogant Kalman filter! Process noise was added to the filter with value $\Phi_s = 1000^2/30$ to indicate large uncertainty in the ballistic coefficient model. Figure 18.7 shows that when the process noise is added, the estimated and actual ballistic coefficients converge after a while.

Figure 18.8 now shows that when realistic process noise is added to reflect large uncertainties, the single flight results and covariance matrix predictions of the error in the estimate of ballistic coefficient are in agreement after the ballistic target has descended below 60 kft. Although the estimates are not great initially, they are continually improving.

We can now revisit the nominal results of Fig. 18.3 when, without a process noise matrix, the arrogant Kalman filter thought its estimates were continually improving as more measurements were taken. If we rerun the nominal case with $\Phi_s = 300^2/30$ to reflect the fact that we have a smaller uncertainty in our knowledge of the ballistic coefficient we get more sobering results as shown in Fig. 18.9. We can see that after a while the filter's estimate of the ballistic does not improve. However, our initial uncertainty

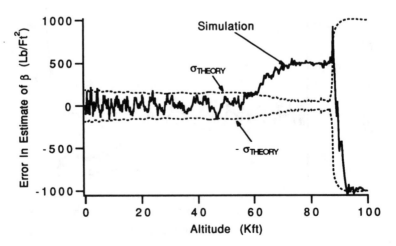

Fig. 18.8 Adding process noise makes covariance matrix predictions more meaningful.

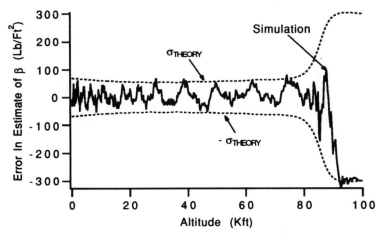

Fig. 18.9   Nominal results are worse when there is process noise but filter is more robust.

in our estimate of the ballistic coefficient has been reduced from the initial guess of 300 lb/ft² to an estimate with slightly under 100 lb/ft² of error. In addition, we now have a filter which is more robust to initialization errors.

Summary

We have seen, using a simplified extended Kalman filter, the difficulties in estimating a target's ballistic coefficient—especially at high altitude where there is very little drag. We have also observed that using zero process noise in the filter gain computations leads to overly optimistic performance projections and makes the filter fragile in the presence of large initialization errors. Adding process noise to the filter's gain computation appears to be the engineering fix when there is large uncertainty. Although adding process noise degrades filter performance under benign conditions, it also enables the filter to perform adequately under more stressing conditions.

References

[1]Gelb, A., *Applied Optimal Estimation*, MIT Press, Cambridge, MA, 1974.
[2]Wolf, P. M., and Koelling, C. P., *Basic Engineering, Science and Business Programs for the Apple II and IIe*, Bradly Communications Co. Inc., Bowie, MD, 1984.

Chapter 19

Ballistic Target Challenges

Introduction

IN this chapter we shall integrate many of the text's concepts in order to illustrate, from a miss distance point of view, additional reasons why ballistic targets are challenging. First, new miss distance formulas will be derived in order to show how the miss due to noise depends on the closing velocity and guidance system time constant. Next, a new formula will be presented showing how the minimum possible guidance system time constant depends on radome slope, closing velocity, and missile turning rate time constant. For head-on scenarios, numerical examples will be presented showing how low-closing velocity aircraft engagements and high-closing velocity ballistic target engagements yield different miss distances even though the error sources may be the same.

Miss Distance Due to Noise

In Chapter 3 closed-form solutions for various deterministic error sources were derived for a single time constant proportional navigation guidance system. We demonstrated in Chapter 6 that although the miss distances generated with the low-order model of the guidance system were serious underestimates of the actual miss, the closed-form solutions were useful because the miss distance normalization factors did not change for higher order guidance systems. We shall use the same methodology in obtaining miss distance formulas due to noise error sources. First we shall obtain noise miss distance closed-form solutions for the single time constant guidance system and then use the brute force method to extend those solutions for a fifth-order binomial guidance system.

As was done with deterministic error sources in Chapter 3, we shall also use the method of adjoints for finding miss distance formulas due to various noise error sources found in homing guidance systems.[1] The noise sources considered are those usually associated with radar homing missiles. Figure 19.1 presents a generalized model of the homing loop similar to Fig. 3.16 except this time the error sources are random rather than deterministic. The first error source is glint or scintillation noise and is caused by random fluctuations of the target radar return. The spectral density of this error source is related to the physical dimensions of the target. Strictly speaking, glint should not be modeled as white noise since it may be highly correlated.[2] For semiactive systems, in which the target is illuminated by a transmitter not on the interceptor, range dependent noise is the thermal

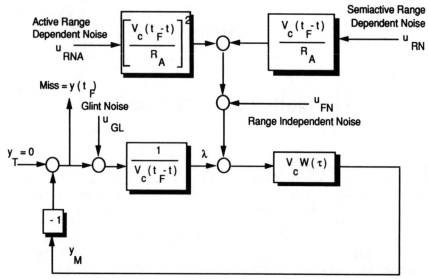

Fig. 19.1   Generalized proportional navigation guidance system with noise sources.

noise produced in the interceptor radar receiver according to the radar range equation. In this simplified model the spectral density of the noise is defined at a reference range R_A. The noise is proportional to the distance from the missile to the target and goes to zero at intercept.[3] For active systems in which the target is illuminated by a transmitter on the interceptor, range dependent noise is proportional to the square of the distance from the missile to the target.[4] Other noise sources are usually lumped together and termed range independent noise.

The spectral densities for the various white noise error sources are given by

$$\Phi_{FN} = \text{Spectral Density of } u_{FN}$$

$$\Phi_{RN} = \text{Spectral Density of } u_{RN}$$

$$\Phi_{RNA} = \text{Spectral Density of } u_{RNA}$$

$$\Phi_{GL} = \text{Spectral Density of } u_{GL}$$

The generalized homing loop adjoint model, which appears in Fig. 19.2, can be found from Fig. 19.1 by using the rules of adjoints developed in Chapters 3 and 4 and then applying some block diagram manipulation. Note that all white noise inputs of the original system become outputs in the adjoint system by squaring, integrating, and multiplying by the spectral density of each of the white noise error sources. Critical points in the adjoint block diagram have been labeled $H(\tau)$, $g(\tau)$, and $f(\tau)$.

To illustrate how noise miss distance formulas can be derived, let us consider a single time constant guidance system with a navigation ratio of

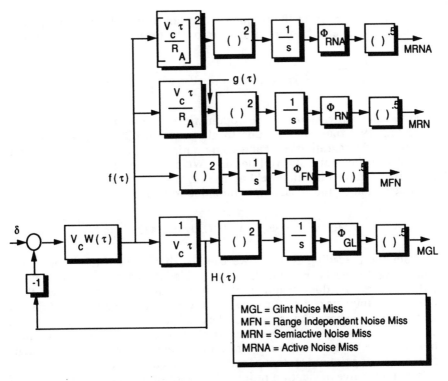

Fig. 19.2   Generalized adjoint homing loop model.

3. Recall from Chapter 3 that for this case W can be represented in the frequency domain as

$$W(s) = \frac{3}{s(1 + sT)}$$

where T is the guidance system time constant. We showed in Chapter 3 that $1 - H$ could be found in the frequency domain from W according to the relationship

$$1 - H(s) = e^{\int W ds} = \frac{s^3}{(s + 1/T)^3}$$

Solving for H by algebraic manipulation of the preceding equation yields

$$H(s) = \frac{1 + 3sT + 3s^2 T^2}{(1 + sT)^3}$$

We can convert H from the frequency domain to the adjoint time domain by taking the inverse Laplace transform of the preceding equation yielding

$$H(\tau) = \frac{e^{\frac{-\tau}{T}}}{T}\left[3 - \frac{3\tau}{T} + \frac{\tau^2}{2T^2}\right]$$

where τ can be interpreted as the homing time or time of flight. We can see from Fig. 19.2 that the miss due to glint noise (MGL) can be found by squaring and integrating $H(\tau)$ and then multiplying the result by the square root of the glint noise spectral density. We can simplify matters and integrate from zero to infinity yielding the closed-form solution for the standard deviation of the steady-state miss due to white glint noise as[5]

$$MGL_{N'=3} = \Phi_{GL}^{0.5}\sqrt{\int_0^\infty H^2(\tau)d\tau} = 1.44T^{-0.5}\Phi_{GL}^{0.5}$$

From the preceding formula we can see that unlike most other error source results we have studied, if the guidance system time constant is reduced, the miss due to glint noise will increase! We can also see that, unlike deterministic error source results, the miss due to glint noise does not go to zero as the homing time approaches infinity. In other words, there will always be some miss distance due to glint noise, no matter how much homing time we have. Closed-form miss distance formulas for the single time constant guidance system can also be derived, in a similar manner, for different effective navigation ratios. The steady-state standard deviation of the miss due to glint noise for effective navigation ratios of four and five can be found to be

$$MGL_{N'=4} = 1.71T^{-0.5}\Phi_{GL}^{0.5}$$

$$MGL_{N'=5} = 1.94T^{-0.5}\Phi_{GL}^{0.5}$$

Note that the miss distance normalization factors do not change with different effective navigation ratios. However the miss distance coefficients due to glint noise increase slightly with increasing effective navigation ratio.

In order to find the steady-state standard deviation of the miss due to range independent noise (MFN), it is first necessary to square and integrate the expression $(1 - H)V_cW$ as can be seen from Fig. 19.2. For a single time constant guidance system with an effective navigation ratio of 3, $(1 - H)V_cW$ in the frequency domain becomes

$$[1 - H(s)]V_cW(s) = \frac{3V_cs^2}{T(s + 1/T)^4}$$

We can convert $(1 - H)V_cW$ to the adjoint time domain by taking the inverse Laplace transform of the preceding equation obtaining

$$f(\tau) = \mathcal{L}^{-1}\{[1 - H(s)]V_cW(s)\} = \frac{3V_c\tau e^{-\tau/T}}{T}\left[1 - \frac{\tau}{T} + \frac{\tau^2}{6T^2}\right]$$

Squaring and integrating the preceding expression from zero to infinity yields the steady-state formula for the standard deviation of the miss distance due to range independent noise as

$$MFN_{N'=3} = \Phi_{FN}^{0.5} \sqrt{\int_0^\infty f^2(\tau)d\tau} = 0.532 V_c T^{0.5} \Phi_{FN}^{0.5}$$

where V_c is the closing velocity. In this case we can see that there is now a geometry dependence on the miss distance because the miss is proportional to closing velocity. Higher closing velocity engagement scenarios will yield more miss distance due to range independent noise. On the other hand, we can see from the preceding expression that, unlike the glint noise case, reducing the guidance system time constant will decrease the miss due to range independent noise. Closed-form miss distance formulas for range independent noise in a single time constant guidance system can also be derived in a similar manner for different effective navigation ratios. The steady-state standard deviation of the miss due to range independent noise for effective navigation ratios of four and five can be found to be

$$MFN_{N'=4} = 0.561 V_c T^{0.5} \Phi_{FN}^{0.5}$$

$$MFN_{N'=5} = 0.588 V_c T^{0.5} \Phi_{FN}^{0.5}$$

Here again we can see that there is a slight increase in the miss distance coefficients as the effective navigation ratio increases.

We can find the standard deviation of the steady-state miss due to semiactive range dependent noise (MRN) by squaring and integrating $g(\tau)$ as shown in Fig. 19.2. The expression for $g(\tau)$ can be found from $f(\tau)$ as

$$g(\tau) = \frac{V_c \tau f(\tau)}{R_A} = \frac{3 V_c^2 \tau^2 e^{-\tau/T}}{R_A T} \left[1 - \frac{\tau}{T} + \frac{\tau^2}{6T^2} \right]$$

Squaring and integrating $g(\tau)$ from zero to infinity yields the standard deviation of the steady-state miss due to semiactive range dependent noise for an effective navigation ratio of three as

$$MRN_{N'=3} = \Phi_{RN}^{0.5} \sqrt{\int_0^\infty g^2(\tau)d\tau} = \frac{1.06 V_c^2 T^{1.5} \Phi_{RN}^{0.5}}{R_A}$$

where R_A is taken to be a reference range. We can see that the closing velocity and time constant dependence of the miss is much greater for semiactive range dependent noise than it was for range independent noise. Steady-state miss distance formulas for semiactive range dependent noise in a single time constant guidance system can be found for higher effective navigation ratios in a similar way and are

$$MRN_{N'=4} = \frac{1.10 V_c^2 T^{1.5} \Phi_{RN}^{0.5}}{R_A}$$

$$MRN_{N'=5} = \frac{1.15 V_c^2 T^{1.5} \Phi_{RN}^{0.5}}{R_A}$$

Again we can see that the miss distance coefficents increase slightly with increasing effective navigation ratio. For active systems miss distance formulas can also be derived for a single time constant system. The steady-state standard deviation of the miss due to active range dependent noise ($MRNA$) for effective navigation ratios of three, four, and five are

$$MRNA_{N'=3} = \frac{4.66 V_c^3 T^{2.5} \Phi_{RNA}^{0.5}}{R_A^2}$$

$$MRNA_{N'=4} = \frac{4.68 V_c^3 T^{2.5} \Phi_{RNA}^{0.5}}{R_A^2}$$

$$MRNA_{N'=5} = \frac{4.82 V_c^3 T^{2.5} \Phi_{RNA}^{0.5}}{R_A^2}$$

We can see that the closing velocity and time constant dependence for active range dependent noise is even stronger than it was for semiactive range dependent noise.

Fifth-Order Binomial Guidance System Miss Distances

In Chapter 6 we saw that once we had closed-form solutions for a single time constant guidance system, we could obtain solutions for higher order systems by the method of brute force because the miss distance normalization factors remained unchanged with system order (i.e., only coefficients change). In this section we shall use the same method to get noise miss distance formulas for higher order systems. The adjoint model for a fifth-order binomial guidance system, first shown in Fig. 6.5, has been modified to include the noise error sources discussed in the previous section and is redrawn in Fig. 19.3. Deterministic error sources are not shown in this diagram. Note that the basic model is unchanged. We have only added new outputs to correspond to the miss due to range independent noise, glint noise, and both semiactive and active range dependent noise. This has been accomplished by squaring and integrating signals proportional to the adjoint variable $y1$ shown in Fig. 19.3.

Adjoint simulation Listing 6.1 has also been modified for noise miss distance calculations and appears in Listing 19.1. The noise spectral densities, closing velocity, guidance system time constant, and reference range have been set to unity so that we can calculate the coefficients for the noise miss distance normalization factors.

Using the method of brute force with the adjoint simulation of Listing 19.1, Table 19.1 was generated for the standard deviation of the steady-state noise miss distances for the fifth-order binomial proportional navigation guidance system under consideration. We can see from Table 19.1 that although the miss distance normalization factors are the same as they were for a single time constant guidance system, the miss distance coefficients are an order of magnitude larger! This means that the miss distances for the higher order system will also be an order of magnitude greater than that of the single time constant guidance system. In addition, we can see that unlike

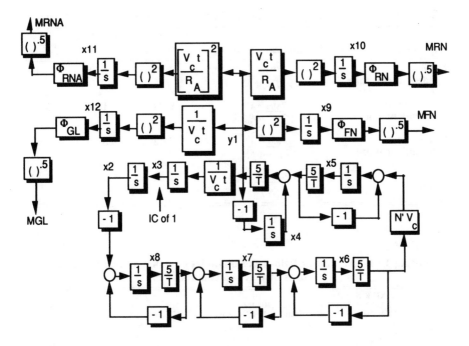

Fig. 19.3   Adjoint of fifth-order binomial guidance system for noise miss distance calculations.

the single time constant guidance system, the effective navigation ratio has a strong influence on the miss distance for the higher order system. Increasing the effective navigation ratio significantly increases the miss distance due to noise.

Minimum Guidance System Time Constant

We saw in Chapter 6 that the radome aberration effects create an unwanted feedback path in the guidance system which can cause stability problems. In the presence of radome slope the guidance system transfer function can be derived from Fig. 6.21 and is given by

$$\frac{n_L}{\dot{\lambda}} = \frac{N'V_c}{\left[1 + \dfrac{sT}{5}\right]^5 + \dfrac{N'V_cR}{V_M}(1 + T_\alpha s)}$$

where R is the radome slope, V_M the missile velocity, T_α an aerodynamic parameter known as the turning rate time constant, and T the guidance system time constant. We can see from the preceding equation that if the radome slope is zero the guidance system transfer function reduces to a fifth-order binomial. For different combinations of guidance system parameters, simulation experiments conducted in Chapter 6 showed that the

Table 19.1 Miss distance formulas for fifth-order binomial guidance system

Error source	Normalization factor	Miss coefficient		
		$N' = 3$	$N' = 4$	$N' = 5$
Range independent noise	$\dfrac{\sigma_{Miss}}{V_c T^{0.5}\Phi_{FN}^{0.5}}$	3.04	5.08	8.19
Semiactive range dependent noise	$\dfrac{\sigma_{Miss} R_A}{V_c^2 T^{1.5}\Phi_{RN}^{0.5}}$	9.47	18.4	33.7
Active range dependent noise	$\dfrac{\sigma_{Miss} R_A^2}{V_c^3 T^{2.5}\Phi_{RNA}^{0.5}}$	41.3	89.4	182
Glint noise	$\dfrac{\sigma_{Miss} T^{0.5}}{\Phi_{GL}^{0.5}}$	1.68	2.35	3.21

Listing 19.1 Adjoint of fifth-order binomial guidance system for noise miss distance calculations

```
      INTEGER STEP
      DATA XNP,TAU,TF,VC/ 3.,1.,10.,1./
      DATA PHIFN,PHIRN,PHIRNA,PHIGL,RA/1.,1.,1.,1.,1./
      T = 0.
      S = 0.
      TP = T + .00001
      X2 = 0
      X3 = 1
      X4 = 0
      X5 = 0.
      X6 = 0.
      X7 = 0.
      X8 = 0.
      X9 = 0.
      X10 = 0.
      X11 = 0.
      X12 = 0.
      H = .02
10    IF(TP > (TF—.00001))GOTO 999
      S = S + H
      X2OLD = X2
      X3OLD = X3
      X4OLD = X4
      X5OLD = X5
      X6OLD = X6
      X7OLD = X7
      X8OLD = X8
      X9OLD = X9
      X10OLD = X10
      X11OLD = X11
      X12OLD = X12
      STEP = 1
      GOTO 200
66    STEP = 2
      X2 = X2 + H*X2D
      X3 = X3 + H*X3D
      X4 = X4 + H*X4D
      X5 = X5 + H*X5D
      X6 = X6 + H*X6D
      X7 = X7 + H*X7D
      X8 = X8 + H*X8D
      X9 = X9 + H*X9D
      X10 = X10 + H*X10D
      X11 = X11 + H*X11D
      X12 = X12 + H*X12D
```

(Listing 19.1 continued on next page.)

Listing 19.1   (cont.) Adjoint of fifth-order binomial guidance system for noise miss distance calculations

```
        TP = TP + H
        GOTO 200
55      CONTINUE
        X2 = (X2OLD + X2)/2 + .5*H*X2D
        X3 = (X3OLD + X3)/2 + .5*H*X3D
        X4 = (X4OLD + X4)/2 + .5*H*X4D
        X5 = (X5OLD + X5)/2 + .5*H*X5D
        X6 = (X6OLD + X6)/2 + .5*H*X6D
        X7 = (X7OLD + X7)/2 + .5*H*X7D
        X8 = (X8OLD + X8)/2 + .5*H*X8D
        X9 = (X9OLD + X9)/2 + .5*H*X9D
        X10 = (X10OLD + X10)/2 + .5*H*X10D
        X11 = (X11OLD + X11)/2 + .5*H*X11D
        X12 = (X12OLD + X12)/2 + .5*H*X12D
        IF(S < .09999)GOTO 10
        S = 0.
        XMFN = SQRT(X9*PHIFN)
        XMFN = SQRT(X10*PHIFN)
        XMFN = SQRT(X11*PHIFN)
        XMGL = SQRT(X12*PHIGL)
        WRITE(9,*)TP,XMFN,XMRN,XMRNA,XMGL
        GOTO 10
200     CONTINUE
        X2D = X3
        Y1 = 5.*(5.(X5/TAU + X4)/TAU
        TGO = TP + .00001
        X3D = Y1/(VC*TGO)
        X4D = —Y1
        X5D = —5.*X5/TAU + 5.*X6*XNP*VC/TAU
        X6D = —5.*X6/TAU + 5.*X7/TAU
        X7D = —5.*X7/TAU + 5.*X8/TAU
        X8D = —5.*X8/TAU—X2
        X9D = Y1**2
        X10D = (Y1*VC*TGO/RA)**2
        X11D = (Y1*((VC*TGO/RA)**2))**2
        X12D = (Y1/VC*TGO))**2
        IF (STEP-1) 66,66,55
999     CONTINUE
        PAUSE
        END
```

guidance system can be unstable. One can show mathematically[6] that if the ratio of the turning rate time constant to the guidance system time constant is greater than unity or

$$\frac{T_\alpha}{T} > 1$$

then the guidance system transfer will be stable only if the following inequality is satisfied

$$-0.79 < \frac{N'V_c R T_\alpha}{V_M T} < 2.07$$

If the radome slope is negative, we can find from the preceding inequality that the minimum guidance system time constant to yield a stable guidance system is

$$T_{\min} = \frac{N'V_c R T_\alpha}{0.79 V_M}$$

We can see from the preceding relationship that engagements with larger closing velocities (i.e., ballistic targets) or those taking place at high altitudes (i.e., larger turning rate time constant) will require a larger guidance system time constant in order to keep the guidance system stable. However, larger guidance system time constants will also tend to increase the miss distance.

Missile Turning Rate Time Constant[7,8]

We saw in Chapter 6 that the missile turning rate time constant T_α had a significant interaction with radome effects. The missile turning rate time constant can be defined as the amount of time it takes to turn the missile flight path angle γ through an equivalent angle of attack α or

$$T_\alpha = \frac{\alpha}{\dot\gamma} = \frac{\alpha V_M}{n_L}$$

where V_M is missile velocity and n_L is missile acceleration. We showed in Chapter 11 the relationship between the lift coefficient C_L and missile acceleration. Substitution of those relationships into the preceding expression yields

$$T_\alpha = \frac{\alpha V_M W}{g Q S_{ref} C_L}$$

where W is the missile weight, S_{ref} is the missile reference area, g is the acceleration of gravity, and Q is the dynamic pressure. If we assume our missile to be a cylinder or flying telephone pole, we showed in Chapter 17 that the lift coefficient could be expressed as

$$C_L = 2\alpha + \frac{1.5 S_{plan} \alpha^2}{S_{ref}}$$

where S_{plan} is the missile planform area. Substitution of the lift coefficient expression into the turning rate time constant formula and expressing the dynamic pressure in more detail yields

$$T_\alpha = \frac{2W}{g \rho V_M S_{ref} \left[2 + \dfrac{1.5 S_{plan} \alpha}{S_{ref}} \right]}$$

We can see that the turning rate time constant depends on altitude (or air density ρ), missile velocity, and angle of attack.

Consider the cylindrical missile of Chapter 17 which was 20 ft long, 1 ft in diameter, and weighed 1000 lb. Figure 19.4 shows that for a missile velocity of 3000 ft/s, the turning rate time constant increases with increasing altitude and decreasing angle of attack. At 50-kft altitude and 20-deg angle of attack the turning rate time constant is approximately 5 s.

We can display the turning rate time constant as a function of altitude for different missile velocities as is done in Fig. 19.5. We can see that the missile

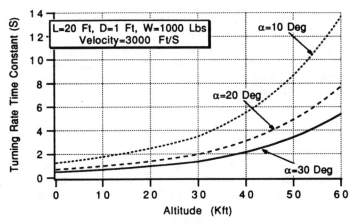

Fig. 19.4 **Turning rate time constant increases with increasing altitude and decreasing angle of attack.**

turning rate time constant increases with decreasing missile velocity. We have already seen in Chapter 6 that larger turning rate time constants exacerbate the radome slope stability problem. In summary, we can say that the radome stability problem will be greatest at the high-altitude, low-missile-velocity portion of the flight envelope.

Checking Minimum Guidance System Time Constant Constraints

To illustrate the increased stability problem caused by ballistic targets let us compare missile acceleration profiles for both aircraft and ballistic targets at 50-kft altitude. We demonstrated in Chapter 17 that a cylindrical missile (i.e., $W = 1000$ lb, $L = 20$ ft, and $D = 1$ ft) has a 7-g capability for

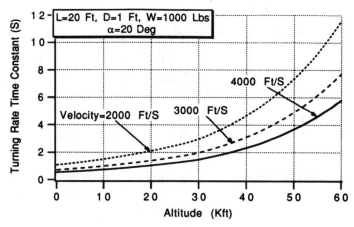

Fig. 19.5 **Turning rate time constant increases with decreasing missile velocity.**

a speed of 3000 ft/s and an angle of attack of 20 deg. In addition, let us assume the radome slope for the interceptor is -0.01. If we consider a head-on case in which an aircraft target is traveling at 1000 ft/s, the resultant closing velocity will be 4000 ft/s. In this chapter we showed that the minimum guidance system time constant permitted for a fifth-order binomial proportional navigation guidance system is

$$T_{min} = \frac{N' V_c R T_\alpha}{0.79 V_M}$$

From Fig. 19.4 we can see that the turning rate time constant for the cylindrical interceptor is 5 s at this flight condition. Therefore the minimum guidance system time constant at this flight condition becomes

$$T_{min} = \frac{3*4000*0.01*5}{0.79*3000} = 0.25 \text{ s}$$

In other words, the interceptor guidance system time constant must be greater than 0.25 s when engaging this particular aircraft threat.

To test the preceding theoretical limit on the minimum allowable interceptor guidance system time constant against the aircraft threat, our multiple run simulation of a fifth-order binomial guidance system with radome effects (Listing 6.2) was modified to investigate single flights. Listing 19.2 shows that the resultant single flight simulation is set up to monitor the relative separation between missile and target y and the acceleration command n_c. The nominal inputs for the aircraft threat we are considering include the 7-g missile acceleration command limit, 4000-ft/s closing velocity, 5-s turning rate time constant, 3000-ft/s interceptor speed, -0.01 radome slope, and effective navigation ratio of 3. A 1-g target maneuver is considered as the only error source.

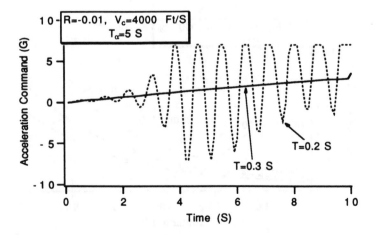

Fig. 19.6   Simulation and theory agree for aircraft threat.

The nominal case was run and the guidance system time constant was made a parameter. Figure 19.6 shows that when the guidance system time constant is 0.2 s (less than the minimum permissible time constant) the acceleration command oscillates between $\pm 7\,g$, indicating that the guidance system is indeed unstable. Increasing the guidance system time constant to 0.3 s (more than the minimum permissible time constant) stabilizes the acceleration command. The resultant acceleration profile is a monotonically increasing straight line, as would be expected for the response due to a step target maneuver. Thus the theoretical formula for the minimum guidance system time constant and the simulation results of Listing 19.2 appear to be in agreement.

If we fly an inverse trajectory with a 3000 ft/s interceptor against a 6000 ft/s ballistic target the resultant closing velocity becomes 9000 ft/s. The minimum guidance system time constant at this flight condition reduces to

$$T_{min} = \frac{3*9000*0.01*5}{0.79*3000} = 0.57 \text{ s}$$

which indicates that the minimum permissible interceptor guidance system time constant against this particular ballistic threat must be greater than 0.57 s. In other words, for the case considered, the missile guidance system time constant must be much greater against a ballistic threat than it has to be against an aircraft threat because of the much higher closing velocities.

The simulation of Listing 19.2 was rerun for the case in which the closing velocity was 9000 ft/s and the guidance system time constant was again made a parameter. Figure 19.7 shows that when the guidance system time constant is 0.5 s (less than the minimum permissible time constant) the acceleration command oscillates between $\pm 7\,g$, indicating that the guidance system is unstable. When the guidance system time constant is increased to 0.7 s (more than the minimum permissible time constant) the acceleration command is stable and approximately monotonically increasing as would be expected for the response due to a step target acceleration. We can also see by comparing Figs. 19.6 and 19.7 that the frequency of oscillation depends on the closing velocity.

Miss Due to Noise for Aircraft and Ballistic Targets

In this chapter we have presented formulas for the miss distance due to various noise sources and have also presented stability requirements for the minimum guidance system time constant in a fifth-order binomial proportional navigation guidance system. In this section we shall illustrate, via a numerical example, how the miss distance due to noise increases when the threat changes from an aircraft to a ballistic target.

All of the formulas for the noise miss distances depended on the spectral density Φ of the noise. Often we talk about noise with a standard deviation σ entering a guidance system every T_s seconds. A useful approximation relating the noise spectral density to the standard deviation is given by

$$\Phi = \sigma^2 T_s$$

Listing 19.2   Simulation of homing loop with radome effects

```
              VC = 4000.
              XNT = 32.2
              XNCLIMG = 7.
              YIC = 0.
              VM = 3000.
              HEDEG = 0.
              TAU = .3
              XNP = 3.
              TA = 5.
              R = —.01
              TF = 10.
              Y = YIC
              YD = —VM*HEDEG/57.3
              YDIC = YD
              XNL = 0.
              ELAMDH = 0.
              X4 = 0.
              X5 = 0.
              TH = 0.
              THH = 0.
              T = 0.
              H = .01
              S = 0.
              XNCLIM = XNCLIMG*32.2
      10      IF(T > (TF—.0001))GOTO 999
              YOLD = Y
              YDOLD = YD
              XNLOLD = XNL
              ELAMDHOLD = ELAMDH
              X4OLD = X4
              X5OLD = X5
              THOLD = TH
              THHOLD = THH
              STEP = 1
              GOTO 200
      66      STEP = 2
              Y = Y + H*YD
              YD = YD + H*YDD
              XNL = XNL + H*XNLD
              ELAMDH = ELAMDH + H*ELAMDHD
              X4 = X4 + H*X4D
              X5 = X5 + H*X5D
              TH = TH + H*THD
              THH = THH + H*THHD
              T = T + H
              GOTO 200
      55      CONTINUE
              Y = .5*(YOLD + Y + H*YD)
              YD = .5*(YDOLD + YD + H*YDD)
              XNL = .5*(XNLOLD + XNL + H*XNLD)
              ELAMDH = .5*(ELAMDHOLD + ELAMDH + H*ELAMDHD)
              X4 = .5*(X4OLD + X4 + H*X4D)
              X5 = .5*(X5OLD + X5 + H*X5D)
              TH = .5*(THOLD + TH + H*THD)
              THH = .5*(THHOLD + THH + H*THHD)
              S = S + H
              IF(S > .09999)THEN
                 S = 0.
                 WRITE(9,*)T,Y,XNC/32.2
              ENDIF
              GOTO 10
      200     CONTINUE
              TGO = TF—T + .00001
              XLAM = Y/(VC*TGO)
              EPS = XLAM—TH—THH + R*THH
              DD = 5.*EPS/TAU
              ELAMDHD = 5.*(DD—ELAMDH)/TAU
              XNC = XNP*VC*ELAMDH
              IF(XNC > XNCLIM)XNC = XNCLIM
              IF(XNC < —XNCLIM)XNC = —XNCLIM
              X4D = 5.*(XNC—X4)/TAU
              X5D = 5.*(X4–X5)/TAU
              XNLD = 5.*(X5—XNL)/TAU
              THD = XNL/VM + TA*XNLD/VM
              THHD = DD—THD
              YDD = XNT—XNL
              IF(STEP—1)66,66,55
      999     CONTINUE
              PAUSE
              END
```

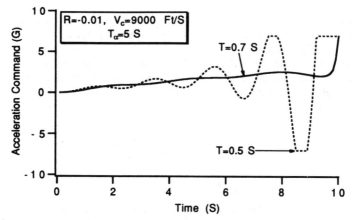

Fig. 19.7 Simulation and theory agree for ballistic threat.

where Φ is measured in units^2/Hz, σ is measured in units, and T_s is measured in seconds. This relationship is identical to the one we used for simulating white noise in Chapter 4 with the sampling time T_s being replaced by the integration interval.

Let us consider an example in which range independent noise with standard deviation 0.001 rad enters a proportional navigation guidance system ($N' = 3$) every 0.01 s.[4,8] The miss distance formula for an effective navigation ratio of 3 expressed in terms of the noise standard deviation can be found from Table 19.1 and is given by

$$\sigma_{\text{Miss}}\bigg|_{\substack{\text{Range}\\\text{Independent}\\\text{Noise}}} = 3.04 V_c T^{0.5} \sigma_{FN} T_s^{0.5}$$

For the aircraft threat with a closing velocity of 4000 ft/s and a minimum guidance time constant of 0.25 s, the minimum miss due to range independent noise is

$$\sigma_{\text{Miss}}\bigg|_{\substack{\text{Range}\\\text{Independent}\\\text{Noise}}} = 3.04*4000*0.25^{0.5}*0.001*0.01^{0.5} = 0.6 \text{ ft}$$

whereas for the ballistic threat with closing velocity of 9000 ft/s and a minimum guidance time constant of 0.57 s, the minimum miss is

$$\sigma_{\text{Miss}}\bigg|_{\substack{\text{Range}\\\text{Independent}\\\text{Noise}}} = 3.04*9000*0.57^{0.5}*0.001*0.01^{0.5} = 2.1 \text{ ft}$$

Although the noise miss is more than three times larger in the ballistic target case than it was in the aircraft threat case, the miss due to range independent noise is negligible.

Let us now consider the influence of semiactive range dependent noise on both targets. The standard deviation of the miss due to semiactive range dependent noise for an effective navigation ratio of three can be found from Table 19.1 as

$$\sigma_{\text{Miss}}\bigg|_{\substack{\text{Semiactive} \\ \text{Range} \\ \text{Dependent} \\ \text{Noise}}} = \frac{9.47 V_c^2 T^{1.5} \sigma_{RN} T_s^{0.5}}{R_A}$$

We notice from the preceding formula that the dependence on closing velocity and guidance system time constant is more significant than it was in the range dependent noise case. Let us now consider a case in which there is 0.02 rad of semiactive noise at 30,000 ft entering the guidance system every 0.01 s.[4,7] For the aircraft threat with a closing velocity of 4000 ft/s and a minimum guidance time constant of 0.25 s, the minimum miss due to semiactive range dependent noise is

$$\sigma_{\text{Miss}}\bigg|_{\substack{\text{Semiactive} \\ \text{Range} \\ \text{Dependent} \\ \text{Noise}}} = \frac{9.47*4000^2*0.25^{1.5}*0.02*0.01^{0.5}}{30,000} = 1.3 \text{ ft}$$

whereas for the ballistic threat with closing velocity of 9000 ft/s and a minimum guidance time constant of 0.57 s, the minimum miss is

$$\sigma_{\text{Miss}}\bigg|_{\substack{\text{Semiactive} \\ \text{Range} \\ \text{Dependent} \\ \text{Noise}}} = \frac{9.47*9000^2*0.57^{1.5}*0.02*0.01^{0.5}}{30,000} = 22 \text{ ft}$$

We can see that the miss due to semiactive noise is very large against ballistic targets because of the strong dependence on closing velocity and guidance system time constant. For this example the ballistic threat miss was nearly 20 times greater than the aircraft threat miss!

Finally, let us now consider the influence of active range dependent noise on both targets. The standard deviation of the miss due to active range dependent noise for an effective navigation ratio of three can be found from Table 19.1 as

$$\sigma_{\text{Miss}}\bigg|_{\substack{\text{Activre} \\ \text{Range} \\ \text{Dependent} \\ \text{Noise}}} = \frac{41.3 V_c^3 T^{2.5} \sigma_{RNA} T_s^{0.5}}{R_A^2}$$

We notice from the preceding formula that the dependence on closing velocity and guidance system time constant is even more significiant than it was in the semiactive noise case. Let us now consider a case in which there is 0.02 rad of active noise at 30,000 ft entering the guidance system every 0.01 s.[4,7] For the aircraft threat with a closing velocity of 4000 ft/s and a minimum guidance time constant of 0.25 s, the minimum miss due to active range dependent noise is

$$\left. \sigma_{\text{Miss}} \right|_{\substack{\text{Active} \\ \text{Range} \\ \text{Dependent} \\ \text{Noise}}} = \frac{41.3*4000^3*0.25^{2.5}*0.02*0.01^{0.5}}{30,000^2} = 0.18 \text{ ft}$$

whereas for the ballistic threat with closing velocity of 9000 ft/s and a minimum guidance time constant of 0.57 s, the minimum miss is

$$\left. \sigma_{\text{Miss}} \right|_{\substack{\text{Active} \\ \text{Range} \\ \text{Dependent} \\ \text{Noise}}} = \frac{41.3*9000^3*0.57^{2.5}*0.02*0.01^{0.5}}{30,000^2} = 16.4 \text{ ft}$$

Although the active noise miss is less than the semiactive noise miss it is nearly 100 times larger for the ballistic threat than for the aircraft threat because the miss depends on the cube of closing velocity and the 2.5 power of the guidance system time constant.

Summary

We have shown that from a noise induced miss distance point of view, ballistic targets are more challenging than the aircraft threat. The high-closing velocity of the ballistic target engagement significantly increases the minimum guidance system time constant required for radome slope stability. The large guidance system time constant and high-closing velocity can make ballistic target noise induced miss distances more than an order of magnitude greater than the miss distances experienced against an aircraft threat. In order to achieve small miss distances against high-closing velocity ballistic targets, methods for reducing the noise and effective radome slope must be found.

References

[1]Travers, P., "Interceptor Dynamics," unpublished lecture notes, Raytheon, circa 1971.

[2]Garnell, P., and East, D. J., *Guided Weapon Control System*, Pergamon, Oxford, 1977.

[3]Macfadzean, R. H. M., *Surface-Based Air Defense System Analysis*, Artech House, Norwood, MA, 1992.

[4]Lin, C. F., *Modern Navigation, Guidance, and Control Processing*, Prentice-Hall, Englewood Cliffs, NJ, 1991.

[5]Howe, R. M., "Guidance," *System Engineering Handbook*, edited by R. E. Machol, W. P. Tanner Jr., and S. N. Alexander, McGraw-Hill, New York, 1965, Chap. 19.

[6]Nesline, F. W., and Zarchan, P., "Radome Induced Miss Distance in Aerodynamically Controlled Homing Missiles," *Proceedings of AIAA Guidance and Control Conference*, AIAA, New York, Aug. 1984.

[7]Jerger, J. J., *System Preliminary Design*, Van Nostrand, Princeton, NJ, 1960.

[8]Nesline., F. W., and Zarchan, P., "Miss Distance Dynamics in Homing Missiles," *Proceedings of AIAA Guidance and Control Conference*, AIAA, New York, Aug. 1984.

Tactical and Strategic Missile Guidance Software

Introduction

IN this appendix examples will be presented to show the interested reader how to use the source code listings presented in *Tactical and Strategic Missile Guidance*. In addition, modified listings will be presented so that the reader will understand examples of specific changes that can be made in order to explore issues beyond the scope of the text. To further emphasize that the text's code can be simulated in any language, the listings in this appendix will be presented in QuickBASIC.

Software Details

To facilitate learning, IBM and Macintosh® formatted floppy disks containing all of the text's FORTRAN source code listings are included. As a special feature for those who do not have or can not afford a FORTRAN compiler, duplicate files which are the QuickBASIC equivalents of the FORTRAN listings are found on each disk.

The source code on the Macintosh formatted disk should run, as is, with either Version 2.3 or 2.4 of the Absoft FORTRAN compiler, or with any version of the Microsoft® QuickBASIC compiler. The source code on the IBM compatible formatted disk should run, as is, with Version 5 of the Microsoft FORTRAN compiler or with any version of the Microsoft Quick-BASIC compiler. Use of different FORTRAN or BASIC compilers, in either the Macintosh or IBM compatible world, may require some slight modification of the source code.

The naming conventions for the source code files on both disks are slightly different. On the Macintosh formatted disk the naming conventions are identical to those of the text (i.e., LISTING 4.2 on the disk corresponds to Listing 4.2 in the text for the FORTRAN version and BLISTING 4.2 for the QuickBASIC version). On the IBM compatible disk the naming convention is CxLy.FOR or CxLy.BAS where x corresponds to chapter number, y corresponds to listing number, and the three-letter extension after the decimal point indicates the language. In other words, C4L2.FOR corresponds to FORTRAN Listing 4.2 of the text (i.e., Chapter 4, Listing 2) and C4L2.BAS is the QuickBASIC equivalent.

Each of the source code files on the enclosed disks has a few lines of extra code to make data files so that the user can plot or store the results after a run is made. The name of the generated data file is DATFIL. The execution

417

time for most of the FORTRAN source code files should vary from a few seconds to several minutes on either 80286 or 68020 class machines with a math coprocessor. Lack of a math coprocessor will degrade running times but the programs will still work and yield the correct answers. Of course, faster Macintosh (i.e., 68030, 68040 series) or IBM compatible (i.e., 80386, 80486 series) computers will significantly improve running times.

The data statements or definition of constants in each of the source code files correspond to those used in the numerical examples presented in the text. The user should first run the program of interest as is to verify that the data file generated corresponds to the appropriate figure in the text. Other cases of interest can be run by either changing constants and recompiling or by modifying the source code to read input from the keyboard.

In the source code listings that make use of random numbers (i.e., uniform or Gaussian noise generators), use has been made of the FOR-TRAN random number generators supplied by Absoft in the Macintosh world and by Microsoft in the IBM compatible world. If other FORTRAN compilers are used, the user will have to invoke the appropriate random number language extension for the particular compiler or may have to write a random number generator (such as the one appearing at the end of this appendix) if it is not supplied by the compiler publisher. QuickBASIC users, in either the Macintosh or IBM compatible world, do not have to worry about random number generators since the BASIC language includes the *RND* statement to simulate a uniformly distributed random number generator.

Integration Example

To demonstrate for QuickBASIC users how the FORTRAN source code has been converted on the enclosed floppy disks, let us revisit the simulation of the sixth-order Butterworth filter presented in Listing 1.1 of Chapter 1. The program has been changed line by line to QuickBASIC and appears in Listing A.1. We can see by comparing Listings 1.1 and A.1 that the QuickBASIC statements and FORTRAN statements are virtually identical. Percentage signs (%) have been added to certain variables to automatically make them integers so that the compiled program will run faster. The system differential equations appear after statement label *INTEGRATE* rather than the nondescriptive statement label 200 in the FORTRAN version (i.e., FORTRAN does not allow labels with names). The QuickBASIC statement *WHILE INKEY$ = " ":WEND* is the equivalent of the *FORTRAN PAUSE* statement and is used to hold the printed results on the computer screen. Running Listing A.1 with a suitable BASIC compiler will yield exactly the same answers as running the FORTRAN version of the program. The nominal answers for a filter natural frequency of 50 rad/s ($\omega_0 = 50$) have already been displayed in Fig. 1.2.

To show how issues beyond the scope of the text can be explored let us consider changing the method of integration used in Listing A.1. We will use the simpler Euler numerical integration method[1] rather than the second-order Runge-Kutta integration technique. Given a first-order differential

Listing A.1   QuickBASIC version of sixth-order Butterworth filter simulation (equivalent to Listing 1.1)

```
DIM X(6),XOLD(6),XD(6)
READ A1,A2,A3,A4,A5,A6,W0
DATA 3.86,7.46,9.13,7.46,3.86,1.,50.
XIN = 1!
OPEN "DATFIL" FOR OUTPUT AS #1
ORDER% = 6
W02 = W0*W0
W03 = W02*W0
W04 = W03*W0
W05 = W04*W0
W06 = W05*W0
FOR I% = 1 TO ORDER%
X(I%) = 0!
NEXT I%
T = 0!
H = .0001
S = 0!
5 :
IF T = .5 GOTO 999
S = S + H
FOR I% = 1 TO ORDER%
XOLD(I%) = X(I%)
NEXT I%
GOSUB INTEGRATE
FOR I% = 1 TO ORDER%
X(I%) = X(I%) + H*XD(I%)
NEXT I%
T = T + H
GOSUB INTEGRATE
FOR I% = 1 TO ORDER%
X(I%) = (XOLD(I%) + X(I%))/2! + .5*H*XD(I%)
NEXT I%
IF S = .004999 THEN
   S = 0!
   PRINT T,X(1)
   WRITE#1,T,X(1)
END IF
GOTO 5
INTEGRATE:
XD(1) = X(2)
XD(2) = X(3)
XD(3) = X(4)
XD(4) = X(5)
XD(5) = X(6)
TEMP = XIN—A5*X(6)/W05—A4*X(5)/W04—A3*X(4)/W03
XD(6) = W06*(TEMP—A2*X(3)/W02—A1*X(2)/W0—X(1))/A6
RETURN
999 :
CLOSE #1
WHILE INKEY$" ":WEND
END
```

equation of the form

$$\dot{x} = f(x,t)$$

Euler integration states that the value of the state x at the next integration interval h is related to the previous value by the recursive relationship

$$x_{K+1} = x_K + hf(x,t)$$

The modified QuickBASIC simulation of sixth-order Butterworth filter using Euler integration appears in Listing A.2. The modified section of code is highlighted in boldface so that the interested reader can quickly identify changes. Note that this program is physically smaller than the one of Listing A.1 because the implementation of Euler integration requires fewer lines of code than does the second-order Runge-Kutta technique.

The price paid for the compact code of Euler integration is less accuracy, compared to other methods, for a given integration interval.[1] If we run Listing A.2 and increase the integration step size H we find that the integration procedure can go unstable, if we are not careful, as shown in Fig. A.1. Being prudent and using small integration step sizes is one way of getting accurate answers with Euler integration. However, sometimes Euler integration does not work at all—no matter how small the integration step size! For this reason second-order Runge-Kutta numerical integration is used in most of the listings in the text.

Random Number Example

In order to show how random numbers can be generated in QuickBASIC, the FORTRAN program to generate probability density functions (Listing 4.2) has been converted. We can see from Listing A.3 that the *RND*

Listing A.2   QuickBASIC simulation of sixth-order Butterworth filter using Euler integration

```
DIM X(6),XOLD(6),XD(6)
READ A1,A2,A3,A4,A5,A6,W0
DATA 3.86,7.46,9.13,7.46,3.86,1.,50.
XIN = 1.
OPEN "DATFIL" FOR OUTPUT AS #1
ORDER% = 6
W02 = W0*W0
W03 = W02*W0
W04 = W03*W0
W05 = W04*W0
W06 = W05*W0
FOR I% = 1 TO ORDER%
X(I%) = 0.
NEXT I%
T = 0.
H = .0001
S = 0.
5:
IF T> = .5 THEN GOTO 999
S = S + H
XD(1) = X(2)
XD(2) = X(3)
XD(3) = X(4)
XD(4) = X(5)
XD(5) = X(6)
XD(6) = W06*(XIN—A5*X(6)/W05—A4*X(5)/W04—A3*X(4)/W03—A2*X(3)/W02
    —A1*X(2)/W0—X(1))/A6
FOR I% = 1 TO ORDER%
X(I%) = X(I%) + H*XD(I%)
NEXT I%
T = T + H
IF S> = .004999 THEN
    S = 0.
    PRINT T,X(1)
    WRITE#1,T,X(1)
END IF
GOTO 5
999:
WHILE INKEY$ = " ":WEND
END
```

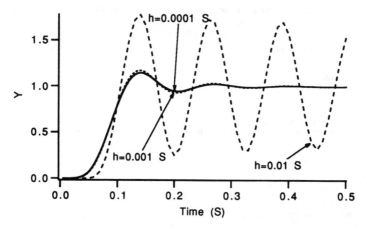

Fig. A.1   Euler integration does not always yield correct answers.

statement is equivalent to a uniform random number generator. In this example we are summing up 12 uniform distributions to yield a Gaussian distribution.

Cases were run with Listing A.3 in which the number of random numbers considered $N\%$ was made a parameter. Figure A.2 shows that when the number of random numbers used is increased from 1000 to 5000, the fit to the theoretical bell-shaped Gaussian distribution is better. The curves also indicate that the random number generator supplied by QuickBASIC is as good as the one supplied by the FORTRAN compiler vendors (i.e., compare Figs. A.2 and 4.6).

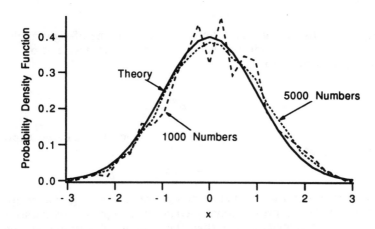

Fig. A.2   More random numbers make Gaussian distribution fit better.

Listing A.3   QuickBASIC program to generate probability density function (equivalent to Listing 4.2)

```
DIM H(10000),X(10000)
OPEN "DATFIL" FOR OUTPUT AS #1
XMAX = 6!
XMIN = —6!
RANGE = XMAX—XMIN
TMP = 1!/SQR(6.28)
N% = 100
BIN% = 50
FOR I% = 1 TO N%
SUM = RND + RND + RND + RND + RND + RND
SUM = SUM + RND + RND + RND + RND + RND + RND—6!
X(I%) = SUM
NEXT I%
FOR I% = 1 TO BIN%
H(I%) = 0
NEXT I%
FOR I% = 1 TO N%
K% = INT(((X(I%)—XMIN)/RANGE)*BIN%) + .99
IF K% < 1THEN K% = 1
IF K% > BIN% THEN K% = BIN%
H(K%) = H(K%) + 1
NEXT I%
FOR K% = 1 TO BIN%
PDF = (H(K%)/N%)*BIN%/RANGE
AB = XMIN + K%*RANGE/BIN%
TH = TMP*EXP(—AB*AB/2!)
PRINT AB,PDF,TH
WRITE#1,AB,PDF,THNEXT K%CLOSE #1
WHILE INKEY$ = " ":WEND
END
```

Pursuit Guidance

In Chapter 2 we convinced ourselves that proportional navigation could hit targets in the absence of guidance lags and acceleration saturation effects. A guidance law that is not as effective as proportional navigation but offers simpler mechanization advantages is known as pursuit guidance. In this guidance law an attempt is made to keep the turning rate of the missile equal to the line-of-sight rate or

$$\dot{\gamma} = \dot{\lambda}$$

where γ is the missile flight path angle and λ is the line-of-sight angle. The turning rate of the missile is related to the missile acceleration n_c and velocity V_M according to

$$\dot{\gamma} = \frac{n_c}{V_m}$$

Therefore we can say that the pursuit guidance law can be expressed mathematically as

$$n_c = V_M \dot{\lambda}$$

When expressed in terms of the line-of-sight rate, pursuit guidance appears to be very similar to proportional navigation except the acceleration depends on missile velocity rather than the closing velocity and the gain is unity rather than an effective navigation ratio.

Listing 2.1, which represents a two-dimensional proportional navigation engagement simulation, was modified to have a pursuit guidance option. Setting the new parameter *PURSUIT* = 0 yields proportional navigation while setting *PURSUIT* = 1 yields pursuit guidance. The slightly modified version of Listing 2.1 appears in QuickBASIC in Listing A.4. Note that the simulation is set up with a − 20-deg heading error and an effective navigation ratio of 4 when proportional navigation is used. The *PRINT* and *WRITE* statements have also been modified so that trajectory information is printed in units of kft and acceleration is printed in units of *g*. In addition, since the BASIC arc tangent function *ATN* does not work in all four quadrants, a special subroutine was written so that the line-of-sight angle could be computed. The arc sine function was used in the FORTRAN version of Listing 2.1 to calculate the missile lead angle. Since BASIC does not have an arc sine function, the QuickBASIC version of the program used trigonometry and the new arc tangent subroutine to compute the missile lead angle. Important differences with the original FORTRAN version of Listing 2.1 have been highlighted in boldface in Listing A.4.

The guidance law in Listing A.4 was made a parameter (*PURSUIT* = 0 and *PURSUIT* = 1) and the nominal case with a 20-deg heading error was run. Trajectory information for both proportional navigation and pursuit

Listing A.4   QuickBASIC engagement simulation with pursuit guidance option (modified Listing 2.1)

```
READ VM,VT,XNT,HEDEG,XNP
DATA 3000.,1000.,0.,−20.,4.
READ RM1,RM2,RT1,RT2
DATA 0.,10000.,40000.,10000.
OPEN "DATFIL" FOR OUTPUT AS #1
PURSUIT = 0
BETA = 0!
VT1 = −VT*COS(BETA)
VT2 = VT*SIN(BETA)
HE = HEDEG/57.3
T = 0!
S = 0!
RTM1 = RT1—RM1
RTM2 = RT2—RM2
RTM = SQR(RTM12 + RTM22)
CALL ATAN2(RTM2, RTM1, XLAM)
CALL ATAN2(VT*SIN(BETA + XLAM),SQR(VM.2—(VT*SIN(BETA + XLAM)).2),XLEAD)
THET = XLAM + XLEAD
VM1 = VM*COS(THET + HE)
VM2 = VM*SIN(THET + HE)
10 :
IF VC<0! GOTO 999
IF RTM<1000! THEN
   H = .0002
ELSE
   H = .01
END IF
BETAOLD = BETA
RT1OLD = RT1
RT2OLD = RT2
RM1OLD = RM1
RM2OLD = RM2
VM1OLD = VM1
VM2OLD = VM2
GOSUB INTEGRATE
BETA = BETA + H*BETAD
RT1 = RT1 + H*VT1
RT2 = RT2 + H*VT2
```

(Listing A.4 continued on next page.)

Listing A.4 (cont.) QuickBASIC engagement simulation with pursuit guidance option (modified Listing 2.1)

```
RM1 = RM1 + H*VM1
RM2 = RM2 + H*VM2
VM1 = VM1 + H*AM1
VM2 = VM2 + H*AM2
T = T + H
GOSUB INTEGRATE
BETA = .5*(BETAOLD + BETA + H*BETAD)
RT1 = .5*(RT1OLD + RT1 + H*VT1)
RT2 = .5*(RT2OLD + RT2 + H*VT2)
RM1 = .5*(RM1OLD + RM1 + H*VM1)
RM2 = .5*(RM2OLD + RM2 + H*VM2)
VM1 = .5*(VM1OLD + VM1 + H*AM1)
VM2 = .5*(VM2OLD + VM2 + H*AM2)
S = S + H
IF S < .09999 GOTO 10
S = 0!
PRINT T,RT1/1000,RT2/1000,RM1/1000,RM2/1000,XNC/32.2
WRITE#1,T,RT1/1000,RT2/1000,RM1/1000,RM2/1000,XNC/32.2
GOTO 10
INTEGRATE:
RTM1 = RT1—RM1
RTM2 = RT2—RM2
RTM = SQR(RTM1^2 + RTM2^2)
VTM1 = VT1—VM1
VTM2 = VT2—VM2
VC = —(RTM1*VTM1 + RTM2*VTM2)/RTM
CALL ATAN2(RTM2, RTM1, XLAM)
XLAMD = (RTM1*VTM2—RTM2*VTM1)/(RTM*RTM)
IF PURSUIT = 0 THEN
   XNC = XNP'VC'XLAMD
ELSE
   XNC = VM'XLAMD
END IF
AM1 = —XNC*SIN(XLAM)
AM2 = XNC*COS(XLAM)
VT1 = —VT*COS(BETA)
VT2 = VT*SIN(BETA)
BETAD = XNT/VT
RETURN
999 :
PRINT T,RT1/1000,RT2/1000,RM1/1000,RM2/1000,XNC/32.2
PRINT RTM
WRITE#1,T,RT1/1000,RT2/1000,RM1/1000,RM2/1000,XNC/32.2
CLOSE #1
WHILE INKEY$ = " ":WEND
END

SUB ATAN2(Y,X,Z)STATIC
IF X<0 THEN
  IF Y<0 THEN
    Z = ATN(Y/X)—3.14159
  ELSE
    Z = ATN(Y/X) + 3.14159
  END IF
ELSE
  Z = ATN(Y/X)
END IF
END SUB
```

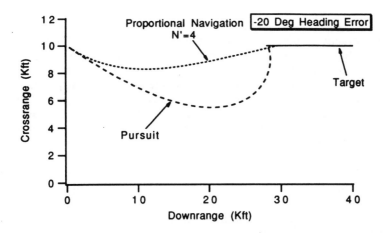

Fig. A.3   Pursuit guidance hits target but ends up in tail chase.

guidance laws are displayed in Fig. A.3. We can see that although both guidance laws appear to be mathematically similar, the resultant trajectories are vastly different. Both proportional navigation and pursuit guidance enable the missile to hit the nonmaneuvering target but the pursuit guidance trajectory has tremendous curvature and ends up in a tail chase.

Figure A.4 shows that the price paid for the tremendous curvature in the pursuit guidance trajectory is very large acceleration requirements when compared to proportional navigation. Unlike proportional navigation, which has a monotonically decreasing acceleration profile against heading error, the acceleration profile for pursuit guidance is monotonically increas-

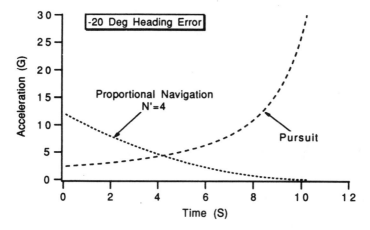

Fig. A.4   Pursuit guidance acceleration requirements are much larger than that of proportional navigation.

ing. In fact, the pursuit guidance command approaches infinity and will cause any practical guidance system to acceleration saturate. The interested reader should conduct more experiments with both proportional navigation and pursuit guidance in which the missile velocity is made a parameter and the target is maneuvering. It will soon become apparent that pursuit guidance is not an effective guidance law against moving targets when the missile and target speeds are comparable. However, Ref. 2 shows that against stationary targets pursuit guidance can be made to work in a very cost effective fashion.

Multiple Target Problem[3]

In endoatmospheric and exoatmospheric engagements there may be an instantaneous apparent shift in target position which can cause unacceptable degradation in homing missile performance. For example, in endoatmospheric tactical radar homing missiles, the interceptor may be guiding on the power centroid of two aircraft flying in close formation. When one of the aircraft falls outside the missile seeker beam, the other aircraft will be resolved. In this case it appears to the pursuing interceptor that the target has instantaneously shifted from the location of the power centroid to the location of the resolved aircraft. In other words, there has been an apparent step change in target position.

Figure A.5 shows two aircraft flying in formation being pursued by a missile. Initially both aircraft are close enough so that the missile, with seeker beamwidth BW, homes on the power centroid of the two aircraft. At the point where one of the aircraft falls outside the seeker beam, resolution takes place and it appears to the missile that the aircraft has been instantaneously displaced a distance y_{TIC}. If the missile and aircraft are traveling at constant speed with closing velocity V_c, the missile will be a distance of $V_c t_F$ from the power centroid at the point of resolution where t_F is the time remaining for guidance after seeker resolution. From trigonometry we can see that the seeker beamwidth is related to the aircraft displacement according to

$$\tan\frac{BW}{2} = \frac{y_{TIC}}{V_c t_F}$$

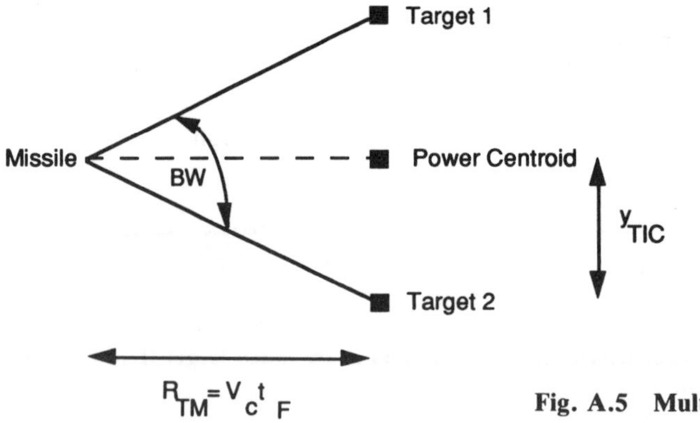

Fig. A.5   Multiple target geometry.

Listing A.5   QuickBASIC fifth-order binomial guidance system adjoint simulation (modified Listing 6.1)

```
READ XNT,XNP,TAU,TF,VC
DATA 32.2,3,.5,5.,4000.
READ XNTD,XNTDD,YIC
DATA 32.2,32.2,200
OPEN "DATFIL" FOR OUTPUT AS #1
T = 0!
S = 0!
TP = T + .00001
X1 = 0
X2 = 0
X3 = 1
X4 = 0
X5 = 0!
X6 = 0!
X7 = 0!
X8 = 0!
X9 = 0!
X10 = 0!
H = .02
10 :
IF TP > (TF—.00001) GOTO 999
S = S + H
X1OLD = X1
X2OLD = X2
X3OLD = X3
X4OLD = X4
X5OLD = X5
X6OLD = X6
X7OLD = X7
X8OLD = X8
X9OLD = X9
X10OLD = X10
GOSUB INTEGRATE
X1 = X1 + H*X1D
X2 = X2 + H*X2D
X3 = X3 + H*X3D
X4 = X4 + H*X4D
X5 = X5 + H*X5D
X6 = X6 + H*X6D
X7 = X7 + H*X7D
X8 = X8 + H*X8D
X9 = X9 + H*X9D
X10 = X10 + H*X10D
TP = TP + H
GOSUB INTEGRATE
X1 = (X1OLD + X1)/2 + .5*H*X1D
X2 = (X2OLD + X2)/2 + .5*H*X2D
X3 = (X3OLD + X3)/2 + .5*H*X3D
X4 = (X4OLD + X4)/2 + .5*H*X4D
X5 = (X5OLD + X5)/2 + .5*H*X5D
X6 = (X6OLD + X6)/2 + .5*H*X6D
X7 = (X7OLD + X7)/2 + .5*H*X7D
X8 = (X8OLD + X8)/2 + .5*H*X8D
X9 = (X9OLD + X9)/2 + .5*H*X9D
X10 = (X10OLD + X10)/2 + .5*H*X10D
IF S < .09999 GOTO 10
S = 0!
XMYIC = X3'YIC
PRINT TP,XMYIC
WRITE#1,TP,XMYIC
GOTO 10
INTEGRATE:
X1D = X2
X2D = X3
Y1 = 5!*(5!*X5/TAU + X4)/TAU
TGO = TP + .00001
X3D = Y1/(VC*TGO)
X4D = —Y1
X5D = —5!*X5/TAU + 5!*X6*XNP*VC/TAU
X6D = —5!*X6/TAU + 5!*X7/TAU
X7D = —5!*X7/TAU + 5!*X8/TAU
X8D = —5!*X8/TAU—X2
X9D = X1
X10D = X9
RETURN
999 :
CLOSE #1
WHILE INKEY$ = " ":WEND
END
```

Using the small angle approximation and solving for the effective time remaining for guidance after seeker resolution we get

$$t_F = \frac{2y_{TIC}}{V_c BW}$$

If a seeker has a beamwidth of 0.1 rad (nearly 6 deg), the two targets are separated by 400 ft and the closing velocity is 4000 ft/s, the time remaining for guidance after resolution will be 1 s or

$$t_F = \frac{2y_{TIC}}{V_c BW} = \frac{400}{4000*0.1} = 1 \text{ s}$$

In other words, the effective homing time after seeker resolution has occured is very small!

We can evaluate the effect of a step target displacement on miss distance by first referring to Fig. 6.5 which displays an adjoint block diagram for the fifth-order binomial guidance system. This figure was used in Chapter 6 in order to find the miss distance sensitivity due to step, ramp, and parabolic target maneuvers. A quick inspection of Fig. 6.5 reveals that the miss due to a step in target displacement can also be found by simply multiplying $x3$ by the magnitude of the step displacement y_{IC}. Listing 6.1, which represents the adjoint simulation of the fifth-order binomial guidance system, was

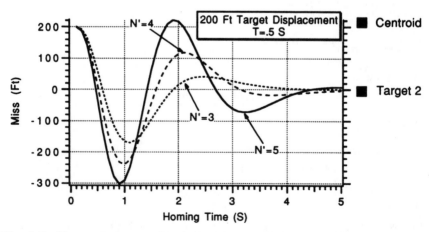

Fig. A.6 Correct target must be resolved as soon as possible for there to be small miss distance.

modified to show the miss distance due to a step in target displacement. The modified QuickBASIC version of the adjoint simulation appears in Listing A.5. We can see that we are now interested in both positive and negative values of the miss (i.e., *ABS* statements have been removed) because of their important physical meaning. In addition, we are considering the case in which the guidance system time constant is 0.5 s, the step in target displacement is 200 ft, and the maximum homing time of interest is 5 s. Recall that a homing time of 1 s, in this example, corresponds to a seeker beamwidth of 6 deg. Longer effective homing times correspond to narrower seeker beamwidths. The statements which have been modified from Listing 6.1 have been highlighted in boldface in Listing A.5.

The nominal case of Listing A.5 was run with the effective navigation ratio *XNP* as a parameter. Figure A.6 shows that the missile will only hit the resolved target (Target 2 in this example) if more than 5 s of homing are available. However, if the seeker beamwidth is 0.1 rad (i.e., approximately 6 deg) and the closing velocity is 4000 ft/s, we have already shown that the effective homing time is 1 s. In this case we can see from Fig. A.6 and the adjoint simulation output that the miss distances will be

$$\text{Miss}_{N'=3} = -165 \text{ ft}$$
$$\text{Miss}_{N'=4} = -238 \text{ ft}$$
$$\text{Miss}_{N'=5} = -288 \text{ ft}$$

The negative sign on the miss distance indicates that the missile did not even end up between the original power centroid and the target. In all three cases the missile would have been better off not resolving the targets (i.e., guiding on the power centroid yields a miss distance of 200 ft in this example). Reducing the guidance system time constant will considerably improve system performance against this important source of error.

Sensitivity of Optimal Guidance to Time to Go Errors

In evaluating the performance of the optimal guidance law we have seen tremendous performance benefits over proportional navigation in the presence of guidance system dynamics. It has been assumed that the time to go information, required by optimal guidance, was perfect. Adjoint Listing 8.2 was modified to include scale factor *SF* and bias *BIAS* errors on the estimated time to go *TGOH* when the optimal guidance option was used ($APN = 2$). An error-free time to go case would require $SF = 1$ and $BIAS = 0$. Time to go errors are not introduced into the proportional navigation option ($APN = 0$) because in practice this guidance law does not require time to go but works directly on the line-of-sight rate. Statements that have been modified from the original Listing 8.2 are highlighted in boldface in Listing A.6.

Cases were rerun for proportional navigation ($APN = 0$), optimal guidance with a time to go scale factor error of 0.9 ($APN = 2$, $SF = 0.9$, $BIAS = 0$) and optimal guidance with a time to go bias error of 0.1 s ($APN = 2$, $SF = 1$, $BIAS = 0.1$). The miss distance sensitivity to a 3-g target maneuver when the guidance system time constant is 1 s is displayed

Listing A.6   QuickBASIC adjoint simulation of optimal guidance system (modified Listing 8.2)

```
READ XNT,XNP,TAU,TF,VM,HEDEG
DATA 96.6,4,1,10,3000.,-20.
READ APN,BIAS,SF
DATA 2,0.,,9
OPEN "DATFIL" FOR OUTPUT AS #1
T = 0!
S = 0!
TP = T + .00001
X1 = 0
X2 = 0
X3 = 1
X4 = 0
XNPP = 0!
H = .02
HE = HEDEG/57.3
10 :
IF TP>(TF-.00001) GOTO 999
S = S + H
X1OLD = X1
X2OLD = X2
X3OLD = X3
X4OLD = X4
GOSUB INTEGRATE
X1 = X1 + H*X1D
X2 = X2 + H*X2D
X3 = X3 + H*X3D
X4 = X4 + H*X4D
TP = TP + H
GOSUB INTEGRATE
X1 = (X1OLD + X1)/2 + .5*H*X1D
X2 = (X2OLD + X2)/2 + .5*H*X2D
X3 = (X3OLD + X3)/2 + .5*H*X3D
X4 = (X4OLD + X4)/2 + .5*H*X4D
IF S<.09999 GOTO 10
S = 0!
XMNT = ABS(XNT*X1)
XMHE = ABS(-VM*HE*X2)
PRINT TP,XMNT,XMHE
WRITE#1,TP,XMNT,XMHE
GOTO 10
INTEGRATE:
TGO = TP + .00001
IF APN = 0 THEN
   C1 = XNP/(TGO*TGO)
   C2 = XNP/TGO
   C3 = 0!
   C4 = 0!
ELSEIF APN = 1 THEN
   C1 = XNP/(TGO*TGO)
   C2 = XNP/TGO
   C3 = .5*XNP
   C4 = 0!
ELSE
   TGOH = SF*TGO + BIAS
   X = TGOH/TAU
   TOP = 6!*X*X*(EXP(-X)-1! + X)
   BOT1 = 2*X*X*X + 3! + 6!*X-6!*X*X
   BOT2 = -12!*X*EXP(-X)-3!*EXP(-2!*X)
   XNPP = TOP/(.0001 + BOT1 + BOT2)
   C1 = XNPP/(TGOH*TGOH)
   C2 = XNPP/TGOH
   C3 = .5*XNPP
   C4 = -XNPP*(EXP(-X) + X-1!)/(X*X)
END IF
X1D = X2 + C3*X4/TAU
X2D = X3 + C2*X4/TAU
X3D = C1*X4/TAU
X4D = -X4/TAU-X2 + C4*X4/TAU
RETURN
999 :
CLOSE #1
WHILE INKEY$ = " ":WEND
END
```

Listing A.7   QuickBASIC version of efficient Lambert subroutine (Listing 14.2)

```
DEFDBL A-H
DEFDBL O-Z
OPEN "DATFIL" FOR OUTPUT AS #1
XLONGMDEG = 45!
XLONGTDEG = 90!
ALTNMT = 0!
ALTNMM = 0!
TF = 1000!
PI = 3.14159
DEGRAD = 360!/(2!*PI)
A = 2.0926E + 07
GM = 1.4077E + 16
ALTT = ALTNMT*6076!
ALTM = ALTNMM*6076!
XLONGM = XLONGMDEG/DEGRAD
XLONGT = XLONGTDEG/DEGRAD
XM = (A + ALTM)*COS(XLONGM)
YM = (A + ALTM)*SIN(XLONGM)
XT = (A + ALTT)*COS(XLONGT)
YT = (A + ALTT)*SIN(XLONGT)
CALL LAMBERT(XM,YM,TF,XT,YT,VRXM,VRYM,XLONGM,XLONGT)
CLOSE #1
WHILE INKEY$ = " ":WEND
END


SUB LAMBERT(XIC,YIC,TFDES,XF,YF,VRX,VRY,XLONGM,XLONGT)STATIC
DEFDBL A-H
DEFDBL O-Z
A = 2.0926E + 07
GM = 1.4077E + 16
RIC = SQR(XIC^2 + YIC^2)
RF = SQR(XF^2 + YF^2)
CPHI = (XIC*XF + YIC*YF)/(RIC*RF)
IF(CPHI < 1!)THEN
   TOP = SQR((RIC*RF)^2—(XIC*XF + YIC*YF)^2)
   CALL ATAN2(TOP,(XIC*XF + YIC*YF),PHI)
END IF
SPHI = SIN(PHI)
R0 = RIC
PI = 3.14159
DEGRAD = 360!/(2!*PI)
ICOUNT = 0
CALL ATAN2((SPHI—SQR(2.*R0*(1.—CPHI)/RF)),(1—CPHI),GMIN)
CALL ATAN2((SPHI + SQR(2.*R0*(1.—CPHI)/RF)),(1—CPHI),GMAX)
GAM = (GMIN + GMAX)/2.
98:
TOP = GM*(1.—COS(PHI))
TEMP = R0*COS(GAM)/RF—COS(PHI + GAM)
BOT = R0*COS(GAM)*TEMP
V = SQR(TOP/BOT)
IF (XLONGT > XLONGM) THEN
    VRX = V*COS(PI/2.—GAM + XLONGM)
    VRY = V*SIN(PI/2.—GAM + XLONGM)
ELSE
    VRX = V*COS(—PI/2. + GAM + XLONGM)
    VRY = V*SIN(—PI/2. + GAM + XLONGM)
END IF
XLAM = R0*V*V/GM
TOP1 = TAN(GAM)*(1—COS(PHI)) + (1—XLAM)*SIN(PHI)
BOT1P = (1—COS(PHI))/(XLAM*COS(GAM)*COS(GAM))
BOT1 = (2—XLAM)*(BOT1P + COS(GAM + PHI)/COS(GAM))
TOP2 = 2*COS(GAM)
BOT2 = XLAM*((2/XLAM—1)^1.5)
TOP3 = SQR(2/XLAM—1)
BOT3 = COS(GAM)/TAN(PHI/2)—SIN(GAM)
CALL ATAN2(TOP3,BOT3,PZ)
TEMP = (TOP2/BOT2)*PZ
TF = R0*(TOP1/BOT1 + TEMP)/(V*COS(GAM))
ICOUNT = ICOUNT + 1
PRINT ICOUNT,57.3*GAM,VRX,VRY,TF
WRITE#1,ICOUNT,57.3*GAM,VRX,VRY,TF
IF((ABS(TFDES—TF)< = .00000001*TFDES) OR ICOUNT > 100)THEN
   GOTO 99
```

(Listing A.7 continued on next page.)

Listing A.7   (cont.) QuickBASIC version of efficient Lambert subroutine (Listing 14.2)

```
END IF
IF TF>FDES THEN
  GMAX = GAM
ELSE
  GMIN = GAM
END IF
IF ICOUNT = 1 THEN
  XNEXT = (GMAX + GMIN)/2.
ELSE
  XNEXT = GAM + (GAM—GOLD)*(TFDES—TF)/(TF—TOLD)
  IF(XNEXT>GMAX OR XNEXT<GMIN)THEN
    XNEXT = (GMAX + GMIN)/2.
  END IF
END IF
GOLD = GAM
TOLD = TF
GAM = XNEXT
GOTO 98
99:
END SUB

SUB ATAN2(Y,X,Z)STATIC
IF X<0 THEN
  IF Y<0 THEN
    Z = ATN(Y/X)—3.14159
  ELSE
    Z = ATN(Y/X) + 3.14159
  END IF
ELSE
  Z = ATN(Y/X)
END IF
END SUB
```

in Fig. A.7. We can see that both scale factor and bias errors degrade the optimal guidance performance. Figure A.7 shows that the performance of optimal guidance with a 0.9 scale factor error is worse than that of proportional navigation for flight times greater than 8 s and with a 0.1-s bias error is worse than that of proportional navigation for flight times greater than 5.5 s.[4] Therefore time to go must be known accurately in order for optimal guidance to perform better than proportional navigation.

Efficient Lambert Subroutine

In this section we shall not perform any new experiments but simply convert Listing 14.2 to QuickBASIC. The reason for this is that the change is not obvious plus we now have to work with double-precison arithmetic. We can see from Listing A.7 that the QuickBASIC statement *DEFDBL* is used to convert variables to double-precision. As was mentioned previously, QuickBASIC does not have an arc tangent statement that is good in all four quadrants, and so a special subroutine has been written to make it equivalent to the FORTRAN *ATAN*2 statement. In addition, since QuickBASIC does not have arc cosine or arc sine statements, trigonometry was used to convert those statements to equivalent arc tangent statements. Note that the *STATIC* statement must be used with QuickBASIC subroutines. The *DO...REPEAT* loop with an *EXIT* statement in the FORTRAN version of Listing 14.2 has also been converted to the inelegant but effective *GOTO* statement in Listing A.7. This program yields identical answers to its FORTRAN counterpart.

Listing A.8 Alternative model of homing loop with radome effects (modified Listing 19.2)

```
OPEN "DATFIL" FOR OUTPUT AS #1
VC = 9000.
XNT = 32.2
XNCLIMG = 7.
YIC = 0.
VM = 3000.
HEDEG = 0.
TAU = .5
XNP = 3.
TA = 5.
R = -.01
TF = 10.
Y = YIC
YD = -VM*HEDEG/57.3
YDIC = YD
XNL = 0.
ELAMDH = 0.
X4 = 0.
X5 = 0.
TH = 0.
D = 0.
T = 0.
H = .01
S = 0.
XNCLIM = XNCLIMG*32.2
10:
IF T > (TF-.0001) GOTO 999
YOLD = Y
YDOLD = YD
XNLOLD = XNL
ELAMDHOLD = ELAMDH
X4OLD = X4
X5OLD = X5
THOLD = TH
DOLD = D
GOSUB INTEGRATE
Y = Y + H*YD
YD = YD + H*YDD
XNL = XNL + H*XNLD
ELAMDH = ELAMDH + H*ELAMDHD
X4 = X4 + H*X4D
X5 = X5 + H*X5D
TH = TH + H*THD
D = D + H*DD
T = T + H
GOSUB INTEGRATE
Y = .5*(YOLD + Y + H*YD)
YD = .5*(YDOLD + YD + H*YDD)
XNL = .5*(XNLOLD + XNL + H*XNLD)
ELAMDH = .5*(ELAMDHOLD + ELAMDH + H*ELAMDHD)
X4 = .5*(X4OLD + X4 + H*X4D)
X5 = .5*(X5OLD + X5 + H*X5D)
TH = .5*(THOLD + TH + H*THD)
D = .5*(DOLD + D + H*DD)
S = S + H
IF S > .09999 THEN
  S = 0.
  PRINT T,Y,XNC/32.2
  WRITE#1,T,Y,XNC/32.2
END IF
GOTO 10
INTEGRATE:
TGO = TF-T + .00001
XLAM = Y/(VC*TGO)
XLAMS = XLAM*(1. + R)-R*TH
DD = 5.*(XLAMS-D)/TAU
ELAMDHD = 5.*(DD-ELAMDH)/TAU
XNC = XNP*VC*ELAMDH
IF XNC > XNCLIM THEN XNC = XNCLIM
IF XNC < -XNCLIM THEN XNC = -XNCLIM
X4D = 5.*(XNC-X4)/TAU
X5D = 5.*(X4-X5)/TAU
XNLD = 5.*(X5-XNL)/TAU
THD = XNL/VM + TA*XNLD/VM
THHD = DD-THD
YDD = XNT-XNL
RETURN
999:
WHILE INKEY$ = " ":WEND
CLOSE #1
END
```

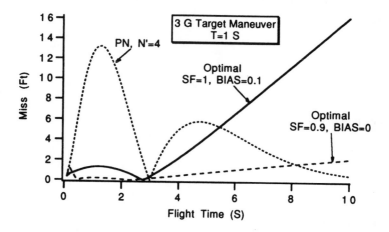

Fig. A.7 **Time to go must be known accurately for optimal guidance to yield performance benefits.**

Alternative Formulation of Radome Effects

In Chapters 6 and 19 the radome refraction angle r was assumed to be proportional to the missile gimbal angle θ_H or

$$r = R\theta_H$$

where R was assumed to be a constant known as the radome slope. Based on that definition stability constraints on the minimum permissible guidance system time constant were derived in Chapter 19. Actually the radome refraction angle is proportional to the missile look angle $\lambda - \theta$ as shown in Fig. A.8. Therefore from Fig. A.8 we can express the measured line of sight

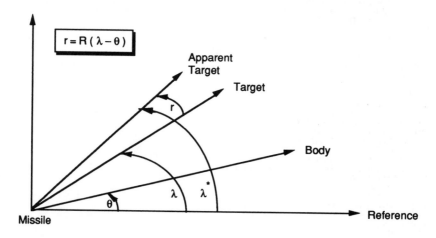

Fig. A.8 **Alternative formulation of radome slope.**

angle λ^* in terms of the radome slope as

$$\lambda^* = \lambda + r = \lambda + R(\lambda - \theta) = \lambda(1 + R) - R\theta$$

Using the preceding relationship, which does not depend on the gimbal angle, the fifth-order binomial model of the guidance system with radome effects simplifies considerably. The alternative guidance system model appears in Fig. A.9.

Listing 19.2, based on the gimbal angle definition of radome slope, was modified to reflect the alternative guidance system formulation of Fig. A.9. The QuickBASIC source code, representing a simulation of the alternative formulation of the fifth-order binomial model of the guidance system with radome effects, appears in Listing A.8. The modifications to the original simulation are highlighted in bold.

The nominal inputs of Listing A.8, representing a ballistic target case, were used and the guidance system time constant TAU was made a parameter. The simulation results were identical to those presented in Fig. 19.7, thus experimentally confirming that the gimbal angle and look angle definitions of the radome slope are approximately the same. This conclusion is also reasonable because the look angle $\lambda - \theta$ and gimbal angle θ_H only differ by an amount smaller than the boresight error (i.e., see Fig. 6.20 which shows $\lambda - \theta - \theta_H = \epsilon - r$). Generally, the boresight error is much smaller than either the gimbal angle or look angle.

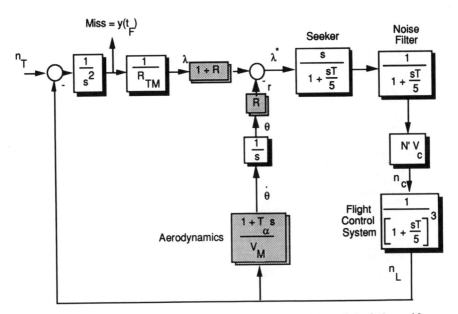

Fig. A.9   Alternative formulation of fifth-order binomial model of the guidance system with radome effects.

Listing A.9 FORTRAN program to generate Gaussian probability density function using the multiplicative congruential method (equivalent to Listing 4.2)

```
        INTEGER BIN
        DIMENSION H(10000),X(10000)
        OPEN(1,STATUS = 'NEW',FILE = 'DATFIL')
        XMAX = 6.
        XMIN = -6.
        RANGE = XMAX-XMIN
        TMP = 1./SQRT(6.28)
        N = 1000
        BIN = 50
        DO 10 I = 1,N
        CALL GAUSS(PZ,1.)
        X(I) = PZ
10      CONTINUE
        DO 20 I = 1,BIN
        H(I) = 0
20      CONTINUE
        DO 30 I = 1,N
        K = INT(((X(I)-XMIN)/RANGE)*BIN) + .99
        IF(K < 1)K = 1
        IF(K > BIN)K = BIN
        H(K) = H(K) + 1
30      CONTINUE
        DO 40 K = 1,BIN
        PDF = (H(K)/N)*BIN/RANGE
        AB = XMIN + K*RANGE/BIN
        TH = TMP*EXP(-AB*AB/2.)
        WRITE(9,*)AB,PDF,TH
        WRITE(1,*)AB,PDF,TH
40      CONTINUE
        PAUSE
        CLOSE(1)
        END

        SUBROUTINE GAUSS(X,SIG)
        SAVE
        SUM = 0.
        DO 14 J = 1,12
        Z = RAND(0)
        SUM = SUM + Z
14      CONTINUE
        X = SUM-6.
        RETURN
        END

        FUNCTION RAND(X)
        SAVE
        REAL*4 REAL4,NORM,SEND
        REAL*8 SEED,MULT,PROD
        INTEGER*4 X,HOLDER
        DATA MULT/16807.D0/
        DATA NORM/4.65661288E-10/
        DATA SEED/524287.D0/
        IF(X.NE.0)SEED = X
        PROD = SEED*MULT
        HOLDER = PROD/2147483647.D0
        SEED = PROD-HOLDER*2147483647.D0
        REAL4 = SEED
        SEND = REAL4*NORM
        RAND = SEND
        RETURN
        END
```

Another Way of Generating Random Numbers

Readers working in a language that does not have a random number generator will have difficulty in duplicating the many Monte Carlo experiments outlined in the text. In this section code will be provided in pure FORTRAN of a Gaussian random number generator based on the multiplicative congruential method which is fully described in Refs. 5 and 6. Listing A.9 is a modified form of Listing 4.2 in which 1000 Gaussian distributed random numbers are generated with the multiplicative congruential and compared to the theoretical probability density function.

The nominal case was run and the resulting probability density function is compared to the Gaussian probability density function in Fig. A.10. We can see that the comparison is excellent and readers should have no problem in using this Gaussian random number generator for Monte Carlo experiments.

Sampling Experiments

In Chapters 7 and 9 we conducted simplified data rate studies with both the digital fading memory and Kalman noise filters. We concluded that the miss distance due to noise and target maneuver tended to decrease as the data rate increased (i.e., sampling time decreased). For simplicity, in the data rate studies, the measurement noise standard deviation was held constant as the data rate changed. In many systems, when one gets into the details of the signal processing, it becomes readily apparent that the data rate and measurement noise standard deviation are *not* independent. In these systems the measurement noise spectral density Φ remains constant, which means that the standard deviation of the simulated digital measurement noise is proportional to the square root of the data rate (i.e., inversely proportional to the square root of the sampling time T_s) or

$$\sigma = \sqrt{\frac{\Phi}{T_s}}$$

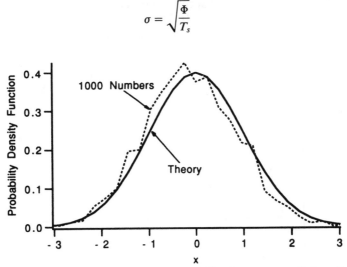

Fig. A.10 **Random numbers based on multiplicative congruential method fits Gaussian distribution.**

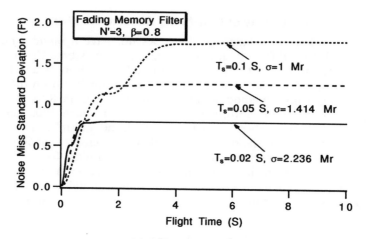

Fig. A.11   Increasing data rate still reduces miss due to digital measurement noise.

Therefore if we double the data rate (i.e., sampling time halved), we must also increase the standard deviation of the simulated digital measurement noise by 41.4% (i.e., $2^{0.5} = 1.414$). In this section we shall repeat the experiments of Chapters 7 and 9 to see if the miss due to digital measurement noise still decreases with increasing data rate when the measurement noise spectral density is held constant.

The miss distance adjoint program of Listing 7.3 represents the adjoint of a digital two-state fading memory filter in the homing loop. The program was modified so that a change in the data rate would cause a change in the standard deviation of the measurement noise according to the preceding relationship under the constant spectral density assumption. It was assumed that a sampling time of 0.1 s (i.e., 10-Hz data rate) corresponded to 1 mr of measurement noise. Adjoint runs were made in which the sampling time

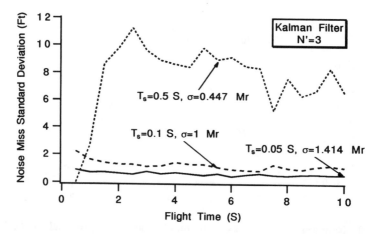

Fig. A.12   Measurement noise miss still increases with decreasing sampling rate.

was considered a parameter. Figure A.11 shows that the standard deviation of the miss distance due to digital measurement noise still decreases with increasing data rate, although not as dramatically as was the case in Fig. 7.22.

The Monte Carlo simulation used to generate Fig. 9.12 was also modified so that the equivalent spectral density of the measurement noise would remain constant and the standard deviation of the digital measurement noise would vary with data rate. Fifty run Monte Carlo sets were run for 20 different values of flight time at data rates of 2 Hz ($T_s = 0.5$ s), 10 Hz ($T_s = 0.1$ s), and 20 Hz ($T_s = 0.05$ s). We can see from Fig. A.12, that although the noise miss distance dependence on data rate is not as dramatic as in Fig. 9.12, the miss distance still decreases with increasing data rate (decreasing sampling time).

In summary, we can say that even in cases in which it is appropriate to hold the measurement noise spectral density constant when data rate studies are conducted, the noise induced miss still decreases with increasing data rate when either a fading memory or Kalman filter is used. Both of these digital noise filters take into account information concerning the data rate so that they can achieve good performance when the data rate changes.

References

[1]Rosko, J. S., *Digital Simulation of Physical Systems*, Addison-Wesley, Reading, MA, 1972.

[2]Chadwick, W. R., and Rose, C. M., "A Guidance Law for General Surface Targets," *Journal of Guidance, Control, and Dynamics*, Vol. 6, Nov.–Dec. 1983, pp. 526–529.

[3]Zarchan, P., "When Bad Things Happen To Good Missiles," *Proceedings of AIAA Guidance, Navigation, and Control Conference*, AIAA, Washington, DC, Aug. 1993.

[4]Nesline, F. W., and Zarchan, P., "A New Look at Classical Versus Modern Homing Guidance," *Journal of Guidance and Control*, Vol. 4, Jan.–Feb. 1981, pp. 78–85.

[5]Knuth, D. E., *The Art of Computer Programming*, Vol. 2, Addison-Wesley, Reading, MA, 1981.

[6]Bell, J., "Fast Random Numbers," *MacTutor*, Vol. 8, July 1992, pp. 16–22.

Units

TO most of the civilized world the units used in this text appear to be unconventional and in violation of everything taught in the universities. However, for many senior U.S. engineers it is not unusual to express altitude in ft, velocity in km/s, and downrange in yards—all in the same breath! As a special favor to those who do not appreciate the importance of the slug, Table B.1 shows how to convert the text's English units (which are no longer used in England) to either the metric system or to more popular units. For those who must pretend that they are familiar with the metric system, simply take the reciprocal of the conversion factor to get back to the text's units.

Table B.1   Unit conversion table

Quantity	Text's units	Multiply by	To get
Angle	rad	57.3	deg
Length	ft	0.305	m
	n.mi.	1.85	km
Velocity	ft/s	0.305	m/s
Acceleration	ft/s^2	0.031	g
		0.305	m/s^2
Area	ft^2	0.093	m^2
Weight	lb	0.45	kg
Air density	slug/ft^3	515	kg/m^3

PROGRESS IN ASTRONAUTICS AND AERONAUTICS
SERIES VOLUMES

*1. Solid Propellant
Rocket Research (1960)
Martin Summerfield
Princeton University

*2. Liquid Rockets
and Propellants (1960)
Loren E. Bollinger
Ohio State University
Martin Goldsmith
The Rand Corp.
Alexis W. Lemmon Jr.
Battelle Memorial Institute

*3. Energy Conversion
for Space Power (1961)
Nathan W. Snyder
*Institute for Defense
Analyses*

*4. Space Power
Systems (1961)
Nathan W. Snyder
*Institute for Defense
Analyses*

*5. Electrostatic
Propulsion (1961)
David B. Langmuir
*Space Technology
Laboratories, Inc.*
Ernst Stuhlinger
*NASA George C. Marshall
Space Flight Center*
J.M. Sellen Jr.
*Space Technology
Laboratories, Inc.*

*6. Detonation and
Two-Phase Flow (1962)
S.S. Penner
*California Institute
of Technology*
F.A. Williams
Harvard University

---

*7. Hypersonic Flow
Research (1962)
Frederick R. Riddell
AVCO Corp.

*8. Guidance and
Control (1962)
Robert E. Roberson,
Consultant
James S. Farrior
*Lockheed Missiles
and Space Co.*

*9. Electric Propulsion
Development (1963)
Ernst Stuhlinger
*NASA George C. Marshall
Space Flight Center*

*10. Technology of
Lunar Exploration (1963)
Clifford I. Cummings
Harold R. Lawrence
Jet Propulsion Laboratory

*11. Power Systems
for Space Flight (1963)
Morris A. Zipkin
Russell N. Edwards
General Electric Co.

*12. Ionization in High-
Temperature Gases (1963)
Kurt E. Shuler, Editor
*National Bureau of
Standards*
John B. Fenn,
Associate Editor
Princeton University

*13. Guidance and
Control—II (1964)
Robert C. Langford
General Precision Inc.
Charles J. Mundo
Institute of Naval Studies

*14. Celestial Mechanics
and Astrodynamics (1964)
Victor G. Szebehely
*Yale University
Observatory*

*15. Heterogeneous
Combustion (1964)
Hans G. Wolfhard
*Institute for Defense
Analyses*
Irvin Glassman
Princeton University
Leon Green Jr.
*Air Force Systems
Command*

*16. Space Power Systems
Engineering (1966)
George C. Szego
*Institute for Defense
Analyses*
J. Edward Taylor
TRW Inc.

*17. Methods in
Astrodynamics and
Celestial Mechanics (1966)
Raynor L. Duncombe
U.S. Naval Observatory
Victor G. Szebehely
*Yale University
Observatory*

*18. Thermophysics and
Temperature Control
of Spacecraft and
Entry Vehicles (1966)
Gerhard B. Heller
*NASA George C. Marshall
Space Flight Center*

---

*Out of print.

*19. Communication Satellite Systems Technology (1966)
Richard B. Marsten
Radio Corporation of America

*20. Thermophysics of Spacecraft and Planetary Bodies: Radiation Properties of Solids and the Electromagnetic Radiation Environment in Space (1967)
Gerhard B. Heller
NASA George C. Marshall Space Flight Center

*21. Thermal Design Principles of Spacecraft and Entry Bodies (1969)
Jerry T. Bevans
TRW Systems

*22. Stratospheric Circulation (1969)
Willis L. Webb
Atmospheric Sciences Laboratory, White Sands, and University of Texas at El Paso

*23. Thermophysics: Applications to Thermal Design of Spacecraft (1970)
Jerry T. Bevans
TRW Systems

24. Heat Transfer and Spacecraft Thermal Control (1971)
John W. Lucas
Jet Propulsion Laboratory

25. Communication Satellites for the 70's: Technology (1971)
Nathaniel E. Feldman
The Rand Corp.
Charles M. Kelly
The Aerospace Corp.

26. Communication Satellites for the 70's: Systems (1971)
Nathaniel E. Feldman
The Rand Corp.
Charles M. Kelly
The Aerospace Corp.

27. Thermospheric Circulation (1972)
Willis L. Webb
Atmospheric Sciences Laboratory, White Sands, and University of Texas at El Paso

28. Thermal Characteristics of the Moon (1972)
John W. Lucas
Jet Propulsion Laboratory

*29. Fundamentals of Spacecraft Thermal Design (1972)
John W. Lucas
Jet Propulsion Laboratory

30. Solar Activity Observations and Predictions (1972)
Patrick S. McIntosh
Murray Dryer
Environmental Research Laboratories, National Oceanic and Atmospheric Administration

31. Thermal Control and Radiation (1973)
Chang-Lin Tien
University of California at Berkeley

32. Communications Satellite Systems (1974)
P.L. Bargellini
COMSAT Laboratories

33. Communications Satellite Technology (1974)
P.L. Bargellini
COMSAT Laboratories

*34. Instrumentation for Airbreathing Propulsion (1974)
Allen E. Fuhs
Naval Postgraduate School
Marshall Kingery
Arnold Engineering Development Center

35. Thermophysics and Spacecraft Thermal Control (1974)
Robert G. Hering
University of Iowa

36. Thermal Pollution Analysis (1975)
Joseph A. Schetz
Virginia Polytechnic Institute
ISBN 0-915928-00-0

37. Aeroacoustics: Jet and Combustion Noise; Duct Acoustics (1975)
Henry T. Nagamatsu, Editor
General Electric Research and Development Center
Jack V. O'Keefe, Associate Editor
The Boeing Co.
Ira R. Schwartz, Associate Editor
NASA Ames Research Center
ISBN 0-915928-01-9

38. Aeroacoustics: Fan, STOL, and Boundary Layer Noise; Sonic Boom; Aeroacoustics Instrumentation (1975)
Henry T. Nagamatsu, Editor
General Electric Research and Development Center
Jack V. O'Keefe, Associate Editor
The Boeing Co.
Ira R. Schwartz, Associate Editor
NASA Ames Research Center
ISBN 0-915928-02-7

39. Heat Transfer with Thermal Control Applications (1975)
M. Michael Yovanovich
University of Waterloo
ISBN 0-915928-03-5

*40. Aerodynamics of Base Combustion (1976)
S.N.B. Murthy, Editor
J.R. Osborn,
Associate Editor
Purdue University
A.W. Barrows
J.R. Ward,
Associate Editors
Ballistics Research Laboratories
ISBN 0-915928-04-3

41. Communications Satellite Developments: Systems (1976)
Gilbert E. LaVean
Defense Communications Agency
William G. Schmidt
CML Satellite Corp.
ISBN 0-915928-05-1

42. Communications Satellite Developments: Technology (1976)
William G. Schmidt
CML Satellite Corp.
Gilbert E. LaVean
Defense Communications Agency
ISBN 0-915928-06-X

*43. Aeroacoustics: Jet Noise, Combustion and Core Engine Noise (1976)
Ira R. Schwartz, Editor
NASA Ames Research Center
Henry T. Nagamatsu,
Associate Editor
General Electric Research and Development Center
Warren C. Strahle,
Associate Editor
Georgia Institute of Technology
ISBN 0-915928-07-8

*44. Aeroacoustics: Fan Noise and Control; Duct Acoustics; Rotor Noise (1976)
Ira R. Schwartz, Editor
NASA Ames Research Center
Henry T. Nagamatsu,
Associate Editor
General Electric Research and Development Center
Warren C. Strahle,
Associate Editor
Georgia Institute of Technology
ISBN 0-915928-08-6

*45. Aeroacoustics: STOL Noise; Airframe and Airfoil Noise (1976)
Ira R. Schwartz, Editor
NASA Ames Research Center
Henry T. Nagamatsu,
Associate Editor
General Electric Research and Development Center
Warren C. Strahle,
Associate Editor
Georgia Institute of Technology
ISBN 0-915928-09-4

*46. Aeroacoustics: Acoustic Wave Propagation; Aircraft Noise Prediction; Aeroacoustic Instrumentation (1976)
Ira R. Schwartz, Editor
NASA Ames Research Center
Henry T. Nagamatsu,
Associate Editor
General Electric Research and Development Center
Warren C. Strahle,
Associate Editor
Georgia Institute of Technology
ISBN 0-915928-10-8

47. Spacecraft Charging by Magnetospheric Plasmas (1976)
Alan Rosen
TRW Inc.
ISBN 0-915928-11-6

48. Scientific Investigations on the Skylab Satellite (1976)
Marion I. Kent
Ernst Stuhlinger
NASA George C. Marshall Space Flight Center
Shi-Tsan Wu
University of Alabama
ISBN 0-915928-12-4

49. Radiative Transfer and Thermal Control (1976)
Allie M. Smith
ARO Inc.
ISBN 0-915928-13-2

50. Exploration of the Outer Solar System (1976)
Eugene W. Greenstadt
TRW Inc.
Murray Dryer
National Oceanic and Atmospheric Administration
Devrie S. Intriligator
University of Southern California
ISBN 0-915928-14-0

51. Rarefied Gas Dynamics, Parts I and II (two volumes) (1977)
J. Leith Potter
ARO Inc.
ISBN 0-915928-15-9

52. Materials Sciences in Space with Application to Space Processing (1977)
Leo Steg
General Electric Co.
ISBN 0-915928-16-7

53. Experimental Diagnostics in Gas Phase Combustion Systems (1977)
Ben T. Zinn, Editor
Georgia Institute of Technology
Craig T. Bowman,
Associate Editor
Stanford University
Daniel L. Hartley,
Associate Editor
Sandia Laboratories
Edward W. Price,
Associate Editor
Georgia Institute of Technology
James G. Skifstad,
Associate Editor
Purdue University
ISBN 0-015928-18-3

54. Satellite Communications: Future Systems (1977)
David Jarett
TRW Inc.
ISBN 0-915928-18-3

55. Satellite Communications: Advanced Technologies (1977)
David Jarett
TRW Inc.
ISBN 0-915928-19-1

56. Thermophysics of Spacecraft and Outer Planet Entry Probes (1977)
Allie M. Smith
ARO Inc.
ISBN 0-915928-20-5

57. Space-Based Manufacturing from Nonterrestrial Materials (1977)
Gerard K. O'Neill, Editor
Brian O'Leary,
Assistant Editor
Princeton University
ISBN 0-915928-21-3

58. Turbulent Combustion (1978)
Lawrence A. Kennedy
State University of New York at Buffalo
ISBN 0-915928-22-1

59. Aerodynamic Heating and Thermal Protection Systems (1978)
Leroy S. Fletcher
University of Virginia
ISBN 0-915928-23-X

60. Heat Transfer and Thermal Control Systems (1978)
Leroy S. Fletcher
University of Virginia
ISBN 0-915928-24-8

61. Radiation Energy Conversion in Space (1978)
Kenneth W. Billman
NASA Ames Research Center
ISBN 0-915928-26-4

62. Alternative Hydrocarbon Fuels: Combustion and Chemical Kinetics (1978)
Craig T. Bowman
Stanford University
Jorgen Birkeland
Department of Energy
ISBN 0-915928-25-6

63. Experimental Diagnostics in Combustion of Solids (1978)
Thomas L. Boggs
Naval Weapons Center
Ben T. Zinn
Georgia Institute of Technology
ISBN 0-915928-28-0

64. Outer Planet Entry Heating and Thermal Protection (1979)
Raymond Viskanta
Purdue University
ISBN 0-915928-29-9

65. Thermophysics and Thermal Control (1979)
Raymond Viskanta
Purdue University
ISBN 0-915928-30-2

66. Interior Ballistics of Guns (1979)
Herman Krier
University of Illinois at Urbana-Champaign
Martin Summerfield
New York University
ISBN 0-915928-32-9

*67. Remote Sensing of Earth from Space: Role of "Smart Sensors" (1979)
Roger A. Breckenridge
NASA Langley Research Center
ISBN 0-915928-33-7

68. Injection and Mixing in Turbulent Flow (1980)
Joseph A. Schetz
Virginia Polytechnic Institute and State University
ISBN 0-915928-35-3

69. Entry Heating and Thermal Protection (1980)
Walter B. Olstad
NASA Headquarters
ISBN 0-915928-38-8

70. Heat Transfer, Thermal Control, and Heat Pipes (1980)
Walter B. Olstad
NASA Headquarters
ISBN 0-915928-39-6

*71. Space Systems and Their Interactions with Earth's Space Environment (1980)
Henry B. Garrett
Charles P. Pike
Hanscom Air Force Base
ISBN 0-915928-41-8

72. Viscous Flow Drag Reduction (1980)
Gary R. Hough
Vought Advanced Technology Center
ISBN 0-915928-44-2

73. **Combustion Experiments in a Zero-Gravity Laboratory** (1981)
Thomas H. Cochran
NASA Lewis Research Center
ISBN 0-915928-48-5

74. **Rarefied Gas Dynamics, Parts I and II** (two volumes) (1981)
Sam S. Fisher
University of Virginia
ISBN 0-915928-51-5

75. **Gasdynamics of Detonations and Explosions** (1981)
J.R. Bowen
University of Wisconsin at Madison
N. Manson
Université de Poitiers
A.K. Oppenheim
University of California at Berkeley
R.I. Soloukhin
Institute of Heat and Mass Transfer, BSSR Academy of Sciences
ISBN 0-915928-46-9

76. **Combustion in Reactive Systems** (1981)
J.R. Bowen
University of Wisconsin at Madison
N. Manson
Université de Poitiers
A.K. Oppenheim
University of California at Berkeley
R.I. Soloukhin
Institute of Heat and Mass Transfer, BSSR Academy of Sciences
ISBN 0-915928-47-7

77. **Aerothermodynamics and Planetary Entry** (1981)
A.L. Crosbie
University of Missouri-Rolla
ISBN 0-915928-52-3

78. **Heat Transfer and Thermal Control** (1981)
A.L. Crosbie
University of Missouri-Rolla
ISBN 0-915928-53-1

79. **Electric Propulsion and Its Applications to Space Missions** (1981)
Robert C. Finke
NASA Lewis Research Center
ISBN 0-915928-55-8

80. **Aero-Optical Phenomena** (1982)
Keith G. Gilbert
Leonard J. Otten
Air Force Weapons Laboratory
ISBN 0-915928-60-4

81. **Transonic Aerodynamics** (1982)
David Nixon
Nielsen Engineering & Research, Inc.
ISBN 0-915928-65-5

82. **Thermophysics of Atmospheric Entry** (1982)
T.E. Horton
University of Mississippi
ISBN 0-915928-66-3

83. **Spacecraft Radiative Transfer and Temperature Control** (1982)
T.E. Horton
University of Mississippi
ISBN 0-915928-67-1

84. **Liquid-Metal Flows and Magnetohydrodynamics** (1983)
H. Branover
Ben-Gurion University of the Negev
P.S. Lykoudis
Purdue University
A. Yakhot
Ben-Gurion University of the Negev
ISBN 0-915928-70-1

85. **Entry Vehicle Heating and Thermal Protection Systems: Space Shuttle, Solar Starprobe, Jupiter Galileo Probe** (1983)
Paul E. Bauer
McDonnell Douglas Astronautics Co.
Howard E. Collicott
The Boeing Co.
ISBN 0-915928-74-4

86. **Spacecraft Thermal Control, Design, and Operation** (1983)
Howard E. Collicott
The Boeing Co.
Paul E. Bauer
McDonnell Douglas Astronautics Co.
ISBN 0-915928-75-2

87. **Shock Waves, Explosions, and Detonations** (1983)
J.R. Bowen
University of Washington
N. Manson
Université de Poitiers
A.K. Oppenheim
University of California at Berkeley
R.I. Soloukhin
Institute of Heat and Mass Transfer, BSSR Academy of Sciences
ISBN 0-915928-76-0

88. **Flames, Lasers, and Reactive Systems** (1983)
J.R. Bowen
University of Washington
N. Manson
Université de Poitiers
A.K. Oppenheim
University of California at Berkeley
R.I. Soloukhin
Institute of Heat and Mass Transfer, BSSR Academy of Sciences
ISBN 0-915928-77-9

89. Orbit-Raising and Maneuvering Propulsion: Research Status and Needs (1984)
Leonard H. Caveny
Air Force Office of Scientific Research
ISBN 0-915928-82-5

90. Fundamentals of Solid-Propellant Combustion (1984)
Kenneth K. Kuo
Pennsylvania State University
Martin Summerfield
Princeton Combustion Research Laboratories, Inc.
ISBN 0-915928-84-1

91. Spacecraft Contamination: Sources and Prevention (1984)
J.A. Roux
University of Mississippi
T.D. McCay
NASA Marshall Space Flight Center
ISBN 0-915928-85-X

92. Combustion Diagnostics by Nonintrusive Methods (1984)
T.D. McCay
NASA Marshall Space Flight Center
J.A. Roux
University of Mississippi
ISBN 0-915928-86-8

93. The INTELSAT Global Satellite System (1984)
Joel Alper
COMSAT Corp.
Joseph Pelton
INTELSAT
ISBN 0-915928-90-6

94. Dynamics of Shock Waves, Explosions, and Detonations (1984)
J.R. Bowen
University of Washington
N. Manson
Université de Poitiers
A.K. Oppenheim
University of California at Berkely
R.I. Soloukhin
Institute of Heat and Mass Transfer, BSSR Academy of Sciences
ISBN 0-915928-91-4

95. Dynamics of Flames and Reactive Systems (1984)
J.R. Bowen
University of Washington
N. Manson
Université de Poitiers
A.K. Oppenheim
University of California at Bereley
R.I. Soloukhin
Institute of Heat and Mass Transfer, BSSR Academy of Sciences
ISBN 0-915928-92-2

96. Thermal Design of Aeroassisted Orbital Transfer Vehicles (1985)
H.F. Nelson
University of Missouri-Rolla
ISBN 0-915928-94-9

97. Monitoring Earth's Ocean, Land, and Atmosphere from Space — Sensors, Systems, and Applications (1985)
Abraham Schnapf
Aerospace Systems Engineering
ISBN 0-915928-98-1

98. Thrust and Drag: Its Prediction and Verification (1985)
Eugene E. Covert
Massachusetts Institute of Technology
C.R. James
Vought Corp.
William F. Kimzey
Sverdrup Technology AEDC Group
George K. Richey
U.S. Air Force
Eugene C. Rooney
U.S. Navy Department of Defense
ISBN 0-930403-00-2

99. Space Stations and Space Platforms — Concepts, Design, Infrastructure, and Uses (1985)
Ivan Bekey
Daniel Herman
NASA Headquarters
ISBN 0-930403-01-0

100. Single- and Multi-Phase Flows in an Electromagnetic Field: Energy, Metallurgical, and Solar Applications (1985)
Herman Branover
Ben-Gurion University of the Negev
Paul S. Lykoudis
Purdue University
Michael Mond
Ben-Gurion University of the Negev
ISBN 0-930403-04-5

101. MHD Energy Conversion: Physiotechnical Problems (1986)
V.A. Kirillin
A.E. Sheyndlin
Soviet Academy of Sciences
ISBN 0-930403-05-3

102. Numerical Methods for Engine-Airframe Integration (1986)
S.N.B. Murthy
Purdue University
Gerald C. Paynter
Boeing Airplane Co.
ISBN 0-930403-09-6

103. Thermophysical Aspects of Re-Entry Flows (1986)
James N. Moss
NASA Langley Research Center
Carl D. Scott
NASA Johnson Space Center
ISBN 0-930403-10-X

104. Tactical Missile Aerodynamics (1986)
M.J. Hemsch
PRC Kentron, Inc.
J.N. Nielsen
NASA Ames Research Center
ISBN 0-930403-13-4

105. Dynamics of Reactive Systems Part I: Flames and Configurations; Part II: Modeling and Heterogeneous Combustion (1986)
J.R. Bowen
University of Washington
J.-C. Leyer
Université de Poitiers
R.I. Soloukhin
Institute of Heat and Mass Transfer, BSSR Academy of Sciences
ISBN 0-930403-14-2

106. Dynamics of Explosions (1986)
J.R. Bowen
University of Washington
J.-C. Leyer
Université de Poitiers
R.I. Soloukhin
Institute of Heat and Mass Transfer, BSSR Academy of Sciences
ISBN 0-930403-15-0

107. Spacecraft Dielectric Material Properties and Spacecraft Charging (1986)
A.R. Frederickson
U.S. Air Force Rome Air Development Center
D.B. Cotts
SRI International
J.A. Wall
U.S. Air Force Rome Air Development Center
F.L. Bouquet
Jet Propulsion Laboratory, California Institute of Technology
ISBN 0-930403-17-7

108. Opportunities for Academic Research in a Low-Gravity Environment (1986)
George A. Hazelrigg
National Science Foundation
Joseph M. Reynolds
Louisiana State University
ISBN 0-930403-18-5

109. Gun Propulsion Technology (1988)
Ludwig Stiefel
U.S. Army Armament Research, Development and Engineering Center
ISBN 0-930403-20-7

110. Commercial Opportunities in Space (1988)
F. Shahrokhi
K.E. Harwell
University of Tennessee Space Institute
C.C. Chao
National Cheng Kung University
ISBN 0-930403-39-8

111. Liquid-Metal Flows: Magnetohydrodynamics and Applications (1988)
Herman Branover,
Michael Mond, and
Yeshajahu Unger
Ben-Gurion University of the Negev
ISBN 0-930403-43-6

112. Current Trends in Turbulence Research (1988)
Herman Branover,
Michael Mond, and
Yeshajahu Unger
Ben-Gurion University of the Negev
ISBN 0-930403-44-4

113. Dynamics of Reactive Systems Part I: Flames; Part II: Heterogeneous Combustion and Applications (1988)
A.L. Kuhl
R & D Associates
J.R. Bowen
University of Washington
J.-C. Leyer
Université de Poitiers
A. Borisov
USSR Academy of Sciences
ISBN 0-930403-46-0

114. Dynamics of Explosions (1988)
A.L. Kuhl
R & D Associates
J.R. Bowen
University of Washington
J.-C. Leyer
Université de Poitiers
A. Borisov
USSR Academy of Sciences
ISBN 0-930403-47-9

115. Machine Intelligence and Autonomy for Aerospace (1988)
E. Heer
Heer Associates, Inc.
H. Lum
NASA Ames Research Center
ISBN 0-930403-48-7

116. Rarefied Gas Dynamics: Space-Related Studies (1989)
E.P. Muntz
University of Southern California
D.P. Weaver
U.S. Air Force Astronautics Laboratory (AFSC)
D.H. Campbell
University of Dayton Research Institute
ISBN 0-930403-53-3

117. Rarefied Gas Dynamics: Physical Phenomena (1989)
E.P. Muntz
University of Southern California
D.P. Weaver
U.S. Air Force Astronautics Laboratory (AFSC)
D. Campbell
University of Dayton Research Institute
ISBN 0-930403-54-1

118. Rarefied Gas Dynamics: Theoretical and Computational Techniques (1989)
E.P. Muntz
University of Southern California
D.P. Weaver
U.S. Air Force Astronautics Laboratory (AFSC)
D.H. Campbell
University of Dayton Research Institute
ISBN 0-930403-55-X

119. Test and Evaluation of the Tactical Missile (1989)
Emil J. Eichblatt Jr.
Pacific Missile Test Center
ISBN 0-930403-56-8

120. Unsteady Transonic Aerodynamics (1989)
David Nixon
Nielsen Engineering & Research, Inc.
ISBN 0-930403-52-5

121. Orbital Debris from Upper-Stage Breakup (1989)
Joseph P. Loftus Jr.
NASA Johnson Space Center
ISBN 0-930403-58-4

122. Thermal-Hydraulics for Space Power, Propulsion and Thermal Management System Design (1989)
William J. Krotiuk
General Electric Co.
ISBN 0-930403-64-9

123. Viscous Drag Reduction in Boundary Layers (1990)
Dennis M. Bushnell
Jerry N. Hefner
NASA Langley Research Center
ISBN 0-930403-66-5

124. Tactical and Strategic Missile Guidance (1990)
Paul Zarchan
Charles Stark Draper Laboratory, Inc.
ISBN 0-930403-68-1

125. Applied Computational Aerodynamics (1990)
P.A. Henne
Douglas Aircraft Company
ISBN 0-930403-69-X

126. Space Commercialization: Launch Vehicles and Programs (1990)
F. Shahrokhi
University of Tennessee Space Institute
J.S. Greenberg
Princeton Synergetics Inc.
T. Al-Saud
Ministry of Defense and Aviation Kingdom of Saudi Arabia
ISBN 0-930403-75-4

127. Space Commercialization: Platforms and Processing (1990)
F. Shahrokhi
University of Tennessee Space Institute
G. Hazelrigg
National Science Foundation
R. Bayuzick
Vanderbilt University
ISBN 0-930403-76-2

128. Space Commercialization: Satellite Technology (1990)
F. Shahrokhi
University of Tennessee Space Institute
N. Jasentuliyana
United Nations
N. Tarabzouni
King Abulaziz City for Science and Technology
ISBN 0-930403-77-0

129. Mechanics and Control of Large Flexible Structures (1990)
John L. Junkins
Texas A&M University
ISBN 0-930403-73-8

130. Low-Gravity Fluid Dynamics and Transport Phenomena (1990)
Jean N. Koster
Robert L. Sani
University of Colorado at Boulder
ISBN 0-930403-74-6

131. Dynamics of Deflagrations and Reactive Systems: Flames (1991)
A. L. Kuhl
Lawrence Livermore National Laboratory
J.-C. Leyer
Université de Poitiers
A. A. Borisov
USSR Academy of Sciences
W. A. Sirignano
University of California
ISBN 0-930403-95-9

132. **Dynamics of Deflagrations and Reactive Systems: Heterogeneous Combustion** (1991)
A. L. Kuhl
Lawrence Livermore National Laboratory
J.-C. Leyer
Université de Poitiers
A. A. Borisov
USSR Academy of Sciences
W. A. Sirignano
University of California
ISBN 0-930403-96-7

133. **Dynamics of Detonations and Explosions: Detonations** (1991)
A. L. Kuhl
Lawrence Livermore National Laboratory
J.-C. Leyer
Université de Poitiers
A. A. Borisov
USSR Academy of Sciences
W. A. Sirignano
University of California
ISBN 0-930403-97-5

134. **Dynamics of Detonations and Explosions: Explosion Phenomena** (1991)
A. L. Kuhl
Lawrence Livermore National Laboratory
J.-C. Leyer
Université de Poitiers
A. A. Borisov
USSR Academy of Sciences
W. A. Sirignano
University of California
ISBN 0-930403-98-3

135. **Numerical Approaches to Combustion Modeling** (1991)
Elaine S. Oran
Jay P. Boris
Naval Research Laboratory
ISBN 1-56347-004-7

136. **Aerospace Software Engineering** (1991)
Christine Anderson
U.S. Air Force Wright Laboratory
Merlin Dorfman
Lockheed Missiles & Space Company, Inc.
ISBN 1-56346-005-5

137. **High-Speed Flight Propulsion Systems** (1991)
S. N. B. Murthy
Purdue University
E. T. Curran
Wright Laboratory
ISBN 1-56347-011-X

138. **Propagation of Intensive Laser Radiation in Clouds** (1992)
O. A. Volkovitsky
Yu. S. Sedunov
L. P. Semenov
Institute of Experimental Meteorology
ISBN 1-56347-020-9

139. **Gun Muzzle Blast and Flash** (1992)
Günter Klingenberg
Fraunhofer-Institut für Kurzzeitdynamik, Ernst-Mach-Institut (EMI)
Joseph M. Heimerl
U.S. Army Ballistic Research Laboratory (BRL)
ISBN 1-56347-012-8

140. **Thermal Structures and Materials for High-Speed Flight** (1992)
Earl A. Thornton
University of Virginia
ISBN 1-56347-017-9

141. **Tactical Missile Aerodynamics: General Topics** (1992)
Michael J. Hemsch
Lockheed Engineering & Sciences Company
ISBN 1-56347-015-2

142. **Tactical Missile Aerodynamics: Prediction Methodology** (1992)
Michael R. Mendenhall
Nielsen Engineering & Research, Inc.
ISBN 1-56347-016-0

143. **Nonsteady Burning and Combustion Stability of Solid Propellants** (1992)
Luigi De Luca
Politecnico di Milano
Edward W. Price
Georgia Institute of Technology
Martin Summerfield
Princeton Combustion Research Laboratories, Inc.
ISBN 1-56347-014-4

144. **Space Economics** (1992)
Joel S. Greenberg
Princeton Synergetics, Inc.
Henry R. Hertzfeld
HRH Associates
ISBN 1-56347-042-X

145. **Mars: Past, Present, and Future** (1992)
E. Brian Pritchard
NASA Langley Research Center
ISBN 1-56347-043-8

146. **Computational Nonlinear Mechanics in Aerospace Engineering** (1992)
Satya N. Atluri
Georgia Institute of Technology
ISBN 1-56347-044-6

147. **Modern Engineering for Design of Liquid-Propellant Rocket Engines** (1992)
Dieter K. Huzel
David H. Huang
ISBN 1-56347-013-6

148.   Metallurgical Technologies, Energy Conversion, and Magneto-hydrodynamic Flows (1993)
Herman Branover
Yeshajahu Unger
Ben-Gurion University of the Negev
ISBN 1-56347-019-5

149.   Advances in Turbulence Studies (1993)
Herman Branover
Yeshajahu Unger
Ben-Gurion University of the Negev
ISBN 1-56347-018-7

150.   Structural Optimization: Status and Promise (1993)
Manohar P. Kamat
Georgia Institute of Technology
ISBN 1-56347-056-X

151.   Dynamics of Gaseous Combustion (1993)
A. L. Kuhl
Lawrence Livermore National Laboratory
J.-C. Leyer
Université de Poitiers
A. A. Borisov
Russian Academy of Sciences
W. A. Sirignano
University of California
ISBN 1-56347-060-8

152.   Dynamics of Heterogeneous Combustion and Reacting Systems (1993)
A. L. Kuhl
Lawrence Livermore National Laboratory
J.-C. Leyer
Université de Poitiers
A. A. Borisov
Russian Academy of Sciences
W. A. Sirignano
University of California
ISBN 1-56347-058-6

153.   Dynamic Aspects of Detonations (1993)
A. L. Kuhl
Lawrence Livermore National Laboratory
J.-C. Leyer
Université de Poitiers
A. A. Borisov
Russian Academy of Sciences
W. A. Sirignano
University of California
ISBN 1-56347-057-8

154.   Dynamic Aspects of Explosion Phenomena (1993)
A. L. Kuhl
Lawrence Livermore National Laboratory
J.-C. Leyer
Université de Poitiers
A. A. Borisov
Russian Academy of Sciences
W. A. Sirignano
University of California
ISBN 1-56347-059-4

155.   Tactical Missile Warheads (1993)
Joseph Carleone
Aerojet General Corporation
ISBN 1-56347-067-5

156.   Toward a Science of Command, Control, and Communications (1993)
Carl R. Jones
Naval Postgraduate School
ISBN 1-56347-068-3

157.   Tactical and Strategic Missile Guidance
Second Edition (1994)
Paul Zarchan
Charles Stark Draper Laboratory, Inc.
ISBN 1-56347-077-2

(Other Volumes are planned.)